FEARLESS FOTH STRIKES AGAIN!

"This is a view through the wrong end of the telescope. It is a fix on a party from afar. It is sympathetic, charitable—and exactly what they deserve."

"I was once at a black-tied dinner of men of staggering intellect which someone described as the greatest meeting of minds since Pierre Trudeau dined alone."

"Pierre Trudeau . . . is the neutron bomb of Liberal politics, destroying all the personalities within while leaving the institution standing (barely)."

"The country needs a shrink more than it needs a prime minister."

"Ottawa—corrupt in its conceit, contented because it knows not what it is. . . . Ottawa, when you get down to it, is the civic equivalent of saltpetre. Only the pensions are indexed; very little else goes up on a regular basis. It's the nature of the place, spontaneity frowned upon and joy severely taxed. A city that lives at the Xerox machine eventually has to suffer some internal damage—mainly a curvature of the imagination."

"Canada . . . a country that boasts no revolutions, brooks no assassinations, spurns class warfare and puts all its money into savings accounts. For over half of the past sixty years it has been run by bachelors who, if they liked women, showed it in a very peculiar way."

MALICE IN BLUNDERLAND

"A collection of gossip and a virtuoso display of vitriol . . . One of those rare books of humor that is much too funny ever to win the Leacock award . . ."

—*Maclean's*

Malice in Blunderland

or
How the Grits Stole Christmas

Allan Fotheringham

SEAL BOOKS
McClelland and Stewart-Bantam Limited
Toronto

This low-priced Seal Book
has been completely reset in a type face
designed for easy reading, and was printed
from new plates. It contains the complete
text of the original hard-cover edition.
NOT ONE WORD HAS BEEN OMITTED.

MALICE IN BLUNDERLAND, OR,
HOW THE GRITS STOLE CHRISTMAS
A Seal Book / published by arrangement with
Key Porter Books

PRINTING HISTORY
Key Porter edition published October 1982
A Book-of-the-Month Club Selection
Serialized in Toronto Life, Ottawa, Vancouver magazines and
The Herald Calgary.
Seal edition / June 1983

ISBN 0-7704-1826-0

*For my mother
who must have taught me
how to laugh.*

Contents

Preface to the Paperback Edition

The Liberals, a shifty party, are ever shifting ground, seeking the expedient middle, stealing an idea here, filching a policy there. Since the hardcover version of this tome has appeared, they have tried yet more ploys, their eyes fixed on their only principle: power.

The first ploy was the three sermonettes-on-the-mound known as the boob tube, the attempt by the Prime Minister to put the nation on a war footing. Instead, he managed only a time zone footing, the brilliantly timed speeches (trying to beat the World Series) coming at a time on the clock when the Western Canada he must win back was still at work or driving home. The Trudeaucrats thus reaffirmed the celebrated remark of Vancouver's John Nichol, once president of the party, that the Liberal view of Canada is everything that Senator Keith Davey can see from the roof of the Royal York on a clear day.

In the new presidential stakes, the Liberals have opted somewhat tremulously for the statuesque Iona Campagnolo, who enters a room as if borne on an Egyptian chair. She will give them trouble because, being indisputably a woman as well as a Westerner and a Northerner, she has not yet been house-broken to Liberal subservience. Her cooperation is sought by the Davey-Trudeau branch of the party (highly unpopular in the country but in power) so as to block the ascendancy of the John Turner branch of the party (highly popular in the country but out of power).

This leads to the supremely Trudeauesque appointment of Don Macdonald, who must face Turner if he aspires to become Prime Minister, as the overseer of the major economic Royal Commission on our future—if any. It has been an appointment roundly criticized but profoundly Liberal: the Natural Governing Party rewards its kind. It does not change. Neither do the opinions updated here.

Allan Fotheringham

Introduction

Someone, God knows, has to save the country. There are those of us who feel so sympathetic to Ottawa—home of all that is good, dedicated and smarmy—that we refuse to reside there. We prefer the perspective of the starship, otherwise known as the People's Republic Airline, home of the toy meals and the geriatric stewardae: Air Canada. Those of us who prefer to view Canada from seven miles high, rather than deal with its depressing reality at street level, spend our fitful lives at luggage carousels, waiting for the mangled remains of our underwear.

The peripatetic life, while ravaging to the liver, the mind and the suitcase, does have one beneficial aspect: it is the view of the *thread*. If one puts down in enough airports, bunks in enough plastic hotel rooms, wrestles often enough with Air Canada cutlery that must have been designed by a vegetarian on a fast, certain patterns become apparent. The skeleton of the land that is not strong becomes clear.

The thread that unites the country is the distaste for the Natural Governing Party, alias the Liberals. Their major mistake, as it turns out, was to snatch that Pyrrhic victory from the boy amateurs of Joe Why on that infamous 1979 budget night. It prevented the Liberals from cleansing their souls, renovating their machinery and scrubbing their leader. Thrust back in power by the incompetence of a nervous Tory prime minister who shot himself in the foot after only seven months, the Liberals discovered they had nothing left in the holster themselves.

Wherever the plane lands, wherever the stomach groans and cries for live food, one finds the same vibrations: these Grits are men (and the occasional woman) who are out of synch with the country. They are not evil, but incompetent. Not corrupt, but bankrupt of ideas. Their

1

arrogance is supreme, their smugness sublime, their ignorance of reality bottomless.

The starship cruises overhead; the traveller gazing down in bewilderment at this collection of brains, led by the finest intellect of our age, a man now cosmically removed from real life, who heads a cabinet that was so eager to regain power for power's sake that it neglected to find any real reason for doing so.

The prisoner in the starship, issuing little yelps of disbelief at what he sees, cruises on.

What follows is a disconnected overview from thirty-five thousand feet of the present political situation. It is not a neat package, but neither is Canada in 1982, thanks to the Grits.

The digressions from slavish theme are purposeful, the wandering thoughts of a reporter who makes a living by bouncing down at airports, snatching insights and gossip and bounding off again, destined for the next deadline. Canada is the second largest country in the world (filled entirely with jealousy). This is not the perfect way to fathom it, but it is preferable, one submits, to sitting in Ottawa in the belief that the capital is relevant to the populace.

It isn't. Its insularity is apparent to all but those who live there and rule from there. It's a sad town, in that it lives on the illusion that it is in touch. Ottawa is the civic equivalent of the man in the insane asylum who contents himself in the belief that he is Napoleon. It needs its head tapped, but those in charge are victims of the same disorder.

What Constant Reader will find here are the author's random inanities on the state of our peril. Some faint traces of outraged thought may be recognized from previous angry periods in both newspaper and magazine scribblings, but no one should be alarmed. Some exquisite assessments are too precious to throw away, some memorable paeans to particular cabinet ministers deserve a second glance. A Reggie Jackson swing, while striking out, deserves to be captured by instant replay and contemplated again.

Landings in Manitoba inspire thoughts pertaining to the permutations in the prime minister's personal entourage; pitstops in Prince Edward Island recall happenings in Nanton, Alberta. The country is connected only by those who flit about it, trailing spider webs of rumour behind them. The journalist's mind is not a solid academic lump; it is stitched together by interconnections, wild leaps and stale anecdotes. The man in the starship is as a stone skipping across the water, making little impact, but touching down often, too often.

These views of the Grits at play have been gathering during fourteen years of writing columns, an indenture coinciding with the term of the Trudeau career as prime minister. They are written, in this summer of 1982, in the belief that a prime minister who went to Ottawa to save one portion of the country has almost succeeded in driving away another section of it.

The views will demonstrate the prejudices and background of a Western Canadian who now lives half the year in Ottawa in an attempt to educate it. I maintain two residences, one in Vancouver and the other in Ottawa, shuttling between them because, as mentioned, God knows someone has to save the country. Those at the top certainly aren't doing it.

If, in the line of duty, I did not persist in the crazy experiment of living in Ottawa two weeks in every month, I would be forced to live there for four weeks a month—something that no sane, civilized man would do. A chap has to nibble at the apple to discover the worm at the core.

Living in two cities does not, as Constant Reader might assume, lead to a permanent state of jet-lag. The human body is remarkably adaptable to most things, save perhaps the verbiage of Allan MacEachen, and becomes accustomed to four-hour-and-forty-five-minute transitions through the Alley Oop 747 time machine.

Although I hate airplanes, air terminals, air dogfood, airline computers and luggage merry-go-rounds, I like being in the air. (The only thing that spoils it is that airlines are in charge of it.) It is the one chance in life, aside from death, when one is spared telephones, ladies from the Red Feather Drive, traffic, and people who want to know in what round Jack Dempsey knocked out Louis Firpo, the Wild Bull of the Pampas.

The journalist is the most interrupted person on earth, everyone assuming that anyone who can solve the daily problems of the globe in one Olympian eight-hundred word chomp does not mind having his tenuous train of thought flagged down at every second paragraph. Only on a plane can one have four hours and forty-five minutes of uninterruption. The best thing about the silver cigar is that it is, usually, packed with complete strangers. One is enveloped in a cocoon of formality; Canadians being as emotionally constricted as they fortunately are, no one is eager to plunge into conversational foreplay if discouraged by a lofty visage. The ordinary earthbound Canadian cannot buy, with whatever money, a week that includes four hours and forty-five minutes of selfish, soulful time to read and ruminate.

The greatest aid to this stealing of silence is the Sony Walkman, which one attaches to one's ears—with the sound off—while gazing out at the limpid ozone over Thunder Bay. When the seatmate ventures some witticism, one only shakes one's head, as if a deaf mute, seemingly oblivious. The disguise works. You can even shake off the dogfood.

To save the country, all that is required is two homes, two cars, two wardrobes and two sets of tennis gear. If anyone would question my devotion to the nation, he need only judge the patriotism required in owning two Prince racquets.

The one insoluble problem is my books. I cannot really clone my library. Dividing them in half, by flipping a coin, doesn't work. Invariably, when the scribbler at 1 AM in Vancouver wants to look up a reference detailing Eugene Whelan's charisma quotient, the book is in Ottawa. And vice versa. The country's salvation may have to await a personal data bank.

Instead of jet-lag, I am twice monthly injected with a most useful syringe of culture shock, the medicine that keeps me so mellow and tolerant, not to mention wise. Flying from the bureaucratic beehive of Ottawa to The Village on the Edge of the Rain Forest is travelling from the edge of night to the edge of the abyss.

Another result of my continually flitting from the ridiculous to the sublime is that Air Canada usually shows a profit in its yearly statements. Take Dr. Foth from its accounts and it is reduced to the revenues of Air Liberia. I will be crushed if my suitcase is not eventually bronzed and mounted in the People's Republic Airline boardroom, alongside the Plasticine bust of Bryce Mackasey.

The qualifications for dispensing the upcoming wisdom are clear. I have now followed Pierre Trudeau and his forelock-tugging forelock-tuggers through five elections. I have chased him through Italy, London, Sweden, Norway and the mental obbligatos of at least four press secretaries. It may not have been quite as much fun as it was going around the world in 80 daze with Joe Clark and his wandering luggage, but it has been useful.

At one stage, I attempted to drive from Halifax to Vancouver, to tap the intellect of every truck-stop waitress and gas jockey in Canada as to the true gut feeling of the populace. About a third of the way through the kidney-jarring expedition, the 1979 election was called and while I interrogated the pizza parlour bus boys of the nation, my mates in the Press Gallery zoomed overhead at thirty-five thousand feet. The starship had become earthbound. (The food on the ground was better.)

Eventually, I abandoned the insane idea at Edmonton and rejoined the political jet-set. Nothing had changed. The press secretaries were still handing out the mandatory "Gainesburgers"—chow to fill the wire services and the thirty-second radio clips—after the regular champagne-and-orange-juice that started each morning's flight.

I toughed it out because I long ago determined that God in Her wisdom placed me on this planet so as to keep the Liberals humble. It's a nasty job, but somebody has to do it.

Those who huddle in the thumb-sucking comfort of Ottawa are automatically disqualified from assessing the Natural Governing Party. The Liberals own the town, and everyone who makes a buck there knows it and must feed off that fact. Only those who owe their allegiance to the boondocks have the perspective, through the wrong end of the telescope, to see the Grits as they are.

This is a view through the wrong end of the telescope. It is a fix on a party from afar. It is sympathetic, charitable—and exactly what they deserve.

1
The Maritimes

Down to the Sea in Rigs

Peckford's bad boy . . .
offshore wrongs . . . the DREE spree, or,
boondoggle in the boondocks . . .
the movable Hatfield . . . the immovable Camp . . .
poor MacEachen

Newfoundland

This journey through the minds of the Trudeaucrats, this incursion into the craniums of those who would steal our patrimony, begins in Newfoundland. It is the home of Liberal icons Joey Smallwood and Don Jamieson—and John Crosbie, once a Liberal, now a Tory, the only man in the House of Commons who doesn't speak either of the two official languages. The fourteen years of Pierre Trudeau hegemony have destroyed Newfie's Grit link: Premier Brian Peckford's April 1982 election returned an astonishing forty-four Conservatives to the legislature of an island brought into Canada by a bow-tied Liberal who is the only living Father of Confederation.

Joey Smallwood, having mother-henned the narrow 1948 Confederation vote, inveigled the gentle Lester Pearson into a prime ministerial open-convertible parade through downtown St. John's. The opening cars of the cavalcade were blocked in traffic causing the Smallwood-Pearson car to come to halt outside a pub, where a bleary citizen shook his fist at the trapped Liberal dignitaries and gave them the benefit of his asterisked eloquence. As a pink-faced Pearson squirmed in discomfort, Joey turned to him and calmly announced, "I think we'll have to put him down as 'undecided.' " Today, there are few Canadians who are undecided about how the once lordly Liberals under Trudeau have dismembered the country.

On that day in 1948 when Newfoundland narrowly decided to join Canada, millionaire's son John Crosbie and his brother Andrew, along with future Newfoundland premier Frank Moores, stood on the dining room table of the exclusive St. Andrew's private school outside Toronto. The Crosbie boys, sent to a Central Canada polishing school, had blacked their faces with shoe polish. The black laces of their rugby boots hung from them in mourning, and with tears streaming down their faces, they sang "I'll Always Be A Newfoundlander."

Perhaps, but not always a Liberal. Crosbie, the Tory, now sits in the Commons, a strangely suspended figure, watching the Liberals, who mocked his 1979 budget and defeated his government on it, flounder on budgets that resemble Swiss cheese. Allan J. MacEachen (Allan J. Ferragamo to insiders)—who devised the Tory downfall—had screwed up far more than Finance Minister John Crosbie ever did, but he did it with unction, a quality unknown to Crosbie, his fellow Maritimer. That Canada should have had successive finance ministers from the most impoverished region of the Dominion may help explain why we are in our present pickle.

Newfoundland is a rock covered with three inches of dirt. Entire grown forests look as if they had been stricken with rickets, resembling thousand-year-old Japanese dwarf trees. Newfie joke: how many Liberals does it take to make chocolate-chip cookies? Six. Two to bake and four to peel the Smarties. Crosbie, a gold medallist at law school who talks like a barroom brawler, has done more to make the Newf patois lovable than anything, including The Mummers. Speaking of loyalty to Joe Clark, he told the Commons: "We stand back to back, cheek to cheek, belly to belly, bum to bum."

The only person who doesn't think he's funny is Joe Clark. But Clark never laughs, at least not in public, which is wise because it makes him sound as if he has been injected with teen-age senility.

Thanks to modern technology, Newfoundlanders no longer lose their sons in fishboats. They lose them in "unsinkable" offshore oil rigs. "If it floats," said an old St. John's fisherman after the *Ocean Ranger* went down, "it can sink."

So can Liberal common sense. With eighty-four dead, most of them Canadians, most of them Newfoundlanders, Ottawa engaged in a struggle with the province as to who would hold the official inquiry into the tragedy. Within weeks, Canadians were treated to the sight of the swift Americans holding their own inquiry, since the rig was U.S. owned. Parents of dead Canadian boys who were drilling for Canadian oil in Canadian waters had to get their first facts on the *Ocean Ranger*'s sinking from hearings in Boston and New Orleans. Bobby Kennedy, bitter over Ottawa's dithering in a Washington crisis, once said, "In an emergency, Canada will offer you all aid short of help." The mothers of the *Ocean Ranger* dead now know the feeling.

The dispute over dead men, so insane from the outside, is at the base of Newfoundland's quarrel with Ottawa. The real struggle is over which government has jurisdiction over the mineral resources offshore. Whoever got to hold the *Ocean Ranger* inquiry might claim it established a precedent. While the two sides in the ghoulish squabble finally agreed on a joint inquiry, we got our basic facts from the speedy Americans.

So wonderful have the relations between the Trudeaucrats and the proud Newfoundlanders become that the two governments refuse to get into the same room together when they exchange money. In February, Transport Minister Jean-Luc Pépin travelled to St. John's to put his signature on a federal-provincial transportation document. It committed the feds to providing seventy-five percent of planned expenditures of some $70 million—mainly for highways and ferry terminals.

After fifteen months of negotiation, much of it acrimonious in the great Canadian tradition, Premier Brian Peckford sat in his office in the Confederation Building, home of the Newfoundland legislature. Pépin sat in the Hotel Newfoundland miles away in downtown St. John's, insisting it was a "convention" that transportation agreements are signed at that hotel. Neither would budge.

So Pépin signed his little piece of paper and forty-five minutes later, Peckford signed it. Two children in their tree forts, sticking their tongues out at each other. So marches the progress of Ottawa's relations with its provinces.

Premier Peckford is an English teacher with the temperament of a four-year-old. He inherited that classic Newfoundland tetchiness toward the condescension of the lords on high from Ottawa, which Pierre Absolutely Trendy carries around with him like after-shave lotion. The prime minister is like catnip to provincial premiers: his arrogance is the best thing they've got going at the polls. If they were smart, they'd send him a cheque in a plain brown wrapper.

The party that brought Newfoundland into Canada is now shut out, seen as a stiff-necked protector of central power. The man's gifts of alienation are marvellous to behold, somewhat like his trampoline backflips.

It seems a peculiar way to run a country in that the prime minister, by insisting on a disputatious style with the ten premiers he clearly regards as inferiors, ensures their popularity at home. It is said that Harold Ballard as a child was so unpleasant they had to tie pork chops around his neck so at least the dog would play with him. Pierre Trudeau displays the same flair for federal-provincial relations.

The best method theatre at the fed-prov confabs, right out of Lee Strasberg, is the eyeball-to-eyeball between new boy Peckford and the man at the head of the horseshoe table.

As luck would have it—seniority actually, as the seating is arranged on the order of entry into Confederation—directly opposite Trudeau, at the other end of the gun barrels of his steely gaze, sits Peckford with the TV cameras boring into the bristles on the back of his neck.

Peckford is shirty, prickly, with eyes that dart like dark cherries plugged into an electric guitar. He epitomizes, in his nervous body language, all the resentments that a new generation of educated Newfies store in their gut against the colonial masters from Ottawa. Newfoundland, as the newcomer among provinces, has yet to get out of her system the feeling that she is regarded as a babe among adults.

Peckford, sparks shooting off him, cannot wait to get his gums into the microphone but must fidget while the familiar litany from the other premiers with seniority is spilled into the maw of the Holy Mother Corporation's cameras.

Trudeau sits at the top of the horseshoe, his eyes glinted into that familiar Egyptian mask configuration, attempting to zap the interloper with ESP electrodes. He is the supreme actor of our time, never more aloof in his role than when the cameras are on him. This is why Clark, by comparison, is such an uncomfortable television figure, his nervous mannerisms too obvious, the fake pomposity that is designed to hide them even more apparent. Trudeau is just as stagey as Clark; the difference is that he is a superb actor. Clark is a lousy one.

Peckford is the adventuresome pup, making tentative darts at Trudeau, the sly old cat who sits, never twitching, oblivious, only occasionally with exquisite timing reaching out to swat the inexperienced intruder. All that's needed is a fireplace and the image of the tabby teaching the pup lessons he will never forget is complete.

The prime minister, in the arch manner that used to so endear him to the farmer premier of P.E.I., Angus MacLean, trots out a favourite quote learned at the Sorbonne, or perhaps the London School of Economics. The former English teacher Peckford, feeling it an aimed insult, snaps back an apt quotation from the reservoir of his memory.

The others who have seen this movie before, Lougheed, the now-departed Blakeney and the wily Davis, smile quietly to themselves and watch the pup lunge at the tabby before the fireplace.

Nova Scotia

Nova Scotia is the refuge of George Bain, the wittiest columnist ever to grace Ottawa, and the Toronto-loving Harry Bruce, who finally decided that a swimming pool in the shape of his ulcer was not his dominant goal in life and retreated to the province that is known as Canada's home for the emotionally tired.

Bruce moved through the media maze in Toronto in successful stints in magazines and newspapers before deciding that Halifax was the last stop. Confounding all the predictions of doom, he was the founding editor of *Atlantic Insight*, a beautifully produced magazine that has walked off with a fistful of awards for design and content. When Bruce returned to Toronto one night to pick up the awards before all his old drinking buddies at the National Magazine Awards banquet, it was like Hannibal coming over the Alps.

Bruce's daring is matched at the other end of the country by *Alberta Report*, the only provincial weekly newsmagazine in the country. It is put out by Ted Byfield, a true believer whose editorials on Trudeau have to be typed while he's wearing asbestos gloves. So violent is he in his condemnation of Ottawa and its goofy energy policies that the pages of his magazine sometimes crinkle in the heat. Anyone in Ottawa who wants to understand Alberta's siege mentality would be wise to read it. No one in Ottawa reads it.

There is Premier John Buchanan, lighter than air, and his hairdresser. Don't leave home without one. Nova Scotia is the sump hole of Canadian tax dollars, where DREE grants speckle the hillside like sheep in Kent.

In the Just Society, Trudeau's 1968 election platform, Trudeau stated, "We must strike at the root of economic disparity, putting behind us the easy subsidized solutions of the past."

The answer was going to be the Department of Regional Economic Expansion, a munificent Santa Claus trailing goodies from Ottawa's basket. The economy would be reformed and unemployment would disappear. As with most Ottawa plans, helped by Liberal muddling, the New Jerusalem did not appear.

What happened is that last year every man, woman and child in Nova Scotia received the equivalent of $66.71 in DREE grants—easily enough to enable each citizen of the province to purchase the three volumes of *The Collected Wit of Herb Gray*. (The DREE grants per capita were $265.56 in Prince Edward Island; $8.51 for every Albertan.)

What happened is that a certain G. McClure joined DREE in 1969. He was director of operations for the East (Atlantic). During his tenure, there were three grants approved for McCain Foods Ltd., run by the millionaire McCain family of New Brunswick who have built an empire on frozen french-fried potatoes and sell McCain products all over the world. The grants totalled $7,772,221. After seventeen months, McClure left DREE to join McCain Foods in a senior capacity.

What happened is that two officers of DREE were suspended without pay in connection with a grant of $736,970 to Silver Shields Mines. The suspensions related to the officials' purchase of stock "at a moment when it was not felt to be proper."

What happened is that Jean Marchand, now Speaker of the Senate, was ultimately responsible for all DREE decisions when he was the minister in charge of the department in the early 1970s. He was also at the time the leader of the federal Liberal party in Quebec. As the 1972 election approached, Quebec's share of DREE grants moved from 36.8 percent of the Canadian total to 74.8 percent of the total.

What happened is that the grants went not only to such deserving paupers as the McCains but to other welfare cases like Michelin ($15 million for starters), Rayonnier Quebec-ITT ($14 million), Noranda Mines, Procter & Gamble, IBM and so on down the breadline.

When a Dr. Springate from the Harvard School of Business testified before the Commons committee on regional development, the government didn't like his findings. After an exhaustive investigation of a sampling of DREE grant recipients, he found that the effect of the grant program on investment decisions was small: "Movement of location of plants within Canada is minimal, and significantly, grants produce few changes in respect to project timing, project size or technology used."

His verdict: "Roughly half of the incentive grants do not influence investment in any significant manner, and can be considered to be windfall gains."

The Economic Council of Canada has been even harder on this boondoggle that Liberal ministers use, while buying votes through employment promises, to ladle out cash to the corporate welfare bums. In 1977 the council did a self-confessedly generous assessment. It found that DREE'S only certain effect was to replace private investment with public money.

"Since most of the projects would have taken place somewhere in Canada if they had not been influenced to locate in particular areas by DREE," the council reported, "there appears to be a loss of real production to the economy as a whole, roughly equal to the amount of DREE money expended."

The study found that, in fact, only about *one-quarter* of DREE grants lived up to the department's mandate to encourage only investments that would otherwise not have been made.

You will be glad to know, gentle reader, that since the program began in 1969, more than $500 million has been spent on these "incentives."

The Liberals keep pumping subsidies into obsolete steel mills and heavy water plants, and all we get back is Allan MacEachen. It doesn't seem a fair trade. Halifax is about to be accepted into the Canadian Football League. This is expected to help the cocaine dealers in town. The annual rainfall in Halifax is higher than that in Vancouver but no one mentions it—1405.0 mm for Halifax to 1068.1 mm for Vancouver. No one, in fact, mentions Halifax. We do not plan to start.

There was that delicious moment in the autumn of 1981 when the Liberal inner cabinet travelled to Cape Breton, a junket designed to show off Allan MacEachen in his own riding. Away from the safe ghetto of Ottawa, the startled figure of External Affairs Minister Mark MacGuigan was accosted by striking coal miners, who had been out for nine weeks and demanded to know what *his* annual salary was. MacGuigan, who seems to wander through the world of diplomacy like little boy lost, is so guileless that—unlike most politicians—he sometimes blurts out the truth by accident. He confessed first of all that he didn't even know there was a strike (delicious!) and then—oh, frabjous joy!—that he couldn't remember how much he was paid. (It was $74,000 a year at the time, but now it's up to $102,100.) One wanted to be a miner at that point.

There was the helpless and bewildered look on the faces of MacEachen and Treasury Board President Don Johnston when their large car was trapped and encircled by irate miners threatening harm. Poor MacEachen, proudly hosting the think tank in his hard-times riding, was so out of touch as to be completely unprepared for the demonstrations and so led his complacent and oblivious colleagues into the ambush—and nationally televized embarrassment. Away from their warm cocoon of Ottawa, they all appear uncomfortable, as if walking on sharp stones in their bare feet.

Prince Edward Island

There is preposterous Prince Edward Island, the islet masquerading as a province. The population is 124,300, approximately the same as that of St. Catharine's, Ont. And Longueuil, Que. However, it still has four senators; British Columbia has six. This is known as co-operative federalism. P.E.I. is the home of the CBC's Mike Duffy, who is larger than three of the beaches. No one can remember the name of the premier. Millions of Canadians are born, go through life and die without ever knowing the name of the premier of Prince Edward Island. His time to speak at federal-provincial conferences is the signal for the press to go out for a beer.

Charlottetown, of course, is the home of Confederation. John Robert Colombo has pointed out that when this country was stillborn in 1867, foreign observers remarked on the remarkable potential ahead. Here was a land that had the fortune to be based on the solidity of the British parliamentary system, with the injection of French culture and American efficiency. It's 115 years later and what do we have? A Canada with the stability of the French political system, with American culture and British efficiency.

Charlottetown is also the place where little Jimmy Coutts, Trudeau's principal secretary, broke into tears backstage while listening to the prime minister make one of his final speeches before losing the 1979 election to Joe Clark. The tears were thought to come because Coutts had just received his private polling update from Toronto revealing that his steed was about to founder.

Coutts is from Nanton ("The finest water in Canada," proclaims a plaque on the main street), a little town just seventeen miles from Clark's High River, and went to the University of Alberta with Joe, where he was the author of the now celebrated assessment that "In this game you have to be a bit of a sonofabitch. Joe doesn't quite have it." Coutts is also widely credited in Ottawa with originating the "wimp" appellation for Clark. He denies it, but the jury is still out. (There are those who think the goal of Coutts, before tripping on his shoelaces in Toronto Spadina, was to succeed his boss Trudeau as leader, thus putting Nanton up against High River in a Huck Finn confrontation. No one, not even in P.E.I., takes Coutts' ambitions seriously.) It is not known what Clark—who, contrary to popular opinion, has a nice dry and wry wit in private—calls Mr. Coutts among intimates. Imagination,

17

however, is rife and suggestions will be entertained for the contest.

I digress. Prince Edward Island is the second province that floats.

New Brunswick

New Brunswick is noted mainly as the refuge of two people, Richard Hatfield and Dalton Camp. Hatfield is the only bachelor among our premiers, which is unusual because they usually populate Ottawa and in fact have run this country for more than one-third of this century, of which more later. Premier Hatfield is said to be the only Canadian who receives invitations to Truman Capote's parties and can spot a good restaurant at a thousand paces. He spends so much of his time in Morocco, New York, Montreal and London that the Liberal opposition once did some research and raised the point in the legislature that the premier had spent 168 days out of the province the previous year. His friend Camp claims that Hatfield told an associate, "I was elected to run New Brunswick. No one said I had to *live* there."

Hatfield is the best leak at federal-provincial conferences. Often you will see emissaries from *As It Happens*, *Morningside*, the *Globe and Mail*, Southam News, Canadian Press, *The National* and *The Journal* lined up outside his hotel suite, being issued numbers as in a butcher shop so they can all get their own version of the truth. The other premiers tend to shun him, mainly because their wives can't figure him out and do not know how to cope with the charm and the boyish wit.

He loves parties and has a beautiful home in Fredericton filled with soft furniture. The other premiers think it is so as to accommodate his brain.

New Brunswick is also the home of Romeo LeBlanc, the longtime minister of fisheries, a nice man who wandered into the wrong field of work in that he was required, in return for groceries, to wobble, muddify and indulge in fuzzification—all requirements of Liberal ministers who want to earn their spurs.

Romeo used to be Trudeau's press secretary, in charge of the care and feeding of the press, and graduated to being the chap responsible for the slaughter of seal pups, there being a certain similarity in the two chores.

LeBlanc is a serious man, as he should be. He was formerly with the CBC in Washington, which would make a serious person out of anyone—with the possible exception of Bob Kaplan. He has the perpetual mien of a doleful spaniel on Friday the thirteenth. This may be due partially to the fact that he represents the dilemma of the country: he is Acadian, representing one-third of the province that is a perfect replica of Canada in that it also has a diminishing third of its population of French-speaking origin.

His problem was that he was trapped in an impossible dream. As a minister from the Maritimes, in charge of a traditionally Maritimes portfolio (the fishery aspect of B.C. is regarded in Ottawa as goldfish decorating hot-tubs), he had to defend the indefensible: the antediluvian seal harvest.

To protect it, Romeo LeBlanc was forced into the embarrassing position of arresting Canadians—the pacifists of the Greenpeace movement—who are trying to protect Canadian seals from "harvesters" (one of the great words of our time).

The situation remains, while world opinion presses in, that for the benefit of the fashion industry the seal "harvest" is the only animal kill in the world that is conducted while the mother of the species is nursing. It will be stopped. It's simply a matter of time. Perhaps that's why Romeo looks so doleful. He has since been shunted to Public Works.

Last spring the New Brunswick legislature, spurred by community anger over sex acts being performed in licensed lounges by strippers and customers, assumed broad new powers to clean up the bars. At issue were lounges in two rural communities which featured strippers who mingled with the audience during their performances or performed oral sex acts.

Church groups, businessmen and women's groups in Perth-Andover and Edmundston had complained to their town councils and legislative members that the sex shows were an affront to community standards of acceptable moral behaviour.

Given royal assent, Bill 69 empowered the New Brunswick Liquor Licensing Board to suspend or revoke liquor permits if it found an establishment guilty of offering indecent, immoral or obscene entertainment.

New Brunswick also produced K. C. Irving and W. A. C. Bennett and raised Charles Lynch, though it shouldn't be held responsible for this. Most millionaires are humourless, but Irving pushes it to the breaking point. It is rumoured he last smiled in 1937. He is so silent that there is one school of thought in New Brunswick that he, like Howard Hughes, is dead but, because of his personality, they can't tell. He will never make Bartlett's.

Camp might. Any man who can tell us that when Richard Nixon proclaimed, "I am not a crook," he immediately became the "only American president in history to insist he was not a crook and tell a lie at the same time" is obviously too useful for hand-to-hand political combat.

Dalton Camp is the Typhoid Mary of Canadian politics, the smartest man in the Conservative party who is forbidden to go near it. He is, thanks to the Diefenbaker legacy, regarded as diseased, and distinguished members of the party cross the street for fear of being seen shaking his hand. Candidates for any high Tory office palpitate if it is bruited about that Camp has anything good to say about them.

Camp sits in his high wood-and-glass home in a lonely field overlooking the soft water in Queens County, thirty-six miles southeast of Fredericton, contemplating with some bemusement, mixed with amusement, the factors that have placed him here in exile, forbidden by group-think to participate in the affairs of the party he loves and despairs of. Dief, the most vindictive man in recent political time, in death has his revenge: Camp, like the Flying Dutchman, can never come home.

Camp's sin, of course, is that he forced on his party the principle of leadership review, a sacrilegious insight in 1966 but now accepted by all three parties as a natural right (and carried to such an extreme elsewhere that the newborn Social Democratic Party in Britain elected Roy Jenkins as leader by a mail vote of all card-carrying party members).

A man of no modesty but much insight, he no doubt

has contemplated one of the more amusing facets of this endlessly amusing country. The Atlantic provinces, which are the poorest of all, seldom make a noise in their indentured poverty while Western Canada, rolling in riches, screams the loudest. (Ontario merely purrs, while Quebec, knowing the real priorities, studies the Expos' box scores.)

2
Quebec

Divorce with Bed Privileges

Belgium-on-the-St. Lawrence . . .
the stale feud between René and Pierre . . .
orphans of the constitution . . .
Ryan won't bet on Canada's future . . .
slip sliding away

Being basically complacent, and a trifle tardy in tolerance, the Anglophone majority in the country makes a terrible blunder on Quebec. (The Anglo-saxophones, the ethnics, can be forgiven a bit, since they feel left out, the ignored bystanders in an old battle.) The mistake is in thinking that the leaders of the Parti Québécois, who want to take Quebec out of Canada, are narrow little men, inward-looking provincial nationalists who cannot see the vision of a larger country.

In fact, the problem is the opposite. *Our* problem, those of us who would like to see this funny collection of fiefdoms hang together, is that the Péquiste leaders are not inward-looking. They are sophisticated outward-looking politicians whose minds and philosophies have been shaped outside Canada. Their thinking was formed abroad and their political models are drawn from abroad.

All of us are products of our backgrounds, and the PQ leaders are products of their international education. They have no real experience of Canada as a country and have no interest in it. Once when I was discussing this with Claude Ryan, then still editor of *Le Devoir*, he pointed out that he had editorial writers at his paper, the most prestigious intellectual newspaper in the country, who had never been to Toronto and had no desire ever to go there. This no doubt will cause an astonishing zoom in *Le Devoir*'s circulation in Moose Jaw and Medicine Hat, but the point is useful. (Ryan, unfortunately, succumbed to the constant peril of the editorial writer—omniscience—and entered politics itself, subsequently proving, as a wise man once said, that any journalist becoming a politician is like a jockey wanting to become a horse.)

When I argue with the Parti Québécois ministers as to the inadvisability of separation, they invariably point to Sweden, with a population of 8.3 million, or Belgium with

9.9 million, or Norway with 4.1 million. Quebec, with a population of 6.4 million, has more resources, more potential, they argue. Why couldn't it survive alone? They draw their examples from the European Common Market; from international analogies.

That is where their background lies. Take a look at the international aspects of the educations of the original PQ cabinet:

Jacques-Yvan Morin: Harvard University and
       Cambridge University
Jacques Parizeau: London School of Economics
Claude Morin: Columbia University
Bernard Landry: University of Paris
Denis Lazure: University of Pennsylvania
Jacques Couture: Speaks Chinese
Louis O'Neill: Theology degree from the Vatican
Yves Berube: Massachusetts Institute of Technology

René Lévesque himself, the world's greatest advertisement for lung cancer, the tiny man in the grubby raincoat with the paster-downer hairstyle, is still underestimated by the rest of Canada. He has been around for so long, puffing into our television screens, so long thought of as an ex-journalist who hit it lucky, that his gifts are overlooked.

He is not just a hothouse nationalist, but a man with an international background equal to that of—and perhaps surpassing—*any* Canadian politician. He obviously could have been a brilliant lawyer (his father was), but he was told to leave his third-year law class at Laval and not to return until he refrained from (wait for it) smoking. The law professor who issued the order was Louis-Philippe Pigeon, later a prickly justice of the Supreme Court of Canada.

Lévesque, instead, joined the U.S. Army as a war correspondent. (Those of us who delight in such things note that Lévesque, the man who wants to take Quebec out of Canada, served in the war for another country while the man who wants to keep it in, Pierre Trudeau, served not at all.)

Lévesque had a very good war. He went through the Blitz in London with Edward R. Murrow, William Shirer,

Walter Cronkite and the other legendary correspondents. He crossed the Rhine with General Patton, and he saw the dead body of Benito Mussolini hanging by the heels in a Milan square. He was one of the first reporters into the Dachau death camp. He interviewed many of the top Nazi generals at the end of the war. Later, he travelled to Moscow with Lester Pearson, representing the CBC, and met Nikita Khrushchev. He was Canada's premier war correspondent in the Korean War while still in the employ of the CBC. He covered the royal tour of the Princess Elizabeth who now, as Queen of England, embodies the link that infuriates him (as it would infuriate any Anglo-Canadian if we had a French-speaking Queen living in Paris.)

On his celebrated Quebec TV show, *Point de Mire*, which thrust him into the limelight so much as to induce the vault into politics, he ranged the world and explained it for his fascinated viewers. Mistaken though his cause may be, he is the finest communicator in Canadian politics.

Pierre Trudeau ranged the world as a young man, but as a well-off gypsy, seeking esoteric revolutions and prankish escapades. There was never any danger of a cheque bouncing. Lévesque's way of seeing the world was in a rather more practical, realistic fashion. Their stars were crossed from the beginning.

There is an amusing flashback clip of Lévesque, the journalist turned politician, being interviewed on TV by a CBC team composed of Larry Zolf and one Pierre Trudeau, who said little and toyed with his notes.

Lévesque nearly slapped Trudeau in a heated argument that broke up in disorder at Jean Marchand's apartment in those heady days when a small coterie of Quebec intellectuals were anticipating the day when the witch Duplessis would be dead. There was André Laurendeau, Pelletier, Trudeau, Jean Marchand and the tentatively accepted newcomer Lévesque, who struck sparks from Trudeau from the moment they met.

The Lévesque-Trudeau relationship was formed early. When Lévesque approached the *Cité Libre* group with the idea of being a contributor, Trudeau loftily asked whether the man who had just been through a war as a U.S. war correspondent "could write."

The antagonism was natural. Lévesque, for all his world-weary appearance, is not an urban animal. He was raised closer to Halifax than Montreal, on the underbelly of the Gaspé Peninsula in the English-monikered town of New Carlisle. It was no surprise that the chain-smoking, rumpled little journalist did not hit it off with the elegant millionaire's son who had dabbled at being a professional student for so long and always wore his intellectual arrogance on a well-tailored sleeve.

We are all now captives of this stale feud. We can only wait, hoping, for one or both to leave the stage. It is rather like a visitor from Mars arriving in the United States and finding that Texas wishes to secede from the union. He then discovers, to his puzzlement, that the two major figures fighting it out are both from Texas. It just wouldn't make sense to the Martian—and it doesn't to the average Canadian.

In the Paul Sauvé Arena in east-end Montreal, six days before the 20 May 1980 separation referendum, the Pierre Elliott Trudeau who can be so good sometimes on the platform and so bad so often put on a brilliant performance. He had an overflow crowd of ten thousand federalists screaming in flag-waving passion as he replied to the Lévesque slur to foreign journalists that Trudeau wasn't really a French-Canadian because of that Elliott in his name.

He traced his Trudeau roots back to the seventeenth century, with his Elliott roots, from his mother's side, almost as long. The Elliotts, he cried, were every bit as much a part of Quebec history as the Trudeaus. He thrashed the petulant Lévesque on that point.

But Trudeau did something else in that same speech. He promised Quebec—as all the headlines recorded the next day—that the reward for a "No" vote in the referendum would be a new constitution. That is the basis for the bitterness, the sense of betrayal that rests in Quebec. When the new constitution came, Quebec was excluded—its premier undisturbed in his sleep while the middle-of-the-night deal was cooked up without him.

The original purpose of the constitution was to lay down new principles, practices and structures that would renew Canadian federalism. The principles were summarized as "pre-eminence of citizens and of their freedoms . . . full respect of native rights . . . full development of two linguistic majorities . . . enhancement of the mosaic of cultures . . . self-development of regions . . . fostering economic integration . . . promoting national solidarity . . . interdependence of two orders of government . . . strengthening of Canada as a united country to serve all Canadians."

Yet, when it was finally patched together with Scotch tape and binder twine, the native peoples opted out and today still cling to Britain as guarantor of their rights, since they have no faith in Ottawa.

The clause on women's rights was forced through only at the last moment.

Property rights were left out in deference to Prince Edward Island.

Some basic legal rights were left out.

And Quebec was left out.

From Quebec's point of view, the push toward patriation of the constitution was always based on the belief that the new constitution would grant Quebec specified powers. Daniel Johnson in 1967 spoke of the need to "establish a new sharing of powers and of resources." In the same year the constitutional committee of the Liberal party referred in its report to "the collective personality of Quebec" and put forward a long list of the powers needed to nurture that personality.

It was Expo year, the hundredth anniversary of the babe of a nation, and Lévesque, still a Liberal then, spoke in Vancouver of a Quebec stifling in "an aging and obsolete Confederation." He said it will "either become an associate state within Canada, with a special status giving it the economic, political and cultural powers required for its expansion as a nation," or else it will become independent.

Trudeau, the new prime minister in 1968, of course always opposed special status for Quebec and instead wanted to expand the constitutional rights of the French language throughout Canada.

In 1971 when Robert Bourassa scuttled the Victoria Conference, Claude Ryan as editor of *Le Devoir* wrote, "There will be no agreement forthcoming from Quebec on an amending formula or patriation without firm assurances that Quebec's key jurisdictional demands will also be included in a new constitution."

With his regained majority in 1974, Trudeau reopened

his constitutional "can of worms," but by 1976 it was Bourassa who had put together a common front among premiers, opposing patriation without a substantial transfer of powers. Lévesque carried on rallying the premiers on the same issue until the 1980 forty-sixty loss on the referendum destroyed his momentum. The feds took the stance that they, not Lévesque, spoke for Quebec, an artful piece of conceit that worked until the Parti Québécois had its mandate renewed at the polls.

Such was the provincial and public distaste for the crazy Trudeau attempt to push through patriation unilaterally that Quebec was accepted as a full member of the Gang of Eight that set out to block it. The Supreme Court ruled they were correct, advising the prime minister that his initiative was legal but "unconstitutional in a conventional sense."

The eventual dog's breakfast of a Kitchen Constitution, patched together in the early morning hours while Lévesque slept, was not liked even by the prime minister. To him, it was an "abject failure."

He should know. He brought it on himself. The man who tried an end run on the provinces and most of public opinion at the finish was on the retreat, the premiers having cornered him through patience (with a little help from Bora and the Supremes).

The whole noble act of creation of a nation's constitution got down to 3:30 AM haggling in a hotel bedroom. All it needed was a private eye on a ladder outside the window of the Château Laurier and the farce would have been complete. A constitution born of adultery.

Pierre Trudeau's concept of nation-building is a peculiar one. The man who came to Ottawa in the first place to keep Quebec within Confederation and to preserve a country decided to cap his career by going to war with the provinces and alienating most of the premiers with whom he had to work. Because the patriation of the constitution (from its silly resting spot across an ocean in the hands of a foreign nation) was the ultimate target of his whole political career, he decided to achieve it by insulting the heads of the provinces, belittling them and calling them mere horse traders.

The result of all this? On that final panic-stricken night in Ottawa, with politicians ricocheting from suite to suite like confused swains in a French comedy, the high-minded feds ended up wheeling and dealing with those despised premiers in a scene that resembled the Casablanca carpet-dealers' convention. Swap this. Swap that. Override this. Override that. This is the way a country is born. Not in full view of the public, as the proud (and more democratic) Americans would have demanded in similar circumstances, but at 3:30 AM in Allan Blakeney's bedroom.

Pierre Trudeau's stubborn vow that he would go to Westminster alone was never going to work. His insistence on deadlines (to fit in with his own personal plans for retirement) was never going to work. His claim that he was justified in acting unilaterally because patriation had been stalled for fifty-four years was nonsense. The usual intellectual flim-flam. The voters had become interested in the issue only in the previous three years, and public opinion had slowly coalesced (to be ignored after midnight in hotel rooms).

We were getting there, in our own fuddling and delaying Canadian way. What the public did not count on was a clutch of conspirators tossing out human rights in all-night sessions like spare cabbages too heavy for the shopping basket.

How is a country built? After the miles of constitutional lawyers have unravelled their tongues? The present unsatisfactory solution comes, partially from a chance meeting between the Saskatchewan and Ontario premiers and their aides in an Ottawa Italian restaurant. A Magna Carta on a checkered tablecloth. Watch the tomato sauce. Wouldn't want it to drip on women's rights.

How is a country built? The Kitchen Constitution that formed the basis for the patchwork compromise that formed the deal that drove Quebec closer to separation that put the sieve in the house that Sir John A. built? Scribbled on bits of paper in a spare pantry, Casablanca rug merchants dealing trades with those who can stay the course.

How is a country built? In that late night in November 1980, proudly announced to the populace on the telly the next morning. Manitoba's Sterling Lyon was no longer there, gone home to put the finishing touches on losing an election. B.C.'s Bill Bennett, a nonlawyer, exhausted at the legal bafflegab, had gone to his pillow, leaving aides to "bargain." P.E.I.'s Angus MacLean, retiring in a few days, wasn't a factor. The fixers from Ontario, Alberta, Saskatchewan and Newfoundland didn't even bother waking René Lévesque, their companion in the long struggle of the Gang of Eight, to inform him that they were settling the flea market. That's the way a country is built, a Rube Goldberg bleary-eyed creation that came apart almost immediately.

The prime minister, in his contempt for the premiers, always maintained their concept of the constitution didn't extend beyond swapping "fish" for "oil." In the end, he did something worse. He swapped human rights like rugs.

The fifty percent of the population that is female? Out the window—forced back in only because of the outcry. Native rights? Out. The Château Laurier was turned into Casablanca because of—as the Supreme Court hinted— Pierre Trudeau's basic lack of understanding of what democracy is all about.

On 16 April 1982, the day before Queen Elizabeth (whose coronation René Lévesque had covered as an employee of a crown corporation) proclaimed on Parliament Hill the constitution that left out one-quarter of Canada, the premier of Quebec said, "We must refuse clearly to be more and more of a minority, more and more dependent, less and less significant. We must decide for ourselves soon— before it is too late—to affirm at least the majority that we are here in Quebec, to decide that Quebec must belong to us . . . as a country, a real country where we can be truly at home."

The Trudeau gamble in becoming the father of a constitution that leaves out his own province is that the Parti Québécois is a mere passing aberration that will fade away so that he or his heirs will then be able to negotiate with a more amenable Quebec government.

It's a great theory. But what if he is wrong?

Separatism wasn't "dead" as he predicted, and the PQ wasn't dead after losing the referendum. After fourteen years, Trudeau has no monopoly on wisdom pertaining to the province that raised him.

Even his fellow Liberal, Claude Ryan, thinks the surprisingly complacent way that Trudeau gave in on the constitution, after his long autocratic stance, makes the breakup of Confederation more likely.

Writing in the summer issue of *Policy Options*, a political science journal, the disillusioned and beleaguered Quebec Liberal leader—before he resigned—concluded, "Mr. Trudeau wanted to reinforce Canadian federalism. On the contrary, what he has done threatens to weaken it where it most urgently needs reinforcement—in Quebec."

Ryan gloomily predicted that the constitutional events of 1982 had given Lévesque's party's argument for independence "the new inspiration it sorely needed. The Parti Québécois predicted things would get worse (in the event of a referendum defeat), and now it can point out that things are getting worse and it's happening in front of our eyes."

By getting the provinces to go along with his idea of Canada, Trudeau had asked Quebec to accept the English-Canadian national image of an independent country "developing in the shadow of the British monarchy."

That does nothing to convince nationalist Quebecers that Canada is their country and "If the prospects of Canada rest on such an artificial foundation, I wouldn't bet much on its future."

Pierre Trudeau previously humiliated an earlier Quebec Liberal premier, Robert Bourassa, by calling him a "hotdog" publicly. Now he is alienated completely from the intellectual Ryan. He seems not able to get along either with adversaries or allies, hotdog or egghead. He seems a strange man to bind a country together. His regard for himself gets in the way.

With Lévesque inching his province toward some sort of sovereignty-association ("Divorce with bed privileges," as Bill Bennett calls it), even the base of the Liberal party is in peril. If Quebec, in some form, goes, there go the Grits as a national party. If the PQ, as threatened, runs candidates in the next federal election, it is likely they could win the dozen or so of Quebec's seventy-five seats that would destroy any Liberal chance of forming a government in Ottawa. The strange thing is that Pierre Trudeau, who went to Ottawa in the first place so as to keep Quebec within Confederation, may both lose Quebec and destroy the Liberal party. The man who called the Liberals gutless when Lester Pearson approved nuclear weapons on Canadian soil may leave it skeleton-less.

3
First Stopover

The Sidewalks of Montreal

The essence of the city is female . . .
a display case for personality . . .
the legend of Nick Auf der Maur . . .
Mordecai Richler on a tear . . .
Drapeau's ediface complex . . . 4 A.M. traffic jams . . .
even the scandals have a flair

$\mathbf{T}$he most civilized of all Canadian cities is also the one where the licence plates make a political statement. Other provinces use their licence plates to boast about their tasty gooseberries or to vilify litterbugs (Can there be a more inane statement anywhere than "Keep Ontario Beautiful"?). Quebec cars, instead, are adorned with "Je Me Souviens"—I Remember. It's a serious business in a city that takes seriously the art of living well.

The essence of Montreal as a city is *female*. Toronto is male. (Vancouver is androgynous and Ottawa is indexed.) Montreal is proud, a show-off, extravagant, vainglorious, impractical and elegant. There is a sense, on the streets, that one is on stage, auditioning for the eyes of all others. Pedestrians do not strut so much as parade. A stroll along Sherbrooke Street is still the finest visual feast in the country, the best-dressed women (Toronto's Bloor Street-Hazelton Lanes enclave is too self-consciously stylish), the most calmly confident men. There is on Montreal streets a bit of the Roman's gift for using the sidewalks as a display case for personality. Other Canadian cities use sidewalks as a thoroughfare for foot traffic; Montreal uses them for entertainment.

It is a city that has been ruled in secrecy for a quarter century by a man who even gets ill in secrecy. Mayor Jean Drapeau, probably the most skilled politician in Canada, has run the city imperiously, with one short interruption, for twenty-five years. When he entered hospital this summer, it was four days before the public was informed he had had a stroke.

He does not give press conferences. He does not speak to reporters, only to his biographers. His stay in hospital was his first "holiday" in twenty-five years. Late at night he likes to drive about the city at great speed by himself,

37

classical music blasting from his stereo. He has emerged unscathed from the greatest public scandal of our time: the disgrace and corruption in the building of the Olympic Stadium. (Vancouver in 1983 will open Canada's first domed stadium; the total cost of $125 million will be less than what it will take to finish the Olympic Stadium roof, with no one yet certain whether it will work.)

(Why is the federal Liberal party like the Big Owe? Because it has a deficit, a large hole in the middle of it and an uncertain future. I digress.)

There is the institution of the Ritz-Carlton, reigning over Sherbrooke Street, home of the Bar Mitzvahs and the five o'clock assignations in the bar, where the nuts are irresistible. Sunday brunch in the Ritz garden, with the *New York Times*, the white ducks paddling in the pond, is one of the more civilized activities in a world filled with plane hijackers, punk rock and the Canadian postal service. (At the end of the summer, the hotel kills the ducks and serves them up.) There is a sedate ritual in the Ritz bar in late afternoon, when preserved-in-aspic matrons from the Westmount ghetto come down the Mount Royal slope and sit quietly over a drink, contemplating past glories. There is in the scene a cameo out of another institution, the Meikles Hotel in Salisbury, now Harare, in Rhodesia, now Zimbabwe, where the patrons seem to be part of the furniture and looking backward over time.

The Ritz is handy. Mordecai Richler's apartment is right across the street. So is Brian Mulroney's office. The Maritime Bar downstairs, once the most comfortable lunch spot in town, hasn't the appeal since it has been redecorated. Some museums need to be preserved.

What sets Montreal apart is the slight air of late-1920s New York to it. There are still *boulevardiers* in Montreal, bon vivants who squeeze every last bit out of the night. One of them is Nick Auf der Maur, a near-legend in his own time, a journalist and politician and provocateur. Living well, as the countess said, is the best revenge, and Auf der Maur follows the principle, sometimes too well. He charts the changing drinking patterns of the Crescent Street regulars in his Montreal Gazette column as assiduously as a chess master, and bistros fall and prosper on his scouting reports.

He was one of the hordes arrested in the War Measures

swoop, an event that has enhanced his career, like someone who has had a good war. As an opposition member of the city council that Drapeau ignores, he wrote a fabulously detailed book on all the Olympic corruption that later formal inquiries confirmed. The Los Angeles 1984 Olympic Games organizers have flown him in to hear his warnings on overspending. He calls himself "the Red Adair of the Olympics movement."

He has a fine mind topped with a manic wit, separated only by a healthy thirst. He is a Montreal original and could not be transplanted anywhere else. His flower would wither and die.

Richler, especially while on a tear, is a *boulevardier* of another stance, a gifted writer who has made a career of mocking his upbringing in the Jewish ambience of St. Urbain street across town. He no longer speaks with his mother and enjoys life in his own bittersweet way. He grows out of the Montreal pavement and he, too, could never be dug up and grafted elsewhere. Montreal has this peculiar early-New York sense, of producing characters who could not possibly *fit* anywhere else. Only Vancouver is similar in this way, in creating some people who would expire from culture shock if shifted to a foreign (i.e., across the mountains) ambience.

Montreal is the only Canadian city with 4 AM traffic jams. The 4 AM traffic jams are filled with Mercedes-Benz taxi cabs. The centre of street life has shifted recently from the boutique-and-bistro glitter of Crescent Street one block west to Bishop, where the midnight air is filled with BMWs, silk and young men with expense account hair.

After the Parti Québécois came to power, the emboldened separatist youth decided to reclaim their own city and established a rival café society on St. Denis, which is the demarcation line to the east end of the city where Drapeau's voters live and love his grandiose edifice complex. On St. Jean Baptiste night, two cultures now compete in street theatre, the true party-goers drifting from rival camp to rival camp. The gonzo successor to St. Urbain's Horseman will be written by someone who can translate that rivalry into an explanation of the new Montreal, financially wounded by the Anglo Boat People taking the 401 escape to Toronto, but being reborn in a more self-controlled way.

Montreal, the home of Pierre Trudeau, has traffic signs that now—unlike Paris—do not say: Arrêt/Stop. It is only Arrêt, thanks to the language police of Bill 101, the tongue-troopers. As Lévesque himself says, he was "humiliated" at having to bring in such a bill, but he had to save Montreal, the second-largest French-speaking city in the world, from becoming an English-speaking city. If Montreal fell, there would be no hope for the rest of the province.

There has never been a situation where a minority acting as if it were a majority did not invite revenge. The Westmount Rhodesians did exploit their comfortable position in Quebec society, and now the revenge-mongers, led by the Grim Reaper Dr. Camille Laurin, are having their innings. Logic will prevail, in the end, but for the moment we must endure the vengeance. Generations have long memories.

The most telling example of how deep runs the bitterness against the slights of the Westmount Rhodesians was the farce of Claude Charron, Lévesque's mercurial House leader, stealing a $130 tweed jacket from Eaton's in downtown Montreal. The department store, no doubt realizing the political implications in the light of the flight of Anglophones from the city, pondered long and hard and went through all the precautionary formalities before filing shoplifting charges.

Immediately—helped along by Lévesque's rather dishonest hints—there was the Francophone outcry of persecution ordered by the "bosses" in Toronto. (The decision to proceed on the charges was made by Francophone executives of Eaton's in Montreal.) While the threats and the hot-lines hummed, it turned out that this was no mere absentminded shoplifter but a cabinet minister who, when questioned at the door, fled for blocks, leaping traffic barricades and risking death by dodging speeding cars before being wrestled to earth by a security guard.

The accusations of Anglo "persecution" of a pure and simple thief were finally silenced by a telling little letter to a Montreal paper by a French-Canadian boy who said that what he apparently was being advised was that it was wrong to steal from French stores but it was okay to steal from English stores. The silence was deafening.

Speaking of that, the single most important player in

the Canadian Football League in 1982 could have been Luc Tousignant, the Trois-Rivières native who was given a chance to quarterback the born-again Montreal Concorde. He was the first chance for the Québécois to shape their own hero and save a franchise in the biggest stadium in Canada (after the club was pillaged and near-ruined by the offhand management of Vancouver buccaneer Nelson Skalbania). Cool Hand Luc was the key to attendance figures—and keeping Montreal in the CFL instead of defecting to Drapeau's dream, a National Football League franchise. Alas Luc grew splinters on the bench.

Drapeau dreams Montreal's dreams. He knows his flock well. He has conditioned them to world standards: Expo '67, the Olympic Games, a showcase subway system, a pioneering subterranean shopping and pedestrian maze. He likes the flamboyant and so does Montreal. Even the scandals have a flair: Lévesque runs over a drunk, Charron steals a sports jacket, Olympic Stadium gravel truck operators drive in one gate and out another, collecting their fee without ever dumping their load and drive around again. *Insouciance* counts in Montreal. Actor Donald Sutherland, the Number One Expos baseball freak, was in Paris during a crucial July series with league-leading St. Louis. He phoned a friend and listened, across the Atlantic, to the games.

Montreal doesn't abide losers (Toronto shrugs and goes back to the money) which is why the Montreal Canadien players dread a summer on the golf course when they don't win the Stanley Cup, having to explain *why* day after endless day on the green. Which is why the city, currently shifting its cultural base from being tenant to being owner, will be a winner again. Trust me.

4
First Digression

Trudeau's Cabinet
or
Journey to the Land of Nod

*Pierre Elliott Reincarnation
and his feckless disciples . . .
Chrétien confides in Fodderingham . . .
an agriculture minister with
foot in mouth disease . . . Senator Phogbound*

Pierre Trudeau, despite the famed reputation for steely discipline and iron command, is, in fact, a lousy leader. In his airy hubris he has driven /scared/sluffed off all the strong Anglos who once populated his ministry. He is the neutron bomb of Liberal politics, destroying all the personalities within while leaving the institution standing (barely).

Paul Hellyer, as a stiff-principled housing minister after forcing all the Canadian armed forces to look like Coca-Cola deliverymen, marched into Mr. Trudeau's office threatening to resign and had the offer ripped out of his hand so fast his church-choir baritone is still squeaky. John Turner went into Mr. Trudeau's office to discuss a promised relief from the dead-end finance portfolio and—after being insulted by being offered the Senate or a spot on the bench—emerged with tears in his eyes, having resigned.

The gutsy Eric Kierans left after determining that his trademark—economic honesty and bluntness—was not appreciated or wanted.

The disputatious Bryce Mackasey, who is nothing if not passionate, resigned one morning in a temper, was persuaded by advisors to recant but, unwisely, had lunch first and grew so agitated during his afternoon repentance session with the PM that he resigned again, which is thought to be a *Guinness Book of World Records* mark for most resignations in one day. His tempestuous career, in and out of the cabinet, then a term in the Quebec legislature, an abortive try at an Ottawa seat and eventually a resting spot in the Ontario federal riding of Lincoln, on the excuse that was where his mother lived, inevitably brought forward the Press Gallery question: "Why is an Edsel running in Lincoln?"

The late Bob Andras, who wanted to be finance minister, left when he saw that the Ping-Pong Trudeau mind was about to flip into one of its nationalist left-leaning modes. He departed for corporate stamp-collecting in Vancouver.

Ron Basford, an honest toiler, left after four cabinet posts—and no one in authority wrote him a letter, thanked him or said, "In your hat."

Mr. Trudeau never dissuades anyone who offers to leave, nor does he think it his responsibility to recruit talented newcomers. Each individual is expected to survive in the vacuum in which Trudeau grooms his own intellect. He doesn't like people, but he does like money and his cheapness, as Margaret's memoirs testify, extends to worn towels and thin linen.

It is amusing that his inherited fortune began as a chain of Montreal Island gas stations which his father sold to Imperial Oil (a.k.a. Esso, a.k.a. Exxon), which ultimately became one of the multinational targets of the disastrous National Energy Policy—the latter-day Trudeau nationalist conversion that turned foreign investors against Canada and destroyed the dollar, the economy and Trudeau's place in history as a triumphant leader. The man dallied over the constitution while the buck burned.

The prime requisite of any leader—in business, politics, academe, publishing or elsewhere—is to assure that there is an acceptable and competent successor in place so as to guarantee continuity. By this criterion, Mr. Trudeau again qualifies as a lousy leader. Proof of this is that in the present Liberal frontbench, where seat assignment is designated by seniority, the man now sitting three chairs away from the prime minister of Canada is Agriculture Minister Eugene Whelan, who only takes his foot out of his mouth to change feet.

The old Ottawa line on Whelan is that he had a bad fire at his house, destroying his entire library. It burned both books and one of them he hadn't finished colouring yet. That is a canard, of course, because we have it on authority that he reads in bed every night until his lips get tired.

Such jollities, prime fodder at press gatherings, are in the same vein as the Liberal minister, well-washed in the brandy one evening, who was asked to fess up as to who the cabinet would nominate as leader "if the PM were run over by a bus tomorrow."

"Easy," was the reply. "The bus driver."

46

The serious part is that Pierre Trudeau, the man who won't recruit and can't retain, has basically destroyed the Liberal party as a national force. It is a regional government attempting to govern nationally. Fifty percent of the Liberal caucus in Parliament is from Quebec. If you take the Quebec factor out of Gallup Poll soundings, the Liberals are running third, behind even the NDP, in the rest of the country.

When Pierre Elliott Reincarnation came to power in 1968, Lester Pearson left him with almost half of Canada—four provinces—under Liberal rule at the provincial level. A fifth and sixth province came later. Today, of course, there is not a single province with a Liberal government.

The combination of Trudeau truculence and indifference has killed the party at the provincial level in Western Canada. In Alberta, it is as dead as the dinosaurs; it is in the grave in Saskatchewan; it is dying in Manitoba and in B.C., to paraphrase John Diefenbaker, it is protected only by the game laws. There isn't a single Liberal left in any of the four Western legislatures, and the only two Western MPs, Lloyd Axworthy and Bob Bockstael, stand almost no chance of re-election.

A further example of Mr. Trudeau's Frisbee-playing with portfolios is the solicitor-general post, thought to be a fairly important position considering its role in the criminal justice system of the country.

When Trudeau became leader in 1968, he shuffled off George McIlraith, one of the Pearson government veterans, into the ministry. By 1970 the unforgettable Jean-Pierre Goyer—incredibly bright and incredibly accident-prone—was given the job. He lasted not two years before Trudeau, shuffling again (not cleaning house, but shuffling) put in the job the sincere and hard-working Warren Allmand.

Allmand set a record under Trudeau (perhaps why he was later bounced from the cabinet): he lasted almost four years in the portfolio.

There next came calligraphy expert Francis Fox, continuing the Trudeau practice of using this potentially dangerous legal role as a sort of training bra post for untried juniors. When Fox had to resign because of his forgetfulness in not telling his boss about personal problems, the ever-smiling Jean-Jacques Blais took over this particular deck chair on the Titanic.

Blais lasted the bare minimum of two years, ducking flak and grenades in the Commons almost every week, a pratfall looking for a place to happen, before being recycled. Bob Kaplan, who had been lusting to get into the cabinet since first being elected in the Trudeaumania sweep of 1968, finally got his reward: the ejector seat also known as solicitor-general.

This bumbling record demonstrates the anomaly in the rigid brain of Pierre Elliott Trudeau. He is famously tough on philosophy, on principles, on issues. But when it comes to changing the men who must apply those principles, he is as dishwater.

He abides to an amazing degree (some shrinks might give you another opinion) helpless victims, men who can't cross the rug without walking on their tongues. A retrospective look at Trudeau's fourteen years with such as André Ouellet and John Munro would make you weep.

Heavy-handed fumblers walking about looking for an open manhole, they foul up, resign and are accepted back into the fold in time by a master who seems, in all honesty, to be so beset by lassitude as not to have the energy to examine the rest of his flock for talent. In truth, it is easier to keep a Munro or an Ouellet around than a Turner or a Kierans. Trudeau takes the easy way out.

Yet there is an air of genial arrogance to the Liberal frontbench, the Natural Governing Party being in such general contempt of both Joe Clark's abilities and the lust of the Tory party to destroy itself that it cruises along, awash in superiority, rather like a Chrysler Air-Flow in overdrive.

Jean Chrétien, puppy-dog frisky, is the most appealing of this bunch but even he has looked somewhat tarnished in his messenger-boy role on the constitution, eager not to irritate his boss since he is attempting the audacious task of succeeding him.

Chrétien's chances of doing so, strangely enough, are being wrecked by what one would think would be his strength: the Quebec caucus. The realization has sunk in among Quebec MPs that if they put their concerted support behind Chrétien—and were successful—it would naturally shatter the unwritten Grit law that has been a key to the party's success: the switching of the leadership between Anglo and Francophone leaders. It has sunk in that if the Quebec wing of the party allows a Francophone to succeed a Francophone, it could lead to a future scenario of a Turner followed by a Macdonald followed by a Fotheringay—and how could Quebec then object?

I once put this notion to Chrétien over dinner and, in his usual irrepressible manner, he said, "Well, Fodderingham, I'll tell you a story."

The story was that Chrétien and Clark always got along well on a personal basis, perhaps because of both being barefoot kids from rather modest backgrounds. In 1975 when Clark was trying to decide if he would assay his rather audacious run at the Tory leadership, he encountered Chrétien at a urinal in the parliamentary washroom. He asked Chrétien's advice as to whether he should try it.

"Joe, I'll guarantee you only one thing," replied Chrétien. "If you don't run, you won't win."

Chrétien turned to me. "Well, Fodderingham, you may be right but I tell you, if I don't run, I won't win."

Chrétien is impossible to dislike, always looking, as Dalton Camp put it, like "the driver of the getaway car." (Cartoonists would be kinder to him if they knew that the famous gangster-out-of-the-corner-of-the-mouth speaking style is because of deafness in one ear.) He is the second youngest of nineteen children, only nine of whom survived. When you come out of Shawinigan, you learn to be a street-fighter.

He is the most solidly married man in Canada. Sequestered as a teen-ager in a church school where girls were not allowed even to visit, he would spend Sunday afternoons walking, trailing fingers, with his sixteen-year-old love, she on the outside of the school fence, he inside. Chrétien arrived in Ottawa in 1963 not speaking a word of English. Adopted as a protégé by Finance Minister Mitchell Sharp, Chrétien was warned by a Quebec colleague after a meeting with high mandarins that the conversations must be regarded as confidential. "You don't have to worry," said Chrétien. "I didn't understand a goddam word."

Alone of the Quebec ministers, he has been a great hit in Western Canada (though is in danger of overdoing it) with his Johnny Baptiste act, telling delighted audiences that he is just a little "pea-souper" who puts "the em-*phas*-is on the wrong sy-*lla*-ble." In fact, he has surprising Western connections. His grandfather, fed up with something, emigrated to Alberta and corresponded with the family constantly on his Prairie experiences. There are some forty-plus Chrétien relatives sprinkled throughout Alberta, ready for the leadership battle.

The street-fighter, naturally, has always been in awe of the elegantly dressed and elegantly egoed leader from Montreal's best salons. Early in his cabinet term, Chrétien found himself in a government plane beside Trudeau on the way to a Liberal event. Struggling for conversation, Chrétien grasped upon the fact that rain had begun to sprinkle his window. "It's raining outside," he ventured helpfully.

"When it's raining, it's always outside," was the bored rejoinder from the prime minister of all Canada. The journey continued in silence.

Allan MacEachen is an explorer, a prober, a Dr. Livingstone of the oratorical art. He is a cartographer of language, someone who finds gullies, crevices, arroyos, dips and undulations on the way to the end of a sentence. He approaches a question period query as he would a bramblebush, carefully meandering his way around it, probing, poking, his fuzzy syntax taking on the qualities of a porcupine, impenetrable, unfathomable, a possible conclusion hidden in a thicket of circumlocutions.

Robert Fulford once wrote that when he listened to a Paul Martin speech he had the feeling his head was being slowly filled with glue. Listening to MacEachen masticating an answer in the House of Commons, ruminating on his choice of prevarications rather like a cow chewing on its cud before depositing it in one of the bifurcations of the stomach, is to witness a master obfuscator, one who uses the language of Shakespeare to conceal rather than to reveal. He is an ecdysiast of the encyclopedia, the Gypsy Rose Lee of the dictionary, a man so used to having his mouth filled with mush that he wouldn't recognize English if he swallowed it.

The first time I met MacEachen was 1968, in his corner station in the Ottawa ice rink, just before the opening ballot in the Liberal leadership race that went to four ballots and featured eight well-qualified candidates, plus the Rev. Lloyd Henderson. (The Rev. Lloyd, mayor of Portage La Prairie, Man., had also run for the leadership in the 1958 convention that chose Lester Pearson. He received one vote and the magnificent Norman Depoe, on national television, consoled him by saying that he at least had the satisfaction of voting for himself. "Oh, I wasn't a voting delegate," confessed Rev. Lloyd. "But my wife and mother-in-law were.")

But I digress. I was introduced to MacEachen by an old friend, Richard Vogel, who went to law school in the Maritimes. Always the diligent reporter, I immediately asked MacEachen where he was going to throw his votes when he was bounced early (as I assumed he knew he would be). Vogel, a consummate gentleman and now B.C.'s deputy attorney-general, rolled his eyes to the roof and looked away in agony, mortified at what he had anticipated would be a genial how-do-you-do introduction. MacEachen blanched and looked stricken, as if someone had told him his fly was open.

He died, of course, on the first ballot, getting only 165 votes. He was so stunned and confused that he didn't get his withdrawal to the convention chairman in time to get his name off the second ballot—which delivered him eleven votes.

It was a defeat so predictable to your scribe and so surprising to MacEachen that it later made more understandable his total misreading of his celebrated budget botch-up that ultimately ruined his career. As a result of my famed diplomacy, we did not speak again for thirteen years, until we were seated opposite one another at the 1981 Parliamentary Press Gallery banquet and could hardly avoid the niceties.

Eugene Whelan sits in the frontbench, seemingly forlorn without the green felt cowboy hat he wears whenever outdoors, and perhaps to bed. He is a large bloodhound, morose, his mangled features never changing, continuing reading his documents when even his less-enthusiastic seatmates are up on their hindlegs pounding their mitts together on some stale excuse for partisan thumping, like fraternity boys in a cafeteria, applauding something of which they know naught, but expressing the bonding of the troupe. Snuffling at the same waterhole.

Whelan keeps to himself, a warthog among dandies

and triflers, tolerated by Trudeau only because, with no Western bodies available, Trudeau must appoint an Ontario agriculture minister to shepherd a portfolio that largely concerns Westerners. Meanwhile Whelan has been steadily courting farm support for his long-planned leadership bid that seems loony, but as he looks about him at some of the other pretenders, he merely shrugs, puts on his hat and goes to bed.

Jean-Luc Pépin, always looking like the comedian in a French bedroom farce, is an unhappy man, a tender poet put among dray horses. He sulks like a cocker spaniel at slights and has been subdued since Trudeau insulted him by shoving him into the meat-and-potatoes transport slot, where his professor's gifts are not exactly suited for boxcars and coal ports. Trudeau does not like him, since Pépin had constitutional ideas of his own and the PM usually does not like anyone who disagrees with him.

The Roberts-Pépin task force on the constitution (Monty Pépin's Flying Circus), a $4,323,736 million test of the elasticity of the taxpayer's wallet, was sunk in the Rideau Canal and hasn't been seen since. Peter Lougheed, by the way, thinks Pépin is a fair person. He sits two seats to the right of Trudeau in the frontbench and they seldom speak.

Marc Lalonde, as David Crombie puts it, would pick a fight on the way to church. The most genial of companions in private, with a grin that stretches from Rimouski to Regina, in public he is the stiff-necked hit man of the Trudeau cabinet. If Chrétien looks like the driver of the getaway car, Lalonde is the guy carrying the violin case.

He shares an affliction, in a strange way, with Robert Stanfield and Joe Clark (both Clark and Lalonde started their political careers devoted to the brilliance of the tragic Davie Fulton, destroyed by Dief's vindictiveness and bounced from the B.C. bench for drunken driving). Stanfield, Clark and Lalonde are comfortable, witty companions in private, in small groups, but once some magic figure is reached—when stepping before, say, thirty people—they are transformed. The former two freeze and perform like marionettes, the latter drops his grin, shifts into his machine-gun mind and lets fire, safety catch forgotten. The first two are intimidated by crowds, the last one attempts to intimidate the world, which is usually mistaken for Alberta.

(Mr. Trudeau has the opposite problem: so engaging when he wants to be in his kiss-trampoline public persona, he is a chilly, encased intellect in private—but that's another book, that has been written thrice.)

Lalonde's lordly manner toward the unwashed comes honestly: he is a solid man whose family has farmed the same land on an island in the St. Lawrence for eight generations. Like Trudeau, he was a civil servant before being persuaded to offer his name on a ballot and so, like his master, brings a father-knows-best attitude to politics, an attitude that accounts for so much of the Liberal party's charm, panache and winsomeness.

Early in his career, Marc Lalonde vowed to rearrange a Canada where insults to French-Canadians were no longer possible. He helped Trudeau achieve that necessary goal, but his hardness, his lack of charity in public comments, has helped to divide the country on an east-west axis.

The failure of the Trudeau era is that the man went to Ottawa for the most noble of purposes, to convince Quebec that it had a place in the capital of Canada. But because of his autocratic manner, he has driven out so many men of talent from the Anglophone end of the world that he had to appoint Lalonde to the essentially Western portfolio of energy and Pépin to the indubitably Western portfolio of transport—knowing that his only possible alternative—Lloyd Axworthy—was too callow for the task. The fault was not Axworthy's, but Trudeau's. The man who thinks recruiting is beneath him reaps the whirlwind.

He is concerned for his country but burnishing his own ego has proven, in the end, more important than his party.

His persona has come before his party. It will be up to history to judge but, one suspects, the process might have been served better if the order of precedence had been readjusted.

I digress, slightly. One of the few interesting faces in the Trudeau crew is Don Johnston, the Economic Development Minister who was Trudeau's personal lawyer in Montreal. He retains his sanity by having a piano in his East Block office and pounds away when the political inanities get to him. The last keeper of the black and white keys in cabinet was Mitchell Sharp, who played

53

sedately as if to fit his parliamentary style. Johnston, playing ragtime in his blue corduroy suit, resembles an antic Yukon piano player in a house of ill repute. (In fact, it's across the way, in the Centre Block.) He is gangly and looks as if he might have trouble in a crosswalk but surprisingly is a terrific tennis player and was on the McGill team. His arms and legs go off in all directions, like Stephen Leacock's horseman, but in truth he's an athletic Joe Clark.

Mines Minister Judy Erola stands out like burnished steel, a widow with a spring in her step, who enters the House each day looking as if just scrubbed from the bath. A tough lady, she would seem to have unlimited potential if Iona Campagnolo (one of The Pretenders) were not lurking in the weeds, waiting for the call.

John Roberts, the Minister in Charge of Acid Rain, a portfolio unfitting to his drawing room gifts, no longer takes himself seriously as a leadership candidate. This is fortunate because his assessment is now attuned to the thoughts of others. What he really needs is a pair of designer gumboots.

Then there's the already mentioned "Hungry Bob" Kaplan. He has been so referred to around Ottawa after encountering, on a parliamentary elevator, Pat Carney, the vigorous Conservative MP for Vancouver Centre, which has the worst child prostitution and street sex problem in Canada. She had demanded in the Commons that the government do something about the disgrace.

On the elevator, the feckless Kaplan, solicitor-general of Canada, tells her that he can't understand her concern, since it must be good for the fast food business in the riding: "Everyone knows that when you get laid, you get hungry."

Hungry Bob, out of elevators, is painfully earnest (he is coauthor with his wife of a tome called *Bicycling in Toronto*) and walks about with an air of innocent puzzlement as to why the world is picking on him.

He defends, then doesn't defend, the RCMP opening our mail. He defends—then reveals he didn't know about—his agents paying $100,000 to a mass-murderer for telling where his corpses were buried. He is terminally stumble-tongued. Ontario County Court Judge Barry Shapiro refused to allow one of Kaplan's helpful letters—a signed character reference for an accused, one of Kaplan's constituents—to be read in court because it was in "poor taste." The judge, rightly, could see it. Kaplan couldn't.

Poor taste is not the word for our prime minister. Poor judgment in men is the proper phrase.

There are others, never-weres and never-will-be's, testaments to the curious Trudeau belief that he is neither responsible for recruiting nor retaining. He almost never sacks anyone; for a man supposedly so strong on principles, on policies, he is strangely reluctant to follow through on his logic to replace those who foul up on his assigned plan.

Those who disgrace themselves (Francis Fox, who couldn't remember his right name; André Ouellet, guilty of contempt of court; John Munro, who phoned a judge) are merely sent into the anteroom to be laundered, then resurface in the cabinet completely cleansed of the lack of judgment they were born with. Lord Carrington, the most respected member of Margaret Thatcher's cabinet, resigned over the Falklands farce as a matter of principle, because he accepted responsibility. Ministers who couldn't carry his spats lounge in Trudeau's cabinet for years and are shuffled about as in checkers. Not chess, checkers.

The unhappy Munro—perspiring, either chain-smoking or endlessly trying to quit—is the only man who has managed to make the bathtub into an offensive weapon. Fox's main accomplishment in Ottawa is still his permanent. It is hard to believe that magazine profiles once pictured the chippy and surly Ouellet as a possible French-Canadian prime minister. His famous complaint, following a disastrous post office strike, that any small businessmen who really relied on the post office for their livelihood had perhaps better find other work is already enshrined in the pantheon of Grit thought, somewhere near the level of the famous pronouncement of the beloved post office union leader Joe Davidson that "the public can go to hell." The sentiments—one from an embittered leader of post office workers, the other from the minister in charge—both came under the aegis of Liberal rule. They have set the tone. Two moronic statements fit and match.

Paul Cosgrove's political career was finished one autumn day in 1981. Angry and worried mortgage-holders, hit with the threat of foreclosures due to zooming interest rates, took a six-hour bus ride from Toronto to protest on Parliament Hill. Cosgrove, a seemingly competent municipal politician from Toronto, was taken into the cabinet as housing minister, what would seem a modest role for a newcomer to the House of Commons.

When the seven hundred middle-class demonstrators arrived on the parliamentary lawn for their orderly protest, not a single Liberal minister, let alone Housing Minister Cosgrove, had the courage or courtesy to come out and address them or accept their petitions. Further, some insensitive twit within the system ordered Mounties to guard Parliament from the people who own it. A government that sends armed police against people who are merely frightened of losing their homes is not a government that deserves support. He has since been made into a delivery boy for Lalonde in Finance.

There are such as Ed Lumley, the poor man's John Turner, and Jim Fleming who sounds like he is delivering a radio commercial (his old trade) every time he tries to issue what is meant to be an important pronouncement.

There is Herb Gray (known in the Press Club as gray Herb), as earnest as his press releases are unreadable. He is the Number One nationalist in cabinet, continually buffeted from success to defeat by Trudeau's detours of philosophy and so serious about his planned leadership bid that he has unleashed North America's second-oldest crewcut (only Mickey Spillane's has lasted longer) and let it grow out, a severe blow to ww Two nostalgia buffs.

There are others, too droll or dull to mention. To represent the three Western provinces, Trudeau has had to dip into the Senate for a puzzling collection of talent. Saskatchewan's representative, Hazen Argue, is a turncoat, who was an ambitious socialist until he was beaten by Tommy Douglas for leader of the New Democratic Party. He jumped to the Liberals in 1961 and when he was appointed to the Senate in 1966, David Lewis rose in the Commons and said, "We have made progress in our civilization. The thirty pieces of silver have now become half a million dollars, which is what Mr. Argue has been paid for being what he was." At forty-five, Argue had a safe thirty years to go in the Senate until mandatory retirement at a then annual wage of $15,000, which would have been worth $450,000. He has since been rewarded three-fold.

The representative from Alberta is another turncoat, Bud Olson, who was a Social Credit MP until induced to become a Liberal and received the usual Senate reward when he was defeated, as all Liberals in these three provinces are.

British Columbia is represented in the cabinet by two men who represent no voter. One, Jack Austin, is a former defeated Liberal candidate. He is an artful dodger with a brilliant mind, a lawyer who turned mining promoter in the bucket-shop days of the Vancouver Stock Exchange. While a mining promoter, he mysteriously became a Queen's Counsel four days before going to Ottawa— arranged with Premier W.A.C. Bennett by Austin's old friend Paul Martin, whom he supported at the 1968 Liberal leadership convention.

Austin lasted just fifteen months as Trudeau's principal secretary before accusations about his past appeared in the press and threatened questions in the Commons by the Tories, speeding his elevation to the Senate. He was just forty-three at the time, and the payoff stretching the thirty-two years until he is seventy-five will total $937,600— an improvement on Argue's reward.

The second B.C. minister is a well-meaning throwback, a stentorian wheelhorse named Ray Perrault who is known as either Senator Phogbound or, in Victoria, Phineas T. Windbag. Thrown out of work by the voters, and before his Senate reward came through, Perrault was fixed with an amorphous job with Jack Davis (then a Trudeau minister before being defeated, turning Social Credit and being sacked from the B.C. cabinet for turning his first class air tickets in for economy seats and pocketing the difference). Enraged by the anti-Trudeaucrat stand taken on CBC Vancouver by commentator Ben Metcalfe, Perrault recorded the critical comments on his own tape recorder and Davis actually raised the issue in the Commons, demanding that this treasonous soul be sacked by the CBC. Mr. Metcalfe no longer appears on the CBC.

A man with a fuse the length of a cigarette butt, Perrault responded thusly to a Vancouver hot-line caller who disagreed with him: "You strike me as not very intelligent, a drag on society." The next woman caller: "Well, I guess I'm just another drag on society." Perrault, who at the time was government leader in the Senate: "Don't phone up here and abuse politicians."

Sometimes you don't have to; they do it to themselves. Perrault, in full flight, often strangles on his own convoluted verbiage and pageboys must be summoned to disentangle him from his syntax before it cuts off his air supply. When he was in the Commons, the word was that he wore out two desk tops per session, his enthusiastic thumping at his leader's eloquence so physical that it reduced the desk top to kindling. Anyone who doubts that Trudeau has a mordant sense of humour only has to note that he has now made the rotund Perrault into a Minister of Sport and Fitness.

The casual way Trudeau approaches the cabinet, its selection and nurturing is illustrated by the consumer and corporate affairs ministry. Pig owners may be better represented in Canada than consumers. The *Directory of Associations* lists seven associations under "Consumer Protection," fifteen under "Swine."

The record of Pierre "Just Society" Trudeau in the struggle between consumers and the business world is a joke. Canada still has the weakest anticombines legislation of any so-called civilized country. Trudeau has used the portfolio as a neglected way station, shuffling ministers through in revolving-door fashion. A look at the record indicates the PM's lack of interest in having an effective watchdog on consumer and corporate interests.

When Ron Basford succeeded John Turner in the early Trudeau years, he introduced Bill C-256, the Competition Act. The *London Sunday Times* called it "the most sweeping antitrust legislation in North American history." That was 1971. A furious and heavily financed lobby from business interests—Basford was called "a dangerous fanatic"—achieved its aim. The bill was killed, Basford was dropped from the ministry in early 1972 and his senior mandarins removed.

In his place, Trudeau planted the compliant Andras, a Lakehead auto dealer who, applauded *The Canadian Grocer*, had "the entrepreneurial wisdom of a successful salesman." Andras, cochairman of the upcoming 1972 election campaign, knew that Liberal bagmen had found slim pickings among infuriated businessmen—a large factor, as it turned out, in the Grits being subsequently dumped into a minority situation. He announced that a revised competition bill would be reintroduced.

After the election, Herb Gray became minister. By April 1974, he had a bill to amend the Combines Investigation Act. The day he opened debate, the Liberal frontbenches were empty. The next month, an election was called and he was dumped from the cabinet. André Ouellet, who succeeded him, had to resign by 1976 when he made some understandable (if inflamed) comments about a judge after Canada's major sugar companies were acquitted in an antitrust case.

Bryce Mackasey was then in and out of the portfolio so fast the revolving door didn't even have time to cool his temper.

The Trudeau genius then appointed Tony Abbott, the genial lightweight who had spent all his previous incarnation in an anticonsumer mode. Son of a former Liberal finance minister, he was executive assistant to that quintessential corporate figure, Robert Winters, and followed him to Brascan, where he was corporate counsel to the food and brewing concerns of the conglomerate.

Next, apprenticing as a champion of consumers, Abbott was president of the Retail Council of Canada, a lobby for the chain stores. In one impassioned speech, he referred to "Comrade Ron" Basford and "Commissar David"—a reference to the respected David Henry, director of investigations and research in the ministry Abbott later was to head. *Beautiful!* Tony Abbott, a flack for corporate interests, is Trudeau's choice as the defender of the consumer.

After little more than a year, Abbott was shuffled to the small business portfolio where he belonged. In came Warren Allmand, a burned-out case after being lied to by the barn-burning Mounties when solicitor-general. And now—you'll never guess. We have the recycled André Ouellet, contrite and cautious, back where he started out.

Just as bad was the treatment of the senior staff. Once it was obvious the Trudeaucrats were backing away from the original Competition Act, Henry resigned to go to the Supreme Court of Ontario. Once it was clear the Liberals would allow Bill C-256 to die on the order paper, deputy minister Jim Grandy left.

In his first ten years in office, the idealist author of The Just Society had seven different ministers and six deputy ministers waft their way through the portfolio. He is now working on his ninth appointment in thirteen years. Does he care? We'll leave it to you.

In toto, Mr. Trudeau has expanded his cabinet to thirty-six bodies, the highest number in Canadian history. It means one-quarter of the entire Liberal caucus, with a majority government, is now in the cabinet. It means that the Trudeaucrat cabinet is now larger than the entire legislature of Prince Edward Island.

It is a cabinet without spark, without wit, without any real oratorical skills, save the now-discredited MacEachen and a Trudeau who less and less often rouses himself. He seldom addresses the House of Commons he disdains in a full speech more than two or three times a year and so debases the coinage. He is a bored man and we are the recipients of his boredom.

It is a cabinet not trusted by the Opposition parties and not respected by the public. It is a testimony to Pierre Trudeau as a leader and selector of what are deemed to be his most talented followers.

5
Second Stopover

*Ottawa Revisited
with a Vengeance*

Hot air and cold warfare . . .
the symbiotic suckling of politicians,
press and swivel servants . . .
mouths stuffed with bafflegab, minds
filled with persiflage . . .
Ennui-on-the-Rideau

Ottawa, Yesterday's City Tomorrow, is at the base of our ills. "Queen Victoria's Mistake," as the city is fondly known, is the coldest capital city in the world next to Ulan Bator. As Casey Stengel used to say, you can look it up.

If Winnipeg's climate can be described as ten months winter and two months hard sledding, Ottawa is best defined as Earmuff and Armpit City. When one isn't in use, the other is. God in Her wisdom, when She invented us, did not really intend human beings to spend their lives in spots with *two* bad seasons. Canadians must suffer because their capital, by error, was planted in a spot that alternates mosquito dive-bombers with Arctic blizzards and the denizens—naturally—wish to share their misery with the rest of their fellow citizens. It is called co-operative federalism.

The residents of Ottawa maintain that bundling up in seven layers of clothing before venturing to the corner Mac's Milk for a pound of prefrozen butter builds character and improves the breed.

It doesn't. It just makes you surly.

Anyone who must shovel his way down the steps, chip the ice from his car, hold a match to the door lock to thaw it and then inch to work behind a snow plow is not going to smile at his desk—he is going to take revenge on his fellow Canadians by venting his spleen on the people in happier circumstances.

Lots of people in Saskatchewan and Newfoundland endure the same day's beginnings, but they have worthwhile work ahead. As the man once said, at any university, the top third of the class goes on to become professors, the second third goes to work for government, and the other third has to go out and earn a living. A bemused outsider, as your faithful agent is, is continually struck by

63

the number of Ottawa residents who actually *think* they lead a normal existence, that this beehive of self-stroking represents reality.

In essence, this is its major sin: it is an artificial city, as artificial as any company town built around a pulp mill on an isolated B.C. inlet. Tennessee Ernie Ford's line, *I owe my soul to the company store*, though he didn't know it, was written for Ottawa. All three species that populate the town—the politicians, the press and the swivel servants—suck off the same giant teat, Mother Government.

There is a natural ambience, a symbiotic relationship (though superficial antagonisms remain, rather like Jack Benny-Fred Allen feuds) since there is a shared experience that is mated, in essence, to a mutual good. Knocking the product, it is felt, is knocking everyone's pay cheque. Ottawa is rather like Detroit: those who dump on this year's model of tin are thought of, in truth, as having a small essence of treason in their souls.

I argue about this with my friends and journalistic colleagues, Charles Lynch and Doug Fisher, settled inhabitants and chroniclers of the upper-middle-class capital of the world. *Of course* it's a comfortable town for those who wish to spend the rest of their lives there, cosseted by the parks, theatres, skating canals and bicycle paths paid for by the unwashed of Moncton and Kamloops. That's the point—why it is such an unreal, artificial place for the dispensing of governmental wisdom. The residents have a vested reason (the journalists included) for maintaining Ottawa's privileged anthill, prepared even to endure the loathsome climate so as to be members of what, perforce, is an exclusive club: i.e., excluding *all* Canadians not privy to the perks.

It is Canada's own Brasilia, its own Canberra, artificially created enclaves, hermetically sealed from the realities that a politician getting on the subway or trying to hail a taxi in London, Paris or even Washington, must endure. In Ottawa, one bicycles, mentally as well as physically. There are designated paths for both. One never freelances.

There have been transplants to Ennui-on-the-Rideau who have been around for years, still wandering around in a daze, their minds stuffed with bafflegab and their mouths filled with persiflage—and vice versa. The first rule that must be remembered is that Rockcliffe matrons, who run

64

the town, speak only to cabinet ministers, who speak only to Pierre Trudeau, who speaks only to God or himself— whichever comes first to mind. I was once at a black-tied dinner of men of staggering intellect, which someone described as the greatest meeting of minds since Pierre Trudeau dined alone.

But I digress. It is impossible to buy a tank of gas in Ottawa after dark. I have encountered towns where they roll up the sidewalks at sundown (a wise man advised that you should never order a martini in a town that still has a high school band—and Ottawa still qualifies) but the capital puzzles in that it assumes no one *drives* after dark. There may be a message there. The gas jockeys of the town, emulating the swivel servants, rush home, when the sun hits the deck, to watch reruns of Desi and Lucy, the most intellectual thing to hit town since they began to show the recreations of Mackenzie King's seances.

(There is a certain justice of the Supreme Court of Canada who, noting the law of the land stipulates that Supreme Court judges must reside within forty miles of Ottawa, says that is his own personal definition of "capital punishment.")

The prime architectural boast is the Château Laurier, which looks as if it were designed by a group of Walt Disney animators who got stoned one night on strange mushrooms. The bellhops are so old they are mistaken for senior citizens and are often helped onto elevators by little old ladies. The CBC has its local radio headquarters in the loft, proving that there are indeed bats in the belfry.

The uniqueness of the cuisine of the town has to do with the arrival—on any important feast day or national holiday—of a fleet of "chip wagons" that descend from the Quebec hills and other unknown depths of the boondocks. These are broken-down buses, looking as if they should be in the graveyards where elephants go to die, with the sides blow-torched out of them, dispensing hot french fries to otherwise deprived gourmands of the capital.

It has not yet been proven that the quality of thought coming out of Ottawa is directly related to the amount of greasy chips that are consumed, winter and summer, man and child, but it is understood that a Carleton University professor is researching a paper on it. He has received a government grant and hopes to be finished, with graduate student help, by 1986.

The locals boast grandly about the Gatineau Hills across the Ottawa River in Quebec. These are mildly undulating mounds of earth that would elsewhere be classified as topographical bumps. The local avid skiers can descend them at approximately 12.5 mph for up to 200 yards, and it is considered a great thrill. Any town raised on the oratorical delights of Mackenzie King and Allan MacEachen is easily thrilled.

One does not want to paint too truthful a picture, but truth must be observed. Ottawans think hot-tubs are located in bathrooms. Condominiums are thought to be a New Brunswick birth control device.

It is the only city in the world where rush hour starts at 3:30, the indexed-pension people fleeing the office early to hit Desi and Lucy. Men wear three-piece blue suits in July. Mandarins wear six-piece minds all year round. The Canadian flag on the Peace Tower goes up and down like a toilet seat as senators die off.

Ottawa (bland on the outside, comatose on the inside) has all the verve of a glass of champagne that has been left standing for two days. I have two favourite vignettes. Sparks Street, the former main drag of this swamp town, has been turned into a pedestrian mall in vain hopes of injecting some humanity into what is basically and irrevocably an inhumane ambience. Scattered sculptures and fainthearted fountains speckle this attempt at pseudo-Rome, and the idea is that a casual, free-flow of pedestrian traffic through what could be a brick Omaha will transfuse a touch of joy into a purse-lipped city.

At each narrow cross street there is a traffic light—designed for the *cars*. But the pedestrians—*Ottawa* pedestrians, conditioned to *obey*—stand dutifully, watching absentmindedly the usually empty two lanes of traffic and refuse to travel the further twelve steps of their casual stroll until the unrelenting red light (their master, their guide, their Ottawa mind-gauge) tells them it's okay to proceed.

Only in Germany have I seen such blind, unblinking obedience at the street level. It is not learned. It is *conditioned*. Ottawa has ways to make you conform.

The second delightful indicator is the elevator of the

Booth Building, 165 Sparks Street. It leads to the National Press Club and a vast clutch of the Ottawa offices of important newspapers, magazines and radio networks. It being Ottawa-run, the numbers on the elevator buttons keep falling off. The repairmen, being Ottawa-run, have lazily patched things up: the "odd" panel reads "1-3-4-6" and the "even" panel, "2-3-5-8."

Strangers enter the elevator, puzzle, and ride up and down for ten minutes searching for their destinations. Little old ladies break out in tears. A sometimes resident of an office up the street, I have watched this tableau with interest for more than a year. The botched-up buttons remain and no one—the tough journalist tenants upstairs who overthrow governments and destroy cabinet ministers—complains. It's accepted. This is Ottawa. You can't get there from here.

You still cannot fly directly from the capital of the country, in the year of Her Lord 1982, to New York on the People's Airline. The only nonstop flight to that regular destination of high snivel servants and other grateful escapees is a recent experiment by the U.S.-owned Pilgrim Airlines, with headquarters in the metropolis of New London, Connecticut, a delightful adventure in Captain Eddy Ricketyback flying. The craft is a two-engine forty-four-seat Fokker, which always gives the impression it is about to land in a jungle clearing to pick up a cache of marijuana. A colleague went aboard with carry-on luggage—and they *lost* it. However, it does get you to New York on one hop, which the People's Airline, run by the People's Government, cannot do eighty-nine years after the Wright Brothers. You still cannot fly from the capital of Canada to the capital of the United States. Complicated arrangements take you through Toronto or Montreal or Baltimore (from Baltimore you make your way by bus). Ottawa is Canada's own Transylvania, a hidden destination off the byways of the nation. It is the Rodney Dangerfield of Canadian cities, never getting any respect because it shies from normal connecting routes. What should be the centrepiece of the country is a wallflower.

The miasma hits at the Ottawa airport, a one-horse structure befitting Medicine Hat, but not the national capital. A plunge into the terminal is a plunge into a sea of briefcases filled with despair, of weekend faces without joy, end-of-day visages abrim to the jowls with the burden of no laughter. A backwater assigned the responsibility of feeling more important than it really is, Ottawa takes itself very seriously. You can tell the permanent residents by the white Plimsoll line on the lower shin line of their trousers, testimony to the salt in the gutter that destroys all automobile fenders, laps over the overshoes and marks a mandarin for life.

There is a significant message in the newsstand—crowded, disorganized and littered with magazines arriving two days after the rest of Canada gets them. The daily papers are cleverly placed at knee-height under an overhanging ledge. To find the name of the paper wanted, one must almost get down on all fours. It is symbolic, educational: to get any information in Ottawa, one must first kneel. It is a most salutory introduction to the town.

Your ink-stained wretch, when he is not spending his time on airplanes, spends it in airport taxis. I am Canada's leading expert on taxis. I am here to say that Ottawa's taxis, for reasons that escape me, are the dirtiest, smelliest, most slovenly taxis in the country.

The Ottawa terminal, shrewdly designed by the same people who run the country, is structured—in this small town—so that one must wrestle one's bag further than in Montreal, Toronto, Vancouver, Winnipeg or elsewhere. There are no luggage carts. Ottawa has yet to discover them.

The taxi lineup has all the discipline of a Chinese fire drill. Montreal cabbies are talkative. In Toronto, they are swift and distracted. In Vancouver, they are likely to be Ph.D.'s in Chaucerian poetry who spend their days at the nude Wreck Beach. In Ottawa? Just surly. I have encountered more surly Ottawa taxi drivers than I have surly politicians in the Liberal cabinet, where I have many friends and admirers.

When the foot-well in the back seat is not full of melted snow (riding in an Ottawa taxi in the winter, I know for the first time how a woman feels in the stirrups), it is full of last week's soggy newspapers. When the lining of the car is not redolent of this day's Col. Sanders, it is reminiscent of terminal sweatsock. Those high people in charge of such things as our airport taxis and our nostrils are unaware of these boring details of ordinary life, as their ministerial limos meeting them at the airport are sprayed twice daily with the afterbreath of an executive assistant. (If they ever banned gin in this town, the political machinery would dry up like the transmission in a 1932 Hupmobile.)

Coma City, Pavlov's secret retreat, has a delightful tableau in summer on the Sparks Street mall, as the swivel servants—drugstore cowboys on high salaries—stand about in their white shoes, glomming the stenographers. (There are a number of them in what we call the Full Winnipeg—white shoes, white belt, white tie.)

Layabouts from the Ottawa Valley, their tick-ridden long locks indicating they have not been informed that the 1960s have ended, pick plaintively at their guitars, their empty-of-dimes cases in front of them, indicating their talents. Government employees stand enraptured at the noon hour, their daily struggle with seniority suspended for one thin sarsaparilla, listening to a free Dixieland band playing on the mall. The subsidy comes not from city hall, but Amnesty International.

There is a suspended animation syndrome to the place. Couriers hand-deliver copies of cabinet ministers' speeches that were delivered a week previously in Moncton or Moosomin. Air Canada delivers tickets, reserved four days previously, in an envelope marked RUSH! Government flacks at garden parties wear three-piece suits of bulletproof wool, their flinty eyes aimed more at promotion than perspiration. It is a town in a constant sweat of anticipation—tenure the goal, pension the heaven. Recession-proof, it is a town that walks in molasses.

Ottawa is a town masquerading as a city, filled with paper and topped with gas. In 1905 Henry James toured Philadelphia and found that on Sunday mornings its boulevards were "vacant of everything but an immeasurable bourgeois blankness." That is Ottawa midweek. Another Philadelphia visitor in the same era was Lincoln Steffens, the famed muckraker, who found it "corrupt and contented." That is Ottawa, corrupt in its conceit, contented because it knows not what it is. A 1905 Philadelphia: not a bad definition of 1982 Ottawa.

People who persist in Ottawa are people who, when you get down to it, enjoy being punished, changing shirts three times daily in the sauna that passes for summer, frigid midgets with rigid digits in the winter, revelling in their suffering. The Marquis de Sade could have had a lot to say about this town—and could possibly expand upon its peculiarities.

The fix the country is in can be explained a lot by the fact that the people who run it, all denizens of this burg, secretly enjoy existing in such punishing sterility and, by transference, wish to pass on the suffering to those out in the boondocks who are deprived of Ottawa's salubrious masochism.

The country needs a shrink more than it needs a prime minister.

6
Second Digression

The Bachelor Party

Mackenzie King as kinky little prototype . . .
Trudeau as the lifetime loner
who dabbled in marriage . . .
MacEachen as the link who missed . . .
wee Jimmy Coutts as the sotto voce
bachelor apparent

There is something strange about Canada. It is the home of The Bachelor Party. It enjoys being run by lonely, selfish men—that being one definition of a bachelor. Does this mean our leaders (Ottawa? the country?) don't like sex? Or does it mean that our leaders (Ottawa? the country?) are promiscuous? A discussion follows.

William Lyon Mackenzie King, that kinky little cutey, ran this nation for twenty-two years in three different spells, 1921 to 1926, a pause, 1926 to 1930, 1935 to 1948. We just kept coming back for more punishment.

Pierre Trudeau, on examination, is a lifetime bachelor who dabbled absentmindedly in marriage for a brief five years with the lovely Margaret and now seems quite the most self-contained single parent in the universe. He lived quite contentedly until he was fifty-one as a bachelor and now, at sixty-three, seems quite contented again.

Bachelorhood seems to be his natural state, the married spasm an aberration. In her first book, *Beyond Reason*, Margaret revealed that he once told her the thing he liked best about his mother was that she never disturbed him. Ah, there lies a true bachelor. There lies a natural leader for Canada, the country that is so polite it never disturbs the saintly reveries of the guru who is so charitable as to lead us.

Here is the key to Canada's survival as a country that boasts no revolutions, brooks no assassinations, spurns class warfare and puts all of its money into savings accounts. For over half of the past sixty years it has been run by bachelors who, if they liked women, showed it in a very peculiar way.

When you examine this turgid country closely, you will find the secret is that it *enjoys* being ruled by lonely, austere bachelors. If the essence, the personality of a

73

country can be judged by the verve of a John Kennedy or the growling lion of a Churchill, Canada is best epitomized by grim, abstemious bachelors pulling the shawls around their feet on February eves.

It fits, therefore, that the game plan of The Bachelor Party, before his hand calculator misfired, was for the second leading bachelor of Ottawa, Allan J. MacEachen, to succeed to the mantle of leadership. At 61, he had well proved his credentials for the job (i.e., avoiding the altar).

Alas, his budget fumblitis killed those chances but The Bachelor Party, always with good bench strength, had a man in reserve. He was wee Jimmy Coutts, who seems to have the *sotto voce* approval of the Big Bachelor himself and certainly has the backing of Senator Keith Davey, The Rainmaker who dispenses dew on the heads of all Grit princes.

Coutts, renowned a bit as a ladies' man and a coveted catch at the right dinner parties, has a good head start on the required credentials by remaining, at forty-four, unsullied and unhitched. He has only to gaze at the leadership of those before him. He hasn't far to go.

Mackenzie King kept on friendly relations with a succession of happily married women, while doing his nighttime missionary projects with prostitutes. (There's the old Ottawa joke about King ending cabinet sessions: "Meeting adjourned. Could any of you fellows lend me ten bucks?")

Trudeau likes young women; so many of his Ottawa dates have an uncanny resemblance to (and are approximately the same age as) Margaret.

Like King, MacEachen's friendships with women tend to be with happily married wives or widows. They're safe. His best friends are Trudeau aide Joyce Fairbairn (Mrs. Michael Gillan; Gillan works for MacEachen) and his personal secretary, Pearl Hunter, a widow who was once secretary to Jimmy Sinclair, Margaret's father.

MacEachen's male friends are mostly bachelors: Alistair Fraser, former clerk of the Commons; John Stewart, the former MP from Antigonish; the priests at St. Francis Xavier University who first boosted him. He goes to mass almost every day. There is a natural link between the brooding Presbyterian King—separated by the pseudo-swinging Trudeau—and the brooding Catholic MacEachen.

It is understandable that Ottawa is a bachelor haven, despite the four to one ratio of females to males in government service. It is a town composed of men who need a committee before they can make a decision. Once home, they are lost without a third party to break the tie. They need a quorum, and that tends to get crowded in the kitchen.

Ottawa, essentially, is a coitus interruptus town. Any place where decisions are two parts delay to one part deny is, perforce, a bad bet in the sheets. It's understandable. Margaret complained in her second book about how Pierre shipped her to a separate bedroom in the attic. That's no surprise. That's a metaphor for what the party has been doing to the rest of the country for years.

Toronto sociologist Dr. Edward Shorter, in a *Saturday Night* piece examining Ottawa's sensuousness, wrote about the way the sexual tension crackled on Friday night around the Press Club bar. The suspicion is that he was listening to the pretzels.

Ottawa, when you get down to it, is the civic equivalent of saltpetre. Only the pensions are indexed; very little else goes up on a regular basis. It's the nature of the place, spontaneity frowned upon and joy severely taxed. A city that lives at the Xerox machine eventually has to suffer some internal damage—mainly a curvature of the imagination.

One of the many disappointments of the Trudeau era is that the expected flowering of the arts and the finer things, anticipated when Camelot North sprung forth from a trampoline, never happened. The home of the rich intellectual, expected to become sort of an Athens-of-the-Arctic, did not materialize. Neither did the city's artistic establishment. Under Trudeau, the capital's national galleries and museums have never been in worse shape.

Sondra Gotlieb, author and wife of Allan Gotlieb, Canadian ambassador to Washington, traces the descent into ennui to the departure of a bundle of lively political wives who fled with their husbands once it was apparent the PM in fact did not intend to reinvent an artistic Nineveh by the Ottawa River: Ruth Macdonald, Geills Turner, Valerie Gibson, Adrian Lang, Jane Faulkner and others of that disappointed era. Just as the tone of any party is set by the mood of the hostess, the tone of Ottawa is determined by the dominant ministerial wives. It is not for nothing that the home of the prime minister is known as 24 Nosex Drive.

Mackenzie King tried to commune with his dead mother and talked to his beloved dog. MacEachen talks to his broken calculator, and Coutts talks to Davey who talks only to Goldfarb. Trudeau (the famous nonnewspaper reader) revealed during the 1981 CBC technicians' strike that it wasn't important because he never listened to radio or watched TV. It is natural. The voters of this country like monks, inward-turning men who are obsessed with self.

It is not an accident that Liberal leaders are bachelors and bachelors are Liberals. It goes with the territory.

7
Ontario

*The Complacency Capital
of the World*

Buttermilk Billy and the Regressive
Conservatives . . . depravity on the silver screen . . .
fag-bashings as election sport . . .
hanging up on the Francophones . . .
a place to withstand

One evening several years ago Dr. Stuart Smith, then the Ontario Liberal leader, delivered a searing, ad lib message from the heart to a collection of fellow Liberals in the basement of a motor hotel in suburban Winnipeg. It was one of those "workshops"—the political buzzword for hair-pulling sessions—and Smith, growing heated, had just dazzled the room with the fever of his feelings on the party's problems.

I upped to him later and said, in admiration, that if he talked like that at home he would be premier of Ontario.

He snorted at my ignorance. "If I talked like that at home," he said, "I'd lose my own seat." A psychiatrist from Montreal who got into Ontario politics via his practice in Hamilton, Smith explained that he had been years in Ontario before he finally realized there are different definitions of the word passionate.

As someone raised in Quebec, he had always thought to be "passionate" was a compliment—a person who felt strongly, who was eager and determined. In Ontario, he found to his eventual sorrow, a "passionate" individual was regarded as slightly unbalanced, demented if not deranged.

"I've only just learned this," he sighed. "And *I'm* a psychiatrist."

All of this explains why Brampton Bill Davis, so dull you can slice it, rules Ontario with a comfortable majority and why Dr. Stuart Smith, suppressed passionate idealist, is now out of politics, having blunted his sword against the forehead of the turgid Ontario voter. If you want to understand Ontario, you must remind yourself that the Regressive Conservative party has now been in power longer than any regime in the universe with the lone exception that comes to mind: Moscow. It is the longest-running political show in what is amusingly called the free world.

In 1943, when the Tories of Ontario began their string, Joe Louis was in his prime. Hitler was still around and kicking. Franklin Delano Roosevelt and Mackenzie King consumed the front pages. Children didn't talk back. Grass was something you mowed.

Bulgaria has not had a government that has lasted as long. Nor Albania or Romania—other bastions of democracy. Even Alberta changes masters more often. Only Ontario, of all the Canadian provinces, remains content with a mandate that will run forty-two years before another election is necessary. There is an electorate of consummate contentment.

Ontario is probably the complacency capital of the world. Cosseted by a 115-year-old policy that deemed the rest of Canada a hinterland for the benefit of Ontario industry, the residents naturally reward their benefactors. The Tories of Buttermilk Bill and predecessors have been in power for twelve straight terms. They have done this by appealing to the most conservative people in Canada, the comfortable burghers of southern Ontario.

To keep these burghers happy, Bill Davis ensured that for five years sophisticated Toronto was the only city in major league baseball where you were not allowed a cardboard cup of beer. (The pinch-faced ban was finally lifted this summer and, at last report, no crazed fans went berserk in the streets, intent on pillage.) To keep these burghers happy, Davis allows his censors to ban *The Tin Drum*, a film that won the Palme d'or at the Cannes Film Festival and an Oscar at the Academy Awards.

Caligula has been running in Vancouver for fifty-five weeks. The residents of the largest and richest and allegedly most advanced city in the country, Toronto, are not allowed to see it, since it would corrupt and deprave them. Ontario has a film censorship policy that would fit well in P.E.I., because Buttermilk Bill is not looking at Toronto, he's looking at the burghers of southern Ontario. Brampton asserts its morals on Bloor Street.

To keep these burghers happy, Davis was prepared to play on the anti-French vote so as to win the majority that escaped him in two previous elections.

Section 133 of the British North America Act (imaginatively retitled the Constitution Act 1867) is the one that gives status to both French and English in the courts and legislature of Quebec. Manitoba, with its small French-speaking population, has been instructed by the courts to honour Section 133. Richard Hatfield's New Brunswick, with its Acadian segment, has voluntarily invoked Section 133.

The Ontario of Bill Davis, with the largest French-speaking community outside Quebec, has stubbornly resisted accepting into law the essential that binds this bilingual country together—acceptance of the fact that a Francophone resident of Ontario has a right (as does an Anglophone resident of Quebec) to a trial in his own language.

Bill Davis, that pink-cheeked, pipe-smoking exemplar of Brampton church-going, is the most expedient politician in Canada. Peter Lougheed is single-minded to the point of inflexibility. Pierre Trudeau is a prisoner of his own ego. René Lévesque is obsessed with giving his own people equality with the lordly Anglos. But Bill Davis, smiling Bill Davis, is superior to all of them in his religiosity, his worshipping before the shrine of power—and what he will do to retain it. What he will do is not pleasant.

To remain top of the heap, Ontario's supposedly solid leaders resorted to trading tricks like a cut-rate streetwalker. It was Davis who was largely responsible for the scuppering of the only Tory government to appear on the federal scene since Jack Pickersgill was a pup. Because Joe Clark, in his fumbling honesty, was prepared to pay Alberta close to fair value for its oil, the Davis government withdrew the awesome slickness of the Big Blue Machine. Davis himself, for his contribution to the 1980 Clark defeat, retreated to the wisdom of his Florida condominium for practically all the campaign.

To remain at what they think is top of the heap, Davis and his Tories willingly deserted the Tory premiers of Alberta, Manitoba, Nova Scotia, Prince Edward Island and Newfoundland by leaping into bed with Pierre Trudeau and his arrogant unilateral stance on the constitution.

In return, of course, for Trudeau's support for the Davis position that Ontario—alone of all its manufacturing competitors in the U.S. and abroad—did not have to pay even close to the world price for the oil it received from Alberta.

81

Protected Ontario industry, which supplies Bill Davis' party funds, refuses to pay the price for oil that its international competitors must pay. So Bill Davis supports Liberal Trudeau in the fight with Tory Lougheed—meanwhile sinking Tory Clark in the election.

In return, also, for the Trudeau blind eye to the fact that Ontario will not give its five hundred thousand Francophones the same equality under the law that Quebec gives its Anglophones. There are ninety-five thousand children in Ontario attending French schools. In a high school in Hamilton, French-language students say they are afraid to speak French in the corridors because they were forever being called "frogs." Bill Davis knows this. So he refuses to accept Section 133.

In return, Ottawa's Liberal-controlled constitutional committee approved—during Davis' 1981 election campaign—a resolution allowing Ontario to wriggle out of Section 133 guarantees. So Pierre Trudeau, who fought valiantly against René Lévesque's Bill 101—insisting that Quebec's Anglophone minority retain its rights—refuses to insist that Bill Davis grant the same rights to his Francophone minority.

It is wheel and deal with principles. It is political Wintario. Bill Davis knows he has the last of the Orange Lodge bigots. Ontario is one of the last places where they still have King Billy parades on 12 July.

(Not a single civil libertarian voice was raised in Ottawa, it should be added, when Toronto police, in crowbar-swinging glee, raided four homosexual bathhouses and hauled in the biggest mass arrest since Trudeau's War Measures Act—a week after Davis had called his election. Fag-bashing is very popular in rural Ontario, coincidentally at election time.)

It's hard to believe, but the Grand Orange Lodge, which came to Canada during the Protestant-Catholic tension in Ireland with a rallying cry of One Flag, One Country and One Language, still has a march through downtown Toronto as King Billy rides his white horse to celebrate the Glorious Twelfth.

King Billy doesn't count that much anymore, but the thought of him still does in the mind of Premier Billy, master manipulator of the shadows of puritanism and antipopery.

To save himself on the constitution, Trudeau went into

the alliance with the Tories of Queen's Park and thus put in peril yet another provincial Liberal party. Both Dr. Smith, who left in despair to head the Science Council of Canada, and new leader David Peterson attempted to distance themselves from their superiors in Ottawa, a link to Trudeau being seen as death at the polling booth.

Ontario at the moment is confused, the locus of Toronto dominating the country but the province as a whole reeling from its unaccustomed relegation into the realm of economic trouble. Bad times were always associated with those whiners in the hinterland. Under Bill Davis, the province has lost the prestige it enjoyed under John Robarts as the linchpin of Confederation connected to Quebec.

That respect has gone and now its economic domination is threatened. It will never be in need of humility pills, but Ontario these days is pondering its future a bit. Any pause for contemplation is greatly appreciated—and watched from afar with small amusement.

8
Third Stopover

Toronto
The Big Lemon

Municipal penis envy . . .
pecuniary mea culpa . . .
S and M at Exhibition Stadium . . .
astronomy of the Sun, the Star and the Globe . . .
Trudeau and the media daisy chain

Just as New York is an entity unto itself, divorced from the rest of America, Toronto is a thing apart, revelling in its chauvinism. It is no more connected with Canada than London is with the Cotswolds, or the moors of Yorkshire, or the downs of Kent. Just as Paris is a world to itself, alien to its rural cousins.

Toronto and the Ontario of Buttermilk Billy are entirely separate. (This is why B.B. has his chauffeur drive him home the twenty-five miles to Brampton most every night; he does not wish to be contaminated by the ambience of a foreign culture.)

The problem with Toronto is that it is imitative. It does not want to be itself. The Big Lemon (as it is known in Western Canada) suffers from municipal penis envy. In shooting through its pubescent era, from the pinch-faced Presbyterian enclave into a fern-bar and Perrier pitstop, it always had role models. New York was its ideal; it also wanted San Francisco's restaurants and Vancouver's clean streets, Atlanta's affluence and Peterborough's rectitude.

That never works. Jealousy is always self-destructive. Toronto, instead, is a failed Boston in that it is always looking over its shoulder, afeared that someone may be gaining. There is a compulsion to create a society on someone else's model. The greatest civic boast is an erection in the sky that beat out a guywire-supported tower in Poland for the record book. This is accomplishment? The Metro Toronto Chairman, Paul Godfrey, has a perm and a jawlift; he succeeds in looking like nothing so much as a superannuated teen-ager in gold chains. Bob Guccione comes to the council table.

There is a reason why the only city in Canada to have its own town fool—Harold Ballard—has also the worst teams in sport, the save-for-this-year Argonauts, the Maple Leafs, the Blue Jays, the Blizzard. Toronto, one must understand, has no collective psyche, no real reason for being other than as a collection plate and siphoning pan for money created elsewhere.

The supposedly failing city of Montreal consistently produces baseball and hockey clubs (and occasionally football teams when shell-game artists from Vancouver are not involved) that are models of good management, pride and performance.

Toronto, in the meantime, has managed to capture a monopoly on the most dreadful collection of spavined hacks and ill-coordinated gorillas ever assembled—all representing this brave new pile of money that is held up as the new Periclean Athens.

The Argos for years secretly kept the country united in shared laughter at their ineptness. The once-mighty Leafs, the goal of every Canadian boy with Eaton's catalogues for shin pads, are now a comic staple. The Blue Jays are baseball's answer to paint-by-number. The money-losing Toronto Blizzard pro soccer team—as inept as their choice of name—completes as stunningly incompetent a clutch of stumblebums as ever represented one city.

Those grim masochists who sat in the CNE grandstand game after game in great numbers to watch the Argos slop around as waves of newly arrived imports, coaches and general managers mill about, tacitly enjoyed the humiliation inflicted upon them by invaders from Regina, Edmonton and other unknown datelines. The Torontonian, knowing deep in his soul that he represents naught but avarice and whose cultural base is about as thin as the mustard on his niggardly hotdog, feels a need for a punishment that will be gone by Monday morning. It's an S-and-M trip but without the scars that would be embarrassing in the golf club Jacuzzi.

The Montreal sports fan goes out into the afternoon or evening proudly, aware that an extension of his being, his love of life, is going to be displayed on ice or diamond within the next few hours. He dresses for the role, flamboyantly, and eats and drinks and sings in a *celebration* of self. Those are not sweaty jocks out there—that is *Quebec*.

The Toronto fan is on a mission of expiation, prepared to pour his guilt to the rest of the nation as if out of a four-gallon maple syrup tin. By the transmission of vibrations, this religious pecuniary *mea culpa* is inexorably injected into the pores of the poor players, who feel the waves of angst wafting down from the grandstands upon them. They swoon. The nation rejoices.

The interesting point about the Toronto of 1982 is that while it controls more of the financial levers in the country than ever before, it is less powerful politically. That is a result of Pierre Trudeau's driving away (or allowing to drift away) the strong men who, coming from the largest and most powerful city in Canada, would naturally be effective spokesmen for the two-thirds of the country that is not Francophone. This is one reason why the country has turned against Trudeau: the strong men refuse to participate in government as long as he is there.

Today mighty Toronto is represented in cabinet by five ministers so junior in rank and respect that even their mothers have trouble remembering their names. John Roberts, Jim Fleming, Paul Cosgrove, Bob Kaplan, Charles Caccia—does anyone have any illusion about how much clout they have around the cabinet table when the going gets rough and the rough get going? It is to laugh.

Ottawa is always nervous/jealous of Toronto's power. When Phil Givens, who was a very popular Toronto mayor, perceived greater roles ahead for himself and went to Ottawa in the 1968 Trudeaumania sweep, he was placed, so as to dilute his ego, in the back row, his bald pate stroking the Commons curtains. In the early months, Givens tried so hard to get the Speaker's attention, flexing his knees in anticipation so often only to be ignored, that he developed the bends. He gave up in disgust and retreated to Toronto.

When Joe Clark, the hiccup of history, came to power for a brief dull moment in 1979, he was presented with possibly the most popular mayor in Toronto's history, David Crombie, the hero of Rosedale after vanquishing the Grit white hope Dr. John Evans, the former University of Toronto president who was billed as leadership potential. Crombie, as ex-boss of the largest city in the country, had the largest budget of anyone in cabinet as health minister—yet the nervous Clark shut him out of the inner cabinet. He feared the tiny perfect one as a rival because of Crombie's street smarts and easy grace with people—two factors that Joe ain't got.

If Toronto lacks the direct political power it once had, it

controls the nation's information, which today is real power. The perceptions flow from Toronto, whether on the TV networks, the excellent CBC radio (the veins of Canada), or the magazines and major newspapers. Thus, because it is insular, Toronto forces insularity on the rest of the country.

The *Toronto Star*, the largest and richest paper in the land, sent a superb reporter, Robert MacKenzie, to Quebec when the stirrings of nationalism and possible separation were apparent. Today, the *Star* has just one reporter covering the four Western provinces. There is the renowned Toronto magazine editor who discovered in recent years, to his surprise, that he was in Calgary for the first time. Magazine editors, particularly, fear to venture west of the Humber River mainly because they hesitate to voluntarily vacate the local gossip circuit—in case they might be the subjects of it.

The *Star*, although it maintains its circulation pre-eminence, is no longer the force it once was. It has strangely never been able to produce a "talk-aboutable" columnist, someone who rivetted the town's attention, since Pierre Berton and then Ron Haggart left. It is full of moral uplift and cheery features, but as a paper it is curiously humourless. The current unlikely combination at the top of the newsroom management, hard-nosed Ray Timson, who is Press Club Incarnate, and Gary Lautens, the former dimpled darling of suburban housewives with his domestic turmoil column, are referred to by their reporters as "Knuckles and Chuckles."

When Alexander Ross, the former *Maclean's* managing editor and *Financial Post* columnist, went to the *Star* to write a column he made it a condition of his employment that he did not have to meet Beland Honderich, the much-feared publisher. Despite my many eons as an ink-stained wretch, I have never met Mr. Honderich, partly by design and partly by accident, and neither of us seems to have suffered grievously as a result.

The *Globe and Mail*—immortalized by columnist Richard J. Needham as the Grope and Flail, or the Mop and Pail—is going through a sticky patch at the moment, mainly due to economic conditions slicing its heavy reliance on national advertising revenue. The *Globe*'s owners, the Thomson chain, accustomed to its docile nonunion empire, were clearly startled at the fierce pride of the *Globe* reporters and editors, who wore Red Guard armbands when management announced staff cuts and then took out an ad in their own paper protesting that news coverage would suffer.

The *Globe*'s brave attempt to become a truly national newspaper via satellite in this geographically impossible country has proven a sometimes thing, oft-times giving the Vancouver reader less Toronto news than he would like and the Toronto reader rather more Calgary news than he would care to absorb. The proprietors must be given top marks for trying, especially since it is so far above their previous Peter Principle level.

If all else fails, there are always the celebrated "Companions Wanted" and "Toronto Introduction Services" meat markets tucked away discreetly in the *Globe*'s classified ad section. They offer an astonishing insight into the modern world not examined in detail in the otherwise staid columns of the *Globe*—a reflection of wants and needs that are not advertised in the other two, supposedly lower-scale, Toronto papers.

Examples:

Hamilton bored housewife looking for discreet encounter with established gentleman. Box 3527, The Globe.

Afternoon delight, registered hotel guests only. Toronto 960-0572.

Attractive, mature gentleman, not into bars, enjoys serving others, seeks dominant male companion who is physically fit and capable of demanding a discreet and responsible association. Box 3485, The Globe.

A female, enquiring over the phone for curiosity's sake, is told that she can rent a male escort for a hundred dollars an hour or five hundred for the night. There are some sixty of these ads running each day. It is not known if Lord Thomson or Buttermilk Bill have heard about it yet.

Presuming Joe Clark wins the next election (one can always presume a lot about Joe and never be disappointed), a most difficult decision he may have to make is whether to put Peter Worthington in the cabinet. Compared to this, moving the Embassy to Jerusalem and dismantling Petro-Canada were mere piffle.

Worthington was the bemused aspirant for the Conservative nomination in the Broadview-Greenwood by-election. Denied his bid by the coalition of two Greek-Canadian candidates, he sulked in his tent for a spell before deciding to run as an independent and frightened the whey out of the Clark forces, finishing a raging second to the NDP with only a short sprint of last-minute campaigning.

Worthington's almost cult status as editor of the phenomenon known as the Toronto *Sun* makes him such a prominent Toronto figure that he would have to command consideration from the Clarkians forming a cabinet, especially since they are not exactly overwhelmed with candidates from Mensa in Toronto. He has now resigned as editor and may very well seek the Tory nomination in a general election. For one thing, he would be the first Conservative minister in history to wear a large tattoo of a schooner on his left forearm. One would pay any money to see the gapes from his colleagues the first muggy Ottawa day when the cabinet decided to get down to shirt sleeves.

The *Sun*, the most successful new paper in North America in an age when old-style newspapers are dying regularly, rose from the ashes of the *Toronto Telegram*. At first it built its success on Fleet Street's proven tabloid formula of sex, sin and soccer—known in more sedate circles as "crime, outrage and underwear."

More recently, however, it has gathered the most interesting array of columnists in any Canadian newspaper: Dalton Camp, Douglas Fisher, Worthington, William F. Buckley, Barbara Amiel, Dr. Morton Shulman, the manic Gary Dunford, Joan Sutton, John Robertson.

The old newspaper joke used to be that the *Sun*'s philosophical position ranged all the way from Worthington on the left to Lubor J. Zink on the right. Now it lurches right across into the psychological ozone of Barbara Amiel, a onetime Marxist who has gone full circle and is described by an admirer as the "best second-hand intellect in town," meaning that George Jonas, her estranged husband, has had an inordinate influence on her. Dr. Foth, as the token simp, the limp-wristed lily-livered limousine liberal, also appears on the pages, meaning that the *Sun* now carries all known colours of the political spectrum and several that haven't been invented yet.

When Peter Newman revealed in *The Acquisitors* that *Sun* publisher Doug Creighton's monthly entertainment bill for the *Sun* from Winston's, the "day-care centre for the Establishment," averaged a whopping amount, everyone in town envied Creighton and thought it a good PR investment on behalf of the paper. Creighton was outraged—apparently out of concern that his little blue-collar readers would be appalled. Instead, he should have recalled the lessons of Adam Clayton Powell, the late U.S. congressman who was never more loved by his impoverished Harlem electorate than when he splashed wads of money around some Caribbean casino. *Sun* readers like flash.

Worthington for his part, is a moralist who was a boxing champion at university. He is also a paper millionaire, as a result of his holdings in *Sun* stock as one of the founders. His father was a general in the Canadian Army and the recent Tory aspirant fought in World War II and the Korean War. He hates communism with a passion and is contemptuous of Pierre Trudeau (whose justice minister once charged Worthington under the Official Secrets Act—thereby enhancing his martyr status among Toronto ethnics and Conservative voters). What Clark would have been able to do with him is difficult to imagine.

Worthington was a throwback to the era when newspaper editors actually had personalities and stood for something. At fity-five, he plays softball, tries to climb Tibetan mountains, wrote a ferocious column and his editorials (the *Sun* runs only one each day, enough for anyone's attention span) were unmistakable in their anger.

He seldom went out for lunch in a town that lives on lunch gossip; he preferred to dine in his paper's cafeteria. (Newspaper lunches aren't what they used to be. They never were up to magazine lunches which, in the good days as my friend Pat Nagle recalls, were composed of "gin and mayonnaise.") But I digress.

Barbara Amiel makes a studied career of being outrageous. She polishes and perfects the role, rather as Zsa Zsa Gabor cultivates her eyelashes. Her right-wing polemics are carefully superior in tone. She is also outrageously

93

beautiful, with a forty-one-year-old waist that would make a teenager—and does make most other women—weep.

Her personal life would fuel an entire Harlequin romance, with enough details left over for an afternoon soap. As associate editor of the *Sun*, she is newly responsible for the most feared feature in Toronto journalism, an anonymous Sunday gossip column called "Panache."

It is suitably vicious stuff, wonderfully bitchy. The column has quickly become *must* reading for the glitterati, all fearful that they might be in it.

Most people on the inside avoid Amiel because of her unfortunate habit of resurrecting, for print, what were assumed to be private conversations some months or even years distant. Those she turns furious often include her own editors. While working for *Maclean's*, she was thrown into jail in Mozambique (after eating her press card in a vain attempt to avoid identification). When she volunteered the details of her adventure to *As It Happens* before *Maclean's* could get into print. *Maclean's* was not amused.

Editor Worthington was on the phone to Amiel when his secretary slipped him a note informing him that the Gouzenko family—friends of Worthington's—were on the other line. Igor Gouzenko had just died and was about to be given a secret burial. The startled Worthington passed on the news to his associate editor, who that minute was on the way to a radio broadcast, and hung up so as to get to the funeral—the only outsider invited.

Amiel proceeded to the *Andy Barrie* show on CJCL and, in her eloquence, delivered a eulogy to Gouzenko, thereby spilling Worthington's world scoop to the, um, *world*. Other radio stations, wire services, eventually the RCMP, phoned to enquire about details of the death of a man they didn't know was dead. Worthington, with a clear beat on every journalist in Canada on what should have been his personal story, was sandbagged by his own innocent associate editor. Amiel is now known around the *Sun*, from the doorman on, as "Scoop."

The point of all this is that Worthington and Amiel, who are shunned by the fashionable Toronto media mafia, are edging into acceptance in some quarters because of the extreme dislike of the lofty Trudeaucrats and the weakness of their cabinet representatives in Toronto.

The Toronto media mafia: it is many layered, multifaceted, a species that can be dissected only by an outsider. In a fey way, one conjures up faint images—in a wild stretch of the imagination—with another daisy chain of intellectual forefrontism, the Bloomsbury group of London. Toronto is not London, and this group is not Bloomsbury, but everything is relative. (This is a digression with a digression.)

The analogy is that an interlocking band of salon partners set the tone—and the standards of those not worthy to join. As Virginia Woolf, Lytton Strachey, E. M. Forster, John Maynard Keynes *et al* established a style that depended mainly on the number of talented persons associated with it, there is, in a playful way, a group in the frontier of grasping Toronto, witty and well-informed, not arrogant about their power, but aware of it.

Rather the major domo of the media mafia is Barbara Frum, the frail-but-tough anchor on the most successful news show in Canadian radio history, *As It Happens*, and now filling the same role on television's *The Journal*, which has changed Canada's sex life as surely as the Manhattan blackout did for New Yorkers that famous fecund evening— by sending the entire country, bewildered but later grateful, to bed an hour earlier each night.

Frum throws the best-planned parties in town, the guests chosen as carefully as cashew nuts, in the elegant home, filled with African art, in a Don Mills glade, all wood and glass since it was designed by the former Vancouver architect Ron Thom. The finest compliment that can be paid the house is that it is the only residence in Toronto that looks as if it could be located in Vancouver.

Murray Frum, who grew so bored being a dentist that he went out and became wealthy as a developer, has the sense of humour of (and looks somewhat like) an elongated Woody Allen. Barbara Frum, for all her gentle ways, is a ferocious trader of information, almost equal to the master of all (high praise indeed), Jack Webster. She is very possibly the kindest person in Canada.

Robert Fulford, the erudite editor of *Saturday Night*, appears as a recreation of Edmund Wilson. He is the amused and aloof arbiter of those who write Canadian books, produce films or need intellectual spanking. He is a nonkinky Hugh Hefner, tending his Bunnyland of print.

When Peter Lougheed wanted to infiltrate Toronto and

burrow into the soft underbelly of Central Canada dogma on his energy fight with Ottawa, he was able to find an entree into the group to apply the message/massage. Trial lawyer Julian Porter, son of an Ontario chief justice, chairman of the Toronto Transit Commission, a light-reined toucher of the levers of power, long-sought as an ideal Tory candidate for any high position up to premier, was the key to the lock.

Anna Porter, his wife, sees herself as the female reincarnation of Maxwell Perkins, the famous American bookman who nurtured and encouraged F. Scott Fitzgerald, Thomas Wolfe and Hemingway, covering their debts, stroking their inadequate egos, picking up their laundry, buying them eggs. (Was Perkins appreciated? No. Did he brood about it? No.)

Lougheed could be introduced at dinner parties to such card-carrying liberals as Fulford and Adrienne Clarkson, the stunning intellect from CBC television who is now Bill Davis' secret weapon in Paris; as Ontario's agent-general, she has the overshadowed Quebec ambassador at Parisian cocktail parties impaling himself on his own swizzle stick.

He could even meet, across the canapés, such regular members of the group as Peter Herrndorf, English network vice-president of the very CBC that Lougheed was suing because of its rough treatment of him in its *Tar Sands* docudrama. It might even have something to do with the fact that, the day the libel trial was to open in Edmonton early this year, the Holy Mother Corp. and the premier made a settlement on the courtroom steps, Lougheed accepting $82,500 in damages. Dinner party companions come to understand each other.

The analogy is not exactly like Tom Wolfe's famous account of the Black Panthers being entertained by the radical chic groupies at Lenny Bernstein's New York pad. The point is that a Western Tory premier, wanting to get his message across, has access to the opinion-moulders in the communications capital because there is a vacuum there.

Pierre Trudeau, once the intellectuals' darling, has out of boredom and lassitude alienated most of those who would confess to being of his political persuasion. He doesn't have any ministers, acolytes or outriders (now that Coutts has left) who would be taken seriously in any drawing room or trivia contest around the white wine and salmon. Fleming? Cosgrove? Kaplan?

Those far-off Conservatives such as Lougheed, and even such local ones as Worthington and Amiel, are allowed to edge their way in, because Ottawa has disappeared as a presence in Toronto.

Pierre Trudeau has let the country's most powerful city slip away from him by not appealing to its talent.

9
Third Digression

*Confessions of a Closet
Enthusiast*

Doesn't Fotheringham like anything? . . .
well, Oysters Florentine, for openers . . .
Eric Kierans and Robert Stanfield . . .
Frank Sinatra-on-records but
not Sinatra-off-records . . . Jack Webster-
on-the-air but not Webster-off-the-air
. . . oranges

Constant Reader, pulling himself up short, irritated, asks: "Doesn't Fotheringham like anything?"

As a matter of fact, it is no problem at all to grant this request. Mr. Fotheringham is a closet enthusiast. He likes an absolutely phantasmagorical number of things.

Mr. Fotheringham, it has been learned, likes Kay Starr. Also Oysters Florentine. He likes Ged Baldwin, Karen Kain and Tuborg. Also Robert Morley. It is hard to imagine him getting enough of Guy Lafleur. He also is very much in favour of Don Shirley.

He is absolutely for Kurt Vonnegut, Iona Campagnolo and Jack Shadbolt. On the other hand, he rather dislikes brussels sprouts and Senator Jack Austin. He likes John Crosbie and Roy MacLaren, Eugene Forsey's letters-to-the-editor. He endures Larry Zolf, a good friend.

The rumour around is that Fotheringham is in favour of Chinese food, Peter De Vries and Barbara Frum's husband. In truth, he likes Japanese food more than Chinese food.

He likes Lawrence Durrell and Dover sole. He has a mad pash for Billy Eckstine. He is in favour of tennis but not golf, the second most stupid sport in the world. The most stupid sport in the world is curling.

Mr. Fotheringham favours politicians who speak the truth. He likes Jean Chrétien, Dave Barrett and Richard Hatfield. His regard lessens when they open their mouths in public.

He likes Dylan Thomas and Woody Allen. Also Gilbert and Sullivan. He has always been in favour of Mary McCarthy. Also sunshine, in moderate amounts. He is in favour of Pommard. Also Cleo Laine, in immoderate amounts.

101

He obviously likes Max Shulman, also John Charles Thomas, Johann Sebastian Bach, John Robert Colombo. But he is able to restrain his enthusiasm for John Philip Sousa. He is much in favour of Housman, A. E., and likes Siegfreid Sassoon—but likes Wilfred Owen more than Sassoon.

He has always liked John Landy but never much fancied Roger Bannister. He has always been a sucker for the underdog. He liked Gordie Drillon over Syl Apps, Whirlaway over Alsab, Swaps over Nashua. He likes oranges.

Fotheringham likes Sinatra-on-records, dislikes Sinatra-off-records. He likes Eric Kierans and Robert Stanfield. He is in favour of B. Goodman, A. J. Liebling and Montreal. What he likes most at the moment is John Irving.

He likes Elizabeth Gray's lascivious laugh and Nicole Belanger's malicious wit. He is in love with a lady called Francesca.

He liked the 1968 Trudeau and admires, but does not much like, the 1982 Trudeau. He likes Jack Webster on-the-air, but not Webster-off-the-air. He is in favour of Spike Milligan and salmon. He can take a lot of Joyce Grenfell and a little of Ogden Nash. He likes Rome, born-again New York and Hong Kong.

There is absolutely no limit to the things Fotheringham is enthusiastic about. He likes Carmen McRae, Gore Vidal, E. B. White, Fats Waller, beaches, hockey-in-the-flesh and Billy Graham-on-TV. He does not like hockey-on-TV and thinks Billy Graham-in-the-flesh would be appalling. He likes Joe Clark in a small room, thinks he's a disaster outside it. He likes John Dempsey and Jean-Paul Riopelle.

He is in favour of Flanders and Swann and mourned at Stanley Holloway. He likes Jacqueline Bissett, even Albert Payson Terhune.

If he could be sure it wouldn't be found out, he might even confess he is in favour of Pierre Berton. He likes John Steinbeck, but not Carol Burnett, Johnny Carson or John McEnroe. In a lifeboat for a length of time, he would prefer as companions Ring Lardner and Peter Ustinov.

He likes green peppers, I. F. Stone, Spain, Anthony Sampson, Sonny Terry and Brownie McGhee, Harry Boyle, Clyde Gilmour, Red Smith's style, Adrienne Clarkson and prawns. He could live on cheese and may have to.

He likes to hear George Burns sing and to read Robert Graves. Constant Reader would be amazed at the number of things about which he is enthusiastic.

I am authorized to speak for Mr. Fotheringham.

10
Manitoba

*The Fun Beneath
the Surface*

Winnipeg, broad-shouldered, rough and garlicky . . .
talent producer to the eastern world . . .
wall-to-wall Bunkerism . . . Beer and Skits . . .
POPE ELOPES! . . . Otto Lang,
the Grit's epitaph in the West

Manitoba is the most sedate of the Western provinces, minus the social fervour of Saskatchewan, the buccaneer drive of Alberta, the looniness of British Columbia. This is because of its unfortunate fate in being planted next to Ontario. A portion of the Central Canada pomposity and turgidity has rubbed off, by osmosis seeping across the border. There is fun beneath the Manitoba surface, but there is that half-Ontario glaze over it.

Manitoba has changed premiers, going from the Conservatives' Sterling Rufus Lyon, who was so mean it was rumoured he threatened to tax the rubber tips on crutches, to the NDP's Howard Pawley, whose idea of fun on a Saturday night is to go down to Eaton's and try on gloves.

Rufus Lyon. There is a fine middle name. Manitoba specializes in this. When Duff Roblin resigned as premier in 1967 to joust unsuccessfully with Robert (Banana) Stanfield for Dief's job, he was succeeded by a portly undertaker from Minnedosa, one Walter Weir—known, naturally, as Minnedosa Fats. A young reporter, diligently doing his job, went to his newspaper library to find out the full name of the new premier so it could be used in all its dignified glory.

There was no mention in Weir's campaign literature of a middle name. The diligent reporter dug deeper. No mention. The further he dug, the more apparent it was that Walter Weir, or his handlers, had buried his full name.

By now fascinated with the mystery, the scribe pursued his quest and—finally—found his evidence. Walter Weir's middle name? Cox-Smith. *Beautiful!* A politician going from platform to platform, rally to rally, forever fearful that an opponent might reveal to the world that he is a Cox-Smith! Our hearts went out, immediately, to undertaker Walter Weir and, on second thought, to his mother.

The dying Manitoba Liberals had a leader called Bobby Bend, and it was suggested that the appropriate election slogan would be: "Go Round the Bend with Bobby."

Winnipeg is a broad-shouldered town, rough and garlicky. The economy is going nowhere, but the city has no self-doubts. While Vancouver gazes, fascinated, in its mirror, and Montreal glances sardonically at grasping Toronto, and Toronto is stricken with awe of New York, Winnipeg is serene, oblivious, profane. It does not envy anybody. It is civic karma.

It produces a steady stream of talent that goes to Toronto and beyond and muscles its way through the media. There is Larry Zolf, offspring of the Marx Brothers (Groucho and Karl); writer Jack Ludwig; critic Martin Knelman; publisher James Lorimer; CBC heavy Peter Herrndorf; Stratford Festival saviour John Hirsch; Tom Hendry, a large influence in the Toronto theatre world.

There is Danny Finkleman, the CBC's licensed eccentric; Adele Wiseman, Beryl Fox, Melinda McCracken. There is Scott Young followed by Neil Young, Trent Frayne, Martin O'Malley, sportswriter Jim Coleman, Ian Sinclair of Canadian Pacific—not to forget the immortal Deanna Durbin.

Winnipeg is wall-to-wall Bunkerism, delighting in raunchy insults that cut across its own racial smorgasbord. When Governor-General Ed Schreyer was elected premier in 1969 (Minnedosa Fats had called a snap election right in the midst of an NDP leadership race), he had French-Canadian René Chartier as his executive assistant and cabinet ministers named Cherniack, Uskin, René Toupin, Rev. Philip Petursson, Burtniak and Borowski.

As a litmus paper test of the town, there is the strange phenomenon of the annual Winnipeg Beer and Skits, the last remaining stag social event in Canada. It is a tribal affair that is the forerunner of the much tamer Ottawa Press Gallery annual dinner and show where cabinet ministers are speared and savaged.

Winnipeg is a throwback—there is a touch of 1940s to the place—and one thousand of the upwardly mobile men in town fight to get tickets to this annual production where Kotex jokes are still considered funny. At a time when females now constitute a good half of any newsroom in the country, the Winnipeg Press Club (filled with women) still bans them from its show. Winnipeg is a throwback.

No one is spared at Beer and Skits. I once sat beside Sterling Rufus Lyon when he was the star target in a skit patterned after *One Flew Over the Cuckoo's Nest*. A doctor in the insane asylum explains that before "the little red-headed fart can be given a lobotomy, we'll have to give him a brain transplant." Lyon beamed bravely, as did Manitoba's lieutenant-governor, who sat down the table.

A prominent lawyer, underlining Winnipeg's cultural strength, did a number in which he explained that Scotch is the only liquor named after a people. "After all, can you buy a mickey of Kraut? A bottle of Bohunk? A fifth of Frog? How about a crock of Wop? A jug of Chink? You can't even get a jigger of Nigger?"

They loved it—including a black member of the cast. It brought down the house. Winnipeg doesn't take itself seriously. (Ottawa does, in spades, and Calgary is getting there.)

A star turn most years is the legendary John Robertson, a Winnipeg character who has twice won National Newspaper Awards but is better known as the subject of song and story in the press bars of the land. At forty-eight, he no longer drinks but, as we say, still has a high lifetime average.

He received his early notoriety by writing such headlines as WORMS GET EARLY BIRD—on the death of the local president of the Early Bird Co. He once caused *Winnipeg Tribune* publisher Ross Munro a near heart attack by running off a few bogus front pages that featured in giant type: POPE ELOPES!

His most famous caper came after he had chased *Toronto Telegram* publisher John Bassett around his office desk "while in the grip of the grape." Later, cold sober, to demonstrate how easily it could be done, he playfully composed a sports story that spelled out—in the leading initial of each paragraph—a message that read: Fuck You, Everybody. It made the paper. Goodbye, Toronto Tely.

In Montreal, he so inflamed listeners of his radio show by rallying more than a hundred thousand signatures protesting Robert Bourassa's language law that he had sixteen bomb threats in one day and his children had to be escorted to school by bodyguards.

On the *Winnipeg Tribune* one Christmas, news editor Al Rogers received a police report on a young man named Oliver who had been stabbed in the vital parts by his wife. He threw it to Robertson to write the headline. Robertson returned it with: YOU SHOULD HAVE SEEN OLIVER TWIST.

Rogers told him to get serious so they could make it to the press club before closing time. Walking there through the snow, Rogers casually asked what he finally wrote. Robertson confessed: SHE DECKED THE HALLS WITH BALLS OF OLLIE.

They sprinted back to the paper and had the presses stopped.

The Dr. Hunter S. Thompson of Canadian journalism ballooned to 260 pounds—"The only exercise I got was climbing the press club steps"—before he decided to save himself from his suicidal lifestyle. He covered the Boston Marathon, and the sight of all those healthy bodies snapped something inside him. Two years later he was back in Boston—to run the race with his fourteen-year-old son.

He finished. He runs forty miles a week. He has raised more than $1 million for the Manitoba mentally retarded. He is a born-again jogger.

He became close to Terry Fox and was with him when Fox had to end his epic run outside Thunder Bay. The one-legged boy told Robertson, "For God's sake, don't wait all your life if you want to do something. Do it before it's too late."

After Fox's death, Robertson as the $74,000-a-year host of Winnipeg's nightly CBC-TV show received a call in late 1981 from Manitoba Senator Nate Nurgitz, suggesting there might be an open Tory nomination in St. Vital, a Winnipeg suburb. Sterling Rufus Lyon hadn't called the election yet, but Robertson recalled Terry Fox and decided to do something.

He was already into taping some pre-election gems: "Sterling Lyon does the work of two men—Laurel and Hardy." Instead, he resigned the $74,000 and the stoic Lyon was there on the platform the night Robertson took the nomination by acclamation—telling his audience he had been out door-knocking "with a bottle of German shepherd-remover in my hand."

He was trounced, of course, as Howard Pawley's NDP

swept Sterling Rufus out of power. The CBC could hardly take back a $74,000 defeated political candidate. In his latest reincarnation, John Robertson has joined the *Toronto Sun* as a sportswriter. To greet him, sports editor George Gross wrote "Welcome John Robertson"—spelled out in the leading initial of each paragraph in his column.

Winnipeg is basic. Ed Schreyer, when he ran Manitoba, lived in a house beside the railway tracks, just past the Esso refinery, which the premier bought at a tax sale after the bootlegger owner had skipped town. Farley Mowat parked his camper in the backyard—and stayed all summer.

My favourite story about His Excellency, Governor-General Edward Schreyer, and Her Excellency, Lily Schreyer, involves the time they decided to leave the four children at home and holiday on a leisurely drive through northern Manitoba. They stopped for gas in a small town and who should appear as the gas jockey but Sylvester, who as a boy had been one of Lily Schreyer's dates.

As Sylvester moved to the rear of the car to fill the tank, Ed Schreyer, with a small grin, said, "Just imagine where you'd be today if you had married him."

Lily Schreyer thought a moment, staring straight ahead, and said, "If I had married him, today I would be the wife of the premier of Manitoba."

Winnipeg is also the home now of Adrian Lang, indefatigable wife of Otto Lang, the last strong Liberal minister from the Prairie provinces where the party is now in oblivion. The incredibly slim-waisted Adrian, named after the last English pope, had the final of her seven children by age twenty-eight—"I wanted nine, but ran out of husband." In her heady whirl through Ottawa in the early Trudeau days as a foil to her stoic husband, she was known as "the power behind the drone."

The dominant—and first—skyscraper in Winnipeg was built by the James Richardson grain people and it sits, naturally, at Portage and Main, which used to be the crossroads of Canada (where now pedestrians are fined if they attempt to walk across the famous intersection rather than using the underground walkway). The tower has the choice clients—Price Waterhouse, Sun Life, Coopers & Lybrand, Midland Doherty, Merrill Lynch—with the Richardsons taking up the top six floors of the thirty stories. On the twenty-fifth floor sits the onetime boy wonder of

Prairie politics, Otto Lang, now the executive vice-president of Pioneer Grain Co. Ltd.

He's an epitaph for the Liberal party in Western Canada. A whiz at school, a Rhodes Scholar, dean of the University of Saskatchewan's law school while still in his early thirties, Otto Lang had a steady rise through the Trudeau cabinet (not helped greatly by Adrian, early on, confiding to a journalist that "Trudeau says Otto is the smartest man in the cabinet").

His much-publicized use of government jets (My Nanny Flies Over the Ocean) and his fights with feminist forces over abortion didn't hurt him as much as his association with a party that was seen in Saskatchewan as completely aloof and Ottawa-bound. He finished a humiliating third in Saskatoon in 1979 to his own priest, the NDP's Rev. Bob Ogle.

Now out of the cabinet, out of politics, out of his own province, Lang's job is to get the crop of Pioneer, the largest independent grain company outside the Wheat Pool, to its terminals in Vancouver, Thunder Bay and Sorel, Quebec. He has to do this under the realization that Prairie farmers, after all these decades under Liberal rule, do not grow anywhere near what they could for a hungry world since Ottawa has never been able to structure a transportation system that can get the grain to the ships that would send it overseas.

Lang, once a transport minister himself, sees the frustration through new eyes as a Westerner. He'll never be back in politics because he knows, as a Liberal, he is dead in the region of his roots. When a man just turned fifty realizes that, it's a measure of how far the Liberals have fallen.

Lang now works for the Richardsons, and they sent their own contribution, Jimmy, to the Trudeaucrats with monumentally disappointing results. James Richardson, from the silk-stocking riding of Winnipeg South, went to Ottawa in the Trudeaumania sweep of 1968 and moved through his cabinet duties in a resolutely pedestrian fashion.

Richardson always strolled to his own drummer (he stopped going to Beer and Skits after complaining to a companion that he didn't get the jokes) and became increasingly alienated from the thrust of the Trudeau cabinet. He finally left the Liberal ranks in 1976 over differences he has never been able to explain in understandable terms but which centre on the fact that he doesn't really like bilingualism. He wanders the political wilderness, rather like Paul Hellyer in his own serene belief that no one really understands him, showing up at federal-provincial conferences, eager to talk to reporters who pay him no mind, an undiscovered prophet.

Richardson finished himself off as being taken seriously by anyone influential when, as defence minister, he submitted himself to a long conversation with reporter Marci McDonald, who was doing a profile on him for *Maclean's*, while on a trans-Atlantic flight in a government plane. The Atlantic is a large ocean. Richardson relaxed with a few drinks and, among the gaucheries that tumbled forth one startling one stood out.

It was that he was rather tired of the complaints of Indians. After all, they had spent all those centuries, before the white man arrived in North America, dragging their belongings on "two sticks" behind their ponies instead of having the wit to invent the wheel.

James Richardson, millionaire, mystic, politician-without-a-party, has thereafter been known in every press and political gathering in the land as "Jimmy Two-Sticks."

The mantle of Liberal heavyweight in Manitoba has fallen upon the thick locks of Lloyd Axworthy, the white hope of Winnipeg until he forgot to count and neglected to remind himself that more than fifty percent of Canadians are female. The eldest of the four Axworthy boys, he has been greatly influenced by his stint at Princeton (at least his wardrobe has) in the Kennedy days.

He has a voice that comes out of the bottom of a rain barrel and is thought to believe that a sense of humour is something found in the Criminal Code. He is known in press circles as "Tank McNamara"—after the comic strip jock announcer.

A supporter of John Turner in past days, he was actually talked of as potential leadership material in late 1979 before Mr. Trudeau rolled back the stone and resurrected himself. Axworthy never recovered from his stiff-necked confrontation with feminist forces on the Status of Women and the Ottawa joke was that he was going downhill faster than Steve Podborski.

Axworthy's mistake was in taking on Doris Anderson,

113

who is herself from the Prairies and has never taken a backward step in a fight with anyone, having left the Maclean-Hunter empire when she felt she could not rise in a male oligarchy, even after her outstanding success as editor of *Chatelaine*.

Anderson was the government-appointed president of the Canadian Advisory Committee on the Status of Women—termed in some quarters as Broads Canada. When this appellation appeared in a newspaper column, a small rat pack of Ottawa female shovers and makers—Anderson; Elizabeth Gray, now the *As It Happens* husky-throated host; Nicole Belanger, now executive producer of *Morningside*; Pam Wallin, now the *Canada AM* star; Stevie Cameron, the Ottawa gossipist supreme; Sondra Gotlieb, now the resident star of the Canadian Embassy in Washington—met in a weekly gathering that they described as a Broads Canada lunch at the National Arts Centre restaurant, overlooking the Rideau Canal. With such massive media guns aimed at his innards, Axworthy didn't have a hope.

There are those of suspicious mind in Ottawa who wondered about the rather puzzling Axworthy appointment in the first place, saddling with the responsibility for women's rights a rookie minister who was going through a marriage breakdown himself and whose views on feminism could be fairly well assessed. Was Lloyd Axworthy set up? Or just tested?

His younger brother Tom is the prime minister's principal secretary, succeeding to that post when Jimmy Coutts did his spectacular pratfall in Spadina. Moustachioed, as witty as Lloyd is dour, he rather resembles a bear being rolled down a hill. He has taught at Eton during summer holidays and is a treasure-house of political trivia. A young lady in Ottawa once asked, "How come Lloyd got all the teeth, hair and voice and Tom got the brains?"

The younger Axworthy is a great fan of the Montreal Expos and in his livelier days was almost personally responsible for the annual profit of Mamma Teresa's, a downtown Ottawa restaurant much given to spaghetti stains and late-night cabals. The place became temporarily famous during the constitution arm-wrestling when aides of Ontario's Bill Davis stumbled upon some emissaries of Saskatchewan's Allan Blakeney one night and, over the groceries and some grape, devised a few of the constitu-

114

tional compromises that supposedly solved all our problems (while leaving out the one-quarter of the country that lives in Quebec). The informal pact immediately became known as the Cannelloni Accord, and it is said that Axworthy has had three red-checked tablecloths, scene of some of his earlier wars, made into family crests in honour of the Pasta Pact.

It is Axworthy who is behind the attempt of the Trudeaucrats to shift the party to the left, particularly on the Prairies, so as to hold off the charging NDP which has succeeded the Liberals as the second party in that portion of the world. The NDP has regained power in Manitoba—Sterling Rufus having blown it all in one term with his Reaganomics—and has an even chance to do the same in British Columbia.

The major thrust and drive in the NDP caucus in Ottawa now come from a gang of young and cocky MPs from the West: Bill Blaikie from Manitoba; Lorne Nystrom from Saskatchewan; and Ian Waddell, Svend Robinson, Nelson Riis and Jim Fulton from B.C. That is Ed Broadbent's major problem—his power base is the dying automobile unions in Oshawa in a province, Ontario, where manufacturing is bleeding profusely, while his caucus is increasingly from Western Canada.

Tom Axworthy, attempting to keep the Grits clinging by their fingertips in the West until perhaps a new leader can remove the hatred, has devised an alliance with the credit unions as a means of undercutting the NDP. The political science theories of the underling are supposed to compensate for the airy attitude of the boss, who views most everything west of Kenora as a wasteland of intellect, a desert of the mind.

The Liberal party has failed in the West because the man who leads it, coming from a different culture and a different region, has never really attempted to understand Western Canada. It puzzles him, and he throws up his famous shrug, a brilliant mind pockmarked with petulance. If he had invested as much effort trying to solve his bewilderment as Western Canada has in attempting to understand Quebec, there would be a different Liberal party today. In keeping it in power, he has vitiated it.

Axworthy, celebrated away from the office for his one-liners, epitomizes something else about Trudeau. Both

Axworthy and his predecessor, Coutts, were star catches at Ottawa parties because of their sense of humour—a quality foreign to the man they worked for.

Pierre Trudeau has wit, as the Irish (Wilde and Shaw, Brendan Behan) have. But he has no sense of humour, as the English have. Wit is directed at others. Sense of humour involves oneself. The droll Robert Stanfield, who could never project in public, each year in Ottawa consistently wiped out Trudeau in the jesting contests at the black-tie Parliamentary Press Gallery dinner. He could make fun of himself, the whole point of these incestuous, in-joke cabarets. Trudeau, reading in bored fashion the constructions of his joke-writers, mistiming the punch lines, cannot. The man who vowed as a boy that he would never allow anyone to hurt him, to intrude on his space, will not allow humour that privilege. He seems genuinely puzzled at so many of the broad-stroking skits, the despairing gallery president having to explain the jokes to him.

(Stanfield, after leaving Ottawa, broke his leg when his sailboat, which he was helping to carry down to the lake, fell on him. When acquaintances spotted the cast and asked the inevitable what-happened question, he replied, deadpan: "Hit by a boat." Puzzled frowns. "Yes," was that celebrated painful drawl. "Got to stop walking on the lake.")

While Axworthy is an antic wit, as funny about his own party as he is about his political enemies, Coutts is renowned as a mimic, a Mickey Rooney-sized cherub who delights dinner parties with his well-honed impersonations of Paul Martin; of the partisan elf, Jack Pickersgill; of Trudeau himself.

There is a strange *discontinuity*—not just between Trudeau and his two most recent witty advisers—but with the entire record of those who have guided the prime minister since 1968. A man noted for the severe discipline of his own mental processes, he seems easily steered when it comes to policy. He keeps himself as tightly sealed as a can of clams but is peculiarly supine in the pure political sense.

A historian reading his report card will determine that he has been all over the map, a chap wandering the Sahara of Liberal principles like a punch-drunk wanderer staggering about in search of water. There is no fixed star in his public career—as opposed to his private.

Charles Lynch, the Southam columnist, once called Trudeau "a physical fitness nut with a high I.Q.." That's not bad. He's not really a politician, but a dazzling personality who dabbles in good works. He always exudes a certain contempt for the common toil of politics and relies on idea men to shape the mould he then polishes. A Churchill he ain't, a Roosevelt he ain't, even a Mackenzie King he ain't.

His career, once he had achieved power, has been remarkably guided by those who have his ear. He is the persona, the star who glistens like the morning sun, but behind him someone else is always steering. For a brilliant mind, he wobbles all over the spectrum once you look at his overall direction.

The principal secretary to the prime minister is the second most powerful man in Ottawa, and therefore in Canada. Cabinet ministers cower before him, mandarins bow and mere mortals quake. He is the gatekeeper to the presence of Himself. He who controls access controls power. When Alexander Haig confided to Richard Nixon that he no longer had pre-eminence in access to Ronnie Reagan, Nixon told him it was ball game over and advised him to quit. Haig quit. In Ottawa, the principal secretary is a supreme being—Haldeman and Ehrlichman wrapped up in one chubby ball.

When Trudeau became prime minister in 1968, he hired for the post Marc Lalonde, a granitic mind—like Trudeau— who had been a lawyer advising the government on constitutional matters. In private, Lalonde can charm the wax from bees, but in official dealings he is cold and ruthless.

He ran Trudeau's office with an iron hand, made a boatload of enemies and the Grits, with all their flowcharts and beautiful people, slid steadily from 1968 to 1972 near-defeat.

Strangely enough, Lalonde was Trudeau's last Francophone principal secretary, all the successors being Anglophones—supervising the process by which their boss has progressively lost support in the Western half of the country where it now does not own a single provincial seat and only two federal.

In 1972, despite having been frightened to death by the

electorate, Trudeau decided to use the vital principal secretary post as an unemployment office. Lalonde having been elected, the title was used as welfare for Martin O'Connell, a dull Toronto cabinet minister who had been defeated and was in need of groceries. Mr. Trudeau, the shining star whose compass had gone astray, was persuaded that the party needed rebuilding, and so a carpenter was sufficient.

By 1974, the nonsparkling Mr. O'Connell safely returned to the House of Commons, there was the need for a new body. It was another eccentric choice, a clever brain from Vancouver, Jack Austin, who had ambitions as long as his controversial career in legal and mining circles. His imagination ranged widely, as evidenced by his key role in formulating Canada's part in the uranium cartel while serving as deputy minister in the department of energy, mines and resources.

One could never discern any pattern in Trudeau's basic political philosophy in flipping from the fierce drive of Lalonde to a defeated politician to the skittering mind of Austin. What was the direction? Where was the link? As many of us had predicted, the gathering questions about Austin's background forced him to the ejector seat into the Senate after just fifteen months in the job. Trudeau's lack of care in the selection process remained as puzzling as ever.

Next choice was Coutts, out of the slick Toronto consulting field, forced on the compliant Trudeau by the party pros, who wanted more manipulation. One is reminded of the woman, married three times, who was asked by a female friend to describe her husbands. The first one, she explained, was a homosexual and it obviously didn't work. The second was a deviant and that was simply ridiculous. The third one, she said, was a public relations man and all he did was sit on the edge of the bed every night telling her how good it was going to be.

However, we digress. Coutts delivered the manipulation, steering the product Trudeau this way and that, ordering him to shut up during election campaigns, blocking interviews with the dreaded press. It was Coutts who arranged the buying of Jack Horner, the super-cynical move that sealed the death of the Liberals in the West.

With Coutts gone down the sump hole of Spadina,

Trudeau simply picked his assistant, Tom Axworthy. He is on the reformist left wing of a party that, after selling out the country to the Americans while under Trudeau, is now trying to buy it back under the same PM. It is interesting that the prime minister's last three principal secretaries have been from Western Canada—and that half of the country has increasingly become contemptuous of him. If they can't teach him, who can?

There's a strange indifference to Trudeau in picking his major aides. He seems not only a bad judge of talent, but an indifferent judge. He has stern views on the constitution and language—but surprisingly docile ones on the economy, i.e., how most people live.

He dazzles, but he has no direction outside his constitution obsession. It's a severe mind, but steered—like a raft on a muddy pond—by a changing crew of boys.

11
Saskatchewan

The Unconscious Force

The meaning of distance out here . . .
a fey wish that Trudeau, Lalonde and Pépin
would travel this road . . . Dr. Foth
is soft on Saskatchewan; he was born there . . .
Tommy Douglas at CCF picnic . . .
Some new Vulgarians . . .
the Uke and Toque Show

The purest water in the world is the water that collects in shallow dips in wheat fields in the late spring. The ponds are the reflected blue of the unending prairie sky and are always scalloped with little ripples from a breeze, origin unknown.

It is a standard thing, of course, to bemoan the ugliness of the Prairies but in fact at this time of year the land is quite pretty. There have been these late rains and the wheat is lush and green, perhaps ten inches high. There is that strange feeling, for someone from the mountains, of looking around and seeing the horizon in a 360-degree sweep. It is as if a Plexiglas dome has been set down on a flat surface.

Just as surely as in the Moroccan desert, or in the medieval remains of southern Italy, you can detect the settlements of humans from the small pockets of trees across the landscape. There is the hum—long forgotten—of telephone wires in the silence. You can hear, uninterrupted, the bobolink's truncated trill. White birds as large as seagulls trail tractors across the summer fallow.

The road in front of the car melts into a liquid with the heat haze. One does not need a map since a route ahead can be devised in geometric patterns, the whisper lines of far-off telephone poles providing the guide to where the roads intersect. Off in the distance, the next town can be detected from the wavering forms of the two or three or four grain elevators that dance and sway through the heat.

Saskatchewan people have the best sense of humour in the land. It is the Regina airport terminal and two teen-age blond boys in shorts, brimming with rural health, stand watching the incoming passengers. Suddenly they sprint forward to a man coming through the entrance, shouting "Daddy! Daddy!" The entire crowd in the small terminal turns to watch the tender emotion. The poor embarrassed man they hold their arms out to is black. An old friend. That's Saskatchewan humour—broad, for public consumption.

There's a bit of prejudice riding on this, you must understand. Dr. Foth was born there, in a little town called Hearne (you remember it, on the Soo Line, some fifty miles south of Moose Jaw, near Rouleau, Briercrest and Avonlea—home of the curling world-champion Campbell brothers).

People from Hearne are called Hearnias. The town was so small we couldn't even afford a village idiot. Everyone had to take turns. (Eventually, however, I moved to British Columbia, which improved the I.Q. of both provinces.)

I went to a one-room schoolhouse, twelve grades in one room, on the bald prairie. We small ones would stand, in anticipation every morning, at the gate as the big hitters of the school raced in on their ponies, the hero-worship reserved for the boy with the most wild-looking pinto stallion, just as the adulation goes now for the smoothie who tools up to a high school with the biggest mufflers mounted on muscle wheels.

The only other person in my grade was Kenny Newans. When we finished our sums we were allowed to go outside and snare gophers, while teacher went on to the higher grades. I seem to have spent most of my early grades outside, snaring gophers. One of us would pour a bucket of water down one end of a gopher hole. When the creature popped up at the other end, soaking and indignant, he would be snared around the neck with a length of binder twine. This proved educational for later use in political journalism.

Kenny Newans is now sports director of Calgary television station CFCN. Which means that of two boys raised in a one-room schoolhouse in the midst of the Depression, one earns his living from his pen and the other with his mouth. Must be something in that old time religion after all. Either that, or it must be useful spending a lot of time around gophers.

The trees on the road west from Winnipeg are gold, stolen from the brush of Cézanne. The prairie at this time of year, suspended in Indian summer, is not dull and bland at all but delicate and beautiful. A traveller on the

124

road west, swallowing the miles between the glimpses of civilization, contemplates only one fey wish. It is that the stern intellects in the Liberal cabinet—Trudeau, Lalonde, Pépin—could travel this road just once to comprehend what distance means to the West.

In these fathomless miles, skies stretching to the horizon in all directions, is the basic Western Canadian belief in land and property and resources. Distance from one's neighbours creates a feel for the earth. Geography becomes a friend, not an enemy. Form dictates content.

The road dips and waves past Portage la Prairie. Towns called Sidney and Melbourne—how did *they* get here? —disappear behind. Carberry, Justice, Two Creeks. We miss Pope, Snowflake and Rapid City. The problem, with the Ottawa mind-set, is the absence of empathy toward the Western feeling on resource ownership. It is one thing not to agree. It is another thing not to understand. The road extends, wavering but never varying from its westward destination, on through the hours.

It is not a concept easily grasped by sophisticated men from tightly packed urban centres in Montreal or Toronto. The miles pound by, the dead porcupine by the road, the squished skunk, the small animals melded into the asphalt. In Central Canada, one gets on airplanes to travel short distances. Out here, one must travel the land. It sets up a bond. The argument over resources is between men who sit in offices and men who have a feeling for the earth.

In the beverage room in the hotel in Moosomin, Sask., there is no talk of constitution as the snooker balls click. The lady in the green sweater borrows ten dollars from her man as she sets out on the most important project in Canada this day: it is the afternoon she conducts thirty-nine Brownies on a hike.

Outside Wapella, past Red Jacket, an object lesson thunders by. A freight train headed back east, its lengths and lengths of automobile carriers empty as it heads to Windsor and Oakville for its next load. One can see Peter Lougheed smiling. His point, exactly. Hewers of wood and drawers of water.

The clouds scud close to the horizon, deformed white blimps against the blue. The Liberals, now an urban party that flies in planes rather than rides in cars, are genuinely puzzled by all the antagonism. They should travel this road.

At Oakshela, the sky darkens, the wind that warns of approaching winter whips the loose soil from the fields, creating a Sahara dust cloud. The wind dies, the windshield reappears. The big trucks dominate the road, creating their own slipstreams and a shuddering blast of air as they thunder by, their jockeys perched on high, steering their rigs like captains at sea, a sea of stubble and hay that stretches as far as the eye can see. The tourists are gone, the swaying trailers fled safely south.

Near Grenfell, a half-dozen giant loaves of bread loom on the horizon, supermarket icons marching off the TV screen. They prove to be, as distance shrinks, storage loaves of fodder, ten yards high, in symmetry. Another train heads eastward, tank cars from Alberta Gas Chemicals, destined for processing in Central Canada rather than the West. One sees Peter Lougheed's smile expanding to a smirk as the imaginary Trudeau/Lalonde/Pépin stand by this road and see resources flowing ever eastward to those who will profit by them. It's an educational road.

Summerberry goes by. Sintaluta. Kipling, Peebles and Odessa are to the left. Gerald, Esterhazy and Stockholm to the right. The farmers, light-years away from the dust bowl, sit on their space age harvesting machines, technicolor in hue, five-figure in value, air-conditioned, tape deck blaring in the earphones. There is no longer awe for men in vests in Ottawa offices that have double doors for security's sake.

The road reaches west. Outside Indian Head, a small airfield holds private planes for these newfound entrepreneurs and landholders who zoom away to potash fields and, one suspects, Arizona. There is no inferiority complex left from the blow-dirt days. Only a sort of weary contempt—and sadness—for those from less changing circumstances who have no idea how once-colonial regions have changed.

Pilot Butte approaches. In Regina, the New York touring company of the Fats Waller Broadway production approaches. Somewhere out there await Conquest, Congress and Climax, Cut Knife, Renown, Outlook, Mozart, Plenty, Unity and Holdfast, Elbow and Eyebrow, Divide,

126

Liberty and Love. The clouds clipper along, lowering to the horizon that never ends and stretches forever.

One only wishes that there were three hitchhikers on this road, learning the lessons of geography, away from the pavement and the airline terminals and the chauffeured limousines. The tumbleweed languidly collides with the front of the car and disintegrates.

> "I feel that here I have made at least a brief acquaintance with the kind of unconscious force which Tolstoy believed is decisive in history."
>
> Hugh MacLennan
> on his 1961 visit to Saskatchewan

Three frisking pinto ponies surge and bump on the grassy slope until they are frozen on the crest against the endless blue sky, like a tableau out of an Old West canvas. In the picnic grounds below, a half-dozen miles northeast of Regina, there are those endless straw boaters, in pastel, adorning the cautious men who wear both belt and suspenders. The plastic folding chairs seek the shade beneath the trees as the old-time fiddle contest begins to tap toes in the rising dust. The horseshoes clank. It is, for one final time, "an old-fashioned CCF picnic," designed to honour the last of the happy warriors, Tommy Douglas, who will not pass this way again, it being 1978 and he does not plan to run again.

Tommy Douglas at this point is seventy-three (like all men of passionate belief, he appears perhaps fifty-three in energy) and there has been a tendency to denigrate him, to regard with wry amusement his outdated marionette mannerisms and dismiss his pulpit style.

One suspects, however, that a reassessment is about in order, that the painful progress of social justice in this tremulous country may spotlight just how much this pugnacious bantam accomplished over time that will someday be perceived as pioneering law, but today is taken for granted.

He is the same five-foot-six as when he was lightweight boxing champ of Manitoba. That carefully tended pompadour bounces above the chipmunk grin. His style was a little too evangelical, too corny ever to make him truly comfortable in skeptical British Columbia where he retreated in 1962 after his galling defeat in Regina, first to a Vancouver suburb, then, defeated again, to his Vancouver Island riding.

But this is his turf here, this picnic, these roots. His barbecued chicken dinner grows cold in the waiting Winnebago while he tries to work his way through the faithful who've driven from all over Saskatchewan for this final chance to grasp the wee chap who gave this province back its pride. "If I'd slept on all the kitchen floors of all the farmhouses as claimed here today," he sighs as he chews on his chicken, "I'd have been around more than Casanova."

Saskatchewan is probably the most misunderstood province of all. Ralph Allen, the man from Oxbow, once wrote of "the union of a very old land and a very young people. . . . The Prairies are older than the Nile, older than the hills of Jerusalem, older than Galilee and the Valley of the Jordan." A million years ago, mile-high glaciers began the process that has produced this silt-rich bread basket.

When Tommy Douglas in 1944 became head of the first socialist government in North America, Saskatchewan had the highest per capita debt in Canada, the second-lowest per capita income. There were a total of 138 miles of paved highway in the entire province. Of one hundred thousand farms, some three hundred were electrified.

Over the distance of time, Douglas' seventeen years as premier were indeed a test pattern for what has happened everywhere else: first Bill of Rights in Canada; first supplementary old age pension; first loan plan for small business; first student aid program; first assistance to the arts—a decade before the Canada Council.

Today, Regina and outskirts have that familiar, pleasantly sated look of upward mobility so prevalent in Alberta, British Columbia and Ontario. M. J. Coldwell, when he met the young Baptist preacher Douglas in Weyburn during the birth of the CCF, was outraged at finding Depression families who had nothing to eat but stewed gophers and coffee made from barley. Now, one of the party's aides from Weyburn worked on the Jimmy Carter campaign, learning about computerized telephone lists. The Regina Inn features a minor Hollywood name in a dinner-theatre production of *Same Time, Next Year*, the Bernie

Slade Broadway classic on how-to-do-it adultery for the middle class.

What Saskatchewan (and Douglas and the CCF) are most celebrated for, of course, is the introduction of medicare. While nervous Ottawa waffled, the audacity of Douglas was rather breathtaking. He did it, in fact, with free enterprise Yanks.

After hiring Dr. Henry Sigerist of Baltimore's Johns Hopkins University, the world's top authority on social medicine, to do a report, Douglas asked him who the best man would be to run such a program in Saskatchewan. "The best possible man" happened to be Dr. Fred Mott, who was untouchable as assistant surgeon-general of the U.S. Army. Douglas phoned *the* U.S. surgeon-general and somehow, with his blarney (the Scottish version) and passion, got a release for Mott who established a scheme that was followed years later by everyone else in tight-assed Canada.

It is somewhat hilarious that the United States, the only advanced country in the world that has yet to introduce medicare (Germany had it in 1896) supplied the two men who enabled socialist Tommy Douglas to lead the way for the rest of nonsocialist Canada.

There are some four thousand victims of nostalgia on the mellow Sunday afternoon. His earthy barnyard jokes, dropped with the precision of a pianist, are the more appreciated for being so familiar. If J. S. Woodsworth was the saint in politics and Coldwell the gentleman, Tommy was always slightly suspect, when he took over, as the laugher. David Lewis was impatient to take over, as he eventually did, because Douglas did not have that urban radical hate.

Baptists don't hate. (They don't let down any barriers, either.) He has few close friends in or out of politics. He has Irma and he has these adoring Depression groupies. Perhaps the critics should merely regard his record instead. The famed mimic somehow could never handle French, but he was the bravest man in the country in his stubborn stand against the War Measures Act.

The Saskatchewan he left now has potash, uranium and oil, in total income surpassing agriculture and may indeed have more future economic security than any of the four Western provinces. (Saskatchewan's economy grew more

129

than twice as fast as Canada's economy in 1981. Real domestic product rose by 5.1 percent while the Canadian economy grew by 2.5 percent. Net farm income rose by 160 percent; wages, salaries and supplementary labour income went up 13.8 percent. According to the Conference Board of Canada, Saskatchewan is the only one of the ten provinces not running a budgetary deficit. Saskatchewan has a $4.1 million surplus).

MacLennan wrote: "These days when I visit Saskatchewan I remember how students from the farms starved during the Depression years in order to get an education. I think how these people cooperated, and thereby upheld the dignity of their species." In that, he saw Tolstoy.

Tommy Douglas stands on a picnic table, the pompadour brushing the red and white stripes of the tent. The sky is now black, and jagged lines of lightning pierce the horizon. He has them howling, remembering their misery. He fits this misunderstood province, the province he remade.

Proof of how far Saskatchewan has come is that it too, though not to the level of its two Western neighbors, has produced some New Vulgarians. There is forty-four-year-old millionaire rancher Colin Thatcher, the energy and mines minister in Premier Grant Devine's new Conservative government. He is the only son of Ross Thatcher, Saskatchewan's last Liberal premier—one more indication that even the progeny are fleeing the party.

Thatcher, called "the J. R. Ewing of Saskatchewan" in the *Globe and Mail*, tools around Regina in his yellow Corvette, tours his fields in an air-conditioned, telephone-equipped farm vehicle or flies off for his winters in Palm Springs.

The headlines have been messy. A bitter divorce from his wife Joanne followed by a lengthy custody battle over son Regan, who then mysteriously disappeared. After continuing court battles—the presiding judge and the warring lawyers all holding press conferences—the child just as mysteriously materialized; the ex-wife was shot in the shoulder by an unknown assailant. All bona fide evidence that the dust bowl has grown up into your basic suburban domestic chaos.

The thoroughly cynical Thatcher has a sign pasted on his office door: "Are you into a change in scene? Would you like new vistas, new horizons? Are you tired of your workmates? Just screw up one more time."

There is Richard Collver, energetic and charming, who single-handedly revived the Tories from their low state but then, with a rush of something to his head, declared himself the head of a new Unionest Party that would separate Western Canada from the rest of the country and join the United States. This loony idea died faster than last year's corn and may have had something to do with the fact that Collver spends much of his time on his properties in Arizona.

Entangled in myriad financial and legal problems, he was fined five hundred dollars after firing a .357 Magnum into the air, while in an exuberant mood, from his apartment window in downtown Regina. (The mysterious Swiss bank account that was unearthed turned out to be, as claimed, for his daughter's education.)

These small indications of egos trying for bit parts in an episode from *Dallas* are proof that Saskatchewan has come of age.

An example of the bankruptcy of Liberal spirit and the corruption of Liberal thought is contained in the object lesson of Roy Romanow. Until Grant Devine's Conservatives upset the astounded Allan Blakeney and his NDP in early 1982, Romanow had been Saskatchewan's attorney-general for almost a decade.

He looks as if he dresses out of *Gentleman's Quarterly*, those ice-chip eyes have the lady reporters doing nip-ups, and he has the clean good looks of a Ukrainian Robert Redford. He is as good on the tennis court as he is before a microphone.

Romanow's father came to Canada as an immigrant in the late 1920s, desperately trying to learn rudimentary English on the boat crossing the Atlantic and, as his boatmates were instructed in like manner, practised on one phrase for the immigration officers: "Me Liberal. Me Mike Romanow."

He went to work for the Canadian National Railways as a labourer in Saskatoon, made well aware that the Natural Governing Party had provided him with a job. He became a strong union man and believed in the CCF after its formation. But when elections came, he was "advised" that he had best vote Liberal, since the Liberals were the

131

ones who had let him into the country. There was a hint there, just a nudge of a threat. The senior Romanow voted Liberal. Had to.

Roy Romanow says, "I've never forgotten that."

When it came time to sell Mr. Trudeau's constitutional package, there was Romanow as cochairman with Jean Chrétien of the road troupe that roamed the country in search of agreement from the squabbling premiers and the autocratic feds. They were billed as "The Uke and Toque Show," two rollicking young risers with a gift for after-hours humour.

There was the attorney-general of little Saskatchewan, given equal billing for months with the justice minister of Canada, coming off very well, thank you. Tune in *As It Happens* and there was Saskatoon's Roy, explaining it all to Barbara Frum. Follow every cameraman's boom mike at the elbowing scrum outside the constitutional doors and there was Roy. A Canadian Club podium in Vancouver? There was Roy, reasonable, conciliatory, charming.

What did it get him? It got him offers, nudge-nudge and wink-wink from the feds.

Romanow had a problem. The handsome A-G was the most eligible premier-in-waiting in the country. He'd been elected four times in a row. He'd been in the NDP caucus for thirteen years. He was so sensitive about his youth, knocked for being "too young" at twenty-eight when he lost to Blakeney in the leadership contest of 1970 that to this day he refuses to list his birthdate in the Parliamentary Guide.

Ottawa knew the man who would make a fine premier of a half-dozen other provinces was locked in behind Blakeney, some thirteen years older and in no mood to step aside. The feds figured on the galling fact that Romanow, the Number Two, was a native son, proud product of Saskatoon, while Blakeney was a brainy Maritimer who moved on to Saskatchewan via the civil service route after his Rhodes Scholarship days at Oxford.

The Grits wanted to buy Romanow, just as they had bought Conservative Jack Horner, with offers of enticing Ottawa positions. Just as they had appointed Ed Schreyer as governor-general—the first Gee-Gee of ethnic persuasion, from Western Canada, the first appointment from a socialist background—thinking it would help them electorally in Western Canada. It didn't. Voters don't like insulting bribes. Schreyer was a fine appointment, in that it demythologized the ceremonial post, but it didn't have the result at the polls the Grits intended.

Romanow hung in, even when the escaped memo from Privy Council's Michael Kirby revealed that the feds had cynically planned on the federal-provincial constitutional conference failing. The Toque, mortified at the exposed Machiavellian dealings of the Trudeaucrats, thereafter never had quite the same relationship with The Uke.

Mr. Trudeau, with his famed gift for names, in early meetings continually addressed Romanow as "Romanoff" —perhaps mistaking him for "Prince" Mike Romanoff, the Hollywood café society figure.

The Trudeau mind, trapped in an airlock, deals only in concepts, not in people. He is famous for his carelessness with names; they simply don't matter to him. His present principal secretary, Tom Axworthy, worked in his office for several years as a policy aide and speech-writer before Trudeau could ever remember his name. "Get me the fat guy," was his signal for Axworthy.

When the PM's popularity was waning in the early 1970s and his reputation had taken on an aura of formal sterility, a speech-writing aide suggested a folksy approach as he was about to address steelworkers in Hamilton. It was the time when Hank Aaron was in the headlines as he verged on breaking Babe Ruth's supposedly inviolate record of 714 home runs, and the aide suggested that the PM, who had barely survived his second election, compare himself to Hank Aaron who never quit after two strikes against him.

"Who's Hank Aaron?"

The aide, swallowing, explained that he was the Atlanta Braves slugger about to break Babe Ruth's record.

"Who's Babe Ruth?"

The aide, perspiration emerging, explained who Babe Ruth was. Once apprised of the approach, Trudeau willingly agreed that it was a good ploy for a speech.

Once before the steelworkers, he made his pitch. Yes, his government perhaps hadn't lived quite up to his expectations of 1968 and yes, it may have been a bit disappointing after 1972, but the 1974 election was a third try and, you know, even though Hank Aaron has one strike

133

on him you don't give up on him—even two strikes, because he still has that third swing to come.

"And you know who Hank Aaron is—he's threatening to break the home run record of Baby Ruth."

George Radwanski, now the editor-in-chief of the *Toronto Star*, author of a sympathetic biography of Trudeau, was given more hours of interviews with the private man for the book than any other author or journalist.

The next time he asked a question at a prime ministerial press conference, Trudeau said, "Yes, Jack?"—and looked around in genuine puzzlement at the hilarity in the press theatre.

Trudeau once had a meeting with Dennis McDermott, president of the Canadian Labour Congress, whom he continually referred to throughout the session as "David."

McDermott, a man of no small ego himself as witness the gold chains and coiffed hairstyle, burned inwardly and finally made the elaborate point that "if I, Dennis McDermott, were presented with such-and-such a proposal, I can tell you, Mr. Prime Minister, what I, Dennis McDermott, would do."

Trudeau listened thoughtfully throughout and, when McDermott had finished, said, "That's a good point, David."

I digress. In the final early-morning cabal that pasted Canada's constitution together (while Quebec's delegation, unwarned, slept across the river in Hull), it was Romanow, Chrétien and Ontario's Roy McMurtry who did the stickum job. This is understandable, since all three are lawyers and all three suffer from the Anthony Eden/John Turner syndrome: growing old while sitting in the waiting room.

McMurtry, a large, slope-shouldered ex-football player with bedroom eyes (they are put to good use; he has six children) has been attorney-general ever since he joined the Bill Davis government. But Davis, who has been at Queen's Park for twenty-three years and premier for eleven, says that he wants to stay around to beat the twenty-seven-year mark of NDP veteran Donald MacDonald, who resigned this summer to allow new NDP leader Bob Rae to contest his seat.

McMurtry is stalled, Chrétien is stalled and the Grits, knowing Romanow was stalled, tried to buy him. They can't grow their own in this territory, so they try to buy others.

Romanow resisted the Ottawa blandishments and, as his reward, was beaten by nineteen votes in the Tory landslide by twenty-two-year-old Jo-Ann Zazalenchuk, a university student who was a gas pump jockey in her father's Petrocan station.

Romanow, as damaged goods, is of no use to the Liberals now. What is useful to remember is that the same party that bullied the father, years later tried to buy the son. These are not nice people. They will be dead for a long time in this territory.

12
Fourth Digression

Notwithstanding Lawyers

Our pockmarked constitution . . .
the legal imbalance in the land . . .
five of ten premiers are unsullied by an LL.D. . . .
a public in awe of mouthpieces

> The first thing we do, let's kill all the lawyers.
> —*Henry VI, Part II*

The famed lexicographer Patrick Nagle maintains that lawyers can pick fly droppings out of pepper while wearing boxing gloves. As evidence, we have only to look at our pockmarked constitution, still quivering, all full of pinpricks, loopholes, crochet work and glue. Only a nation whose leaders are lawyers could construct a new Magna Charta built on a "notwithstanding" clause.

That is the metaphor for Canada: notwithstanding. A perfect Mackenzie King word. Notwithstanding that it excludes one of our two founding races and the native people, notwithstanding we have a pluperfect lawyer mind.

It is why the most overlooked event of 1982 is that some tiny progress in the creep of civilization has been achieved. We actually acquired a new premier without adding to the legal imbalance of the land. Grant Devine took over Saskatchewan and, glory be, he is not a lawyer. No one seemed to notice it, but those of us put here to supervise the legal profession marked it down as a significant act, just short of Harold Ballard's brain transplant. It means the never-ending struggle to keep our affairs from being dominated completely by nitpickers in laced shoes is still in a holding pattern, not yet swamped beyond repair.

Since Premier Devine is an agricultural economist, it means that a remarkable five of the ten premiers still hold their heads high, unsullied by the millstone of an LL.D. They are allowed to walk about in public, small boys do not stone them and dogs greet them with a friendly wag of the tail. They are a rare breed, these five, due for extinction eventually like the three-toed wombat, and we should

139

cherish them. One cannot remember when the public last received such a break, since the leadership of the land has been dominated for so long by the legal beagles, everyone had lost count.

James Matthew Lee took over Prince Edward Island and, to everyone's surprise, turned out not to be a lawyer. He is a realtor, which is a fancy name for someone who sells houses. William Richards Bennett of British Columbia is not a lawyer on account you gotta attend university to be one, and MiniWac grew so impatient that he didn't finish the niceties of high school, eager to get out and make a million, which he did.

Bennett is a believer in corporate baron Bud McDougald who, when he died, owned most of Canada. McDougald once confessed: "Left school at 14 and I've regretted it all my life. Should have left when I was 12!" The reason Bennett, who was chairman of the Gang of Eight, was fast asleep at 3:00 AM when the "notwithstanding" nonsense was shoe-horned into the final constitutional bargain in a Château Laurier bedroom was that, not being a lawyer, his mind grew exhausted at all the legal mumbo-jumbo and his body gave him a signal. If you listen to lawyers talking for too long, it makes you sterile. You can look it up.

René Lévesque is not a lawyer, but it was a close call. With that Gallic gift of the gab, the courts might have been on overtime. When he was kicked out of Laval law school for smoking, he joined the U.S. Army as a war correspondent, and journalism—not law—must take the blame for what has followed.

Lucky Brian Peckford is not a lawyer. The Newfoundland premier is probably the only passionate high school English teacher in captivity and achieved the satisfaction of shoving across the table the final compromise solution that supposedly solved the constitution muddle. Peckford's brimstone soul is fired like a furnace at the sight of Pierre Trudeau across the federal-provincial table because the Cartesian mind of the PM is so bloodless (Where's Poland?) that it inflames someone who thinks words should be used to communicate, not obfuscate. If Shakespeare hadn't said it, Peckford would have.

A chap called Plato talked of lawyers' "small and righteous" souls. We are run by them. Always have been. Of

242 federal cabinet ministers between 1867 and 1940, forty-eight percent were lawyers. Dr. John Porter, in his monumental *The Vertical Mosaic*, showed how the percentage is increasing and how lawyers are far more prevalent in our political system than in Britain or Australia. There is one office building in downtown Toronto that contains more QCs than there are in the British Isles. Lawyers make up fifty percent of all United States senators and representatives and seventy percent of all presidents, vice-presidents and cabinets. Is it any wonder the world is in such a notwithstanding mess?

Keats wrote, "I think we may class the lawyer in the natural history of monsters." We somehow are cowed by monsters, mainly monsters of the language. Ontario's Bill Davis uses words like jungle camouflage, hiding himself as if a Vietnam combat veteran with his voice box as the uniform. When he intones "finally" in one of his short speeches, you can go out for a hamburger and be assured of returning for the final cliché. Saskatchewan's Allan Blakeney always approached the English language carefully, as a bomb-disposal expert creeping up on an explosive car, ever circling, until the bomb defused for lack of air.

Joe Clark expired, among other reasons, because the public was slightly nervous over a chap who—given the choice of two law schools, Dalhousie and the University of B.C.—flubbed them both. Joe's distaste for the law was his greatest gift, but the public is in awe of the mouthpiece. The chances are the next leaders (Macdonald and Turner on one side, Mulroney and Crosbie on the other) will rise from the legal beagles. Notwithstanding. We are brutes for punishment.

13
Alberta

*Man-Boys
in the Promised Land*

What makes Lougheed ride? . . .
oil, cowboys and nouveau riche swagger . . .
the key to understanding Alberta
is androgen, the male sex hormone . . .
a whiff of Dallas . . .
the specific gravity of Joe Clark's head . . .
Gordon Kesler, the Louis Riel
of the bronco set

In 1938, a ten-year-old boy broke into a twenty-six-room house in Calgary. The mansion, known as Beaulieu, was up for public auction the next day after being seized for tax arrears. The boy was Peter Lougheed, and the reason he broke into the house was that it had been owned by his grandfather, the grandest man in Alberta, and it was the symbol of the family fortune and reputation that had been destroyed.

The house—filled with teak and brass and eight Italian marble fireplaces—had once entertained British royalty and now was being stripped. Peter Lougheed, from a secret hiding place in the house he knew so well, watched as the entire library—volumes bound in leather—went for twenty-two dollars. Peter Lougheed has a long memory, and a low forgiveness factor, to this day.

Any one of us, one suspects, would have been pierced by the experience of that ten-year-old. Those from Quebec have centuries of grievances. Those from Alberta have similar feelings that run back only a few generations, but the bitterness can be equated.

Lougheed's grandfather graduated from Osgoode Hall and articled with a Toronto law firm. When he saw the potential of making a fortune in the West with the building of Sir John A. Macdonald's transcontinental railway, he persuaded Sir William Van Horne to make him CPR solicitor in Calgary.

His knowledge of CPR plans allowed Jimmy Lougheed to make judicious land purchases. His buildings eventually dominated the Calgary skyline. For several years after 1914, Lougheed was assessed *half* the taxes in the city of Calgary. When he was made Senator Lougheed, he was the youngest member of the Canadian Senate: thirty-five.

There was something uncanny in his maiden speech when he intimated that Calgary could in time replace

145

Ottawa as the capital and went on to state that the province's resources "when developed, I am satisfied, will eventually make Alberta the dominant portion of the Dominion." That was, gentle reader, in 1889—the last appointment to the Senate Sir John A. would make.

Grandfather's law partner was R. B. Bennett, the prime minister. Grandfather became, in 1916, Sir James Alexander Lougheed, the first and only Albertan ever knighted. When he died, he left a fortune to Lady Lougheed and heirs.

The Depression, as it seared Western Canada more than Ottawa thinkers yet realize fifty years later, ruined the family. The Metropolitan Life Insurance Co. of Ottawa, which held most of the mortgages on the Loughheed properties, made Royal Trust of Montreal the trustee and put Peter Lougheed's father, Edgar, on a "salary."

Edgar Lougheed, complaining bitterly about how his family was "brought to its heels by the callous moneylenders from the East," turned into a drinker. Peter Lougheed's mother, Edna, suffered a nervous breakdown and underwent psychiatric treatment. The magnificent Beaulieu was turned into a residence for the WACs during the Second World War and is now Red Cross Headquarters in Calgary.

Peter Lougheed, as a result of his family's humiliation, became a fighter, a constant competitor. As a teen-ager, his nickname was "The Demander," because of his insistence on turning everything into a contest. Harold Millican, a schoolmate who later worked with Lougheed in government, recalls: "All of his games, whether cowboys and Indians, table tennis or football, were set up as win-or-lose situations."

University of Alberta political scientist Larry Pratt, in *The Tar Sands*, writes: "What Peter Lougheed articulates so well are the politics of resentment, the frustrated aspirations of a second-tier elite for so long dismissed as boorish cowboys, as yahoos with dung on their boots, by the smug, ruling Anglo-French establishment of Ontario and Quebec."

The first time Marc Lalonde travelled by train from Montreal to his national capital in Ottawa, he found that the conductors on the government's railway couldn't speak to him in his own language. He has devoted his years in

Ottawa to setting such outrages aright. It's too bad he didn't have the tolerance, when he was energy minister of Canada, to understand other bitter minorities.

Someone who does understand the situation is Richard Milo, sports editor of *Le Devoir*. After the superbly prepared Edmonton Eskimos had humiliated the Hamilton Tiger-Cats in the 1980 Grey Cup game, he wrote of the winners: "They are to Alberta what Les Canadiens used to be to Quebec. They are the flagship, the showcase. They have to win. It means so much to the whole province. Players realize this. Alberta's honor is at stake, as well as the result of a football game."

So true. If a Quebec sportswriter can recognize it, why can't Marc Lalonde and Pierre Trudeau? Because they are prisoners of their own pilgrimage. That same year, in the College Bowl, a contest in Toronto's Varsity Stadium that would decide the Canadian university football championship, the University of Alberta took great pleasure in running up a 35-0 half-time lead over a befuddled University of Ottawa.

At the intermission, the Alberta star, a five-foot-six-inch quarterback by name of Forrest Kennerd, was asked if his team would ease up in the second half and not make the debacle even more embarrassing.

No chance, he replied quite calmly. His team was still smarting over some supposed slight in the Toronto press and, he emphasized, there wasn't the proper respect for the calibre of Western Canadian collegiate football. Furthermore, his mates represented not just Alberta but the whole West. No respect. The Depression complex runs deep. Instead of the usual Dick-and-Jane inanity of these jockdom interviews, we had a little touch of political science.

The pride runs deep. In 1981 the Golden Bears were defending their title (their fourth trip to the championship game in eleven years) against Nova Scotia's Acadia University—which is the exact opposite of the regional authenticity of the Alberta team. Acadia is a football factory. Only twenty-one of its forty-four players were from the Atlantic provinces. Fourteen of them were imported from Ontario, two from Quebec and seven from the United States.

Forty of the fifty-one Golden Bears were born and raised in Edmonton. Only four were from outside the province.

They are the expression of a province, not hired mercenaries. (The mercenaries won in the last minute of play.)

The key to understanding Alberta is androgen. Androgen rules business. Androgen permeates politics. Androgen affects Alberta's relations with the outside world.

Androgen is the male sex hormone, and the aura it projects, the insecurities it hides, the locker-room mentality it bolsters, explain the new rich kid on the block—the province of oil and cowboys and nouveau riche swagger. It is a strange province, aggressive in its new stance and surprisingly chippy toward outsiders. There is some question of whether it is willing to tolerate those areas of the country with differing cultural backgrounds.

Alberta is the male animal on display. The need to prove oneself in the primitive manner of a bull in rut makes the atmosphere of the place resemble an entire province posing for a hairy-chested after-shave lotion. There can be nothing more ludicrous than a grown man with a paunch teetering about Calgary on the high heels and pointed toes of embroidered cowboy boots, attempting to capture a reminder of some distant past. If the foot is a sex object, as a trendy new doctor claims, Alberta is abrim with eroticism.

These are man-boys playing in the make-believe world of their own playpen—exposed as pseudo-machismo caricatures only when they stray beyond their own borders. The costume parade—affected by otherwise normal businessmen—is, of course, a sham, because Alberta is not the stage for John Wayne it makes itself out to be. Since the Second World War, Canada has had the fastest urban growth rate of any country in the world, and Calgary is the fastest-growing city in the country.

It will be a fine city, as they say, when they finish uncrating it. Calgary has less green space per square foot in its downtown core than any city in Canada. In the race toward Mammon, green space got left behind. The skyline of the city is now a cardboard cutout, the towers reminiscent of the Metropolis backdrop for a Superman comic. The new towers make even more ridiculous the insane bulbous knob of the Calgary Tower, another example of the municipal fascination with such symbols that induced Toronto to add its own Disneyland touch to its view with its CN Tower.

The two towns perhaps have something in common—a lust for power and sway at the sacrifice of sensitivity. While Toronto is merely superior in its isolation, Calgary takes an aggressive stance against the rest of Canada. It was there, in this city famed for Western hospitality, in the professionally printed banners that hung in the Calgary Corral, the hockey rink, when Quebec Nordiques paid their first visit after the Calgary Cowboys' Rick Jodzio was suspended for his brutal attack on the Nordiques' top scorer Marc Tardif. The banners read: FROGS ARE BACK JUMPERS. Other signs in the arena showed the same delicate taste: JODZIO EATS FROGS and QUEBEC LES TURKEYS.

Somehow, there is the need to exert muscular dominance. Albertans do not pick and choose, they stampede. After enduring thirty-six straight years of sanctimonious rule under Social Credit, the electorate—one might have imagined—would have preferred some balance in the parliamentary system. Instead, they shy from providing an opposition that can be some check on government excess— they give Peter Lougheed's Tories seventy-three of the seventy-nine seats.

Albertans don't vote when they enter the polling booth as much as they anoint. The opposition is in effect composed of one member, the NDP's lonely Grant Notley who has now been joined by a colleague. Two of every three Albertans vote the same way—an aberration in the political mosaic that makes up the rest of Canada. They are conformists with a vengeance—the only province that sends only one party to Ottawa. Twenty-one solid Conservatives.

Lougheed comes across as pensive on Joe Clark—who was once almost an office boy for him—saying the correct, necessary things as an executive would about a onetime junior.

No intellectual himself but a fiercely determined worker, Lougheed declined the opportunity to sit across the floor from Trudeau as leader of the Opposition. He did not even stay in the Ottawa Civic Arena for the final ballot of the Tory leadership contest in 1976. What his vote might have been is unknown, but all we know is that he didn't vote for Clark on the clinching ballot. He didn't vote for anyone.

There is one link with Quebec: the populations of the

two precincts tend to veer toward uniformity of thought. They love landslides. If democracy is not entirely a frail flower in Alberta, the lack of opposition members does make for quite the dullest legislature in the country. It is an unusual week when Lougheed is asked an interesting question. For years, the cameras that televise the sittings were aimed at the government benches, capturing only the backs of the heads of the sparse opposition members. The general atmosphere is that of a nunnery at recess.

The mistake is to misjudge the province of rough faces and new wallets. Bruised pride is everything. When Premier Lougheed toured Europe in 1975, his entourage— including wives and press—totalled 110.

The mystique of the frontier male wafts over the province as thick as musk. There are few outstanding Alberta women who would come to mind for the average Canadian. There is not a single woman among the twenty-one MPs. The locker-room syndrome was most apparent among the tightly knit coterie of ex-athletes and thrusty success stories in Lougheed's first cabinets. A reporter observing them move like a phalanx around King Peter, as he was then known, at federal-provincial conferences always expected them to snap into a huddle and call the next play.

The base of it all, the folk rite that reveals the soul, is the anachronism called the Calgary Stampede, which every summer allows the abandoning of the frontier strictures that are in play the rest of the year. It is like some ancient Greek festival, when societal rules were set in abeyance for a set duration. Men who decline to swear in front of their secretaries are suddenly revealed as raunchy gropers who establish that the barriers are down in the after-office parties at the Calgary Inn (which I refuse to call The Westin). They treat women as they would a horse.

It is, in fact, the Canadian version of *Fasching*, the permissive celebrations of the flesh in Bavarian towns when the year's normal restrictions on conduct are abandoned. Stampede Week is when the Albertan climbs down out of his aftershave lotion ad and attempts to emulate the caricature. The boy-men are out of school.

Edmonton is more interesting than Calgary, a more livable city. The river valley of the North Saskatchewan that divides the town is one of the great assets of any Canadian city in winter and summer. But it is too cold. Brass monkeys change airline tickets just to avoid the place. It will become a less interesting town since the publisher of the *Edmonton Journal*, J. Patrick O'Callaghan, has just moved to take up the same post at the *Calgary Herald*. J. P. O'C.—as he's known to his staff—has been likened to a cannon loose on the deck of a frigate in a storm. With O'Callaghan and Ted Byfield in the same town at the same time the city may have to order more fire extinguishers.

Red Deer is the birthplace of Marjorie Nichols, the Victoria journalist, and one day it will erect a plaque in her honour. ("She doesn't have ulcers," it will say, "but she's a carrier.") When she starred in Ottawa as the Pearl Mesta of the journalistic set, she used to host parties to which she would invite Margaret but not Pierre. "He kills parties," she would explain. "They fall flat kerplunk on the floor when he arrives." She meant the social variety. Now he's killed the other variety.

Albertans, with their siege mentality, don't really mind the taunt that they have the only one-party government this side of Albania. They like less the suggestion that, to paraphrase Toynbee, Alberta may be the only jurisdiction in history that has gone from poverty to decadence without passing through civilization. Unlike the residents of Saskatchewan, who know their hearts are pure and God in Her socialist or Tory beneficence will take care of them, and unlike British Columbians, who simply don't give a damn, knowing golf is just around lunch, Albertans have a nonamused view of the rest of Canada, especially Ottawa, suspicious that the Eastern bastards want to steal their riches now that they've dug themselves out of Depression days.

One night in the Owl's Nest, the bar of the Calgary Inn, a visitor got up to say goodnight and tapped on the shoulder—as a method of saying farewell—one of the men seated around the table. A hand shot backward, an iron grip seized the visitor's arm, and he was warned, in threatening tones, that this "Eastern condescension" had gone on for too many years and Western grievances were going to be settled and on and on. Finally prising himself loose with some difficulty, the perplexed visitor—who

151

happened to be from Vancouver—made his way to his bed. The chap issuing the threats turned out to be a transplant from Ontario. Marc Lalonde let loose a lot of hidden anger.

As a diplomat, he'd make a great piano-mover. With the province seething with rage over the effects of the National Energy Policy and the oil rigs heading south, the man who imported expensive oil from Venezuela for Eastern Canada while denying Alberta the world price for oil travelled to Cold Lake and Edmonton on a fence-mending tour in late January of 1981.

The trip was rare enough to make major news in Alberta, because the failure of the Liberal heavy hitters to show their faces in the province since their celebrated energy policy the previous October had further contributed to the anger. Lalonde, who has never lacked courage, was gaining points on his two-day tour until he came up with another of his gems.

Multinational oil companies always act strongly when countries start to limit outside control over oil production, he said in an address to Alberta Indians. Then he thoughtfully added, "At least they have not brought the CIA in, like they did in certain foreign countries."

If there is an insult to be had, Lalonde will find it with the unerring gift of a water diviner. By giving the sly nudge that there might somehow be a connection with what went on in places such as Chile and what could go on in Alberta, Lalonde was playing for cheap applause before a minority group. That's a class act?

A University of Alberta professor's wife, who has lived in the United States, says there is a "whiff of Dallas" to the political air. She finds it chilling. J. O. Karpinka, president of Oleum Exploration Ltd., says in a letter to the *Calgary Herald* that the day the NEP was introduced, "budget day, Oct. 28, 1980, must rank as a day of infamy in this nation's history." He refers to that intrinsic emotion called freedom—"the very substance which people of our world are prepared to die for." One keeps running into references to death in conversations in Alberta this year. It is not a pleasant atmosphere.

Albertans, regarded as funny-money freaks by the outside world for those three and a half decades under the descendants of Bible Bill Aberhart, are further embittered by another factor. The lonely Tory toffs of the province have good reason for their frustration. For thirty-six years they wandered unappreciated outside the mainstream of Canadian political life as the mumbo-jumbo artists of Social Credit-ruled Alberta.

The leaders of the province were, in effect, regarded as lepers elsewhere in Canada. There was certainly no connecting bond of patronage with Ottawa. Then, a decade ago, there was a further waft of alienation when Alberta was a lonely island of capitalism in a sea of socialism, with the NDP controlling the governments of Manitoba, Saskatchewan and affluent British Columbia (the latter fact completely befuddling materialistic Albertans). The siege mentality and xenophobia simply increased. Earlier, when Peter Lougheed did his magnificent repair job on the provincial Conservative party, at least the nabobs of Calgary and Edmonton were plugged into one of the two major political parties—though they had to remain outside the federal trough as the Grits seemed destined to reign forever.

Then came Joe Clark. There's the basis of the further embitterment. Clark is not much respected in his home province, mainly because he can't ride a horse. In a culture that still retains the illusion that it is a cameo out of a Zane Grey novel, this apparently means a lot. Clark, admittedly, is one of the more uncoordinated specimens ever to tread the public stage.

He once confessed into my tape recorder in his office that the reason he can't swim has to do with a problem with his head. "It floats?" I asked in my famed suave manner. "No," he said, "I shouldn't tell *you* this, but it . . . um . . . *sinks*." At this his aide, Donald Doyle, who was seated behind him out of Clark's view, twisted his body into the fetal crouch and his lips formed a silent primordial scream, realizing what demons were to emerge later from my typewriter.

To this day, at my Saturday night parties when readings from *The Collected Wit of Herb Gray* pall and guests grow tired of my snapshot album showing the CNR double-tracked all the way from Larry Zolf's kosher log cabin in Winnipeg to the shores of the Pacific, I bring out my tape of Joe Clark explaining why his head is heavier than water.

153

But, to be fair—my constant weakness—there is a medical, or at least military diagnosis for Clark's coordination problems. I was walking with him one day and kept feeling as if I had three left feet, continually doing a quick shuffle, trying to keep in step. I finally realized why I could never do it. Most people, when they walk, move their left arm forward as their right foot goes forward—and vice versa.

Joe Clark, when he walks, swings his right arm forward with his right leg, his left arm with his left leg. He suffers from ambulatory dyslexia. I explained this discovery to my close buddy Marjorie Nichols, the *Vancouver Sun* columnist who regularly operates without anaesthetic on the politicians in the B.C. legislature. "That's right!" she cried. "If he'd been born a horse, he'd be a pacer!"

But, it must be explained, I said *most* people. Not everyone. The Canadian Army discovered the anomaly during the latest of our wars. There are some recruits, it found, who indeed cannot march in unison: they walk the way Clark does. The army has even devised a word for this. These incipient mercenaries are "zunters." That's now an official army word. So Joe Clark, when you puzzle over him on TV, is "zunting."

Mackenzie King, when you think of it, would never have survived the age of television. Joe Clark, if present conditions prevail, has a good chance of being our next prime minister and, just as Mackenzie King was our first PM who talked with his dead mother and his dog, Clark was our first and (quite possibly) will be our second PM who zunts.

However, I digress. The advent of Clark in 1979 as prime minister (only one Alberta MP supported his leadership bid) at last promised to bring the lonely millionaires of Alberta into the national fold. It was fully expected that the decision-making bodies and all those nonelected boards in Ottawa would suddenly flower with these energetic and tough-minded Alberta men who had been denied their say for so long. The highest per capita income-earners in Canada being denied a role in running the country? It had been an unnatural state and was now to end.

There was talk of an Alberta figure heading the CBC and another getting a major position in the CNR. Once young Joe found the levers of power in Ottawa, it was expected (a natural expectation) that all those havens of patronage filled with fatted Liberals would be cleansed with lean-jawed Tories, a good percentage of them from Alberta.

Instead, as the violins whined and the rye turned to hemlock in the Petroleum Club, poor Clark and his Boy Amateurs did the kamikaze act in record time and the Albertans, just about to taste the national goodies, had them snatched away again.

It is sometimes hard to discern which is the strongest—the distaste for Pierre and the Reincarnates, or the contempt for the inability of Clark to accomplish what was expected of him. That is, a quick replacing of the movable bodies. The eminently fair and meticulous manner in which Clark's lady of patronage Jean Pigott, the Godmother, was sifting eager aspirants was subsequently viewed, in Alberta, as juvenile. The propertied class of Alberta bitterly saw itself shut out yet again for years ahead.

Considering its lonely existence for so long in the past, it was more understandable when there was a sudden spate of frustrated cries for a Western sovereign state unblemished by language promises and DREE grants. Pierre Trudeau's energy policies and constitutional obsessions certainly didn't help the situation, but at the base of the separatism mutterings was the anger (Tory anger at Tories, if you will) at seeing salvation so close, but then watching it slip away again.

Clark, sternly warning the prime minister from platform after platform that Western Canada is dangerously ripe for the separatist myth, passes on a mood that has gripped a certain small slice of Alberta society. But he must be nagged by the knowledge that he himself, by his ineptitude, unwittingly fanned the small flame.

If Clark is uncomfortable with his own province, Trudeau is mystified/indifferent by/to it. As a man who believes that his intellect can pierce steel plate at forty glances, Trudeau tends—when thwarted—to sulk and seek easier targets. This is the basis of his failures in Western Canada over fourteen years: being Number Two, he doesn't try harder.

This is even more peculiar because his principal advisers, over the period of his greatest failure have been from Alberta itself, the impenetrable castle. His brains have been steered by Ivan Head, Jimmy Coutts and Joyce Fairbairn, all Albertans who gravitated as adults to Ottawa and therefore would be presumed to be able to influence or educate a man who was past fifty before he spent much time west of Ottawa.

Head was a University of Alberta law professor who for ten years was Trudeau's heavy thinker and a writer of his more important speeches. He seems to have reserved his rented genius for global affairs, seldom casting his eye on Red Deer. Over the years he has had about as much influence on Trudeau's understanding of Western Canada as Wayne Gretzky has.

Joyce Fairbairn was a pert blond reporter from Alberta who, with a well-turned ankle in the front row of press conferences in the miniskirt era, was often the subject of Trudeau's playful flirtations. She joined his office, and as his legislative assistant prepares him for the probable line of debate in question period every day. She is married to Michael Gillan, a former *Globe and Mail* reporter and saxophone player who has long been an executive assistant to Allan MacEachen. It is widely believed that Trudeau will place Fairbairn, forty-two, in the Senate before he departs his job. She does the verbal do-si-do when you mention it to her.

Coutts of course is an Alberta product, grew up there, took his law degree there and presumably would still have had some contacts in his home province that he could have passed on to the prime minister. It was Coutts and Fairbairn who convinced Trudeau to bribe Jack Horner to cross the floor, the worst political decision since Rudolf Hess parachuted into Scotland.

If there is anything the land of the cowboy detests it is a traitor, and lifetime Tory Horner, running as a Liberal, was trounced twice in Crowfoot by young Tory Arnold Malone, who is known around Ottawa as "Mortimer Snerd" from the Edgar Bergen days, because of his speaking style.

So Trudeau's main spokesmen to win the hearts and minds of Western Canadians were turncoats. Horner was a turncoat, Senator Argue, as we've seen, was a turncoat. Senator Olson was a turncoat. A Tory-turned-Liberal, a socialist-turned-Liberal, a Socred-turned-Liberal. It seems a strange way to build a political base. (The effectiveness of Senators Argue, Olson and Perrault, when they were the three senators in Trudeau's cabinet, can be judged by the fact that they were known as "Winken, Blinken and Nod" in their wanderings through this Liberal wasteland.)

The strange thing about Trudeau is that with his office full of Westerners, he still can't fathom the territory—and has given up trying. "I came to Ottawa to save Quebec," he told Joe Clark while discussing the transfer of power to the Tories after his 1979 defeat, "someone else is going to have to save the West."

His last three principal secretaries have been from the West: Austin from B.C., Coutts from Alberta, Axworthy from Manitoba. But none of the intelligence seems to take root.

It's not that there hasn't been *enough* advice. The fault lies in the receiving set. The sender was working. The receiver wasn't tuned in—or turned on.

A most important point that Trudeau and the panjandrums of Central Canada most dangerously ignore is that Alberta feels frustrated, trapped, the only province besides serene Saskatchewan without access to the sea. Alberta is a musclebound Switzerland. She aims to do something about it.

Peter Lougheed, a polite, pleasant man sits on a flowered couch in his huge office in Edmonton. He is free to admit that the reason he shocked his free enterprise friends by buying the Vancouver-based Pacific Western Airlines and moving it to Alberta is that his province will no longer abide being a prisoner of transportation systems controlled from afar. (Calgary is the only major city in Canada where the CPR lines still carve the downtown core like a Berlin Wall, forcing streets to duck under or rise above.)

As soon as the Supreme Court of Canada disagreed with Ottawa's objections and approved Alberta's PWA purchase, it was discovered the airline was talking merger with Transair, another line that sweeps across the northern prairie and into Toronto.

Now that Lougheed had his own airline, did he also want a route to the sea? He acknowledges the opening of the Mackenzie Valley corridor to the Arctic has been an Alberta (and family) dream since grandfather Sir James

Lougheed advocated the project in the Senate. Some Albertans refer to Inuvik, in the Mackenzie delta, as "Alberta's port."

Mel Hurtig, the Edmonton publisher, used to say that there were more left-handed Mormon streakers in Western Canada than there were separatists. That's not quite true anymore, but there still aren't that many real live separatists out there. What you do have is a clutch of cowards.

A coward is someone who, faced with a fight, cuts and runs away. That is what a Western separatist is (Quebec is another question). Confronted with the need to work out an accommodation with the insular rulers of Ottawa, the separatist turns and runs, seeking thumb-sucking independence rather than a tiresome family quarrel. That's a coward.

Gordon Kesler, the Louis Riel of the bronco set, is not going to frighten any democracy. He went to a Utah college on a rodeo scholarship. (For those who keep track of items of the symbolism of certain classic movies, it should be recorded that one of the five children of Gordon Kesler is named Shane.) He makes his living as an oil patch spy using binoculars and contacts with oil rig workers to find out up-to-date drilling intelligence which he then sells to competing oil companies. It is common practice in the oil patch and, while not exactly illegal, certainly flirts in the unethical arena.

It is industrial espionage, in fact, a strange trade for a man calling for a new code of conduct in politics.

Olds-Didsbury, the riding that Kesler won for the Western Canada Concept (in Alberta, the Liberal party is now referred to as the "Eastern Canada Concept"), was the most susceptible seat in the province for his brand of Poujadism. It has never been represented by any of the old-line parties.

Always out there on the right-wing fringe, Olds-Didsbury was previously held for twenty-one years by now-retired Social Credit leader Bob Clark. A farming area halfway between Calgary and Edmonton—the town of Olds has eight grain elevators and now a waterbed store—the seat before going Socred was held by the United Farmers of Alberta. Any group of voters who feels that Peter Lougheed

158

is too far to the *left* is breathing a special type of air denied most Canadians.

Kesler is so sophisticated that he told the microphones within minutes of being elected in February that "if we're lucky" Pierre Trudeau "will have a heart attack in the next five minutes."

Wiser minds convinced him to apologize for the remarks several days later, but at the WCC convention in July, some members displayed posters that said: COME WEST, TRUDEAU. They were decorated with a noose.

The voters in the Olds-Didsbury byelection went to the polls just after hearing about Westminster giving second-reading approval to Trudeau's new constitution which Kesler claimed would rob Albertans of property rights. Obviously a number of people believed him.

The fruitcake quality of the Alberta separatist movement can be judged by the fact that the man who founded it in 1975 is a laywer from Victoria—which doesn't have to break away from Canada since it never joined it. Doug Christie has those evangelical eyes of an Elmer Gantry that burn like cigarette butts. He is in continual dispute with his Alberta brethren and is alternately tossed in and out of the WCC, in jurisdictional disputes that only a PTA meeting could admire. He fits Churchill's definition of a fanatic: someone who can't change his mind and won't change the subject.

Kesler, abandoning the voters of Olds-Didsbury who elected him so he could operate closer to his home in High River, got what he deserved when Lougheed romped back with another landslide in October. Kesler and the rest of the Western Cowardly Canadians were wiped out at the polls by an electorate sending a signal to Central Canada.

Basically, it is the politics of cowardice. A Western Canada that survived the humiliation and the disasters of the Depression is now in the "have" haven in the provincial pecking order, loaded with resources, full of space and beckoning population. To advocate that the part of the country with the most potential of all should now cut and run is sad.

Separatists are sad, as are most cowards.

The essential problem is not separatism but Trudeau. What is taken for hatred of Ottawa is hatred of Trudeau.

159

His confrontation style, his inability to work interestedly when he has no adversary, has poisoned the attitudes of those who think that in the Western Canada Concept lies their salvation. If Trudeau goes, Western separatism will disappear like a snowbank before a chinook.

14
British Columbia

Narcissus-on-the-Pacific

Valium West has a quality all its own . . .
Victoria, God's waiting room . . .
voters weaned on kooks . . .
Wacky Bennett, or, Orson Welles lurching out
of a space bubble . . . Miniwac's menagerie . . .
the Grits as the last remnant of the class system . . .
Polynesian Paralysis

In the Maritimes, politics is a disease; in Quebec a religion; in Ontario a business; on the Prairies a cause. In British Columbia? Entertainment.

Angus MacInnis, legendary CCF figure

We are now in British California. Bennett Columbia. Home of Social Credit and the Sasquatch (the Sasquatches are the ones with the *big* feet). Those in the Bill Bennett cabinet who are not millionaires are car dealers. In fact, there's a rumour that the entire province is going to be put on a two-year, 50,000-mile warranty.

Valium West has a quality all its own. It was the most affluent jurisdiction in the world ever to democratically elect a socialist government when it chose the NDP to govern it in 1972. The new premier, Dave Barrett, was forty-three years of age and took office having never been to Montreal in his life. The first Jewish premier in Canadian political history had been to Seattle, where he studied under the Jesuits, and he had been to St. Louis, where he went to graduate school and became an adoring expert on Franklin Delano Roosevelt. But he had never been to Montreal. It is our ignorance that binds our country together.

To understand B.C. politics (millions of Canadians would rather not try), one must understand that the province was run for twenty years by a man named Wacky Bennett who had as his most popular minister the Rev. Phlying Phil Gaglardi while Vancouver was administered by Mayor Tom Terrific Campbell. To be a politician in B.C., one

163

must tap-dance, juggle and, if necessary, drop one's pants.

This is in large part because Victoria, God's Waiting Room, is the only capital in the country that is physically detached from the vast majority of the people it governs. (Ottawa is detached mentally.) The result of this is that there is the constant sense of being afloat. Stern mothers, who knew what they were doing from their own experience, used to advise their daughters never to go to a party on a yacht. There is a detachment from reality, with subsequent consequences. Victoria can be described as Political Love Boat. Some of the characters are interchangeable.

It was no real surprise that within a year of Barrett taking power, a cabinet minister had to be sacked for being caught *in flagrante delicto* in a car within a fifty-yard view of the premier's office window. Or that the social hostess of the stately Empress Hotel complained about two NDP ministers, installed in a suite close by the one reserved for Prince Philip, who were cooking their meals by hotplate and leaving the beer bottles rolling about the Persian carpet. Or the Social Credit lady MLA who had to request that the Empress management switch her room because of the steady tattoo of passion exerted on the wallboards of the adjoining room due to the amorous nightly adventures of one particularly randy NDP minister.

All of this is in keeping with the great traditions of B.C. politics. Voters in the nethermost province have been weaned on kooks, from the day more than a hundred years ago when an itinerant from the California goldfields, one William Smith, felt his name was too commonplace. He changed it to Amor de Cosmos—lover of the universe— became B.C.'s second premier and once delivered a speech lasting seven hours. He founded the *Victoria Colonist*, the oldest newspaper on the entire North American Pacific coast (now put into a bastard merger with the *Victoria Times* by the money-squeezing Thomson owners). A bizarre and eccentric character, he sat for a while in the House of Commons and in his last speech there expressed the view—extremely advanced for the time—that Canada should have the power to negotiate her own commercial treaties.

Down through the years, the longing for slightly deranged statesmen has persisted. One of W.A.C. Bennett's ministers, who now earns his living as a piano-tuner, became the first minister in Commonwealth history to be sent to jail for accepting bribes, most of which he spent on indifferent rugs and tacky furniture.

There was the famed Socred MLA Lydia Arsens, who fought fluoridation and once proposed to the legislature that all householders be required to have three garbage cans, in three colours, to make life easy for the dustman—since the red can would contain tins, the white one waste paper and the blue one such mundane things as coffee grounds and soggy tea bags.

It didn't quite rank, really, with the crowd-pleasing antics of Phlying Phil, the evangelical speed freak who saved thousands of souls in his Kamloops Sunday School empire in splendiferous Oral Roberts fervor while also roaming the continent in government jets, sometimes neglecting to remember who was paying for it. While upholding the law as B.C. highways minister, he was convicted of speeding and careless driving offenses, had his driver's licence suspended, was fined $1,000 for contempt of court and once sped away after running over a dog, only to be overtaken by an irate motorist—and voter.

The Reverend Gaglardi, in a passionate plea for understanding, one day cried in the legislature, "If I tell a lie it's only because I think I'm telling the truth!"

There was Wacky Bennett himself, an abstemious teetotaler who dressed in a black homburg and a funeral director's suit, roamed the province in a black limousine, zoomed around the mountain passes and descended on small towns rather like Orson Welles lurching out of a space bubble.

In some perverse way, he collected around him a technicolor retinue of flacks, touts, rounders and sycophants. They reeked of hair oil and loud socks, chain-smokers who furtively hid in the end car on the premier's train, drinking rye late at night like boys behind the barn, hiding out from the boss who sedately played bridge up ahead with his constant companion, a terrible-tempered minister named Waldo Skillings who once hit a female Conservative opponent during a radio debate and had a habit of falling up the down escalators.

One of Bennett's retainers—all of whom looked as if they'd failed the early auditions for *Guys and Dolls*—went to jail for forging the premier's signature on a letter to the prime minister's office; another used his name to call phony press conferences for mining promoters and a third wrote a fawning book on Bennett that was so dreadful it almost won, unentered, the Stephen Leacock Medal for Humour.

Wacky's successor, Dave Barrett, regularly saved voters from wasting their time watching *Hee Haw*. On stage, he was something fit only for a home movie: wrenching off his jacket, his tie, on occasion even his shoes. Short, fat, profane—a socialist Buddy Hackett—he had John Diefenbaker's timing crossed with Lenny Bruce's vocabulary.

He consumed Chinese food by the bushel, travelled to Japan to play on his Old-Timers rugby team (where he was in constant danger of losing his pants)—and lasted only three years in office.

The probable turning point was when he rounded a corner outside the legislative chamber one day and spotted columnist Marjorie Nichols, who had been savaging him in her usual surgical way and at the time was chatting with his executive assistant. "Fuck you! Fuck you! Fuck you!" screamed Dave Barrett.

Ms. Nichols, who had heard the word before, began her column the next day: "A short rotund man in a blue suit approached me in a corridor of the B.C. Legislature yesterday. I recognized him immediately as the premier of British Columbia, because he was shouting . . ." Mr. Barrett never really recovered politically after that.

The B.C. demand for balminess affects even those hired to represent the Queen's dignity. Speaker Gordon Dowding, an NDP lawyer, got into a row in the House after it was revealed he used the legislative dining room to cater a private party and the telltale cherry tomatoes were sprinkled down the legislative steps. Premier Barrett, watching the robed Dowding march stiffly down the corridor in his tricorne, cracked, "I think the job has gone to his three-cornered head."

Barrett's attorney-general, Alex Macdonald, in kilt and sporran, played tennis with Bobby Riggs on the Empress lawn, doing a striptease throughout until he emerged in his shorts. The powerful doctrinaire socialist, Resources Minister Bob Williams, used to reply to reporters' tough questions by smiling sweetly and saying: "Kiss my ass, daddy."

There was the celebrated Agnes Kripps, a gushing Socred

of yellow coiffure who one day aroused snoozing MLAs with an earnest speech explaining that there were too many sniggers about the word "sex," it was embarrassing to children and that she proposed replacing it with an entirely new word—bolt—for Biology of Living Today.

There was a thunderous clatter as MLAs of all parties sat up with a start. "I'm bolt upright just listening to you," cried an NDP backbencher. As poor, flustered Mrs. Kripps tried to flounder on, a Socred shouted, "It's okay for the bolts, but what about the nuts?"

Mrs. Kripps, refusing to quit when she was behind, finally attempted to silence the hilarity all about her by pleading to the chair: "Mr. Speaker! Mr. Speaker! Won't you please bang that thing of yours on the table!"

Today's legislature has some of the same characteristics that have made B.C. politics so justifiably renowned from sea to shining sea. Mr. Bennett's majority is down to three seats, the last Speaker had a heart bypass operation, another member is on a pacemaker and the Socred government whip, who is seventy-four, has been cited as the correspondent in a divorce case involving adultery in the back seat of a white Cadillac convertible. (You think I'm making this up, but this is British California.)

As a result, the fate of the Bennett government rests not so much on politics as on the medical profession. Considering the government's most recent war with doctors over fees, I'd hate to be the first Socred cabinet minister who enters hospital for an appendectomy. He may emerge with a vasectomy.

Beside all this, the premier, a card-carrying workaholic, finds it rather hard to compete. He is unique in the Commonwealth, certainly in Canada, part of a unique father-son act that had the senior Bennett premier for twenty years and now his son heading into his eighth year in the same role. They are different, of course. For one thing, when Bill Bennett goes from Vancouver to the legislature in Victoria, he takes the ferry. His father used to walk.

Bill Bennett is energetic, alert, rich, dedicated—all those things that moved journalist Christina Newman, after two hours with him, to conclude that he had "a relentless dullness" and was "eminently forgettable." Another female reporter, in the midst of a TV profile designed to reveal the real man behind the political mask, in frustration demanded, "Don't you ever *indulge* yourself in anything?"

"Well, yes," replied Miniwac solemnly, "peanut butter sandwiches." He held his fingers apart before the camera to indicate the sinful thickness of the crime.

He cannot compete with his underlings, who speckle his pristine image with juvenile excesses, like Fuller brush salesmen given their first out-of-town trip with a credit card. Consumer Affairs Minister Peter Hyndman, champion of the downtrodden, is detected charging $374.57 for a dinner for six, including four bottles of $37.50 Pouilly-Fuisse, and is deposed. Labour Minister Bob McClelland is detected with a $1,298 New York expense account, including $325 for tickets to *Sugar Babies*, the raunchy Mickey Rooney burlesque musical. Finance Minister Hugh Curtis, at a time when Bennett is preaching restraint to the unwashed, has his records reveal $1,200 on Broadway tickets that include a research trip to *The Best Little Whorehouse in Texas*. W. A. C. Bennett groans in his grave and turns on his side.

The reason why you must entertain British Columbians before they will listen to your philosophy is that they are hedonists. They enjoy the best quality of life, which is different from (i.e., better than) the best standard of living in Canada—which means in the world. Industrialists moan about B.C. having the highest hourly wages in North America, about the boy spraying lettuce in the Vancouver supermarket for twelve dollars an hour, the woman slicing pies on the B.C. ferries who makes fourteen dollars an hour.

British Columbians, with the highest percentage of unionized workers on the continent (the possible exception being coal-mining West Virginia), feel there is nothing wrong with this. Since this is the best place in the cosmos to live, why should not the wages be the highest?

Residents of B.C. in fact have achieved the ultimate of the consumer/acquisitive society as preached nightly on colour TV. There is a fuzzing over of class lines, and plumbers, butchers and piano-movers—obeying what they are taught by TV and magazine ads—feel they deserve the same sailboats, ski cabins and cantilevered waterfront homes as doctors, lawyers and stockbrokers. This is distinctive B.C. logic: to prove that there is a classless society, there

168

must be strikes all the time, those on strike demonstrating that their monthly payments on the boat are just as onerous as those paid by their dentist. It is not so much the revolution of the blue collar as what could be called the osmosis creep. There's the Shaughnessy Heights story of the man whose sink plugged up on a Sunday night so he had to call a plumber. The workman stayed fifteen minutes and charged seventy-five dollars.

The householder exploded. "Look," he fumed, "I'm a lawyer and even I couldn't charge those rates."

"Oh, I know," sympathized the plumber. "Neither could I when I was a lawyer."

The reason the Liberals disappeared in B.C. is that they defied this rule. They were the last remnants of the class system. The federal Liberals drew their guidance from that table in the Vancouver Club ruled over by Senator deB. Farris. Patronage flowed to the selected law firms, and the masters of the party failed to notice that the province was becoming filled up with newcomers from the Prairies who owed their allegiance to protest parties called NDP and Social Credit.

The provincial wing of the party, with its upper middle class tastes, became hived into the silk stocking ridings in Vancouver and Victoria that had yacht clubs and tennis clubs. If a child had braces on its teeth, you could bet its father was a Liberal. It became not so much a political party as a cocktail party.

The small coterie of provincial Liberal MLAS were cut from such a mould (out of *Esquire*, wives by Junior League) that they began to resemble the *Sports Illustrated* Silver Anniversary All-American basketball team. One of them, Allan Williams, was so dignified it was said that he fell down one day and broke his suit. It was suspected he slept in a Birks box.

Mr. Williams today is B.C.'s attorney-general, eventually leaping (after years of denials) at the standing offer of top cabinet posts in Miniwac's Socred government. This act of philosophical consistency, of course, endeared the Liberal party further in the eyes of local voters.

The only one who refused to succumb to the bribes was Gordon Gibson, son of a millionaire, once the provincial leader, three times an unsuccessful federal candidate, formerly the most bushy-tailed Liberal cheerleader in the province.

Gibson, as a political aide in Ottawa in 1967, was one of the very first men to put together the organization that convinced Pierre Trudeau to run for the leadership. He worked in the PM's office, was close to him, in fact, was the trusted one chosen to drive Trudeau to his secret wedding.

Today Gibson is so livid at what federal policies and indifference have done to Liberal fortunes in B.C. that he has publicly denounced the government and refused to attend the celebrated fund-raising dinner at which Trudeau lectured Vancouverites on their inability to climb their own mountains. Gibson and a small group of supporters toyed with the idea this spring of Gibson openly declaring himself a contender for the Liberal leadership as a champion of Western Canadian interests—a race he never could have won but which would have been designed to smoke out Trudeau and make him declare more clearly his resignation timetable.

An example of the Gibson disillusionment with the blind masters of obfuscation in Ottawa was the delightful scam known as the Canada Development Corporation.

When Gibson still had some influence with the prime minister, he convinced him of the necessity of giving the West some sense of having a say in some of the national decision-making bodies—especially in the financial field. (This was in the era a decade ago when the Trudeaucrats marched out to Calgary for the much-trumpeted Western Economic Opportunities Conference. When it was over an irritated Trudeau, buffeted by Western premiers, muttered that this was the first "and last" such conference. It was.)

There was a great thunder of headlines in Vancouver papers when Ottawa announced that the CDC, son of Walter Gordon, would have its headquarters established in The Village on the Edge of the Rain Forest. Gibson beamed. Ottawa was sincere about decentralization.

There was just one problem, it turned out. CDC president Tony Hampson, a good Eastern product, didn't want to live in Vancouver. He preferred to stay in Toronto, close to the Ottawa mothership.

The CDC opened its "head office" in Vancouver in the most expensive property, high in a waterfront tower with the best view in town of the harbour and mountains, filled it with the right art and furniture—while Hampson collected *his* staff around him in Toronto.

On his token trips to Vancouver, hammered by reporters at press conferences, I used to greet him with, "Welcome to Vancouver, Mr. Hampson. Find your way in from the airport okay?"

Eventually, to cover its embarrassment, the CDC hired a retired Vancouver banker, John Ellis, as "chairman"—to give the castrated head office that wasn't a head office some supposed clout.

When those of us who are paid to do such things continued to heap abuse on the fraud, the CDC next hired a Vancouver-based public relations man. *Wonderful!* When you're not telling the truth in the first place, hire a flack. The poor shill was assigned to convince the locals that while the president and his operating officers remained in Toronto, running the show, the collection of secretaries and nonentities cluttering up the exquisite offices overlooking the sea was really the head office after all. It was a typical Liberal operation, like the storefronts in a Hollywood horse opera, all sham, no backup.

Still a favourite tale is the time the directors of the CDC forced the local directors into a 7:00 AM board meeting so they could catch the great silver bird back to Toronto without disturbing their body clocks.

Early in 1981, on a Friday the thirteenth, Ellis as token chairman was replaced by Winnipeg industrialist Frederick W. Sellers. Less than three months later, the Trudeaucrats decided to make a move on the Winnipegger who had replaced a Vancouverite on the Vancouver-based $3.4 billion operation that was run from Toronto.

Their choice was the celebrated Maurice Strong (an abortive Liberal candidate in Toronto) who confessed that Finance Minister Allan MacEachen (since bounced into External Affairs) had offered him the job.

The astonishing attempted putsch was beaten back at the annual meeting after the press revealed the sly plot. But the federal craniums, trying to win the West, got their way. They placed on the board such as Paul Martin, Jr., the Montreal shipping executive who allows that he will be into Liberal politics in time, and Halifax lawyer William

Mingo, a member of the Liberal federal executive, recruited for the CDC by MacEachen.

They joined such as Mary Lamontagne, who happens to be the wife of Defence Minister Gilles Lamontagne. When the little coup was finished, it meant that only two of the twenty-one directors (including Sellers) were from the West. It meant that all three Vancouver representatives were off the board, leaving Vancouver, where the CDC was supposedly based, without a voice in the body.

Even this outrage finally penetrated the bunker in Ottawa and, four months later, there was a shamefaced shuffle. Two Vancouver Liberal bodies were airlifted aboard: a mining executive and—surprise!—former cabinet minister Bob Andras.

In June of 1982, of course, it was announced that the CDC was to be sold off, loosed from denmother Ottawa. It was the culmination of Liberal hypocrisy: the federal government did not have either the guts to move it to the Toronto money markets where it probably belonged in the first place, or the courage to admit to Vancouver that it was all fakery. So endeth the lesson.

There are varying theories, of course, as to why the inhabitants of Narcissus-on-the-Pacific are so different from the rest of dull Canadians. There is the belief that Polynesian Paralysis, the *mañana* disease, comes with the Pacific currents and induces executives into hot-tubs when they should be knee-deep in accounts.

There is the theory, also, that the dregs of humanity drift to the edge of the frontier and, being unable to swim to Japan, stay to interbreed and multiply.

The real difference, it has come to me, is that people in British Columbia don't wear hats.

Each month as I migrate between Upper Canada and the Lotus Eaters, my system clogged with Air Canada toy food, I am left with a puzzled air, a culture-shocked refugee who finds something slightly uneasy about street scenes, something slightly off-key.

It suddenly became apparent the other day. No one in Vancouver wears headgear. When you retreat from an Ottawa or Montreal where the locals must protect their ears as they would their jewels, the sight of all these bare heads open to the elements portends a strange new tribe. British Columbians go through life from womb to tomb without ever putting anything on their headbone, a circumstance that leads to differences as well as luxuriant natural fur on top.

Outsiders would claim that this ability to exist without a cranium blanket merely accounts for the fact that the brain in B.C. has a convertible roof and simply leaks out the top. This, they claim, accounts for the production of politicians who go by such aforementioned names as Wacky, Phlying Phil and Tom Terrific.

This has nothing to do with it. British Columbians simply insist—since they have to put up with politicians—that they be entertainers also. (Was not Churchill a great entertainer, i.e., performer? JFK? Hitler? Fiorello La Guardia? Trudeau? Dief? It's the reason Joe Clark has such a struggle: he can't entertain.) W.A.C. Bennett, in fact, wore a homburg, and one of the reasons he stayed in power for twenty years is that he was the only B.C. citizen most voters had ever seen who wore a hat. They assumed it was a crown.

One of the reasons John Kennedy was elected president was that he never wore a hat. Since most people look ridiculous in hats, he reasoned that he would eliminate the possibilities of being photographed in one.

Americans recognized in JFK a free spirit (as subsequent revelations have proven). If he'd been a Canadian, he would have been a British Columbian, possibly almost as popular as Tom Terrific Campbell, the Vancouver mayor who didn't even go into a phone booth to don his cape and beat up hippies.

The hatless state accounts for the suspicion and mistrust that the natives have for their blood brothers who dwell across the mountains. Every night, British Columbians sit before their television sets, puzzling at the strange scenes before them out of Ottawa and way points, all those people marching about the streets with their creative juices wrapped in stifling headgear.

It is somewhat like watching a ritual out of Pago Pago, people who don't dress like *real* Canadians, i.e., British Columbians. They dress *funny*. Can they really be fellow citizens to be trusted?

People in Vancouver, mostly women, do carry protective devices over their heads when out in the open, to ward off the dew, but they are folded and shucked once indoors. There isn't a single woman in the province who knows how to wear a hat, where it goes or what it is supposed to protect. It's why they look so out of place once they have to venture out of civilization to other portions of the Dominion.

Men in B.C. regard umbrellas essentially as they do abortion: they don't think about it and don't want to get involved.

The result of all this hatlessness is that the inhabitants are different from the rest of Canadians. The breezes blowing over their naked scalps stimulate both the left and the right portions of the brain, making it all loosey-goosey and amenable to exotic strains (i.e., Social Credit) and forbidden fruits (i.e., tennis in December) denied to their earmuffed cousins.

One feels more free when one has reached the age of forty without ever owning a pair of gloves or a single hat. It is liberating and puts one in concert with nature. Thoreau could explain it (and get elected here).

There are the Boat People and the Village People and the Displaced People. If you wish to understand B.C. (not everyone wishes to), think of it as the home of the Hatless People and everything will come clear.

15
Fourth Stopover

*The Village on the Edge
of the Rain Forest*

Vancouver: the worst weather in the world
and the best climate . . . downtown martini-land
to complete wilderness in twenty minutes . . .
the last retreat of hot-line shows . . .
the mouth that roared . . .
home again

Vancouver is the hot-tub and waterbed concession of the land, the Canadian equivalent of the Italian economy: nothing seems to work but everyone is contented, heading for the water. Vancouver is unreal, as unreal a microcosm of Canada as Ottawa is unreal, but it's a good slap in the face after a spell in the capital. It's as useful as shock treatment. An alternative to the yin and yang might be Sudbury. But I've been to Sudbury.

Vancouver is like London. It has the worst weather in the world and the best climate. There is a difference. Ottawa, the most unfortunately situated capital of any allegedly advanced country, has two wretched seasons, relieved only by a delightful autumn that can last up to forty-three days and some minutes, and a spring that sometimes can consume ninety-six hours. Its residents cower, from birth, before Mother Nature. Vancouverites pat her on the head and paddle off.

People who gravitate to Vancouver are essentially simple people in that they do not like bother. They do not like the bother, the fuss, of having to own two wardrobes. All you need in Vancouver is a light raincoat, a strong ego and $40,000 a year so as to stay above the basic poverty level.

At any party in Upper Canada, the chap standing about with a puzzled expression on his puss is a B.C. refugee, watching the elaborate fifteen-minute ritual of removing galoshes, scarves, mufflers, mitts, overcoats, hats, earmuffs and frost-free clavicle-protectors. By the time you do this at the start of the evening and then have to prepare for the same ritual at leaving, there's hardly time left in the evening to discuss the charisma of Sinclair Stevens.

Basically, there's the difference. Vancouverites are cowards when it comes to discomfort. We are only here three score and ten. It has always mystified me, for example, why millions of people suffering from the shilling gas meter and bone-searching chill, live in Liverpool and Manchester when they could be in Alicante or Sorrento.

Vancouver people feel the same way. They are not provincial. They are merely content. Newscasts about Eastern Canadian blizzards are ignored. They are not interested in anyone who does not share their hedonism. To be truthful, they view other Canadians with an air of amused pity.

This is the reason why British Columbia has never provided a prime minister. The wives won't allow it. The brightest and best in B.C.—those lawyers with strong jaws, silvered temples, golden tonsils and a good squash racquet—never run for federal office because their wives can read. They read the Ottawa weather report in the newspaper and, zap, there goes the political career.

The Cardiac Special (the overnight Air Canada flight from Vancouver to Ottawa) has ruined more marriages than the pro at the golf club. It takes little devotion to the nation to be a member of the Tuesday-to-Thursday Club— those Quebec and Ontario MPs who get an early start and a late arrival on their weekends. (On some Mondays the Tory ranks in the Commons resemble Dresden, circa 1945 and you could lob a watermelon into the Grit backbenches and not splatter one of those rural Quebec ties that look as if they had been purchased at the wallpaper store.) It takes rather more devotion to live three time zones away in Narcissus-on-the-Pacific—that's a lot of dogfood—and attempt to fly home every other weekend to acquaint your constituents with the latest arithmetical wizardry of Allan MacEachen's boffins, who somehow turned a $10 billion deficit into a $20 billion deficit.

That's why B.C. never has dominant cabinet ministers, when it has any. All the smart chaps are on their yachts, their ski slopes, or in their hot-tubs. (Their wives are with the golf club pro.) None of them is in Ottawa.

The main point about Vancouver is that it is probably the largest city in the world so close to immediate wilderness. This was pointed out some twenty-five years ago by the *New York Times* in a most telling incident when three foolish Sunday afternoon hikers on a North Shore mountain in winter ventured beyond the limits of their endurance and daylight. Dressed in light clothes as darkness and rain closed in, they grew exhausted, confused and finally panicky.

Stumbling down a mountain stream, they lost their shoes; one died in a fall and the second somehow found his way down the mountain, leaving the third huddled in a cave.

For days, in the pelting rain and chilling nights, just above suburban split-level range on the mountain, searchers combed the slopes for the lost and unhappy hiker. The *Times*, in a front-page passage, tried to explain this inconceivable picture to its teeming masses: how the trapped man could look down on the lights of a modern city, with rescuers only thirty minutes away, but still be held in the grip of complete wilderness—before finally being rescued.

It's true. You can get more quickly into the primeval forest than in any city anywhere—from downtown martini-land in twenty minutes (quicker if you've had two). You can cross the Lions Gate Bridge to the North Shore mountains and—if it were possible—walk straight to the North Pole with the strong possibility that you would never encounter another human being on the way.

That sort of sense tends to do something to you. It doesn't tend to make you want to become prime minister.

In the elevator leading to the famous Top of the Mark bar in the Mark Hopkins Hotel in San Francisco—the best view in that most civilized of American cities—there is a sign that states there are six spectacular cities in the world. They are listed, in no particular order: Hong Kong, Rio de Janeiro, San Francisco, Sydney, Vancouver, Cape Town.

Of the six, I have yet to see Rio but will concede it number one spot on track record and on what I have seen and heard of it from afar.

Of the others, Vancouver is certainly number two or three.

San Francisco, for all its soft pastel beauty and undulating hills, lacks the truly arresting geographical features. Sydney, too, for all the beauty of its winding harbour and the architectural shock of that billowing-sails opera house, has the absence of a sharp vertical lift in a visual sense.

Hong Kong is the reverse of Vancouver, the residential side on the flat and the throbbing financial-hotel section across the water on Victoria Peak which rises as sharply as Vancouver's mountains—its exotic colours and vibrant millions perhaps exaggerating its geographical gifts.

Cape Town, ignored in the purdah of South Africa's current rank in world opinion, is so stunning with the looming presence of Table Mountain and its remarkably groomed leafy drives that it ranks with Hong Kong as a legitimate competitor to Vancouver, which is a babe among its rivals.

So what we have here is one of the three most beautiful cities in the world in the realm of physical setting. It is one of the two cities of the globe (Beirut is the other) where the skiers can look down on the bikinis and, at a certain selected time in the spring, switch places.

Inside the skin of The Village on the Edge of the Rain Forest there is, ahem, another animal.

All this beautiful scenery does, however, make for some interesting logistical challenges. Everywhere you go in Vancouver you have to get on a bridge to get somewhere else. The downtown core is in effect an island, with five of the six accesses to it by bridge or viaduct. This naturally shapes the traffic routes, the traffic mentality and, eventually, the *personality* of the city. One of the newspaper chains recently decided against establishing a third paper in Vancouver because its research showed a community chopped up by water, creating pockets of tinier communities rather than a homogeneous whole.

In Vancouver, everyone hates everyone else. The unions hate management. The teachers hate the government. The government hates the doctors. Those who wear bathing suits at the beach hate those who refuse to wear anything. City council fights with Victoria which fights with Ottawa. It's why foreign wars and disasters sometimes have trouble making the front page of the local papers; there's so much local blood.

Fiery radicals bent on class warfare dominate city council in a place that has the easiest lifestyle in the country. The polls are topped each election by Alderman Harry Rankin, a rumpled Marxist who can hurl eloquent insults at an opponent for fifteen minutes without once repeating himself. Because of his politics, the Vancouver Bar Association attempted to prevent him from practising his calling when he graduated from the University of B.C. law school—even though he had just come back from fighting a war for Canada. A second alderman, Bruce Yorke, is a Communist black sheep from a wealthy Vancouver family. A third, a reformed alcoholic, terrorizes Skid Road hotels where, like Carrie Nation, he preaches against the Demon Rum and harasses them into cleaning up their act. He knows their tables. He used to sleep under them.

The mayor, Mike Harcourt, is a thirty-nine-year-old socialist lawyer who lives on the trendiest townhouse street, which overlooks False Creek and the mountains and is due for a beautification scheme—after a civic election is safely out of the way.

Because of all this verbal violence, Vancouver is the last retreat of hot-line shows, otherwise known as open-mouth radio. The airwaves tingle with the cries of the wounded, and politicians regularly carry on their wars via the wireless, shouting down old age pensioners and the unemployed. It's a day-long circus of the tonsils.

As proof of the seriousness of the game, last year the Hon. Rafe Mair, B.C.'s minister of health, shucked his cabinet post for the delights of becoming a hot-line host on a Vancouver radio station. If this would appear strange, we should only remind ourselves of the growing link between politics and show biz.

There is a new shortcut between the two provided by those to the south of us. Since the most successful politicians are those who can become supreme actors in public, the Americans in their practical way have eliminated one step in the process by electing an actor. No learning process is required. Ronnie Reagan can dimple and prevaricate and obfuscate without any apprenticeship, a born bluffer right out of the starting gate. The crossbreeding between politicians and entertainers is stepping up, complete with fuzzification of the line dividing bafflegab and bubble gum.

Just as California leads the Excited States of America in innovation, so too does B.C. in Canada. To understand the political nuances you must realize that Mr. Mair, in his decision to promote himself from the public interest to the esoteric heights of open mouthery, replaced host John Reynolds, who himself plunged into radio because he felt his previous role—serving the public as a member of Joe Clark's caucus—was not commensurate with his talents (and he therefore grabbed a mike instead).

Premier Bennett, retaliating swiftly, filled Mr. Mair's post of health minister with the duck-tailed Jim Nielsen who (you've got to follow this closely) was a former hot-line host on the same station that recycled Mr. Reynolds, a Tory, in favor of Mr. Mair, a former Liberal who is now Social Credit. The same station, to demonstrate its ecumenical nature, nearly lured former premier Dave Barrett out of politics with a $100,000 offer to vent his tonsils for the greater good of advertisers rather than waste them on deaf public ears.

In all, this is an admirable trend, proof incarnate that the trade of politics is a sort of kindergarten course on the way to the riches of the marketplace, a way station on the path to true stardom which, as we all know, involves presiding at the opening of new service stations on Saturday afternoons. (Ronnie, having proven his credentials as a shill for General Electric and 20 Mule Team borax cleanser on TV before entering politics, thereby demonstrated that he understood the basis of politics.)

Rafe Mair, who practised law for years and did well in real estate, for some time was B.C.'s minister in charge of federal-provincial relations and travelled to London and Europe on the tortuous path to a new constitution. By decreeing that there is a higher calling still, answering housewives' complaints and lecturing electronically, he has given us all a lesson in priorities political.

It should come as no surprise, this crossover between earnest good works and dollar-a-holler radio. The federal minister of sport, Gerry Regan, was a sports announcer before he was premier of Nova Scotia. Jim Fleming, the Liberals' minister of propaganda and ethnic advertising boondoggling, is a Toronto radio product. Don Jamieson, the famed Golden Pipes, baffled his gab on behalf of Newfoundland private radio before inflicting it on puzzled foreigners as Canada's external affairs minister. Geoff Scott, a Hamilton Tory MP and high school friend of Rich Little, was celebrated when a TV reporter in the Press Gallery for his devastating imitations of Robert Stanfield and Joe Clark—a gift that has now strangely disappeared from his repertoire. Chuck Cook, an invisible Tory MP from North Vancouver-Burnaby, was an open-mouth host on that same Vancouver station that acts as a farm team for politicians who are either rising or falling on their luck.

The reason B.C. broadcasters want to be politicians (and vice versa) is that they all wallow in the slipstream of The Mouth That Roared, Jack Webster, a superb journalist who inherited the ham of Harry Lauder and now makes some $300,000 annually with five months off. Blather McHaggis has been in the country for thirty-five years but every time he gets a raise his accent gets thicker. If his income increases any more, he'll be speaking Croatian. He is truly B.C.'s ombudsman because of the clout of his radio hot-line show, which he has now moved to television. He has been nominated for an honorary degree from Simon Fraser University in honour of his gifts, plans to entitle his memoirs *Bullshit is My Business* and regularly refuses overtures from all political parties on the grounds that he can't afford the demotion to either his wallet or his power.

The rewards in this crazy field are such that some grow greedy. Before the late Judy LaMarsh became a Vancouver radio host, she was sued for libel by Ed Murphy, a testy broadcaster who this year was sent to jail for conspiring to offer a $100,000 bribe to a Social Credit cabinet minister who turned out to be the aforementioned Mr. Nielsen who has succeeded Mr. Mair who succeeded Mr. Reynolds.

All of them pale into insignificance before the late Rene Castellani, a promotion manager for the most successful Vancouver station, who set out on a marathon flagpole sitting stunt on behalf of the station's favourite charity. The only problem was that Castellani had a habit, after dark, of sneaking down the pole and, on the way to his girl friend's, visiting his ailing wife in hospital where he fed her milkshakes laced with arsenic. Sent up the river for murder, he spent his weekends playing drums in the prison band which called itself The Hangman's Five. Ronnie Reagan has a lot to answer for. . . .

The best way to detect the new fabric of the town is to glance at the graduation pictures of one of the city's tonier private girls' schools, where faces from well-fixed Hong Kong and Southeast Asian families make up half the class. The reason Vancouver has the highest real estate prices in the country is that it is the home of the good life, the most comfortable spot in Canada to live. With the British lease on the crown colony of Hong Kong running out in 1997, money is being tucked safely into B.C. properties. Bob

Lee, one Vancouver real estate salesman, has become a millionaire by selling off most of downtown Vancouver to Hong Kong and Southeast Asian money. One would not be surprised to see Stanley Park go next.

The Vancouver newspapers have some of the oldest staffs in the country, defying the usual vagabond nature of the trade, simply because the living is so pleasant that the vagabonds, once discovering Valhalla, refuse to move on. There is nowhere near the flux there is in papers in, say, Toronto. Publishers moan about this, while heading for the golf course.

Vancouver has its faults, of course. Visitors from the Prairies say that it is a nice place, but it is too bad the mountains spoil the view. They also complain that they built the cliffs too close to the roads. Behind the Tweed Curtain, in Victoria, you can't see the retired wheat farmers for the lawn bowling clubs. (They like the flat surfaces).

If Vancouver has a philosophy, it is that life is not so important as lifestyle. Since there is no alternative to birth and death, the only solution is to smell the flowers on the way through. While the economy supposedly flounders and the nation goes bankrupt, some ninety miles north of Vancouver is Whistler Mountain, the conspicuous consumption capital of the land. At Whistler, money oozes out of the ground, it soars in architectural shapes, it slides down the slopes, money crawls out of the microwaves, money comes on four-wheeled drives and blasts out of the stereos, money sticks to the trunks of the trees.

The weekending Vancouver families prance about on their cowboy heels, adding to the Gross National Product. They zip down the mountain, technicolor streaks against the snow, guardians of our fiscal integrity, selflessly keeping the dollar afloat. Without Whistler, the nation's coffers would choke up and rust.

The genius bringing about this salvation of the Canadian currency comes, appropriately enough, with the mating of Hollywood and the Taxpayer. The newest aspect of the Whistler opulence—development of a whole new mountain, Blackcomb—is a joint operation of Twentieth Century-Fox and Ottawa's Federal Business Development Bank. It is only proper. The illusion of the film world melded with the illusion of fiscal responsibility.

Twentieth Century-Fox's Aspen Ski Corp., which has

made that Colorado resort the sex, drugs and rock 'n' roll centre of the universe, has been given a fifty-year lease by the B.C. government to work its hedonistic magic with Blackcomb along with its partner, the feds' bank. It is a marriage made in snow heaven.

Whistler sits in the valley of five lakes—Alpha, Nita, Alta, Green and Lost—two of them connected by the aptly named River of Golden Dreams. It is the river of condominium dreams, one side containing the White Gold Estates, the other side the modest ski chalets of Alpine Meadows, awash in bidets and Gucci-embroidered Jacuzzis.

The new Whistler Village, set on fifty-eight acres between Whistler and Blackcomb, rises splendiferously like a Flash Gordon version of a Bavarian ski town. Some $350 million has been invested so far. There are soaring turrets, clock towers, flying buttresses, steeply banked roofs, tons of stone and copper and angled glass. At night, it looms out of the valley darkness, lights gleaming, like some giant battleship come aground. The Trapp family would freak out. It is Sun Valley updated to the 1980s, the railway barons of the past who built ski resorts replaced by John Q. Public and the men from movie financing who wear tinted shades and forty dollars' worth of haircut.

Arnold Palmer designed the golf course. In condo-world, there is Tantalus. Windwhistle. Brandywine Park Lodge. Wedgeview Centre. The Arthur Erickson-designed Hearthstone. Saunas and whirlpools, hot-tubs and cold champagne. The deli in Whistler Village features Romanoff caviar, canned kumquats and chocolate-covered grasshoppers. The bag lunch packed for skiers is a special gourmet repast: roughing it in the wilderness. The covered parking for condo guests reaches three floors underground.

Whistler is a monster of a mountain. To reach it requires a spectacular, twisting cliffside sprint along one of the B.C. fiords, as beautiful as the Amalfi Drive south of Naples, and then a portage through a canyon that resembles the face of the moon.

The mountain intimidates. One ski run is ten miles long. Thirteen-year-olds rocket by, every one of them wearing a thousand dollars worth of designer pastels. The two hundred dollar moulded plastic boots resemble a piece of modern sculpture stolen from an art gallery. Whistler is named after the marmots that live in the upper region of the mountain. The marmots cower at the colours and shield their eyes. A helicopter whisks jaded skiers to the glacier above. Pierre Trudeau makes his annual pilgrimage and often stays at the condo of his Vancouver dentist. He appreciates the mountain and likes his dentist but doesn't comprehend B.C. anymore than he did his bride who came from here.

Spiffiest of all are the skiers from Tokyo; entire families, tape decks strapped to their chests, earphones injecting John Lennon into their heads, boogie down the mountain. It is the fad of the high-speed skier, enclosed in his own cocoon of sound, with Beethoven or the Grateful Dead, as he sails through the powder snow wrapped in stereo, oblivious to all around, oblivious to the cares of the world, the prototype Vancouverite.

The ultimate in the sybaritic life—and what sums up Vancouver—is the newest fashionable restaurant, L'Orangerie, cunningly stationed within a shanked punt of the new domed stadium that will open in 1983—if the eighteen-dollar-an-hour construction workers can get in off their yachts, after time off for strikes, in time to finish it. One of the owners, Peter Brown, is a former stock market bad boy who has now reformed. A fortyish millionaire, he is the new chairman of the Vancouver Stock Exchange and likes to order Dom Perignon by the bushel for his friends until the table is awash, rather resembling the plastic tops in beer parlours where they have noon-hour strippers on stage.

The feature of L'Orangerie, copied from an old Paris restaurant, is a sliding glass roof that extends and withdraws at the touch of a finger of a waiter who keeps his eyes peeled for clouds. One usually can go through six changes of season before the brandy arrives.

16
Fifth Digression

The Pretenders

Blue-eyed exile in Winston's . . .
Macdonald was willin' but PET rolled back
the stone . . . Mulroney, the candidate
from Whimsy . . . a tiny, perfect run up the middle . . .
Joe Maybe

Τ he weeds are full of potential successors to Pierre Elliott Reincarnation. The closets echo with their pants of excitement. The curtains rustle as they fidget impatiently, not wanting to disturb the master, who is notoriously stiletto-shy. They await his nod, pawing in the dirt.

John Turner: The Duke of Windsor of Canadian politics, on his own Elba in the left corner banquette in Winston's, the Toronto restaurant that serves, in Peter Newman's phrase, as "the day-care centre for the Establishment." When he was a small child in Ottawa, his mother bought him a dog and he went out on the daily route that Mackenzie King took with his dog. They met. His path was set, foreordained, as boy, youth and man acquiring credentials that can only be topped with the prime ministership. Trudeau doesn't like him because (a) he believes Turner to be not a Liberal at all but a Conservative born accidentally into a Liberal family (true); (b) he suspects Turner fomented gossip about Trudeau's personal life. It is thought that Trudeau will do anything to prevent Turner from taking over, ruining Canada if necessary. He may succeed. Turner pulled back last time when private polls showed he wasn't a sure thing. He has a lot to give up, in the family and pecuniary sense, but he's more in demand this time, the country being in worse shape. Abstinence makes the heart grow fonder.

Don Macdonald: Left with a slight smear of egg on his face last time, after displaying his willingness, when Trudeau rolled back the stone. Would be the choice of party regulars—if there weren't such a thing as popularity polls. Has less hair than Bobby (Jungle Transplant) Hull. Business community likes him. Has thrown careful bread on the water by floating his cautious economic views in the *Globe and Mail*'s Report on Business, the Koran of Bay

189

Street. Would immediately restore the clout of Toronto to the cabinet table. A tough operator, though somewhat mellowed from the Commons days when as Grit House leader he was known as "Thumper" and customarily stepped on the fingers of any Tories hanging from their windowsills. As a careful loyalist to Trudeau, he is still second choice in the public mind to Turner, who has not been. Perhaps there's a lesson there.

Jean Chrétien: Still slightly soiled by his previous stint in finance. He knows he must run this time, since sneaking up behind him in soft loafers is House leader Yvon Pinard, who looks as if he could be, and perhaps should be, on the cover of *Paris Match*. His main handicap is that he is seen as a good, lively Number Two but not quite with the heft for the big job. It would be almost impossible to overcome the determination of Southern Ontario and Western Canada not to have another Francophone following Trudeau. There is practically no one who dislikes Chrétien, but his organizational abilities are suspect. He lives on his nerves and his nerves may be giving out—waiting for the boss to leave.

David Crombie: How much does Joe Clark fear him? Plenty. Is unassailable in key Toronto riding of Rosedale. Preparing quietly for an assault if Clark falters, while letting Brian Mulroney act as the heat-seeking missile. He would like to do, in fact, what Clark did in 1976: sneak up the middle as Mr. Nice Guy while more volatile adversaries take the flak from the flanks. Is an uncommonly adept communicator, which is why Clark has kept him shunted to the sidelines in Tory duties in the Commons.

Brian Mulroney: The jaw that walks like a man may have shot his bolt with his too-publicized national speaking tour that was designed to raise Tory funds. In fact it raised Mulroney's over-weening profile a trifle too high just at a time when MacEachenomics was sending Joe Was into the stratosphere. The Liberal swan dive hurt Mulroney as much as it helped the long-suffering Clark. The Candidate from Whimsy, who wants to start at the top, is not forgiven by large dollops of the party for his reluctance to run a risk. He will not run in a byelection unless he is certain he can win. Politics does not allow that luxury. A man of enormous charm and platform ability, he in fact is trying a remarkable gamble. He is

190

testing whether the Canadian parliamentary system can accommodate an American idea: picking leaders occasionally from the outside who are not actively involved in a formal political role. Mulroney is resentful that, although he has worked in the party as long as Clark (since they were both seventeen) he is regarded as a newcomer. Can he pull off his gamble? Not while Mac Trudeau sends the Tories soaring in the polls with their present tenacious leader. It says something about the present bizarre state of Ottawa politics that the three people who most want to become prime minister—Turner, Macdonald and Mulroney—refuse to be a part of the Ottawa scene. The difference is that Turner and Macdonald are seen to have put their families through the gruelling apprenticeship once and are supposedly allowed to rest on the oars of their corporate directorships while in the weeds waiting for the departure of the man who, as someone said of Horace Greeley, fancies himself a self-made man who's in love with his creator.

Paul Hellyer: The Harold Stassen of Canadian politics. A sure-fire entry. The old joke used to be that Hellyer, after bombing as a candidate at both the 1968 Liberal Convention and the 1976 Conservative convention for the same reason—a disastrous leadership speech that he kept secret from his advisors—was headed for the Arctic to teach lemmings how to swim. In fact, he has a good enough sense of humour to mock himself, in his church choir voice, in the skits at the Parliamentary Press Gallery annual dinner now that he is a fairly dull newspaper columnist. Trudeau, from the front row, looks at Hellyer with some puzzlement. Why would a man once seeking the top job in the land mock himself on stage? Hellyer does it because, like practically all politicians, he is a ham. It is why Joe Clark is not a good politician: he does not have the confidence to be a ham in public. Robert Stanfield was appalled at the prospect. William Lyon Mackenzie succeeded because he was his own self-parody.

I digress.

Iona Campagnolo: the one chance for some excitement in the Liberal leadership race. Has the face of an Inca goddess. Would be the Grit equivalent of Rosemary Brown at the NDP Winnipeg convention that chose Ed Broadbent—with no real chance of winning but frightening the whey

191

out of the male contenders. The feminist factor is actually infiltrating the Grit grimace. She is almost as gray as John Turner and even better looking. Liberal men don't trust her ambition and her desire to play the outsider while keeping the umbilical cord slightly attached to the Ottawa Mothership. The constricted Tories of Britain elected, to their surprise, a woman. Would The Bachelor Party be frightened at the contemplation of a woman as a real leadership threat? You betcha.

John Crosbie: a millionaire from one of the four families that own all Newfoundland, a gold medallist at two universities, he discovered early on that his shyness was inhibiting his political ambitions. The solution? Public speaking lessons. Now he knocks them dead while on his feet, but the shyness remains, rolling his eyes upward when asked a question, as a reporter put it, as if contemplating the insides of his eyelids. The rollicking barroom style, laying about him with pun and insult with great gusto, is like a man swinging a broomstick in a crowded Volkswagen van. Probably the best platform performer, all fake outrage, in either party. Unfortunately, his comic gifts and the demands for him to appear as an entertainer at fundraisers have stereotyped him a bit. The smartest man in a political party is seldom the leader. The ill-confident Clark, who doesn't like rivals with strong personalities, achieved his aim in purposely shifting the ex-finance minister from the much-publicized finance critic post to the shadowland of external affairs critic. He has disappeared from your screen. Some of the boys around Clark play hardball. It is difficult to build a leadership base from "this poor bald rock," as Joey Smallwood calls it.

Bill Davis: He can read. He can especially read Gallup Polls that push the Conservatives, even under Joe Clark, forward when Pierre MacEachen and Allan Trudeau fall behind. So Bill Davis has announced he will stay at Queen's Park, where he has represented Brampton for twenty-four years and where he plans to surpass the twenty-seven years established by former NDP leader Donald MacDonald. Queen's Park always did regard itself as superior to Ottawa.

Peter Lougheed: Is insulted at the suggestion he must go to Ottawa to prove himself. Regards his role in Alberta as the national stage. Is sincere in his desire for a more peaceful private life. Does not regard Ottawa, run by the mandarinate, as reality. He is not a factor in any Conservative search for a new national leader.

Gerald Regan: The former Nova Scotia premier, now Minister of Trade among the Trudeaucrats, has two funny quirks in his life. The first is his tennis serve, which starts behind his left ear and emerges from somewhere. The second is his belief that he will be in the leadership race. The serve is only slightly funnier.

Michael Wilson: The tall Tory, a former securities executive, looks like a nonsmoking Randolph Scott and is so straight he would help Boy Scouts across the street. Regards politics as serious business and wouldn't recognize a giggle in a carload. A Clark loyalist up to now, he would be in there slogging if a leadership contest opened.

Edward Schreyer: It has always been the suspicion of this typewriter, which is eternally suspicious, that it has always been the wish of Pierre Trudeau and Edward Schreyer that the one succeed the other. The appointment as governor-general of the first socialist, the first man from the West, the first of ethnic persuasion, was designed by the Grits to win them love, affection and votes in the West. They are now zero for three. However this does not alter the fact that inevitably the Liberals and the NDP are headed for some sort of a merger in Western Canada and social democrat Schreyer can see himself as the link. Underemployed and bored in his current ceremonial role, his problem is how to launder himself so as to be acceptable in active politics again. The only question is: could Lily accept the demotion?

Darcey McKeough: The real white hope dark horse if Clark loses another election. McKeough, big, bluff and hearty, is the John Turner of the Regressive Conservatives: stacked up behind Bill Davis in a holding pattern as Ontario treasurer, he decided to exile himself for a while in business to await a landing spot. As head of Union Gas, he has been collecting corporate directorships like grapes. Big Business loves him. How he would fare in Medicine Hat, with his pinstripes that make him look like a refugee from *Guys and Dolls*, is a moot point.

Eugene Whelan: You think I'm kidding, but he's serious.

Joe Clark: The bland leading the bland. The man who secretly suffers from the disease known as amsirahc—

charisma spelled backwards. The man who books a hall that sleeps three hundred. Joe Clark has a strange gift. When he enters a room, people instinctively look up and say, "Who's left?" Joe Was has become Joe Maybe, helped along by pain. His face now shows the signs of a man who has been through fire and has emerged, not safely, but emerged. There are signs of character in it now. Wise political journalist W. A. Wilson has pointed out that while Clark is not strong, he has another quality: resiliency. He has the resiliency of a Brillo pad. Everyone kicks sand in his face, and he returns to the beach for another hotdog. As the Rodney Dangerfield of politics, he can't get no respect. His spine is steeled by the determined, and now stylish, Maureen McTeer. Prematurely frumpish when her husband was elected leader, she was taken to Montreal by Tory girlfriends and pointed in the right directions. She is now, arguably, the best-dressed woman in Canadian politics. Another measure of her will. She hungers for revenge with a white heat. Clark's major problem remains that the talented people one needs to survive in politics will not work for him. His body language gives off negative sparks. His greatest asset is Pierre Trudeau, who may turn him into Joe Gallup.

17
Finale

*Trudeau Today
is Nowhere at All*

Portrait of Pierre as a non-leader
learning his trade in middle age . . .
Dr. Foth and the PM:
a pleasant little war turned sour . . .
the War Measures Act:
out of the mouth of Spiro Agnew . . .
fade to disillusion

The first time I met Pierre Trudeau was one March Sunday morning in 1968 when we boarded a clumsy Grumman Goose in Vancouver to skip over the Gulf Islands and land in Victoria harbour in front of the Empress Hotel. I was impressed, I see by the back copies, by his "lynx face with high cheekbones and slightly gopher teeth."

Carrying his battered briefcase that contained his change of shirt, he was just one step removed from the international boy vagabond who had never really stuck at any one pursuit—or had to.

A small reception at the Empress, before popeyed matrons and the right sort of Victoria lawyers, was part of his soundings tour to determine if there really was enough national support to push him into the April leadership race.

In the Empress suite, the new hotshot leadership possibility is shaking hands and having tea with twittering party delegates. The press is excluded. But a reporter, hiding behind a teacup, remains unmolested against the wall.

Trudeau moves to the mantel, beneath an immense ornate painting of an obscure English battle. He rests one foot against the hearth, beckons the women in the room to sit at his feet and begins to talk, softly, amusingly, supremely confident, toying with a sandwich. It is the Trudeau of Montreal society, entertaining a few guests at a Saturday soiree.

The women are enraptured, their teacups frozen in their hands. It is easy to see why he prefers small groups. It is easy to see why he masters TV. The charm has an operative range of fifty feet.

After the Goose got us back to Vancouver late that afternoon, there was an excited young girl with tight reddish curls, even then magnetic in her attractiveness, pushing her way through the front row of a crowd that was waiting for the ballroom doors to open in the Hotel Vancouver for yet another reception. When Trudeau appeared, she gave him a quick kiss on the cheek and asked if he "remembered" her from their first meeting in Tahiti. Margaret Sinclair was nineteen.

Over the fourteen years since, there has been the usual cat-and-mouse relationship always endemic to the politician-journalist connection. Reporters and politicians in fact exist in a symbiosis much like prison guards and inmates: in their own peculiar way they are more closely connected to each other than either group is to society at large. They share common interests—and fascinations.

In 1972, your scribbler did a long interview with Prime Minister Trudeau in a hastily requisitioned bedroom in the Fraser Arms Motel in Vancouver—raucous haunt of the University of B.C. beer drinkers—that had a meter on the wall with a message: "This bed is equipped with a massaging unit which quickly carries you off to tingling relaxation and ease. Magic fingers. 25¢ for 15 minutes. Home adaptor unit available."

The Fraser Arms seemed a rather unusual setting to interview a prime minister. It was chosen, one presumed, because it was in the riding of Vancouver South, where Trudeau's former aide Gordon Gibson was attempting to get elected as a Liberal MP, and this exercise was deemed to help. (It didn't. Gibson was defeated, before moving across the water to North Vancouver and trying twice, unsuccessfully, from there. He is now back in the neighbourhood.)

Ignoring the meter, I reminded the prime minister that he took the job almost on a dare, almost as a joke—as he had said at the time—that the press was playing on the country. How had four years of power affected Pierre Trudeau?

He grew quite animated at analyzing himself.

"I never imagined myself as a leader. I was always a loner—even during the *Cité Libre* days. That's why I had to have Pelletier as a coeditor—to hold the thing together. I wasn't the type."

He said he had always liked individual sports, "not team sports. Climbing, hiking, canoeing—there were always

198

four-to-six of us in a group. I was never someone who was the leader, though I was forced into it in some circumstances."

How had the job changed him?

"As a professor, as a lawyer, as a writer, I've always been my own man. I called the shots. I made the rules. I can't do this now. This morning I can't just get up and say, 'I'm going to do what I want.' It doesn't work that way."

He explained that when he was "flirting with politics, I could never see myself as part of a team. But when I did go in I realized, 'I'm giving up some of my freedom.'

"I've always been inner-directed. There's the discipline now. More subject to a timetable. At two o'clock every day I have to be in the Commons." For this man, the ordinary disciplines of young manhood didn't come until he was forty-nine.

He talked of the difficulties—meaning the difficulties of a lifetime loner—in running cabinet meetings. "It's more difficult when there's no clear consensus. You have to make sure the team doesn't fall apart."

I got the sense then of someone who had made a career of being a nonleader painfully attempting to grasp the rudimentary tools of running a group of men. It fitted in with the frequent criticism that his cabinet colleagues could never figure out exactly where he stood on issues. Here was a man trying to learn an entirely new trade—while close to the age of fifty-three, two-thirds of his life behind him.

In 1968, Dr. Foth was a cheering fan, climbing off the fence most astonishingly. It's most educational to trip back through the newspaper files and observe my transition in opinion.

5 February 1968—"Who wants a prime minister who goes around in his bare feet? Exactly! I do."

16 March 1968—"For anyone who is puzzled by Trudeau, who is thinking about supporting him—or who thinks he is an evil threat to the country—this collection of his writings [*Federalism and the French Canadians*] provides most of the answers.

"Most of all, there is the clear demonstration of a man who is concerned first with ideas. Whether such an intellectual can master the practical side of the complex world

199

of politics is another matter. Here is a man who has been thinking seriously and pronouncing himself for over a decade on the constitutional and racial problems that have overtaken Canadian politics in the last year or so.

"Trudeau, goes the line, would be a gamble as a prime minister. Of course he's a bit of a gamble. Who wasn't?

"Canada has yet to be run by a leader who has been born in this century. I think that a country that produced Expo should be able to produce as prime minister someone other than a jaded warhorse or a reconverted civil servant. Let's live a little."

2 April 1968—"I think Pierre Elliott Trudeau would be the best choice from what is available because he holds promise. He would be a good choice to lead a country that holds the same. Trudeau is a pragmatist. He always has been. I would trust him to adjust to the realities once he was saddled with the responsibilities of dealing with a province which, after all, is his homeland."

24 June 1968—"Since no one has offered the main reason why Pierre Elliott Trudeau will sweep the country tomorrow, it is donated here, free of charge. Eight years ago, Canadians suffered a frustrated longing as they watched Americans elect a president who was young, handsome, rich, intellectual and stylish. He shattered the political taboos. You could feel the Canadian envy. In 1968 Canadians found someone just as attractive. (Canada's choice tomorrow, by the way, will be between two millionaire graduates of Harvard.)

"The Canadian inferiority complex toward Americans has turned into smugness, as we compare what we have with what is now available to Americans. In Oregon last month, James Reston of the *New York Times* queried me intently about this man whose reputation has gone south of the border. U.S. reporters were very interested. For the first time within memory, many Yanks are looking in envy at what we have. We're smug. But if Jack Kennedy had not existed, Pierre Elliott Trudeau would not exist."

16 January 1969—"The bleat from Mr. P. E. Trudeau concerning the press supposedly interfering with his private romantic life reminds me of Frank Sinatra. Both have achieved fantastic success—in Mr. Sinatra's case, in show biz; in Mr. Trudeau's case, a variation of show biz: politics— exactly because both have received so much publicity con-

cerning their free-swinging, independent ways. Now that they are in power, *they* want to determine which is good publicity and which is bad publicity.

"The point is that Trudeau simply isn't much interested in the press. He won the newspapers over so easily with his casual charm and unorthodox manner last spring, it's natural—human nature being what it is—that he now spurns the panting throng."

26 May 1970—"It's puzzling that a prime minister of Canada can have this attitude. This attitude, I mean, that he can still determine by his edict what will be printed in the papers and what won't be. That he, in fact, will do the deciding what is 'news' and what isn't.

"There was the sadly familiar story out of Australia last week, Mr. Trudeau and his aides 'furious' that a Sydney paper had front-paged a picture of the prime minister, clad in a brightly-patterned open-neck shirt and beads, dancing snugly in the Taboo Nightclub with an attractive television girl called Bobo.

"Does he really think that photographers would look blissfully the other way if an Australian prime minister visited a Vancouver nightclub wearing beads? The fact that Mr. Trudeau is capable of kissing girls in New Zealand and dancing in Sydney is one of the reasons this country flocked to this intriguing man. But his hypocritical view on the reporting of these activities reveals an autocratic streak that is not very attractive."

15 October 1970—"Yes, indeed things have been perilous these last few days. But try a little test. Take those tough words of Pierre Elliott Trudeau of yesterday on reduction of civil liberties and put them in the mouth of Spiro Agnew. Would you notice any difference?"

4 November 1970—"The sad fact of the Trudeau government, charged with saving Quebec from itself, is that it is not telling us the truth. Anything less than the whole truth is not the truth.

"We hear, day upon day, hedging hints from minister upon minister that 'if we only knew the truth' we would understand. As each day passes, the suspicion grows— and is supported by talkative cabinet ministers—that the War Measures Act was invoked for political reasons rather than fears of an insurrection.

"We are told to trust the government. But the government, supported by an overwhelming majority of Canadians who have backed Ottawa's action on faith, does not trust us enough to spell out the unpleasant truth."

13 May 1971—"Mr. Trudeau, drifting along on the swell of his own ego, has been increasingly reluctant to face the grubby minions of the press in full conflict. In fact, he has held fewer press conferences in the past eon than did that reluctant tiger Lester Pearson, never exactly a Georgie Jessel before the mike."

14 October 1971—"A young reporter for the dying *Toronto Telegram* did a piece the other day on the changing mores of Our Leader, one Pierre Easily Trendeau. Our Leader, recounted the reporter, had displayed an interesting switch in tactics lately, in line with his changing status in the opinion polls.

"Our leader, it was detailed, had taken to actually talking to backbench Liberal MPs. Our Leader, it was said, was getting absolutely chummy with the ink-stained wretches who chase him down the halls. The other day, in a chat with some minions, he playfully punched one of them in the stomach and nudged another in jest.

"So yesterday, emerging from Question Period, Our Leader was beset by the same group of reporters in quest of the usual daily information. In mock imitation of the article, he playfully punched one of the two girl reporters, both under 30, in the throng of a dozen males.

"No, he didn't want to comment on that. Don't you have anything to say, the retreating figure was asked? Yes, he playfully replied as he went through the door, and the phrase rang out from Our Leader's lips, 'Fuck off.' Most instructional, it is, to do the social round these days."

And so on. For a long time there was a good adversarial atmosphere, a mutual needling. Deadpan, Trudeau would step on my foot as he emerged from press conferences. Once, when my newspaper editorial board hosted him at lunch, he entered the dining area, shook hands solemnly with all present, and then punched me in the chest. It was a pleasant little war, both sides enjoying it.

But over the years, as the needling sharpened into something stronger, there was a change. While the PM claims never to read the newspapers, he is in fact supplied with daily selected press clippings by aide Joyce Fairbairn. As

Richard Gwyn pointed out in his brilliant book on Trudeau, *The Northern Magus*, the reason he pretends not to know what is in the press is that he can't stand being criticized.

I was writing during the first Trudeau decade for the *Vancouver Sun*, which at that time had the second-highest circulation in Canada and was the largest paper in Western Canada. As the Liberals sank lower in fortunes in our end of the world, it seemed logical that the party would like to use its prize communicator to explain its no-doubt-misunderstood message. Requests for interviews became Byzantine struggles, translated through scores of nervous aides and often killed near the top by such as Senator Perrault, who had the puzzling philosophy that those who criticized should be punished by being sent to Coventry.

Eventually, as the manipulators (and the nervous ones) around Trudeau purposely shut off access to anyone who might be rough on him, the relationship simply hardened into war. Between 1976 and 1978, they loosed their tiger to fifty-three sessions on radio and television, fifteen encounters with the foreign press—and only thirteen to Canadian print journalists. More foreigners were allowed to interview Canada's prime minister than Canadian reporters—an accurate gauge of the distaste felt by the PMO for the increasingly critical national press.

During his winning 1980 election campaign, Trudeau gave a total of twelve interviews (as opposed to ten while losing in 1979). Just three of them were to the despised pencil press.

(I was granted another long interview in his Centre Block office some years after the Fraser Arms episode. The relationship went downhill from there.)

Perhaps it is time to dispel the standard misconception that still rests among some portions of the public, namely that the press "elected" Trudeau in 1968. The press did no such thing (oh, that we had the power). The press is simply a radar system, a DEW-line, as McLuhan said, out there ahead of the public, paid to sniff the wind.

The press, along with its junior cousins in the electronic jockey field, was out in front of the public on the 1968 Trudeau because it could detect an incipient public interest. In the same way that the press soured on Trudeau before the public did—the voter disillusion subsequently followed. That's what radar is for.

(These sins of the press come when it isn't far *enough* in front of the public—as in the Parti Québécois sweep in Quebec, or the Olds-Didsbury byelection.)

At the close of the Economic Summit in Venice in the summer of 1980, Trudeau held a press conference for Canadian reporters and I asked him, since he would be host at the 1981 summit in Ottawa, if that would fulfill his goals and would he then proceed to his retirement as he had earlier indicated.

He replied that "there are stranger things in politics than are written in the stars and, as to my retirement, one can only speculate and—in your case—hope."

The next night, in Rome, after Trudeau had taken his son Justin to see the Pope, he was to have a small midnight dinner at the penthouse apartment of Roloff Beny, the Medicine Hat photographer who had become an international name for his posh coffee table books, including the unfortunately timed tribute to the Shah of Iran.

I was invited along by Suzanne Perry, a Trudeau press secretary. It was a magnificent summer night. Beny's sumptuous three-floor apartment as exquisitely decorated as could be imagined, overlooked from its rooftop garden the sluggish Tiber below with the lights of Rome beyond. We sat under the potted trees as several ladies prepared scrambled eggs filled with smoked salmon, and when Trudeau realized your shy agent was present, said, "Oh, God, *Fotheringham*. I can't go *anywhere* but you're there."

One thing about Fotheringham he admired, he went on to the assembled guests, "is that you make enemies so easily. You remind me in that way of Cyrano de Bergerac. If you had any culture, you'd know"—and he launched into a passage of Cyrano in French.

"Oh, Mr. Prime Minister," I said, "I couldn't possibly have any culture. I'm from Western Canada."

Trudeau left shortly after. That encounter two years ago was really the last. After that, the Trudeaucrats hived into their bunker mentality vis-à-vis Western Canada. Your scribbler, I suppose, now reflects the general Western attitude: the government and its leader have given up on half the country. It's simply a matter of waiting them out.

Most all Canadians underestimate what a freak Pierre

Trudeau is—a freak in the sense of how long he has been around. He is the longest-reigning leader in the western democracies. The United States has gone through five presidents since Trudeau came to power: Lyndon Johnson, Richard Nixon, Gerald Ford, Jimmy Carter and now Ronnie Reagan.

The Brits have gone through five prime ministerial terms: Harold Wilson, Edward Heath, Wilson again, James Callaghan and now Maggie Thatcher. When Trudeau was elected, Chancellor Kiesinger was running West Germany, followed by Willy Brandt and Helmut Schmidt. France has moved from Couve de Murville to Gisgard d'Estaing to Mitterand in the same time span. Italy has circulated a Rubik's cube of names, which are as forgettable as those Prince Edward Island premiers.

If Trudeau wishes to beat the longevity record of French-Canadian prime ministers, as he has hinted, he would stay until April 1984, to beat the term of Sir Wilfrid Laurier. The record for a democratically elected leader is Prime Minister Tage Erlander of Sweden, in power for 22 years, 357 days.

Trudeau has now been in power himself longer than all the Progressive Conservative leaders since World War I. He has been more successful, in terms of political longevity, than Messrs. Meighen, Bennett, Manion, Bracken, Drew, Diefenbaker, Stanfield and Clark put together.

The problem, from our point of view—me and thee voter—is that as his quite underestimated seniority advances, his real interest in the country at large diminishes, rather than increases. He has a shrinking vision of Canada, dominated by his constitutional obsession, but is incapable of venturing much beyond that. He is a brilliant, but limited, man.

During the Depression, doomed Prime Minister R. B. Bennett wore a top hat throughout. Pierre Trudeau, in the worst unemployment and economic conditions since the Depression, wears a fresh rose in his lapel morning, noon and evening. There is a link.

Only history, of course, will assess Trudeau, but there have been preliminary attempts. Richard Gwyn concluded that he was a magician, and a dull, stolid country of the cold north was fascinated by such a quicksilver character. My friend George Radwanski, in his more sympathetic treatment, has been jibed a trifle too much for his assessment that Trudeau is not so much a failure as "unfulfilled." (The Argentine forces were not defeated in the Falklands; they were unfulfilled.)

This corner suspects that the judgment of time will applaud Trudeau for what is currently regarded as his greatest failure: Quebec. The criticism is that the man who went to Ottawa to save Quebec has had to watch while a separatist government was voted into power. In fact, his brave and stubborn determination to impose official bilingualism on an ostensibly bilingual country (with a streak of prejudice still running underground) probably stalled the progress of the independantistes.

If he had not arrested the smug superiority of English-Canada and alerted it to its responsibilities, Quebec would have, one suggests, embraced a separatist-bent party even sooner than it did. Trudeau couldn't halt the progress of cultural forces in his own province, but he did bend them a bit and bought some time.

His faults lie in another direction. Relentless in his determination when it comes to things that interest him, he descends into lassitude and indifference when it comes to things that don't. It's why he has allowed the Liberal party to die in the four Western provinces where the future growth of population is headed.

There is the strange impulse that moved him, on one of his rare forays into Regina, to twit the locals about their "hysteria" over the gas and oil slump caused by his National Energy Policy. The same impulse, almost a political death wish, impelled him to lecture a Liberal gathering in Banff this spring on the Alberta delegates' unseemly obsession with oil and gas, a stunning insight that taken to its uttermost, might dissuade Maritimers from being too concerned with fish or British Columbians from being too worried about their failing lumber markets. It is a lordly attitude, ethereal, infuriating, contemptuous.

The disappointment in him is devastating. In 1967, Peter Newman wrote in the *Toronto Star*: "Unlike the unreconstructed political dinosaurs of the Liberal party who still occupy most of the positions of power, Trudeau is an agent of ferment, a critic of Canadian society, questioning its collected conventional wisdom . . . [He makes] our national future appear very bright indeed." In 1982

Newman as editor of *Maclean's* called for his resignation. The *Globe and Mail* does the same, saying of a man heading a majority government that still has a three-year mandate ahead of it: "He cannot solve our problems because he is the problem."

Especially in my part of the country. Because he does not understand the West, he has given up on it—and, in the process, vitiated his party.

Last year, Vancouver's Simon Fraser University (Margaret's alma mater, a school that Trudeau has never visited in his fourteen years of power) had a two-day conference honouring F. R. Scott, the legendary Montreal socialist, poet and constitutional lawyer. Trudeau attended a reception in a downtown hotel for the great man, who was eighty-one, as old as the century. It might have been useful for him to recall what Frank Scott wrote in *The Dance is One*, a 1973 collection of his poems:

By moving West
I learned how to go East . . .
    Wanting to go somewhere
I started in the other direction
At last I know where I am
I am nowhere at all.

Pierre Trudeau is nowhere at all. Despite his 1971 resolve, he never mastered being a team man and so gave up on it. He didn't try to keep a team together and the players are now on the outside, waiting for his removal.

In the end, the vigorous sixty-three-year-old on the trampoline proved to be a *lazy* leader. He gave evidence, in the final judgment, to support the worst charge against him in the beginning: he is a dilettante.

Acknowledgements

This book would not have been written without the inspiration, encouragement and support of Anna Porter, a publisher whose determination is exceeded only by her sense of humour. Both were sorely tested in this project. It owes much to the hand-holding of Don Obe, the skillful steering of Paula Goepfert and the sharp eyes of Judith Brooks. Their tolerance is greatly appreciated.

I am grateful to my employer, Southam News, and to *Maclean's*, under whose banner I have gathered the material over the years that provided the evidence for this diatribe. My acknowledgments are due Allan Hustak's *Lougheed* and the late David Lewis' *Corporate Welfare Bums*.

I must pay tribute to the unique contributions made by Alexander Ross, Jack Batten, the tape of Supertramp and Ballantine's. Without them, this page would not exist.

ABOUT THE AUTHOR

ALLAN FOTHERINGHAM was born in Hearne, Saskatchewan on August 31, 1932. "The town," he writes, "was so small we couldn't afford a village idiot; everyone had to take turns." He went to a one-room schoolhouse (containing 12 grades), where he spent most of his time outdoors, snaring gophers with a length of binder twine. "This," he says, "proved educational for later use in political journalism."

Eventually he moved to B.C. ("which improved the IQ of both provinces") with his family. He went to Chilliwack High School, where he wrote a column for the school paper, and the University of British Columbia, where, naturally, he wrote a column for the *Ubyssey*. He joined the sports department of the Vancouver *Sun* after graduation, leaving three years later to travel and write in Britain, Europe and Russia. He returned to the *Sun* as a travel writer, then spent a sabbatical year at the University of Toronto on a Southam Fellowship. For the next four years, he sharpened his outrage as a member of the *Sun*'s editorial board. He was given a column in 1968 and for 11 years used his notoriously cutting style to expose every bit of sham, cant and outright double dealing he could find. But, his work had another significance, as Ron Haggart, a fine columnist himself, now turned TV producer, has pointed out: "Fotheringham brought Vancouver a wider view of the nation than the narrow B.C. outlook. It was a major contribution; it had a real effect."

It also brought him national attention. In 1975, while still at the *Sun*, he began his reign of the back page of *Maclean's*, a bi-monthly, then weekly forum that sent him on his way to becoming Canada's most controversial columnist. In 1979, he left the *Sun* to write a national column for the FP News Service in Ottawa; he switched to the Southam chain just before FP News folded in 1980. His column appears in the 15 Southam papers and is syndicated to five others. He continues to be the best-read feature in *Maclean's*.

These days, he practises a kind of shuttle journalism, living two weeks of the month in Vancouver ("the hot tub and water bed concession of the world") and two in Ottawa ("Ennui-on-the-Rideau," where "minds are stuffed with bafflegab and mouths filled with persiflage—and vice versa"). He has been called—quite correctly—"the greatest cobweb blower and guff-remover in Canadian journalism."

SEAL BOOKS

Offers you a list of outstanding fiction, non-fiction and classics of Canadian literature in paperback by Canadian authors, available at all good bookstores throughout Canada.

The Canadian Establishment	Peter C. Newman
A Jest of God	Margaret Laurence
Lady Oracle	Margaret Atwood
The Snow Walker	Farley Mowat
St. Urbain's Horseman	Mordecai Richler
The Stone Angel	Margaret Laurence
The Back Doctor	Hamilton Hall
Consequences	Margaret Trudeau
Empire Inc.	Clarke Wallace
Lunatic Villas	Marian Engel
Jake and the Kid	W. O. Mitchell
Daddy's Girl	Charlotte Vale Allen
Preparing for Sabbath	Nessa Rapoport
My Country	Pierre Berton
The Diviners	Margaret Laurence
Sunday's Child	Edward Phillips
Ransom Game	Howard Engel
High Crimes	William Deverell
Bronfman Dynasty	Peter C. Newman
Men for the Mountains	Sid Marty
The Canadians (6 volumes)	Robert E. Wall
The Tent Peg	Aritha van Herk
A Woman Called Scylla	David Gurr
Never Cry Wolf	Farley Mowat
Children of My Heart	Gabrielle Roy
Life Before Man	Margaret Atwood
The Wild Frontier	Pierre Berton
Who Has Seen the Wind	W. O. Mitchell
The Acquisitors	Peter C. Newman
Destinies	Charlotte Vale Allen
The Serpent's Coil	Farley Mowat
Bodily Harm	Margaret Atwood
Joshua Then and Now	Mordecai Richler

THE INTERNATIONALLY ACCLAIMED

MORDECAI RICHLER

Comic and tragic, raucous and saucy, abrasive and tender—this is Mordecai Richler. His original and satirical stories have made him one of Canada's leading novelists. *Newsweek* says of one of his books, "... a novelist as stunningly talented as he is prolific... inventive... outrageously funny... a minor masterpiece."

☐ 01635-7	**COCKSURE**	$2.75
☐ 01656-X	**JOSHUA THEN AND NOW**	$3.95
☐ 01665-9	**JACOB TWO-TWO MEETS THE HOODED FANG** (juvenile)	$2.50
☐ 01697-7	**ST. URBAIN'S HORSEMAN**	$3.95

Seal Books are available in paperback in bookstores across Canada, or use this handy coupon.

THE DIARY OF A YOUNG GIRL

"Anne Frank's diary is too tenderly intimate a book to be frozen with the label 'classic,' and yet no lesser designation serves. It is a warm and stirring confession, to be read over and over for insight and enjoyment." —*The New York Times*

"Her longings are expressed in language beautiful and womanly." —*Catholic World*

"Against the grim background of the Jewish pogrom, the commonplaces of a teenage girl are much more than usually touching. Anne's romance with Peter Van Daan is the very type and model of early love—but with death itself standing just beyond." —*Commonweal*

Translated into nineteen languages, ANNE FRANK: THE DIARY OF A YOUNG GIRL has been read and loved by over five million people around the world. A best-selling book, a Pulitzer Prize-winning play, an Academy Award-winning motion picture, it is undoubtedly a classic of our time.

Anne Frank:

THE DIARY OF A YOUNG GIRL

TRANSLATED FROM THE DUTCH
BY B. M. MOOYAART-DOUBLEDAY
WITH AN INTRODUCTION
BY ELEANOR ROOSEVELT

AND A NEW PREFACE
BY GEORGE STEVENS

PUBLISHED BY POCKET BOOKS NEW YORK

Produced as a Broadway play October 5, 1955 under the title *The Diary of Anne Frank*

Anne Frank: The Diary of a Young Girl has been published in the following countries: Argentina, Brazil, Czechoslovakia, Denmark, Finland, France, Germany, Great Britain, Greece, Iceland, Israel, Italy, Japan, The Netherlands, Norway, Poland, Portugal, Spain, Sweden, Turkey.

POCKET BOOKS, a Simon & Schuster division of
GULF & WESTERN CORPORATION
1230 Avenue of the Americas, New York, N.Y. 10020

Copyright 1952 by Otto H. Frank; Preface copyright © 1958
by Simon & Schuster, a division of Gulf & Western Corporation

Published by arrangement with Doubleday & Company, Inc.

ISBN: 0-671-82449-X

First Pocket Books printing December, 1953

82nd printing

Trademarks registered in the United States and other countries.

Printed in the U.S.A.

FIRST PUBLISHED IN 1947 IN HOLLAND
BY CONTACT, AMSTERDAM, UNDER THE TITLE *Het Achterhuis*

Het Achterhuis, the Dutch title of this book, refers to that part of the building which served as a hiding place for the two families who took shelter there between 1942 and 1944. *Achter* means "behind" or "in back of" and *huis* is Dutch for "house." In Amsterdam's old buildings the apartments overlooking a garden or court may be divided from those overlooking the street, thus providing two separate suites within the same apartment. Het Achterhuis or, literally, "the house behind" is situated on the Prinsengracht, one of the city's canals.

To simplify the English text, we have called that part of the house the Secret Annexe, although it is not an annex in the proper sense of the word.

PREFACE

Of all the many remarkable things about Anne Frank, I believe the most important is the fact of her survival—a survival contained between the covers of a small red-checkered cloth-covered diary book.

Within this diary exists a young girl touched with a perceptive genius on one hand and an almost consuming sensitivity on the other. And combined with these is a most exquisite sense of feeling and knowledge of life at its finest. "I believe in the good of man," said Anne, with her quiet smile. "My mission is to destroy and exterminate," hoarsely shouted the leader of the great forces of Nazi Germany.

In 1943, this seemed quite a hopeless and unequal contest. All the communications machinery of a powerful nation was projecting the voice of its Fuehrer, and his words were heard around the world. At the same time, Anne was quietly penning her words in the little diary seen only by herself.

Today, the shouting voice is no longer heard, but daily more and more people of many tongues are repeating and reflecting on what Anne Frank had to say.

This destiny to survive was illustrated dramatically in a conversation I had with Mr. Otto Frank in 1957. We were sitting in a cramped attic in Amsterdam and I was holding in my hand a printed edition of *The Diary of a Young Girl*. It was in this building that Mr. Frank had sheltered his little group while they hid from the Nazis. After serious hesitation, I asked Mr. Frank a question to which I felt I must have the answer—"Can you tell me something about what occurred when the Gestapo broke into this room? Their mission was to destroy—how was it they did not find and destroy the diary?"

While Mr. Frank bravely described what happened on that fateful day, I looked at the little volume in my hand and realized that Anne's persistent belief in the triumph of the good in human nature was best exemplified by the very survival of her writing.

On that day in August, 1944, Sergeant Silverbauer, of the Green Police, and four subordinates were executing just another phase of what Hitler and Goebbels had conceived as the "final solution of the Jewish problem." Their mission was to remove the Jews from Holland. While so doing, they were to loot and to plunder and, most importantly, they were to leave no record or documentation of this work.

While searching the attic, the sergeant picked up Mr. Frank's brief case. He asked if there were any jewels. Mr. Frank said there was nothing but papers. The sergeant opened it. Disappointed, he threw the papers and the diary to the floor and put the silverware and the Hanukkah candlestick into the brief case. The little group which had spent the last twenty-five months in this attic was led away. The room was left in disarray.

However, there remained on the floor the diary of a young girl. The Nazi soldiers had failed in their mission. They had left behind a statement to the world. They had left behind a comment on their work. They had left behind a story of a girl in adolescence, her troubles with her parents, and her young love.

In this diary which was to be discovered later remained a story of great adventure which was to symbolize a triumph of the human spirit. Through the survival of this book, the thoughts, the hopes and the beliefs of Anne Frank will endure forever.

—GEORGE STEVENS

INTRODUCTION

This is a remarkable book. Written by a young girl—and the young are not afraid of telling the truth—it is one of the wisest and most moving commentaries on war and its impact on human beings that I have ever read. Anne Frank's account of the changes wrought upon eight people hiding out from the Nazis for two years during the occupation of Holland, living in constant fear and isolation, imprisoned not only by the terrible outward circumstances of war but inwardly by themselves, made me intimately and shockingly aware of war's greatest evil—the degradation of the human spirit.

At the same time, Anne's diary makes poignantly clear the ultimate shining nobility of that spirit. Despite the horror and the humiliation of their daily lives, these people never gave up. Anne herself—and, most of all, it is her portrait which emerges so vividly and so appealingly from this book—matured very rapidly in these two years, the crucial years from thirteen to fifteen in which change is so swift and so difficult for every young girl. Sustained by her warmth and her wit, her intelligence and the rich resources of her inner life, Anne wrote and thought much of the time about things which very sensitive and talented adolescents without the threat of death will write—her relations with her parents, her developing self-awareness, the problems of growing up.

These are the thoughts and expression of a young girl living under extraordinary conditions, and for this reason her diary tells us much about ourselves and about our own children. And for this reason, too, I felt how close we all are to Anne's experience, how very much involved we are in her short life and in the entire world.

Anne's diary is an appropriate monument to her fine

spirit and to the spirits of those who have worked and are working still for peace. Reading it is a rich and rewarding experience.

ELEANOR ROOSEVELT

*Ik zal hoop ik aan jou alles kunnen
toevertrouwen, zoals ik het nog aan
niemand gekunt heb, en ik hoop dat
jij een grote steun voor me zult zijn.*

Anne Frank. 12 Juni 1942.

I hope I shall be able to confide in you completely, as I
have never been able to do in anyone before, and I hope
that you will be a great support and comfort to me.

Anne Frank:

THE DIARY OF A YOUNG GIRL

On Friday, June 12th, I woke up at six o'clock and no wonder; it was my birthday. But of course I was not allowed to get up at that hour, so I had to control my curiosity until a quarter to seven. Then I could bear it no longer, and went to the dining room, where I received a warm welcome from Moortje (the cat).

Soon after seven I went to Mummy and Daddy and then to the sitting room to undo my presents. The first to greet me was *you,* possibly the nicest of all. Then on the table there were a bunch of roses, a plant, and some peonies, and more arrived during the day.

I got masses of things from Mummy and Daddy, and was thoroughly spoiled by various friends. Among other things I was given *Camera Obscura,* a party game, lots of sweets, chocolates, a puzzle, a brooch, *Tales and Legends of the Netherlands* by Joseph Cohen, *Daisy's Mountain Holiday* (a terrific book), and some money. Now I can buy *The Myths of Greece and Rome*—grand!

Then Lies called for me and we went to school. During recess I treated everyone to sweet biscuits, and then we had to go back to our lessons.

Now I must stop. Bye-bye, we're going to be great pals!

Monday, 15 June, 1942

I had my birthday party on Sunday afternoon. We showed a film *The Lighthouse Keeper* with Rin-Tin-Tin, which my school friends thoroughly enjoyed. We had a lovely time. There were lots of girls and boys. Mummy always wants to know whom I'm going to marry. Little does she guess that it's Peter Wessel; one day I managed, without blushing or flickering an eyelid, to get that idea right out of her mind. For years Lies Goosens and Sanne Houtman have been my best friends. Since then, I've got to know Jopie de Waal at the Jewish Secondary School. We are together a lot and she is now my best girl friend. Lies is more friendly with another girl, and Sanne goes to a different school, where she has made new friends.

Saturday, 20 June, 1942

I haven't written for a few days, because I wanted first of all to think about my diary. It's an odd idea for someone like me to keep a diary; not only because I have never done so before, but because it seems to me that neither I—nor for that matter anyone else—will be interested in the unbosomings of a thirteen-year-old schoolgirl. Still, what does that matter? I want to write, but more than that, I want to bring out all kinds of things that lie buried deep in my heart.

There is a saying that "paper is more patient than man"; it came back to me on one of my slightly melancholy days, while I sat chin in hand, feeling too bored and limp even to make up my mind whether to go out or stay at home. Yes, there is no doubt that paper is patient and as I don't intend to show this cardboard-covered notebook, bearing the proud name of "diary," to anyone, unless I find a real friend, boy or girl, probably nobody cares. And now I come to the root of the matter, the reason for my starting a diary: it is that I have no such real friend.

Let me put it more clearly, since no one will believe that a girl of thirteen feels herself quite alone in the world, nor is it so. I have darling parents and a sister of sixteen. I know about thirty people whom one might call friends—I have strings of boy friends, anxious to catch a glimpse of me and who, failing that, peep at me through mirrors in class. I have relations, aunts and uncles, who are darlings too, a good home, no—I don't seem to lack anything. But it's the same with all my friends, just fun and joking, nothing more. I can never bring myself to talk of anything outside the common round. We don't seem to be able to get any closer, that is the root of the trouble. Perhaps I lack confidence, but anyway, there it is, a stubborn fact and I don't seem to be able to do anything about it.

Hence, this diary. In order to enhance in my mind's eye the picture of the friend for whom I have waited so long, I don't want to set down a series of bald facts in a diary like most people do, but I want this diary itself to be my friend, and I shall call my friend Kitty. No one will grasp what I'm talking about if I begin my letters to Kitty just out of the blue, so albeit unwillingly, I will start by sketching in brief the story of my life.

My father was thirty-six when he married my mother, who was then twenty-five. My sister Margot was born in 1926 in Frankfort-on-Main, I followed on June 12, 1929, and, as we are Jewish, we emigrated to Holland in 1933, where my father was appointed Managing Director of Travies N.V. This firm is in close relationship with the firm of Kolen & Co. in the same building, of which my father is a partner.

The rest of our family, however, felt the full impact of Hitler's anti-Jewish laws, so life was filled with anxiety. In 1938 after the pogroms, my two uncles (my mother's brothers) escaped to the U.S.A. My old grandmother came to us, she was then seventy-three. After May 1940 good times rapidly fled: first the war, then the capitulation, followed by the arrival of the Germans, which is when the sufferings of us Jews really began. Anti-Jewish decrees followed each other in quick succession. Jews must wear a yellow star,[1] Jews must hand in their bicycles, Jews are banned from trains and are forbidden to drive. Jews are only allowed to do their shopping between three and five o'clock and then only in shops which bear the placard "Jewish shop." Jews must be indoors by eight o'clock and

[1] To distinguish them from others, all Jews were forced by the Germans to wear, prominently displayed, a yellow six-pointed star.

cannot even sit in their own gardens after that hour. Jews are forbidden to visit theaters, cinemas, and other places of entertainment. Jews may not take part in public sports. Swimming baths, tennis courts, hockey fields, and other sports grounds are all prohibited to them. Jews may not visit Christians. Jews must go to Jewish schools, and many more restrictions of a similar kind.

So we could not do this and were forbidden to do that. But life went on in spite of it all. Jopie used to say to me, "You're scared to do anything, because it may be forbidden." Our freedom was strictly limited. Yet things were still bearable.

Granny died in January 1942; no one will ever know how much she is present in my thoughts and how much I love her still.

In 1934 I went to school at the Montessori Kindergarten and continued there. It was at the end of the school year, I was in form 6B, when I had to say good-by to Mrs. K. We both wept, it was very sad. In 1941 I went, with my sister Margot, to the Jewish Secondary School, she into the fourth form and I into the first.

So far everything is all right with the four of us and here I come to the present day.

Saturday, 20 June, 1942

Dear Kitty,

I'll start straight away. It is so peaceful at the moment, Mummy and Daddy are out and Margot has gone to play ping-pong with some friends.

I've been playing ping-pong a lot myself lately. We ping-pongers are very partial to an ice cream, especially in summer, when one gets warm at the game, so we usually finish up with a visit to the nearest ice-cream shop, Delphi or Oasis, where Jews are allowed. We've given up scrounging for extra pocket money. Oasis is usually full and among our large circle of friends we always

4

manage to find some kindhearted gentleman or boy friend, who presents us with more ice cream than we could devour in a week.

I expect you will be rather surprised at the fact that I should talk of boy friends at my age. Alas, one simply can't seem to avoid it at our school. As soon as a boy asks if he may bicycle home with me and we get into conversation, nine out of ten times I can be sure that he will fall head over heels in love immediately and simply won't allow me out of his sight. After a while it cools down of course, especially as I take little notice of ardent looks and pedal blithely on.

If it gets so far that they begin about "asking Father" I swerve slightly on my bicycle, my satchel falls, the young man is bound to get off and hand it to me, by which time I have introduced a new topic of conversation.

These are the most innocent types; you get some who blow kisses or try to get hold of your arm, but then they are definitely knocking at the wrong door. I get off my bicycle and refuse to go further in their company, or I pretend to be insulted and tell them in no uncertain terms to clear off.

There, the foundation of our friendship is laid, till tomorrow!

Yours, Anne

Sunday, 21 June, 1942

Dear Kitty,

Our whole class B1 is trembling, the reason is that the teachers' meeting is to be held soon. There is much speculation as to who will move up and who will stay put. Miep de Jong and I are highly amused at Wim and Jacques, the two boys behind us. They won't have a florin left for the holidays, it will all be gone on betting. "You'll move up," "Shan't," "Shall," from morning till night. Even Miep pleads for silence and my angry outbursts don't calm them.

According to me, a quarter of the class should stay

where they are; there are some absolute cuckoos, but teachers are the greatest freaks on earth, so perhaps they will be freakish in the *right* way for once.

I'm not afraid about my girl friends and myself, we'll squeeze through somehow, though I'm not too certain about my math. Still we can but wait patiently. Till then, we cheer each other along.

I get along quite well with all my teachers, nine in all, seven masters and two mistresses. Mr. Keptor, the old math master, was very annoyed with me for a long time because I chatter so much. So I had to write a composition with "A Chatterbox" as the subject. A chatterbox! Whatever could one write? However, deciding I would puzzle that out later, I wrote it in my notebook, and tried to keep quiet.

That evening, when I'd finished my other homework, my eyes fell on the title in my notebook. I pondered, while chewing the end of my fountain pen that anyone can scribble some nonsense in large letters with the words well spaced but the difficulty was to prove beyond doubt the necessity of talking. I thought and thought and then, suddenly having an idea, filled my three allotted sides and felt completely satisfied. My arguments were that talking is a feminine characteristic and that I would do my best to keep it under control, but I should never be cured, for my mother talked as much as I, probably more, and what can one do about inherited qualities? Mr. Keptor had to laugh at my arguments, but when I continued to hold forth in the next lesson, another composition followed. This time it was "Incurable Chatterbox," I handed this in and Keptor made no complaints for two whole lessons. But in the third lesson it was too much for him again. "Anne, as punishment for talking, will do a composition entitled 'Quack, quack, quack, says. Mrs. Natterbeak.'" Shouts of laughter from the class, I had to laugh too, although I felt that my inventiveness on this subject was exhausted. I had to think of something else, something entirely original. I was in luck, as my friend Sanne writes good poetry and offered to help by doing the whole composition in verse. I jumped for joy. Keptor wanted to make a fool of me with this absurd theme, I would get my own back and make him the laughing-stock of the whole class. The poem was finished and was perfect. It was about a mother duck and a father swan who had three baby ducklings. The baby ducklings were bitten to death by Father because they chattered too much. Luckily Keptor saw the joke, he read the poem out loud to the class, with comments, and also to various other classes.

Since then I am allowed to talk, never get extra work, in fact Keptor always jokes about it.

Yours, Anne

Wednesday, 24 June, 1942

Dear Kitty,

It is boiling hot, we are all positively melting, and in this heat I have to walk everywhere. Now I can fully appreciate how nice a tram is; but that is a forbidden luxury for Jews—shank's mare is good enough for us. I had to visit the dentist in the Jan Luykenstraat in the lunch hour yesterday. It is a long way from our school in the Stadstimmertuinen; I nearly fell asleep in school that afternoon. Luckily, the dentist's assistant was very kind and gave me a drink—she's a good sort.

We are allowed on the ferry and that is about all. There is a little boat from the Josef Israelskade, the man there took us at once when we asked him. It is not the Dutch people's fault that we are having such a miserable time.

I do wish I didn't have to go to school, as my bicycle was stolen in the Easter holidays and Daddy has given Mummy's to a Christian family for safekeeping. But thank goodness, the holidays are nearly here, one more week and the agony is over. Something amusing happened yesterday, I was passing the bicycle sheds when someone called out to me. I looked around and there was the nice-looking boy I met on the previous evening, at my girl friend Eva's home. He came shyly towards me and introduced himself as Harry Goldberg. I was rather surprised and wondered what he wanted, but I didn't have to wait

7

long. He asked if I would allow him to accompany me to school. "As you're going my way in any case, I will," I replied and so we went together. Harry is sixteen and can tell all kinds of amusing stories. He was waiting for me again this morning and I expect he will from now on.

Yours, Anne

Tuesday, 30 June, 1942

Dear Kitty,

I've not had a moment to write to you until today. I was with friends all day on Thursday. On Friday we had visitors, and so it went on until today. Harry and I have got to know each other well in a week, and he has told me a lot about his life; he came to Holland alone, and is living with his grandparents. His parents are in Belgium.

Harry had a girl friend called Fanny. I know her too, a very soft, dull creature. Now that he has met me, he realizes that he was just daydreaming in Fanny's presence. I seem to act as a stimulant to keep him awake. You see we all have our uses, and queer ones too at times!

Jopie slept here on Saturday night, but she went to Lies on Sunday and I was bored stiff. Harry was to have come in the evening, but he rang up at 6 P.M. I went to the telephone, he said, "Harry Goldberg here, please may I speak to Anne?" "Yes, Harry, Anne speaking."

"Hullo, Anne, how are you?"

"Very well, thank you."

"I'm terribly sorry I can't come this evening, but I would like to just speak to you; is it all right if I come in ten minutes?"

"Yes, that's fine, good-by!"

"Good-by, I'll be with you soon."

Receiver down.

I quickly changed into another frock and smartened up my hair a bit. Then I stood nervously at the window watching for him. At last I saw *him* coming. It was a wonder I didn't dash down at once; instead I waited pa-

8

tiently until he rang. Then I went down and he positively burst in when I opened the door. "Anne, my grandmother thinks you are too young to go out regularly with me, and that I should go to the Leurs, but perhaps you know that I am not going out with Fanny any more!"

"No, why is that, have you quarreled?"

"No, not at all. I told Fanny that we didn't get on well together, so it was better for us not to go out together any more, but she was always welcome in our home, and I hope I should be in hers. You see, I thought Fanny had been going out with another boy and treated her accordingly. But that was quite untrue. And now my uncle says I should apologize to Fanny, but of course I didn't want to do that so I finished the whole affair. That was just one of the many reasons. My grandmother would rather I went with Fanny than you, but I shan't; old people have such terribly old-fashioned ideas at times, but I just can't fall into line. I need my grandparents, but in a sense they need me too. From now on I shall be free on Wednesday evenings. Officially I go to wood-carving lessons to please my grandparents, in actual fact I go to a meeting of the Zionist Movement. I'm not supposed to, because my grandparents are very much against the Zionists. I'm by no means a fanatic, but I have a leaning that way and find it interesting. But lately it has become such a mess there that I'm going to quit, so next Wednesday will be my last time. Then I shall be able to see you on Wednesday evenings, Saturday afternoon, Sunday afternoon, and perhaps more."

"But your grandparents are against it, you can't do it behind their backs!"

"Love finds a way."

Then we passed the bookshop on the corner, and there stood Peter Wessel with two other boys; he said "Hello" —it's the first time he has spoken to me for ages, I was really pleased.

Harry and I walked on and on and the end of it all was that I should meet him at five minutes to seven in the front of his house next evening.

Yours, Anne

9

Dear Kitty,

Harry visited us yesterday to meet my parents. I had bought a cream cake, sweets, tea, and fancy biscuits, quite a spread, but neither Harry nor I felt like sitting stiffly side by side indefinitely, so we went for a walk, and it was already ten past eight when he brought me home. Daddy was very cross, and thought it was very wrong of me because it is dangerous for Jews to be out after eight o'clock, and I had to promise to be in by ten to eight in future.

Tomorrow I've been invited to his house. My girl friend Jopie teases me the whole time about Harry. I'm honestly not in love, oh, no, I can surely have boy friends— no one thinks anything of that—but one boy friend, or beau, as Mother calls him, seems to be quite different.

Harry went to see Eva one evening and she told me that she asked him, "Who do you like best, Fanny or Anne?" He said, "It's nothing to do with you!" But when he left (they hadn't chatted together any more the whole evening), "Now listen, it's Anne, so long, and don't tell a soul." And like a flash, he was gone.

It's easy to see that Harry is in love with me, rather fun for a change. Margot would say, "Harry is a decent lad." I agree, but he is more than that. Mummy is full of praise: a good-looking boy, a well-behaved, nice boy. I'm glad that the whole family approves of him. He likes them too, but he thinks my girl friends are very childish, and he's quite right.

Yours, Anne

Sunday morning, 5 July, 1942

Dear Kitty,

Our examination results were announced in the Jewish Theater last Friday. I couldn't have hoped for better. My report is not at all bad, I had one *vix satis*, a five for algebra, two sixes, and the rest were all sevens or eights. They were certainly pleased at home, although over the question of marks my parents are quite different from most. They don't care a bit whether my reports are good or bad as long as I'm well and happy, and not too cheeky: then the rest will come by itself. I am just the opposite. I don't want to be a bad pupil; I should really have stayed in the seventh form in the Montessori School, but was accepted for the Jewish Secondary. When all the Jewish children had to go to Jewish schools, the headmaster took Lies and me conditionally after a bit of persuasion. He relied on us to do our best and I don't want to let him down. My sister Margot has her report too, brilliant as usual. She would move up with *cum laude* if that existed at school, she is so brainy. Daddy has been at home a lot lately, as there is nothing for him to do at business; it must be rotten to feel so superfluous. Mr. Koophuis has taken over Travies and Mr. Kraler the firm Kolen & Co. When we walked across our little square together a few days ago, Daddy began to talk of us going into hiding. I asked him why on earth he was beginning to talk of that already. "Yes, Anne," he said, "you know that we have been taking food, clothes, furniture to other people for more than a year now. We don't want our belongings to be seized by the Germans, but we certainly don't want to fall into their clutches ourselves. So we shall disappear of our own accord and not wait until they come and fetch us."

"But, Daddy, when would it be?" He spoke so seriously that I grew very anxious.

"Don't you worry about it, we shall arrange everything. Make the most of your carefree young life while you can." That was all. Oh, may the fulfillment of these somber words remain far distant yet!

Yours, Anne

Dear Kitty,

Years seem to have passed between Sunday and now. So much has happened, it is just as if the whole world had turned upside down. But I am still alive, Kitty, and that is the main thing, Daddy says.

Yes, I'm still alive, indeed, but don't ask where or how. You wouldn't understand a word, so I will begin by telling you what happened on Sunday afternoon.

At three o'clock (Harry had just gone, but was coming back later) someone rang the front doorbell. I was lying lazily reading a book on the veranda in the sunshine, so I didn't hear it. A bit later, Margot appeared at the kitchen door looking very excited. "The S.S. have sent a call-up notice for Daddy," she whispered. "Mummy has gone to see Mr. Van Daan already." (Van Daan is a friend who works with Daddy in the business.) It was a great shock to me, a call-up; everyone knows what that means. I picture concentration camps and lonely cells—should we allow him to be doomed to this? "Of course he won't go," declared Margot, while we waited together. "Mummy has gone to the Van Daans to discuss whether we should move into our hiding place tomorrow. The Van Daans are going with us, so we shall be seven in all." Silence. We couldn't talk any more, thinking about Daddy, who, little knowing what was going on, was visiting some old people in the Joodse Invalide; waiting for Mummy, the heat and suspense, all made us very overawed and silent.

Suddenly the bell rang again. "That is Harry," I said. "Don't open the door." Margot held me back, but it was not necessary as we heard Mummy and Mr. Van Daan downstairs, talking to Harry, then they came in and closed the door behind them. Each time the bell went, Margot or I had to creep softly down to see if it was Daddy, not opening the door to anyone else.

Margot and I were sent out of the room. Van Daan

12

wanted to talk to Mummy alone. When we were alone to-gether in our bedroom, Margot told me that the call-up was not for Daddy, but for her. I was more frightened than ever and began to cry. Margot is sixteen; would they really take girls of that age away alone? But thank good-ness she won't go, Mummy said so herself; that must be what Daddy meant when he talked about us going into hiding.

Into hiding—where would we go, in a town or the country, in a house or a cottage, when, how, where . . . ?

These were questions I was not allowed to ask, but I couldn't get them out of my mind. Margot and I began to pack some of our most vital belongings into a school satchel. The first thing I put in was this diary, then hair curlers, handkerchiefs, schoolbooks, a comb, old letters; I put in the craziest things with the idea that we were going into hiding. But I'm not sorry, memories mean more to me than dresses.

At five o'clock Daddy finally arrived, and we phoned Mr. Koophuis to ask if he could come around in the eve-ning. Van Daan went and fetched Miep. Miep has been in the business with Daddy since 1933 and has become a close friend, likewise her brand-new husband, Henk. Miep came and took some shoes, dresses, coats, under-wear, and stockings away in her bag, promising to return in the evening. Then silence fell on the house; not one of us felt like eating anything, it was still hot and every-thing was very strange. We let our large upstairs room to a certain Mr. Goudsmit, a divorced man in his thirties, who appeared to have nothing to do on this particular eve-ning; we simply could not get rid of him without being rude; he hung about until ten o'clock. At eleven o'clock Miep and Henk Van Santen arrived. Once again, shoes, stockings, books, and underclothes disappeared into Miep's bag and Henk's deep pockets, and at eleven-thirty they too disappeared. I was dog-tired and although I knew that it would be my last night in my own bed, I fell asleep immediately and didn't wake up until Mummy called me at five-thirty the next morning. Luckily it was not so hot as Sunday; warm rain fell steadily all day. We put on heaps of clothes as if we were going to the North Pole, the sole reason being to take clothes with us. No Jew in our situation would have dreamed of going out with a suitcase full of clothing. I had on two vests, three pairs of pants, a dress, on top of that a skirt, jacket, summer coat, two pairs of stockings, lace-up shoes, woolly cap, scarf, and still more; I was nearly stifled before we started, but no one inquired about that.

Margot filled her satchel with schoolbooks, fetched her bicycle, and rode off behind Miep into the unknown, as far as I was concerned. You see I still didn't know where our secret hiding place was to be. At seven-thirty the door closed behind us. Moortje, my little cat, was the only creature to whom I said farewell. She would have a good home with the neighbors. This was all written in a lettter addressed to Mr. Goudsmit.

There was one pound of meat in the kitchen for the cat, breakfast things lying on the table, stripped beds, all giving the impression that we had left helter-skelter. But we didn't care about impressions, we only wanted to get away, only escape and arrive safely, nothing else. Continued tomorrow.

Yours, Anne

Thursday, 9 July, 1942

Dear Kitty,

So we walked in the pouring rain, Daddy, Mummy, and I, each with a school satchel and shopping bag filled to the brim with all kinds of things thrown together anyhow.

We got sympathetic looks from people on their way to work. You could see by their faces how sorry they were they couldn't offer us a lift; the gaudy yellow star spoke for itself.

Only when we were on the road did Mummy and Daddy begin to tell me bits and pieces about the plan. For months as many of our goods and chattels and necessities of life as possible had been sent away and they were sufficiently ready for us to have gone into hiding of our own accord on July 16. The plan had had to be speeded up ten days because of the call-up, so our quarters would not be so well organized, but we had to make the best of it. The hiding place itself would be in the building where Daddy has his office. It will be hard for outsiders to understand, but I shall explain that later on. Daddy didn't have many people working for him: Mr. Kraler, Koophuis, Miep, and Elli Vossen, a twenty-three-year-old typist who all knew of our arrival. Mr. Vossen, Elli's father, and two boys worked in the warehouse; they had not been told.

I will describe the building: there is a large warehouse on the ground floor which is used as a store. The front door to the house is next to the warehouse door, and inside the front door is a second doorway which leads to a staircase (A). There is another door at the top of the stairs, with a frosted glass window in it, which has "Office" written in black letters across it. That is the large main office, very big, very light, and very full. Elli, Miep, and Mr. Koophuis work there in the daytime. A small dark room containing the safe, a wardrobe, and a large cupboard leads to a small somewhat dark second office. Mr. Kraler and Mr. Van Daan used to sit here, now it is only Mr. Kraler. One can reach Kraler's office from the passage, but only via a glass door which can be opened from the inside, but not easily from the outside.

From Kraler's office a long passage goes past the coal store, up four steps and leads to the showroom of the whole building: the private office. Dark, dignified furniture, linoleum and carpets on the floor, radio, smart lamp, everything first-class. Next door there is a roomy kitchen with a hot-water faucet and a gas stove. Next door the W.C. That is the first floor.

A wooden staircase leads from the downstairs passage to the next floor (B). There is a small landing at the top. There is a door at each end of the landing, the left one leading to a storeroom at the front of the house and to the attics. One of those really steep Dutch staircases runs from the side to the other door opening on to the street (C).

The right-hand door leads to our "Secret Annexe." No

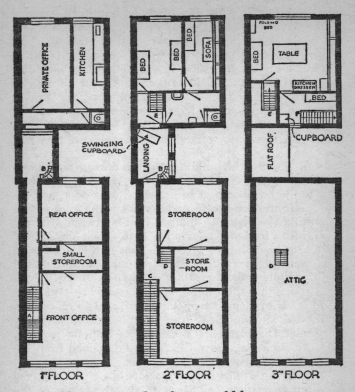

1ST FLOOR

PRIVATE OFFICE

KITCHEN

SWINGING CUPBOARD

B

REAR OFFICE

SMALL STOREROOM

A   FRONT OFFICE

2ND FLOOR

BED

BED

BED

SOFA

E

LANDING

B

STOREROOM

D   STORE-ROOM

C

STOREROOM

3RD FLOOR

FOLDING BED

BED

TABLE

KITCHEN DRESSER

BED

E

F

FLAT ROOF

CUPBOARD

D   ATTIC

1ST FLOOR   2ND FLOOR   3RD FLOOR

one would ever guess that there would be so many rooms hidden behind that plain gray door. There's a little step in front of the door and then you are inside.

There is a steep staircase immediately opposite the entrance (D). On the left a tiny passage brings you into a room which was to become the Frank family's bed-sitting-room, next door a smaller room, study and bedroom for the two young ladies of the family. On the right a little room without windows containing the washbasin and a small W.C. compartment, with another door leading to Margot's and my room. If you go up the next flight of stairs and open the door, you are simply amazed that there could be such a big light room in such an old house by

16

the canal. There is a gas stove in this room (thanks to the fact that it was used as a laboratory) and a sink. This is now the kitchen for the Van Daan couple, besides being general living room, dining room, and scullery.

A tiny little corridor room will become Peter Van Daan's apartment. Then, just as on the lower landing, there is a large attic. So there you are, I've introduced you to the whole of our beautiful "Secret Annexe."

Yours, Anne

Friday, 10 July, 1942

Dear Kitty,

I expect I have thoroughly bored you with my long-winded descriptions of our dwelling. But still I think you should know where we've landed.

But to continue my story—you see, I've not finished yet —when we arrived at the Prinsengracht, Miep took us quickly upstairs and into the "Secret Annexe." She closed the door behind us and we were alone. Margot was already waiting for us, having come much faster on her bicycle. Our living room and all the other rooms were chock-full of rubbish, indescribably so. All the cardboard boxes which had been sent to the office in the previous months lay piled on the floor and the beds. The little room was filled to the ceiling with bedclothes. We had to start clearing up immediately, if we wished to sleep in decent beds that night. Mummy and Margot were not in a fit state to take part; they were tired and lay down on their beds, they were miserable, and lots more besides. But the two "clearers-up" of the family—Daddy and myself—wanted to start at once.

The whole day long we unpacked boxes, filled cupboards, hammered and tidied, until we were dead beat. We sank into clean beds that night. We hadn't had a bit of anything warm the whole day, but we didn't care; Mummy and Margot were too tired and keyed up to eat, and Daddy and I were too busy.

On Tuesday morning we went on where we left off the

day before. Elli and Miep collected our rations for us, Daddy improved the poor blackout, we scrubbed the kitchen floor, and were on the go the whole day long again. I hardly had time to think about the great change in my life until Wednesday. Then I had a chance, for the first time since our arrival, to tell you all about it, and at the same time to realize myself what had actually happened to me and what was still going to happen.

Yours, Anne

Saturday, 11 July, 1942

Dear Kitty,

Daddy, Mummy, and Margot can't get used to the sound of the Westertoren clock yet, which tells us the time every quarter of an hour. I can. I loved it from the start, and especially in the night it's like a faithful friend. I expect you will be interested to hear what it feels like to "disappear"; well, all I can say is that I don't know myself yet. I don't think I shall ever feel really at home in this house, but that does not mean that I loathe it here, it is more like being on vacation in a very peculiar boardinghouse. Rather a mad idea, perhaps, but that is how it strikes me. The "Secret Annexe" is an ideal hiding place. Although it leans to one side and is damp, you'd never find such a comfortable hiding place anywhere in Amsterdam, no, perhaps not even in the whole of Holland. Our little room looked very bare at first with nothing on the walls; but thanks to Daddy who had brought my film-star collection and picture postcards on beforehand, and with the aid of paste pot and brush, I have transformed the walls into one gigantic picture. This makes it look much more cheerful, and, when the Van Daans come, we'll get some wood from the attic, and make a few little cupboards for the walls and other odds and ends to make it look more lively.

Margot and Mummy are a little bit better now. Mummy felt well enough to cook some soup for the first time yesterday, but then forgot all about it, while she was downstairs

18

talking, so the peas were burned to a cinder and utterly refused to leave the pan. Mr. Koophuis has brought me a book called *Young People's Annual*. The four of us went to the private office yesterday evening and turned on the radio. I was so terribly frightened that someone might hear it that I simply begged Daddy to come upstairs with me. Mummy understood how I felt and came to. We are very nervous in other ways, too, that the neighbors might hear us or see something going on. We made curtains straight away on the first day. Really one can hardly call them curtains, they are just light, loose strips of material, all different shapes, quality, and pattern, which Daddy and I sewed together in a most unprofessional way. These works of art are fixed in position with drawing pins, not to come down until we emerge from here.

There are some large business premises on the right of us, and on the left a furniture workshop; there is no one there after working hours but even so, sounds could travel through the walls. We have forbidden Margot to cough at night, although she has a bad cold, and make her swallow large doses of codeine. I am looking for Tuesday when the Van Daans arrive; it will be much more fun and not so quiet. It is the silence that frightens me so in the evenings and at night. I wish like anything that one of our protectors could sleep here at night. I can't tell you how oppressive it is *never* to be able to go outdoors, also I'm very afraid that we shall be discovered and be shot. That is not exactly a pleasant prospect. We have to whisper and tread lightly during the day, otherwise the people in the warehouse might hear us.

Someone is calling me.

Yours, Anne

Friday, 14 August, 1942

Dear Kitty,

I have deserted you for a whole month, but honestly, there is so little news here that I can't find amusing things to tell you every day. The Van Daans arrived on July 13.

We thought they were coming on the fourteenth, but between the thirteenth and sixteenth of July the Germans called up people right and left which created more and more unrest, so they played for safety, better a day too early than a day too late. At nine-thirty in the morning (we were still having breakfast) Peter arrived, the Van Daans' son, not sixteen yet, a rather soft, shy, gawky youth; can't expect much from his company. He brought his cat (Mouschi) with him. Mr. and Mrs. Van Daan arrived half an hour later, and to our great amusement she had a large pottie in her hat box. "I don't feel at home anywhere without my chamber," she declared, so it was the first thing to find its permanent resting place under her divan. Mr. Van Daan did not bring his, but carried a folding tea table under his arm.

From the day they arrived we all had meals cozily together and after three days it was just as if we were one large family. Naturally the Van Daans were able to tell us a lot about the extra week they had spent in the inhabited world. Among other things we were very interested to hear what had happened to our house and to Mr. Goudsmit. Mr. Van Daan told us:

"Mr. Goudsmit phoned at nine o'clock on Monday morning and asked if I could come around. I went immediately and found G. in a state of great agitation. He let me read a letter that the Franks had left behind and wanted to take the cat to the neighbors as indicated in the letter, which pleased me. Mr. G. was afraid that the house would be searched so we went through all the rooms, tidied up a bit, and cleared away the breakfast things. Suddenly I discovered a writing pad on Mrs. Frank's desk with an address in Maastricht written on it. Although I knew that this was done on purpose, I pretended to be very surprised and shocked and urged Mr. G. to tear up this unfortunate little piece of paper without delay.

"I went on pretending that I knew nothing of your disappearance all the time, but after seeing the paper, I got a brain wave. 'Mr. Goudsmit'—I said—'it suddenly dawns on me what this address may refer to. Now it all comes back to me, a high-ranking officer was in the office about six months ago, he appeared to be very friendly with Mr. Frank and offered to help him, should the need arise. He was stationed in Maastricht. I think he must have kept his word and somehow or other managed to get them into Belgium and then on to Switzerland. I should tell this to any friends who may inquire. Don't, of course, mention Maastricht.'

"With these words I left the house. Most of your friends know already, because I've been told myself several times by different people."

We were highly amused at the story and, when Mr. Van Daan gave us further details, laughed still more at the way people can let their imagination run away with them. One family had seen the pair of us pass on bicycles very early in the morning and another lady knew quite definitely that we were fetched by a military car in the middle of the night.

Yours, Anne

Friday, 21 August, 1942

Dear Kitty,

The entrance to our hiding place has now been properly concealed. Mr. Kraler thought it would be better to put a cupboard in front our door (because a lot of houses are being searched for hidden bicycles), but of course it had to be a movable cupboard that can open like a door.

Mr. Vossen made the whole thing. We had already let him into the secret and he can't do enough to help. If we want to go downstairs, we have to first bend down and then jump, because the step has gone. The first three days we were all going about with masses of lumps on our foreheads, because we all knocked ourselves against the low doorway. Now we have nailed a cloth filled with wood wool against the top of the door. Let's see if that helps!

I'm not working much at present; I'm giving myself holidays until September. Then Daddy is going to give me lessons; it's shocking how much I've forgotten already.

There is little change in our life here. Mr. Van Daan and I usually manage to upset each other, it's just the opposite with Margot whom he likes very much. Mummy sometimes treats me just like a baby, which I can't bear. Otherwise things are going better. I still don't like Peter any more, he is so boring; he flops lazily on his bed half the time, does a bit of carpentry, and then goes back for another snooze. What a fool!

It is lovely weather and in spite of everything we make the most we can of it by lying on a camp bed in the attic, where the sun shines through an open window.

Yours, Anne

Wednesday, 2 September, 1942

Dear Kitty,

Mr. and Mrs. Van Daan have had a terrific quarrel, I've never seen anything quite like it before. Mummy and Daddy would never dream of shouting at each other. The cause was so trivial that the whole thing was a pure waste of breath. But, still, everyone to his own liking.

Naturally it is very unpleasant for Peter, who has to stand by. No one takes him seriously, he is so frightfully touchy and lazy. Yesterday he was badly upset because he found that his tongue was blue instead of red; this unusual phenomenon of nature disappeared just as quickly as it had come. Today he is going about with a scarf on, as he has a stiff neck; in addition "M'lord" complains of lumbago. Pains around the heart, kidneys, and lungs are not unusual either, he is a real hypochondria (that's the word for such people, isn't it?)! It is not all honey between Mummy and Mrs. Van Daan; there is plenty of cause for unpleasantness. To give a small example, I will tell you that Mrs. Van Daan has taken all three of her sheets out of the common linen cupboard. She takes it for granted that Mummy's sheets will do for all of us. It will be a nasty surprise for her when she finds that Mummy has followed her good example.

Also, she is thoroughly piqued that her dinner service

and not ours is in use. She is always trying to find out where we have actually put our plates; they are closer than she thinks, they are in a cardboard box behind a lot of junk in the attic. Our plates are unget-at-able as long as we are here, and a good thing too. I always have bad luck; I smashed one of Mrs. Van Daan's soup plates into a thousand pieces yesterday. "Oh!" she cried angrily. "Couldn't you be careful for once—that's the last one I've got." Mr. Van Daan is all sugar to me nowadays. Long may it last. Mummy gave me another frightful sermon this morning; I can't bear them. Our ideas are completely opposite. Daddy is a darling, although he can sometimes be angry with me for five minutes on end. Last week we had a little interruption in our monotonous life; it was over a book about women—and Peter. First I must tell you that Margot and Peter are allowed to read nearly all the books that Mr. Koophuis lends us, but the grownups held back this particular book on the subject of women. Peter's curiosity was aroused at once. What was it the two of them were not allowed to read in this book? He got hold of the book on the sly, while his mother was downstairs talking, and disappeared with his booty to the attic. All went well for a few days. His mother knew what he was doing, but didn't tell tales, until Father found out. He was very angry, took the book away, and thought that that would finish the whole business. However, he had not allowed for his son's curiosity, which waxed rather than waned because of his father's attitude. Peter, determined to finish it, thought of a way to get hold of this enthralling book. In the meantime, Mrs. Van Daan had asked Mummy what she thought about it all. Mummy thought this particular book was not suitable for Margot, but she saw no harm in letting her read most books.

"There is a great difference, Mrs. Van Daan," said Mummy, "between Margot and Peter. In the first place, Margot is a girl and girls are always more grownup than boys, secondly, Margot has read quite a lot of serious books, and does not go in search of things that are forbidden her, and thirdly, Margot is far more developed and intelligent, shown by the fact of her being in the fourth form at school." Mrs. Van Daan agreed, but still thought it was wrong in principle to let children read books which were written for grownups.

In the meantime Peter had found a time of the day when no one bothered about him or the book: seven-thirty in the evening—then everyone was in the private office listening to the radio. That was when he took his treasure to the attic again. He should have been downstairs again by eight-thirty, but because the book was so thrilling he forgot the time and was just coming downstairs as his father came into the room. You can imagine the consequences! With a slap and a snatch, the book lay on the table and Peter was in the attic. That's how matters stood as we sat down to table. Peter stayed upstairs—no one bothered about him, and he had to go to bed without any supper. We went on with the meal, chattering gaily, when suddenly we heard a piercing whistle; we all stopped eating and looked with pale changed faces from one to another. Then we heard Peter's voice, calling down the chimney, "I say, I'm not coming down anyway." Mr. Van Daan sprang to his feet, his napkin fell to the floor, and scarlet in the face he shouted, "I've had enough of this." Daddy took his arm, afraid of what might happen, and the two men went together to the attic. After a good deal of resistance and stamping, Peter landed up in his room with the door closed and we went on eating. Mrs. Van Daan wanted to save one slice of bread for the dear boy, but his father stood firm. "If he doesn't apologize soon, he will have to sleep in the attic." Loud protests from the rest of us, as we thought missing supper was quite enough punishment. Besides, Peter might catch cold and we couldn't call a doctor.

Peter did not apologize; he was already in the attic. Mr. Van Daan did nothing more about, but I noticed the next morning that Peter's bed had been slept in. Peter was back in the attic at seven o'clock, but Daddy managed with a few friendly words to persuade him to come down again. Sour faces and obstinate silences for three days and then everything went smoothly once more.

Yours, Anne

Dear Kitty,

Today I'm going to tell you our general news.

Mrs. Van Daan is unbearable. I get nothing but "blow-ups" from her for my continuous chatter. She is always pestering us in some way or other. This is the latest: she doesn't want to wash up the pans if there is a fragment left; instead of putting it into a glass dish, as we've always done until now, she leaves it in the pan to go bad.

After the next meal Margot sometimes has about seven pans to wash up and then Madame says: "Well, well, Margot, you have got a lot to do!"

I'm busy with Daddy working out his family tree: as we go along he tells me little bits about everyone—it's terribly interesting. Mr. Koophuis brings a few special books for me every other week. I'm thrilled with the *Joop ter Heul* series. I've enjoyed the whole of Cissy van Marxveldt very much. And I've read *Een Zomerzotheid* four times and I still laugh about some of the ludicrous situations that arise.

Term time has begun again, I'm working hard at my French and manage to pump in five irregular verbs per day. Peter sighs and groans over his English. A few schoolbooks have just arrived; we have a good stock of exercise books, pencils, rubbers, and labels, as I brought these with me. I sometimes listen to the Dutch news from London, heard Prince Bernhard recently. He said that Princess Juliana is expecting a baby about next January. I think it is lovely; it surprises the others that I should be so keen on the Royal Family.

I was being discussed and they decided that I'm not completely stupid after all, which had the effect of making me work extra hard the next day. I certainly don't want to still be in the first form when I'm fourteen or fifteen.

Also the fact that I'm hardly allowed to read any decent books was mentioned. Mummy is reading *Heeren,*

Vrouwen en Knechten now, which I'm not allowed (Margot is). First I must be more developed, like my talented sister. Then we talk about my ignorance of philosophy and psychology, about which I know nothing. Perhaps by next year I shall be wiser! (I looked up these difficult words quickly in *Koenen*.)

I have just woken up to the disturbing fact that I have one long-sleeved dress and three cardigans for the winter. I've received permission from Daddy to knit a jumper of white sheep's wool; it's not very nice wool, but as long as it's warm that's all that matters. We have some clothes deposited with friends, but unfortunately we shall not see them until after the war, that is if they are still there then. I had just written something about Mrs. Van Daan when in she came. Slap! I closed the book. "Hey, Anne, can't I just have a look?"

"I'm afraid not."

"Just the last page then?"

"No, I'm sorry."

Naturally it gave me a frightful shock, because there was an unflattering description of her on this particular page.

Yours, Anne

Friday, 25 September, 1942

Dear Kitty,

Yesterday evening I went upstairs and "visited" the Van Daans. I do so occasionally to have a chat. Sometimes it can be quite fun. Then we have some moth biscuits (the biscuit tin is kept in the wardrobe which is full of moth balls) and drink lemonade. We talked about Peter. I told them how Peter often strokes my cheek and that I wished he wouldn't as I don't like being pawed by boys.

In a typical way parents have, they asked if I couldn't get fond of Peter, because he certainly liked me very much. I thought "Oh dear!" and said: "Oh, no!" Imagine it!

I did say that I thought Peter rather awkward, but that it was probably shyness, as many boys who haven't had much to do with girls are like that.

I must say that the Refuge Committee of the "Secret Annexe" (male section) is very ingenious. I'll tell you what they've done now to get news of us through to Mr. Van Dijk, Travies' chief representative and a friend who has surreptitiously hidden some of our things for us! They typed a letter to a chemist in South Zeeland, who does business with our firm, in such a way that he has to send the enclosed reply back in an addressed envelope. Daddy addressed the envelope to the office. When this envelope arrives from Zeeland, the enclosed letter is taken out, and is replaced by a message in Daddy's handwriting as a sign of life. Like this, Van Dijk won't become suspicious when he reads the note. They specially chose Zeeland because it is so close to Belgium and the letter could have easily been smuggled over the border, in addition no one is allowed into Zeeland without a special permit; so if they thought we were there, he couldn't try and look us up.

Yours, Anne

Sunday, 27 September, 1942

Dear Kitty,

Just had a big bust-up with Mummy for the umpteenth time; we simply don't get on together these days and Margot and I don't hit it off any too well either. As a rule we don't go in for such outbursts as this in our family. Still, it's by no means always pleasant for me. Margot's and Mummy's natures are completely strange to me. I can understand my friends better than my own mother—too bad!

We often discuss postwar problems, for example, how one ought to address servants.

Mrs. Van Daan had another tantrum. She is terribly moody. She keeps hiding more of her private belongings. Mummy ought to answer each Van Daan "disappearance" with a Frank "disappearance." How some people do adore bringing up other people's children in addition to their own. The Van Daans are that kind. Margot doesn't need it, she is such a goody-goody, perfection itself, but I seem to have enough mischief in me for the two of us put together. You should hear us at mealtimes, with reprimands and cheeky answers flying to and fro. Mummy and Daddy always defend me stoutly. I'd have to give up if it weren't for them. Although they do tell me that I mustn't talk so much, that I must be more retiring and not poke my nose into everything, still I seem doomed to failure. If Daddy wasn't so patient, I'd be afraid I was going to turn out to be a terrific disappointment to my parents and they are plenty lenient with me.

If I take a small helping of some vegetable I detest and make up with potatoes, the Van Daans, and Mevrouw in particular, can't get over it, that any child should be so spoiled.

"Come along, Anne, have a few more vegetables," she says straight away.

"No, thank you, Mrs. Van Daan," I answer, "I have plenty of potatoes."

"Vegetables are good for you, your mother says so too. Have a few more," she says, pressing them on me until Daddy comes to my rescue.

Then we have from Mrs. Van Daan—"You ought to have been in our home, we were properly brought up. It's absurd that Anne's so frightfully spoiled. I wouldn't put up with it if Anne were my daughter."

These are always her first and last words "if Anne were my daughter." Thank heavens I'm not!

But to come back to this "upbringing" business. There was a deadly silence after Mrs. Van Daan had finished speaking yesterday. Then Daddy said, "I think Anne is extremely well brought up; she has learned one thing anyway, and that is to make no reply to your long sermons. As to vegetables, look at your own plate." Mrs. Van Daan was beaten, well and truly beaten. She had taken a minute helping of vegetables herself. But *she* is not spoiled! Oh, no, too many vegetables in the evening make her constipated. Why on earth doesn't she keep her mouth shut about me, then she wouldn't need to make such feeble excuses. It's gorgeous the way Mrs. Van Daan blushes. I don't and that is just what she hates.

Yours, Anne

Monday, 28 September, 1942

Dear Kitty,

I had to stop yesterday, long before I'd finished. I just must tell you about another quarrel, but before I start on that, something else.

Why do grownups quarrel so easily, so much, and over the most idiotic things? Up till now I thought that only children squabbled and that that wore off as you grew up. Of course, there is sometimes a real reason for a quarrel, but this is just plain bickering. I suppose I should get used to it. But I can't nor do I think I shall, as long as I am the subject of nearly every discussion (they use the word "discussion" instead of quarrel). Nothing, I repeat, nothing about me is right; my general appearance, my character, my manners are discussed from A to Z. I'm expected (by order) to simply swallow all the harsh words and shouts in silence and I am not used to this. In fact, I can't! I'm not going to take all these insults lying down, I'll show them that Anne Frank wasn't born yesterday. Then they'll be surprised and perhaps they'll keep their mouths shut when I let them see that I am going to start educating them. Shall I take up that attitude? Plain barbarism! I'm simply amazed again and again over their awful manners and especially . . . stupidity (Mrs. Van Daan's), but as soon as I get used to this—and it won't be long—then I'll give them some of their own back, and no half measures. Then they'll change their tune!

Am I really so bad-mannered, conceited, headstrong, pushing, stupid, lazy, etc., etc., as they all say? Oh, of course not. I have my faults, just like everyone else, I know that, but they thoroughly exaggerate everything.

29

Kitty, if only you knew how I sometimes boil under so many gibes and jeers. And I don't know how long I shall be able to stifle my rage. I shall just blow up one day.

Still, no more of this, I've bored you long enough with all these quarrels. But I simply must tell you of one highly interesting discussion at table. Somehow or other, we got on to the subject of Pim's (Daddy's nickname) extreme modesty. Even the most stupid people have to admit this about Daddy. Suddenly Mrs. Van Daan says, "I too, have an unassuming nature, more so than my husband."

Did you ever! This sentence in itself shows quite clearly how thoroughly forward and pushing she is! Mr. Van Daan thought he ought to give an explanation regarding the reference to himself. "I don't wish to be modest—in my experience it does not pay." Then to me: "Take my advice, Anne, don't be too unassuming, it doesn't get you anywhere."

Mummy agreed with this too. But Mrs. Van Daan had to add, as always, her ideas on the subject. Her next remark was addressed to Mummy and Daddy. "You have a strange outlook on life. Fancy saying such a thing to Anne; it was very different when I was young. And I feel sure that it still is, except in your modern home." This was a direct hit at the way Mummy brings up her daughters.

Mrs. Van Daan was scarlet by this time. Mummy calm and cool as a cucumber. People who blush get so hot and excited, it is quite a handicap in such a situation. Mummy, still entirely unruffled, but anxious to close the conversation as soon as possible, thought for a second and then said: "I find, too, Mrs. Van Daan, that one gets on better in life if one is not over-modest. My husband, now, and Margot, and Peter are exceptionally modest, whereas your husband, Anne, you, and I, though not exactly the opposite, don't allow ourselves to be completely pushed to one side." Mrs. Van Daan: "But, Mrs. Frank, I don't understand you; I'm so very modest and retiring, how can you think of calling me anything else?" Mummy: "I did not say you were exactly forward, but no one could say you had a retiring disposition." Mrs. Van Daan: "Let us get this matter cleared up, once and for all. I'd like to know in what way I am pushing? I know one thing, if I didn't look after myself, I'd soon be starving."

This absurd remark in self-defense just made Mummy rock with laughter. That irritated Mrs. Van Daan, who added a string of German-Dutch, Dutch-German expressions, until she became completely tongue-tied; then she rose from her chair and was about to leave the room.

Suddenly her eye fell on me. You should have seen her. Unfortunately, at the very moment that she turned round, I was shaking my head sorrowfully—not on purpose, but quite involuntarily, for I had been following the whole conversation so closely.

Mrs. Van Daan turned round and began to reel off a lot of harsh German, common, and ill-mannered, just like a coarse, red-faced fishwife—it was a marvelous sight. If I could draw, I'd have liked to catch her like this; it was a scream, such a stupid, foolish little person!

Anyhow, I've learned one thing now. You only really get to know people when you've had a jolly good row with them. Then and then only can you judge their true characters!

Yours, Anne

Tuesday, 29 September, 1942

Dear Kitty,

Extraordinary things can happen to people who go into hiding. Just imagine, as there is no bath, we use a washtub and because there is hot water in the office (by which I always mean the whole of the lower floor) all seven of us take it in turns to make use of this great luxury.

But because we are all so different and some are more modest than others, each member of the family has found his own place for carrying out the performance. Peter uses the kitchen in spite of its glass door. When he is going to have a bath, he goes to each one of us in turn and tells us that we must not walk past the kitchen for half an hour. He seems to think this is sufficient. Mr. Van Daan goes right upstairs; to him it is worth the bother of carrying hot water all that way, so as to have the seclusion of his own room. Mrs. Van Daan simply doesn't bathe at all at present; she is waiting to see which is the best place. Daddy has his bath in the private office, Mummy behind a fire guard in the kitchen; Margot and I have chosen the front office for our scrub. The curtains there are drawn on Saturday afternoons, so we wash ourselves in semi-darkness.

However, I don't like this place any longer, and since last week I've been on the lookout for more comfortable quarters. Peter gave me an idea and that was to try the large office W.C. There I can sit down, have the light on, lock the door, pour my own bath water away, and I'm safe from prying eyes.

I tried my beautiful bathroom on Sunday for the first time and although it sounds mad, I think it is the best place of all. Last week the plumber was at work downstairs to move the drains and water pipes from the office W.C. to the passage. This change is a precaution against frozen pipes, in case we should have a cold winter. The plumber's visit was far from pleasant for us. Not only were we unable to draw water the whole day, but we could not go to the W.C. either. Now it is rather indecent to tell you what we did to overcome this difficulty, however, I'm not such a prude that I can't talk about these things.

The day we arrived here, Daddy and I improvised a pottie for ourselves; not having a better receptacle, we sacrificed a glass preserving jar for this purpose. During the plumber's visit, nature's offerings were deposited in these jars in the sitting room during the day. I don't think this was nearly as bad as having to sit still and not talk the whole day. You can't imagine what a trial that was for "Miss Quack-Quack." I have to whisper on ordinary days; but not being able to speak or move was ten times worse. After being flattened by three days of con-

32

tinuous sitting, my bottom was very stiff and painful. Some exercises at bedtime helped.

Yours, Anne

Thursday, 1 October, 1942

Dear Kitty,

I got a terrible shock yesterday. Suddenly at eight o'clock the bell rang loudly. Of course, I thought that someone had come; you'll guess who I mean. But I calmed down a bit when everyone said it must be some urchins or perhaps the postman.

The days are becoming very quiet here. Lewin, a small Jewish chemist and dispenser, works for Mr. Kraler in the kitchen. He knows the whole building well and therefore we are always afraid that he'll take it into his head to have a peep in the old laboratory. We are as quiet as mice. Who, three months ago, would ever have guessed that quicksilver Anne would have to sit still for hours—and, what's more, could?

The twenty-ninth was Mrs. Van Daan's birthday. Although it could not be celebrated in a big way, we managed a little party in her honor, with a specially nice meal, and she received some small presents and flowers. Red carnations from her husband; that seems to be a family tradition. To pause for a moment on the subject of Mrs. Van Daan, I must tell you that her attempts to flirt with Daddy are a source of continual irritation for me. She strokes his face and hair, pulls her skirt right up, and makes so-called witty remarks, trying in this way to attract Pim's attention. Pim, thank goodness, doesn't find her either attractive or funny, so he doesn't play ball. Mummy doesn't behave like that with Mr. Van Daan, I've said that to Mrs. Van Daan's face.

Now and then Peter comes out of his shell and can be quite funny. We have one thing in common, from which everyone usually gets a lot of amusement: we both love dressing up. He appeared in one of Mrs. Van Daan's very narrow dresses and I put on his suit. He wore a hat and I a cap. The grownups were doubled up with laughter and we enjoyed ourselves as much as they did. Elli has bought new skirts for Margot and me at Bijenkorf's. The material is rotten, just like sacking, and they cost 24.00 florins and 7.50 florins respectively. What a difference compared with before the war!

Another nice thing I've been keeping up my sleeve. Elli has written to some secretarial school or other and ordered a correspondence course in shorthand for Margot, Peter, and me. You wait and see what perfect experts we shall be by next year. In any case it's extremely important to be able to write in a code.

Yours, Anne

Saturday, 3 October, 1942

Dear Kitty,
There was another dust-up yesterday. Mummy kicked up a frightful row and told Daddy just what she thought of me. Then she had an awful fit of tears so, of course, off I went too; and I'd got such an awful headache anyway. Finally I told Daddy that I'm much more fond of him than Mummy, to which he replied that I'd get over that. But I don't believe it. I have to simply force myself to stay calm with her. Daddy wishes that I would sometimes volunteer to help Mummy, when she doesn't feel well or has a headache; but I shan't. I am working hard at my French and am now reading *La Belle Nivernaise*.

Yours, Anne

Friday, 9 October, 1942

Dear Kitty,
I've only got dismal and depressing news for you today. Our many Jewish friends are being taken away by the dozen. These people are treated by the Gestapo without a shred of decency, being loaded into cattle trucks and

sent to Westerbork, the big Jewish camp in Drente. Westerbork sounds terrible: only one washing cubicle for a hundred people and not nearly enough lavatories. There is no separate accommodations. Men, women, and children all sleep together. One hears of frightful immorality because of this; and a lot of the women, and even girls, who stay there any length of time are expecting babies.

It is impossible to escape; most of the people in the camp are branded as inmates by their shaven heads and many also by their Jewish appearance.

If it is as bad as this in Holland whatever will it be like in the distant and barbarous regions they are sent to? We assume that most of them are murdered. The English radio speaks of their being gassed.

Perhaps that is the quickest way to die. I feel terribly upset. I couldn't tear myself away while Miep told these dreadful stories; and she herself was equally wound up for that matter. Just recently for instance, a poor old crippled Jewess was sitting on her doorstep; she had been told to wait there by the Gestapo, who had gone to fetch a car to take her away. The poor old thing was terrified by the guns that were shooting at English planes overhead, and by the glaring beams of the searchlights. But Miep did not dare take her in; no one would undergo such a risk. The Germans strike without the slightest mercy. Elli too is very quiet: her boy friend has got to go to Germany. She is afraid that the airmen who fly over her home will drop their bombs, often weighing a million kilos, on Dirk's head. Jokes such as "he's not likely to get a million" and "it only takes one bomb" are in rather bad taste. Dirk is certainly not the only one who has to go: trainloads of boys leave daily. If they stop at a small station en route, sometimes some of them manage to get out unnoticed and escape; perhaps a few manage it. This, however, is not the end of my bad news. Have you ever heard of hostages? That's the latest thing in penalties for sabotage. Can you imagine anything so dreadful?

Prominent citizens—innocent people—are thrown into prison to await their fate. If the saboteur can't be traced,

35

the Gestapo simply puts about five hostages against the wall. Announcements of their deaths appear in the papers frequently. These outrages are described as "fatal accidents." Nice people, the Germans! To think that I was once one of them too! No, Hitler took away our nationality long ago. In fact, Germans and Jews are the greatest enemies in the world.

Yours, Anne

Friday, 16 October, 1942

Dear Kitty,

I'm terribly busy. I've just translated a chapter out of *La Belle Nivernaise* and made notes of new words. Then a perfectly foul math problem and three pages of French grammar. I flatly refuse to do these math problems every day. Daddy agrees that they're vile. I'm almost better at them than he is, though neither of us are much good and we often have to fetch Margot. I'm the furthest on of the three of us in shorthand.

Yesterday I finished *The Assault*. It's quite amusing, but doesn't touch *Joop ter Heul*. As a matter of fact, I think Cissy van Marxveldt is a first-rate writer. I shall definitely let my children read her books. Mummy, Margot, and I are as thick as thieves again. It's really much better. Margot and I got in the same bed together last evening, it was a frightful squash, but that was just the fun of it. She asked if she could read my diary. I said "Yes—at least, bits of it"; and then I asked if I could read hers and she said "Yes." Then we got on to the subject of the future. I asked her what she wanted to be. But she wouldn't say and made a great secret of it. I gathered something about teaching; I'm not sure if I'm right, but I think so. Really, I shouldn't be so curious!

This morning I was lying on Peter's bed, having chased him off at first. He was furious with me, not that I cared very much. He might be a bit more friendly with me for once; after all I did give him an apple yesterday.

I asked Margot if she thought I was very ugly. She

said that I was quite attractive and that I had nice eyes. Rather vague, don't you think?

Till next time,

Yours, Anne

Tuesday, 20 October, 1942

Dear Kitty,

My hand still shakes, although it's two hours since we had the shock. I should explain that there are five fire extinguishers in the house. We knew that someone was coming to fill them, but no one had warned us when the carpenter, or whatever you call him, was coming.

The result was that we weren't making any attempt to keep quiet, until I heard hammering outside on the landing opposite our cupboard door. I thought of the carpenter at once and warned Elli, who was having a meal with us, that she shouldn't go downstairs. Daddy and I posted ourselves at the door so as to hear when the man left. After he'd been working for a quarter of an hour, he laid his hammer and tools down on top of our cupboard (as we thought) and knocked at our door. We turned absolutely white. Perhaps he had heard something after all and wanted to investigate our secret den. It seemed like it. The knocking, pulling, pushing, and wrenching went on. I nearly fainted at the thought that this utter stranger might discover our beautiful secret hiding place. And just as I thought my last hour was at hand, I heard Mr. Koophuis say, "Open the door, it's only me." We opened it immediately. The hook that holds the cupboard, which can be undone by people who know the secret, had got jammed. That was why no one had been able to warn us about the carpenter. The man had now gone downstairs and Koophuis wanted to fetch Elli, but couldn't open the cupboard again. It was a great relief to me, I can tell you. In my imagination the man who I thought was trying to get in had been growing and growing in size until in the end he appeared to be a giant and the greatest fascist that ever walked the earth.

Well! Well! Luckily everything was okay this time. Meanwhile we had great fun on Monday. Miep and Henk spent the night here. Margot and I went in Mummy and Daddy's room for the night, so that the Van Santens could have our room. The meal tasted divine. There was one small interruption. Daddy's lamp blew a fuse, and all of a sudden we were sitting in darkness. What was to be done? There was some fuse wire in the house, but the fuse box is right at the very back of the dark storeroom—not such a nice job after dark. Still the men ventured forth and after ten minutes we were able to put the candles away again.

I got up early this morning. Henk had to leave at half past eight. After a cozy breakfast Miep went downstairs. It was pouring and she was glad not to have to cycle to the office. Next week Elli is coming to stay for a night.

Yours, Anne

Thursday, 29 October, 1942

Dear Kitty,

I am awfully worried, Daddy is ill. He has a high temperature and a red rash, it looks like measles. Think of it, we can't even call a doctor! Mummy is letting him have a good sweat. Perhaps that will send his temperature down.

This morning Miep told us that all the furniture has been removed from the Van Daans' home. We haven't told Mrs. Van Daan yet. She's such a bundle of nerves already, and we don't feel like listening to another moan over all the lovely china and beautiful chairs that she left at home. *We* had to leave almost all our nice things behind; so what's the good of grumbling about it now?

I'm allowed to read more grown-up books lately. I'm now reading *Eva's Youth* by Nico van Suchtelen. I can't see much difference between this and the schoolgirl love stories. It is true there are bits about women selling themselves to unknown men in back streets. They ask a packet of money for it. I'd die of shame if anything like

38

that happened to me. Also it says that Eva has a monthly period. Oh, I'm so longing to have it too; it seems so important.

Daddy has brought the plays of Goethe and Schiller from the big cupboard. He is going to read to me every evening. We've started with *Don Carlos*.

Following Daddy's good example, Mummy has pressed her prayer book into my hand. For decency's sake I read some of the prayers in German; they are certainly beautiful but they don't convey much to me. Why does she force me to be pious, just to oblige her?

Tomorrow we are going to light the fire for the first time. I expect we shall be suffocated with smoke. The chimney hasn't been swept for ages, let's hope the thing draws.

Yours, Anne

Saturday, 7 November, 1942

Dear Kitty,

Mummy is frightfully irritable and that always seems to herald unpleasantness for me. Is it just a chance that Daddy and Mummy never rebuke Margot and that they always drop on me for everything? Yesterday evening, for instance: Margot was reading a book with lovely drawings in it; she got up and went upstairs, put the book down ready to go on with it later. I wasn't doing anything, so picked up the book and started looking at the pictures. Margot came back, saw "her" book in my hands, wrinkled her forehead and asked for the book back. Just because I wanted to look a little further on, Margot got more and more angry. Then Mummy joined in: "Give the book to Margot; she was reading it," she said. Daddy came into the room. He didn't even know what it was all about, but saw the injured look on Margot's face and promptly dropped on me: "I'd like to see what you'd say if Margot ever started looking at one of your books!" I gave way at once, laid the book down, and left the

39

room—offended, as they thought. It so happened I was neither offended nor cross, just miserable. It wasn't right of Daddy to judge without knowing what the squabble was about. I would have given Margot the book myself, and much more quickly, if Mummy and Daddy hadn't interfered. They took Margot's part at once, as though she were the victim of some great injustice.

It's obvious that Mummy would stick up for Margot; she and Margot always do back each other up. I'm so used to that that I'm utterly indifferent to both Mummy's jawing and Margot's moods.

I love them; but only because they are Mummy and Margot. With Daddy it's different. If he holds Margot up as an example, approves of what she does, praises and caresses her, then something gnaws at me inside, because I adore Daddy. He is the one I look up to. I don't love anyone in the world but him. He doesn't notice that he treats Margot differently from me. Now Margot is just the prettiest, sweetest, most beautiful girl in the world. But all the same I feel I have some right to be taken seriously too. I have always been the dunce, the ne'er-do-well of the family, I've always had to pay double for my deeds, first with the scolding and then again because of the way my feelings are hurt. Now I'm not satisfied with this apparent favoritism any more. I want something from Daddy that he is not able to give me.

I'm not jealous of Margot, never have been. I don't envy her good looks or her beauty. It is only that I long for Daddy's real love: not only as his child, but for me—Anne, myself.

I cling to Daddy because it is only through him that I am able to retain the remnant of family feeling. Daddy doesn't understand that I need to give vent to my feelings over Mummy sometimes. He doesn't want to talk about it; he simply avoids anything which might lead to remarks about Mummy's failings. Just the same, Mummy and her failings are something I find harder to bear than anything else. I don't know how to keep it all to myself. I can't always be drawing attention to her untidiness, her sarcasm, and her lack of sweetness, neither can I believe that I'm always in the wrong.

We are exact opposites in everything; so naturally we are bound to run up against each other. I don't pronounce judgment on Mummy's character, for that is something I can't judge. I only look at her as a mother, and she just doesn't succeed in being that to me; I have to be my own mother. I've drawn myself apart from them all; I am my own skipper and later on I shall see where I come to land. All this comes about particularly because I have in my mind's eye an image of what a perfect mother and wife should be; and in her whom I must call "Mother" I find no trace of that image.

I am always making resolutions not to notice Mummy's bad example. I want to see only the good side of her and to seek in myself what I cannot find in her. But it doesn't work; and the worst of it is neither Daddy nor Mummy understands this gap in my life, and I blame them for it. I wonder if anyone can ever succeed in making their children absolutely content.

Sometimes I believe that God wants to try me, both now and later on; I must become good through my own efforts, without examples and without good advice. Then later on I shall be all the stronger. Who besides me will ever read these letters? From whom but myself shall I get comfort? As I need comforting often, I frequently feel weak, and dissatisfied with myself; my shortcomings are too great. I know this, and every day I try to improve myself, again and again.

My treatment varies so much. One day Anne is so sensible and is allowed to know everything; and the next day I hear that Anne is just a silly little goat who doesn't know anything at all and imagines that she's learned a wonderful lot from books. I'm not a baby or a spoiled darling any more, to be laughed at, whatever she does. I have my own views, plans, and ideas, though I can't put them into words yet. Oh, so many things bubble up inside me as I lie in bed, having to put up with people I'm fed up with, who always misinterpret my intentions. That's why in the end I always come back to my diary. That is

41

where I start and finish, because Kitty is always patient. I'll promise her that I shall persevere, in spite of everything, and find my own way through it all, and swallow my tears. I only wish I could see the results already or occasionally receive encouragement from someone who loves me.

Don't condemn me; remember rather that sometimes I too can reach the bursting point.

Yours, Anne

Monday, 9 November, 1942

Dear Kitty,

Yesterday was Peter's birthday, he was sixteen. He had some nice presents. Among other things a game of Monopoly, a razor, and a lighter. Not that he smokes much; it's really just for show.

The biggest surprise came from Mr. Van Daan when, at one o'clock, he announced that the British had landed in Tunis, Algiers, Casablanca, and Oran. "This is the beginning of the end," everyone was saying, but Churchill, the British Prime Minister, who had probably heard the same thing in England, said: "This is not the end. It is not even the beginning of the end. But it is, perhaps, the end of the beginning." Do you see the difference? There is certainly reason for optimism. Stalingrad, the Russian town which they've already been defending for three months, still hasn't fallen into German hands.

But to return to affairs in our secret den. I must tell you something about our food supply. As you know, we have some real greedy pigs on the top floor. We get our bread from a nice baker, a friend of Koophuis. We don't get so much as we used to at home, naturally. But it's sufficient. Four ration cards have also been bought illegally. Their price is going up all the time; it has now gone up from twenty-seven florins to thirty-three. And all that for a little slip of printed paper! In order to have something in the house that will keep, apart from our 150 tins of vegetables, we have bought 270 pounds of dried peas and beans. They are not all for us, some are for the office people. They are in sacks which hang on hooks in our little passage (inside the hidden door). Owing to the weight of the contents, a few stitches in the sacks burst open. So we decided it would be better to put our winter store in the attic and Peter was given the job of dragging it all up there.

He had managed to get five of the six sacks upstairs intact, and he was just busy pulling up number six, when the bottom seam of the sack split and a shower—no, a positive hailstorm of brown beans came pouring down and rattled down the stairs. There were about fifty pounds in the sack and the noise was enough to waken the dead. Downstairs they thought the old house with all its contents was coming down on them. (Thank God there were no strangers in the house.) It gave Peter a moment's fright. But he was soon roaring with laughter, especially when he saw me standing at the bottom of the stairs, like a little island in the middle of a sea of beans! I was entirely surrounded up to my ankles in beans. Quickly we started to pick them up. But beans are so slippery and small that they seemed to roll into all the possible and impossible corners and holes. Now, every time anyone goes downstairs they bend down once or twice, in order to be able to present Mrs. Van Daan with a handful of beans.

I'd almost forgotten to mention that Daddy is quite better again.

Yours, Anne

P.S. The news has just come over the radio that Algiers has fallen. Morocco, Casablanca, and Oran have been in British hands for several days. Now we're waiting for Tunis.

Tuesday, 10 November, 1942

Dear Kitty,

Great news—we want to take in an eighth person. Yes, really! We've always thought that there was quite enough room and food for one more. We were only afraid of giving Koophuis and Kraler more trouble. But now that the appalling stories we hear about Jews are getting even worse, Daddy got hold of the two people who had to decide, and they thought it was an excellent plan. "It is just as dangerous for seven as for eight," they said, and quite rightly. When this was settled, we ran through our circle of friends, trying to think of a single person who would fit in well with our "family." It wasn't difficult to hit on someone. After Daddy had refused all members of the Van Daan family, we chose a dentist called Albert Dussel, whose wife was fortunate enough to be out of the country when war broke out. He is known to be quiet, and so far as we and Mr. Van Daan can judge from a superficial acquaintance, both families think he is a congenial person. Miep knows him too, so she will be able to make arrangements for him to join us. If he comes, he will have to sleep in my room instead of Margot, who will use the camp bed.

Yours, Anne

Thursday, 12 November, 1942

Dear Kitty,

Dussel was awfully pleased when Miep told him that she had got a hiding place for him. She urged him to come as soon as possible. Preferably Saturday. He thought that this was rather doubtful, since he had to bring his card index up to date first, see to a couple of patients, and settle his accounts. Miep came to us with this news this morning. We thought it was unwise of him to put it off. All these preparations entail explanations to a number of people, whom we would rather keep out of it. Miep is going to ask if he can't manage to come on Saturday after all.

Dussel said no; now he is coming on Monday. I must say I think it's pretty crazy that he doesn't jump at the proposal—whatever it is. If he were to get picked up outside, would he still be able to do his card index, settle his finances, and see to his patients? Why delay then?

I think it's stupid of Daddy to have given in. No other news—

Yours, Anne

Tuesday, 17 November, 1942

Dear Kitty,

Dussel has arrived. All went well. Miep had told him that he must be at a special place in front of the Post Office at eleven o'clock, where a man would meet him. Dussel was standing at the rendezvous dead on time. Mr. Koophuis, who knows Dussel too, went up to him and told him that the said gentleman could not come, but asked whether he would just go to Miep at the office. Koophuis got into a tram and went back to the office, while Dussel walked in the same direction. At twenty past eleven Dussel tapped at the office door. Miep helped him off with his coat, so that the yellow star would not be seen, and took him to the private office, where Koophuis engaged him in conversation until the charwoman had gone. Then Miep went upstairs with Dussel under the pretext that the private office was needed for something, opened the swinging cupboard, and stepped inside before the eyes of the dumfounded Dussel.

We all sat around the table upstairs, waiting with coffee and cognac to greet the newcomer. Miep showed him into our sitting room first. He recognized our furniture at once, and had not the remotest idea that we were there, above his head. When Miep told him he nearly passed out with surprise. But luckily Miep didn't give him much time and took him straight upstairs.

Dussel sank into a chair, speechless, and looked at us all for a while, as if he had to really take it all in first. After a while he stuttered "But . . . *aber, sind* you not in Belgium then? *Ist der Militär nicht* come, *das Auto,* the escape is *sie nicht* successful?"

We explained everything to him, that we had spread the story about the soldiers and the car on purpose to put

45

people, and especially the Germans, on the wrong track, should they try to find us.

Dussel was again struck dumb by such ingenuity and, when he had explored further our superpractical exquisite little "Secret Annexe," he could do nothing but gaze about him in astonishment.

We all had lunch together. Then he had a little nap and joined us for tea, tidied up his things a bit (Miep had brought them beforehand), and began to feel more at home. Especially when he received the following typed "Secret Annexe Rules" (Van Daan product).

PROSPECTUS AND GUIDE TO THE "SECRET ANNEXE"

Special institution as temporary residence
for Jews and suchlike.

Open all the year round. Beautiful, quiet, free from woodland surroundings, in the heart of Amsterdam. Can be reached by trams 13 and 17, also by car or bicycle. In special cases also on foot, if the Germans prevent the use of transport.

Board and lodging: Free.

Special fat-free diet.

Running water in the bathroom (alas, no bath) and down various inside and outside walls.

Ample storage room for all types of goods.

Own radio center, direct communication with London, New York, Tel Aviv, and numerous other stations. This appliance is only for residents' use after six o'clock in the evening. No stations are forbidden, on the understanding that German stations are only listened to in special cases, such as classical music and the like.

Rest hours: 10 o'clock in the evening until 7:30 in the morning. 10:15 on Sundays. Residents may rest during the day, conditions permitting, as the directors indicate. For reasons of public security rest hours must be strictly observed!!

Holidays (outside the home): postponed indefinitely.

Use of language: Speak softly at all times, by order! All civilized languages are permitted, therefore no German!

Lessons: One written shorthand lesson per week. English, French, Mathematics, and History at all times.

46

Small Pets—Special Department (permit is necessary): Good treatment available (vermin excepted).

Mealtimes: breakfast, every day except Sunday and Bank Holidays, 9 A.M. Sundays and Bank Holidays, 11:30 A.M. approximately.

Lunch: (not very big): 1:15 P.M. to 1:45 P.M.

Dinner: cold and/or hot: no fixed time (depending on the news broadcast).

Duties: Residents must always be ready to help with office work.

Baths: The washtub is available for all residents from 9 A.M. on Sundays. The W.C. kitchen, private office or main office, whichever preferred, are available.

Alcoholic Beverages: only with doctor's prescription.

END

Yours, Anne

Thursday, 19 November, 1942

Dear Kitty,

Dussel is a very nice man, just as we had all imagined. Of course he thought it was all right to share my little room.

Quite honestly I'm not so keen that a stranger should use my things, but one must be prepared to make some sacrifices for a good cause, so I shall make my little offering with a good will. "If we can save someone, then everything else is of secondary importance," says Daddy, and he's absolutely right.

The first day that Dussel was here, he immediately asked me all sorts of questions: When does the charwoman come? When can one use the bathroom? When is one allowed to use the lavatory? You may laugh, but these things are not so simple in a hiding place. During the day we mustn't make any noise that might be heard downstairs; and if there is some stranger—such as the charwoman for example—then we have to be extra careful. I explained all this carefully to Dussel. But one thing amazed me: he is very slow on the uptake. He asks

47

everything twice over and still doesn't seem to remember. Perhaps that will wear off in time, and it's only that he's thoroughly upset by the sudden change.

Apart from that, all goes well. Dussel has told us a lot about the outside world, which we have missed for so long now. He had very sad news. Countless friends and acquaintances have gone to a terrible fate. Evening after evening the green and gray army lorries trundle past. The Germans ring at every front door to inquire if there are any Jews living in the house. If there are, then the whole family has to go at once. If they don't find any, they go on to the next house. No one has a chance of evading them unless one goes into hiding. Often they go around with lists, and only ring when they know they can get a good haul. Sometimes they let them off for cash—so much per head. It seems like the slave hunts of olden times. But it's certainly no joke; it's much too tragic for that. In the evenings when it's dark, I often see rows of good, innocent people accompanied by crying children, walking on and on, in charge of a couple of these chaps, bullied and knocked about until they almost drop. No one is spared—old people, babies, expectant mothers, the sick—each and all join in the march of death.

How fortunate we are here, so well cared for and undisturbed. We wouldn't have to worry about all this misery were it not that we are so anxious about all those dear to us whom we can no longer help.

I feel wicked sleeping in a warm bed, while my dearest friends have been knocked down or have fallen into a gutter somewhere out in the cold night. I get frightened when I think of close friends who have now been delivered into the hands of the cruelest brutes that walk the earth. And all because they are Jews!

Yours, Anne

Friday, 20 November, 1942

Dear Kitty,

None of us really knows how to take it all. The news about the Jews had not really penetrated through to us until now, and we thought it best to remain as cheerful as possible. Every now and then, when Miep lets out something about what has happened to a friend, Mummy and Mrs. Van Daan always begin to cry, so Miep thinks it better not to tell us any more. But Dussel was immediately plied with questions from all sides, and the stories he told us were so gruesome and dreadful that one can't get them out of one's mind.

Yet we shall have our jokes and tease each other, when these horrors have faded a bit in our minds. It won't do us any good, or help those outside, to go on being as gloomy as we are at the moment. And what would be the object of making our "Secret Annexe" into a "Secret Annexe of Gloom"? Must I keep thinking about those other people, whatever I am doing? And if I want to laugh about something, should I stop myself quickly and feel ashamed that I am cheerful? Ought I then to cry the whole day long? No, that I can't do. Besides, in time this gloom will wear off.

Added to this misery there is another, but of a purely personal kind; and it pales into insignificance beside all the wretchedness I've just told you about. Still, I can't refrain from telling you that lately I have begun to feel deserted. I am surrounded by too great a void. I never used to feel like this, my fun and amusements, and my girl friends, completely filled my thoughts. Now I either think about unhappy things, or about myself. And at long last I have made the discovery that Daddy, although he's such a darling, still cannot take the place of my entire little world of bygone days. But why do I bother you with such foolish things? I'm very ungrateful, Kitty; I know that. But it often makes my head swim if I'm jumped

49

upon too much, and then on top of that have to think about all those other miseries!

Yours, Anne

Saturday, 28 November, 1942

Dear Kitty,

We have used too much electricity, more than our ration. Result: the utmost economy and the prospect of having it cut off. No light for a fortnight; a pleasant thought, that, but who knows, perhaps it won't happen after all! It's too dark to read in the afternoons after four or half past. We pass the time in all sorts of crazy ways: asking riddles, physical training in the dark, talking English and French, criticizing books. But it all begins to pall in the end. Yesterday evening I discovered something new: to peer through a powerful pair of field glasses into the lighted rooms of the houses at the back. In the daytime we can't allow even as much as a centimeter's chink to appear between our curtains, but it can't do any harm after dark. I never knew before that neighbors could be such interesting people. At any rate, ours are. I found one couple having a meal, one family was in the act of taking a home movie; and the dentist opposite was just attending to an old lady, who was awfully scared.

It was always said about Mr. Dussel that he could get on wonderfully with children and that he loved them all. Now he shows himself in his true colors; a stodgy, old-fashioned disciplinarian, and preacher of long, drawn-out sermons on manners.

As I have unusual good fortune (!) to share my bed-room—alas, a small one—with His Lordship, and as I'm generally considered to be the most badly behaved of the three young people, I have a lot to put up with and have to pretend to be deaf in order to escape the old, much-repeated tickings-off and warnings. All this wouldn't be too bad, if he wasn't such a frightful sneak and he didn't pick on Mummy of all people to sneak to every time. When I've already just had a dose from him,

50

Mummy goes over it all again, so I get a gale aft as well as fore. Then, if I'm really lucky, I'm called on to give an account of myself to Mrs. Van Daan and then I get a veritable hurricane!

Honestly, you needn't think it's easy to be the "badly brought-up" central figure of a hypercritical family in hiding. When I lie in bed at night and think over the many sins and shortcomings attributed to me, I get so confused by it all that I either laugh or cry: it depends what sort of mood I am in.

Then I fall asleep with a stupid feeling of wishing to be different from what I am or from what I want to be; perhaps to behave differently from the way I want to behave, or do behave. Oh, heavens above, now I'm getting you in a muddle too. Forgive me, but I don't like crossing things out, and in these days of paper shortage we are not allowed to throw paper away. Therefore I can only advise you not to read the last sentence again, and certainly not to try to understand it, because you won't succeed anyhow!

Yours, Anne

Monday, 7 December, 1942

Dear Kitty,

Chanuka and St. Nicholas Day came almost together this year—just one day's difference. We didn't make much fuss about Chanuka: we just gave each other a few little presents and then we had the candles. Because of the shortage of candles we only had them alight for ten minutes, but it is all right as long as you have the song. Mr. Van Daan has made a wooden candlestick, so that too was all properly arranged.

Saturday, the evening of St. Nicholas Day, was much more fun. Miep and Elli had made us very inquisitive by whispering all the time with Daddy, so naturally we guessed that something was on.

And so it was. At eight o'clock we all filed down the wooden staircase through the passage in pitch-darkness (it made me shudder and wish that I was safely upstairs again) into the little dark room. There, as there are no windows, we were able to turn on a light. When that was done, Daddy opened the big cupboard. "Oh! how lovely," we all cried. A large basket decorated with St. Nicholas paper stood in the corner and on top there was a mask of Black Peter.

We quickly took the basket upstairs with us. There was a nice little present for everyone, with a suitable poem attached. I got a doll, whose skirt is a bag for odds and ends; Daddy got book ends, and so on. In any case it was a nice idea and as none of us had ever celebrated St. Nicholas, it was a good way of starting.

Yours, Anne

Thursday, 10 December, 1942

Dear Kitty,

Mr. Van Daan used to be in the meat, sausage, and spice business. It was because of his knowledge of this trade that he was taken on in Daddy's business. Now he is showing the sausagy side of himself, which, for us, is by no means disagreeable.

We had ordered a lot of meat (under the counter, of course) for preserving in case we should come upon hard times. It was fun to watch, first the way the pieces of meat went through the mincer, two or three times, then how all the accompanying ingredients were mixed with the minced meat, and then how the intestine was filled by means of a spout, to make the sausages. We fried the sausage meat and ate it with sauerkraut for supper that evening, but the Gelderland sausages had to be thoroughly dried first, so we hung them over a stick tied to the ceiling with string. Everyone who came into the room began to laugh when they caught a glimpse of the row of sausages on show. They looked terribly funny!

The room was in a glorious mess. Mr. Van Daan was wearing one of his wife's aprons swathed round his substantial person (he looked fatter than he is!) and was busy with the meat. Hands smothered in blood, red face, and the soiled apron, made him look like a butcher. Mrs. Van Daan was trying to do everything at once, learning Dutch from a book, stirring the soup, watching the meat being done, sighing and complaining about her injured rib. That's what happens to elderly ladies (!) who do such idiotic exercises to reduce their large behinds!

Dussel had inflammation in one eye and was bathing it with camomile tea by the fire. Pim, who was sitting on a chair in a beam of sunlight that shone through the window, kept being pushed from one side to the other. In addition, I think his rheumatism was bothering him, because he sat rather hunched up with a miserable look on his face, watching Mr. Van Daan at work. He looked exactly like some shriveled-up old man from an old people's home. Peter was doing acrobatics round the room with his cat. Mummy, Margot, and I were peeling potatoes; and, of course, all of us were doing everything wrong because we were so busy watching Mr. Van Daan.

Dussel has opened his dental practice. For the fun of it, I must tell you about his first patient. Mummy was ironing; and Mrs. Van Daan was the first to face the ordeal. She went and sat on a chair in the middle of the room. Dussel began to unpack his case in an awfully important way, asked for some eau de cologne as a disinfectant and vaseline to take the place of wax.

He looked in Mrs. Van Daan's mouth and found two teeth which, when touched, just made her crumple up as if she was going to pass out, uttering incoherent cries of pain. After a lengthy examination (in Mrs. Van Daan's case, lasting in actual fact not more than two minutes) Dussel began to scrape away at one of the holes. But, no fear—it was out of the question—the patient flung her arms and legs about wildly in all directions until at one point Dussel let go of the scraper—that remained stuck in Mrs. Van Daan's tooth.

Then the fat was really in the fire! She cried (as far as it was possible with such an instrument in one's mouth), tried to pull the thing out of her mouth, and only succeeded in pushing it further in. Mr. Dussel stood with his hands against his sides calmly watching the little comedy. The rest of the audience lost all control and roared with laughter. It was rotten of us, because I for one am quite sure that I should have screamed even louder. After much turning, kicking, screaming, and calling out, she got the instrument free at last and Mr. Dussel went on with his work, as if nothing had happened!

This he did so quickly that Mrs. Van Daan didn't have time to start any fresh tricks. But he'd never had so much help in all his life before. Two assistants are pretty useful: Van Daan and I performed our duties well. The whole scene looked like a picture from the Middle Ages entitled "A Quack at Work." In the meantime, however, the patient hadn't much patience; she had to keep an eye on "her" soup and "her" meal. One thing is certain. Mrs. Van Daan won't be in such a hurry to allow herself to be treated again!

Yours, Anne

Sunday, 13 December, 1942

Dear Kitty,

I'm sitting cozily in the main office, looking outside through a slit in the curtain. It is dusk but still just light enough to write to you.

It is a very queer sight, as I watch the people walking by; it looks just as if they are all in a terrible hurry and nearly trip over their own toes. With cyclists, now, one simply can't keep pace with their speed. I can't even see what sort of person is riding on the machine.

The people in this neighborhood don't look very attractive. The children especially are so dirty you wouldn't want to touch them with a barge pole. Real slum kids with running noses. I can hardly understand a word they say.

Yesterday afternoon Margot and I were having a bath here and I said, "Supposing we were to take the children who are walking past, one by one, hoist them up with a fishing rod, give them each a bath, wash and mend their clothes, and then let them go again, then . . ." Margot interrupted me, "By tomorrow they would look just as filthy and ragged as before."

But I'm just talking nonsense; besides, there are other things to see—cars, boats, and rain. I like particularly the screech of the trams as they go by.

There is no more variety in our thoughts than there is for ourselves. They go round and round like a roundabout—from Jews to food and from food to politics. By the way, talking of Jews, I saw two Jews through the curtain yesterday. I could hardly believe my eyes; it was a horrible feeling, just as if I'd betrayed them and was now watching them in their misery. There is a houseboat immediately opposite, where a bargeman lives with his family. He has a small yapping dog. We only know the little dog by his bark and his tail, which we can see when he runs round the deck. Ugh! Now it's started to rain and most of the people are hidden under umbrellas. I see nothing but raincoats and occasionally the back of someone's hat. Really I don't need to see more. I'm gradually getting to know all the women at a glance, blown out with potatoes, wearing a red or a green coat, troddendown heels and with a bag under their arms. Their faces either look grim or kind—depending on their husbands' dispositions.

Yours, Anne

Tuesday, 22 December, 1942

Dear Kitty,

The "Secret Annexe" has heard the joyful news that each person will receive an extra quarter of a pound of butter for Christmas. It says half a pound in the newspapers, but that's only for the lucky mortals who get their ration books from the government, not for Jews who have gone into hiding, who can only afford to buy four illegal ration books, instead of eight.

We are all going to bake something with our butter.

I made some biscuits and two cakes this morning. Everyone is very busy upstairs and Mummy has told me I must not go there to work or read, until the household jobs are done.

Mrs. Van Daan is in bed with her bruised rib, complains the whole day long, allows herself to be given fresh dressings all the time, and isn't satisfied with anything. I shall be glad when she's on her feet again and tidies up her own things, because I must say this for her: she's exceptionally industrious and tidy, all the while she is healthy in mind and body. She is cheerful too.

Just as if I didn't hear enough "ssh-ssh" during the day, for making too much noise, my gentleman bedroom companion now repeatedly calls out "ssh-ssh" to me at night too. According to him, I am not even allowed to turn over! I refuse to take the slightest notice of him, and shall go "ssh-ssh" back at him the next time.

He makes me furious, on Sundays especially, when he turns the light on early to do his exercises. It seems to take simply hours, while I, poor tormented creature, feel the chairs, which are placed at the head of my bed to lengthen it, slide backwards and forwards continually under my sleepy head. When he has ended with a couple of violent arm-waving exercises to loosen his muscles, His Lordship begins his toilet. His pants are hanging up, so to and fro he must go to collect them. But he forgets his tie, which is lying on the table. Therefore once more he pushes and bumps the chairs to get it.

But I won't bore you any longer on the subject of old men. It won't make things any better and all my plans of revenge (such as disconnecting the lamp, shutting the door, hiding his clothes) must be abandoned in order to keep the peace. Oh, I'm becoming so sensible! One must apply one's reason to everything here, learning to obey, to hold your tongue, to help, to be good, to give in, and I don't know what else. I'm afraid I shall use up all my brains too quickly, and I haven't got so very many. Then I shall not have any left for when the war is over.

Yours, Anne

Wednesday, 13 January, 1943

Dear Kitty,

Everything has upset me again this morning, so I wasn't able to finish a single thing properly.

It is terrible outside. Day and night more of those poor miserable people are being dragged off, with nothing but a rucksack and a little money. On the way they are deprived even of these possessions. Families are torn apart, the men, women, and children all being separated. Children coming home from school find that their parents have disappeared. Women return from shopping to find their homes shut up and their families gone.

The Dutch people are anxious too, their sons are being sent to Germany. Everyone is afraid.

And every night hundreds of planes fly over Holland and go to German towns, where the earth is so plowed up by their bombs, and every hour hundreds and thousands of people are killed in Russia and Africa. No one is able to keep out of it, the whole globe is waging war and although it is going better for the Allies, the end is not yet in sight.

And as for us, we are fortunate. Yes, we are luckier than millions of people. It is quiet and safe here, and we are, so to speak, living on capital. We are even so selfish as to talk about "after the war," brighten up at the thought of having new clothes and new shoes, whereas we really ought to save every penny, to help other people, and save what is left from the wreckage after the war.

The children here run about in just a thin blouse and clogs; no coat, no hat, no stockings, and no one helps them. Their tummies are empty, they chew an old carrot to stay the pangs, go from their cold homes out into the cold street and, when they get to school, find themselves in an even colder classroom. Yes, it has even got so bad in Holland that countless children stop the passers-by and beg for a piece of bread. I could go on for hours about

57

all the suffering the war has brought, but then I would only make myself more dejected. There is nothing we can do but wait as calmly as we can till the misery comes to an end. Jews and Christians wait, the whole earth waits; and there are many who wait for death.

Yours, Anne

Saturday, 30 January, 1943

Dear Kitty,

I'm boiling with rage, and yet I mustn't show it. I'd like to stamp my feet, scream, give Mummy a good shaking, cry, and I don't know what else, because of the horrible words, mocking looks, and accusations which are leveled at me repeatedly every day, and find their mark, like shafts from a tightly strung bow, and which are just as hard to draw from my body.

I would like to shout to Margot, Van Daan, Dussel—and Daddy too—"Leave me in peace, let me sleep one night at least without my pillow being wet with tears, my eyes burning and my head throbbing. Let me get away from it all, preferably away from the world!" But I can't do that, they mustn't know my despair, I couldn't bear their sympathy and their kindhearted jokes, it would only make me want to scream all the more. If I talk, everyone thinks I'm showing off; when I'm silent they think I'm ridiculous; rude if I answer, sly if I get a good idea, lazy if I'm tired, selfish if I eat a mouthful more than I should, stupid, cowardly, crafty, etc., etc. The whole day long I hear nothing else but that I am an insufferable baby, and although I laugh about it and pretend not to take any notice, I *do* mind. I would like to ask God to give me a different nature, so that I didn't put everyone's back up. But that can't be done. I've got the nature that has been given to me and I'm sure it can't be bad. I do my very best to please everybody, far more than they'd ever guess. I try to laugh it all off, because I don't want to let them see my trouble. More than once, after a whole string of undeserved rebukes, I have flared up at Mummy:

"I don't care what you say anyhow. Leave me alone: I'm a hopeless case anyway." Naturally, I was then told I was rude and was virtually ignored for two days; and then, all at once, it was quite forgotten, and I was treated like everyone else again. It is impossible for me to be all sugar one day and spit venom the next. I'd rather choose the golden mean (which is not so golden), keep my thoughts to myself, and try for *once* to be just as disdainful to them as they are to me. Oh, if only I could!

Yours, Anne

Friday, 5 February, 1943

Dear Kitty,

Although I haven't written anything about our rows for a long time, there still isn't any change. The discord, long accepted by us, struck Mr. Dussel as a calamity at first. But he is getting used to it now and tries not to think about it. Margot and Peter aren't a bit what you would call "young," they are both so staid and quiet. I show up terribly against them and am always hearing, "You don't find Margot and Peter doing that—why don't you follow their example?" I simply loathe it. I might tell you I don't want to be in the least like Margot. She is much too soft and passive for my liking and allows everyone to talk her around, and gives in about everything. I want to be a stronger character! But I keep such ideas to myself: they would only laugh at me, if I came along with this as an explanation of my attitude. The atmosphere at table is usually strained, though luckily the outbursts are sometimes checked by "the soup eaters"! The "soup eaters" are the people from the office who come in and are served with a cup of soup. This afternoon Mr. Van Daan was talking about Margot eating so little again. "I suppose you do it to keep slim," he added, teasing her. Mummy, who always defends Margot, said loudly: "I can't bear your stupid chatter any longer." Mr. Van Daan turned scarlet, looked straight in front of him, and said nothing. We often laugh about things; just recently Mrs. Van

Daan came out with some perfect nonsense. She was recalling the past, how well she and her father got on together and what a flirt she was. "And do you know," she went on, "if a man gets a bit aggressive, my father used to say, then you must say to him, 'Mr. So and So, remember I am a lady!' and he will know what you mean." We thought that was a good joke and burst out laughing.

Peter too, although usually so quiet, sometimes gives cause for mirth. He is blessed with a passion for foreign words, although he does not always know their meaning. One afternoon we couldn't go to the lavatory because there were visitors in the office; however, Peter had to pay an urgent call. So he didn't pull the plug. He put a notice upon the lavatory door to warn us, with "S.V.P. gas" on it. Of course he meant to put "Beware of gas"; but he thought the other looked more genteel. He hadn't got the faintest notion it meant "if you please."

Yours, Anne

Saturday, 27 February, 1943

Dear Kitty,

Pim is expecting the invasion any day. Churchill has had pneumonia, but is improving slowly. The freedom-loving Gandhi of India is holding his umpteenth fast. Mrs. Van Daan claims to be fatalistic. But who is the most scared when the guns go off? No one else but Petronella.

Henk brought a copy of the bishop's letter to church-goers for us to read. It was very fine and inspiring. "Do not rest, people of the Netherlands, everyone is fighting with his own weapons to free the country, the people, and their religion." "Give help, be generous, and do not dismay!" is what they cry from the pulpit, just like that. Will it help? It won't help the people of our religion.

You'd never guess what has happened to us now. The owner of these premises has sold the house without informing Kraler and Koophuis. One morning the new owner arrived with an architect to have a look at the house. Luckily, Mr. Koophuis was present and showed the gentlemen everything except the "Secret Annexe." He professed to have forgotten the key of the communicating door. The new owner didn't question any further. It will be all right as long as he doesn't come back and want to see the "Secret Annexe," because then it won't look too good for us.

Daddy has emptied a card index box for Margot and me, and put cards in it. It is to be a book card system; then we both write down which books we have read, who they are by, etc. I have procured another little notebook for foreign words.

Lately Mummy and I have been getting on better together, but we still *never* confide in each other. Margot is more catty than ever and Daddy has got something he is keeping to himself, but he remains the same darling.

New butter and margarine rationing at table! Each person has their little bit of fat put on their plate. In my opinion the Van Daans don't divide it at all fairly. However, my parents are much too afraid of a row to say anything about it. Pity, I think you should always give people like them tit for tat.

Yours, Anne

Wednesday, 10 March, 1943

Dear Kitty,

We had a short circuit last evening, and on top of that the guns kept banging away all the time. I still haven't got over my fear of everything connected with shooting and planes, and I creep into Daddy's bed nearly every night for comfort. I know it's very childish but you don't know what it is like. The A.A. guns roar so loudly that you can't hear yourself speak. Mrs. Van Daan, the fatalist, was nearly crying, and said in a very timid little voice, "Oh, it is so unpleasant! Oh, they are shooting so hard," by which she really means "I'm so frightened."

It didn't seem nearly so bad by candlelight as in the dark. I was shivering, just as if I had a temperature, and begged Daddy to light the candle again. He was relentless, the light remained off. Suddenly there was a burst of machine-gun fire, and that is ten times worse than guns. Mummy jumped out of bed and, to Pim's annoyance, lit the candle. When he complained her answer was firm: "After all, Anne's not exactly a veteran soldier." And that was the end of it.

Have I already told you about Mrs. Van Daan's other fears? I don't think so. If I am to keep you informed of all that happens in the "Secret Annexe," you must know about this too. One night Mrs. Van Daan thought she heard burglars in the attic; she heard loud footsteps and was so frightened that she woke her husband. Just at that moment the burglars disappeared and the only sounds that Mr. Van Daan could hear were the heartbeats of the frightened fatalist herself. "Oh, Putti [Mr. Van Daan's nickname], they are sure to have taken the sausages and all our peas and beans. And Peter, I wonder if he is still safely in bed?" "They certainly won't have stolen Peter. Listen, don't worry and let me go to sleep." But nothing came of that. A few nights after that the whole Van Daan family was woken by ghostly sounds. Peter went up to the attic with a torch—and scamper—scamper! What do you think it was running away? A swarm of enormous rats! When we knew who the thieves were, we let Mouschi sleep in the attic and the uninvited guests didn't come back again; at least not during the night.

Peter went up to the loft a couple of evenings ago to fetch some old newspapers. He had to hold the trap door firmly to get down the steps. He put his hand down without looking . . . and went tumbling down the ladder from the sudden shock and pain. Without knowing it he had put his hand on a large rat, and it had bitten him hard. By the time he reached us, as white as a sheet and with his knees knocking, the blood had soaked through his pajamas. And no wonder; it's not very pleasant to stroke a large rat; and to get bitten into the bargain is really dreadful.

Yours, Anne

Friday, 12 March, 1943

Dear Kitty,

May I introduce someone to you: Mama Frank, champion of youth! Extra butter for the young; the problems of modern youth; Mummy defends youth in everything and after a certain amount of squabbling she always gets her way. A bottle of preserved sole has gone bad; gala dinner for Mouschi and Boche. You haven't met Boche yet, although she was here before we went into hiding. She is the warehouse and office cat and keeps down the rats in the storerooms. Her odd political name requires an explanation. For some time the firm had two cats; one for the warehouse and one for the attic. Now it occasionally happened that the two cats met; and the result was always a terrific fight. The aggressor was always the warehouse cat; yet it was always the attic cat who managed to win—just like among nations. So the storehouse cat was named the German or "Boche" and the attic cat the English or "Tommy." Tommy was got rid of later; we are all entertained by Boche when we go downstairs.

We have eaten so many kidney beans and haricot beans that I can't bear the sight of them any more. The mere thought of them makes me feel quite sick. Bread is no longer served in the evenings now. Daddy has just said that he doesn't feel in a good mood. His eyes look so sad again—poor soul!

I can't drag myself away from a book called *The Knock at the Door* by Ina Boudier-Bakker. The story of the family is exceptionally well written. Apart from that, it is about war, writers, the emancipation of women; and quite honestly I'm not awfully interested.

Horrible air raids on Germany. Mr. Van Daan is in a bad mood; the cause—cigarette shortage. Discussions over the question of whether we should, or should not, use our canned vegetables ended in our favor.

I can't get into a single pair of shoes any more, except ski boots, which are not much use about the house. A pair of rush sandals costing 6.50 florins lasted me just one week, after which they were out of action. Perhaps Miep will scrounge something under the counter. I must cut Daddy's hair. Pim maintains that he will never have another barber after the war, as I do the job so well. If only I didn't snip his ear so often!

Yours, Anne

Thursday, 18 March, 1943

Dear Kitty,

Turkey is in the war. Great excitement. Waiting in suspense for the news.

Yours, Anne

Friday, 19 March, 1943

Dear Kitty,

An hour later joy was followed by disappointment. Turkey is not in the war yet. It was only a cabinet minister talking about them soon giving up their neutrality. A newspaper in the Dam[1] was crying, "Turkey on England's side." The newspapers were torn out of his hands. This is how the joyful news reached us too; 500- and 1000-guilder notes have been declared no longer valid. It is a trap for black marketeers and suchlike, but even for people who have got other kinds of "black" money, and for people in hiding. If you wish to hand in a 1000-guilder note you must be able to declare, and prove, exactly how you got it. They may still be used to pay taxes, but only until next week. Dussel has received an old-fashioned foot-operated dentist's drill, I expect he'll soon give me a thorough check-over. The "Führer aller Germanen" has been talking to wounded soldiers. Listening-in to it was

[1] A square in front of the Royal Palace.

64

pitiful. Question and answer went something like this:

"My name is Heinrich Scheppel."

"Wounded where?"

"Near Stalingrad."

"What kind of wound?"

"Two feet frozen off and a broken joint in the left arm."

This is exactly what the frightful puppet show on the radio was like. The wounded seemed to be proud of their wounds—the more the better. One of them felt so moved at being able to shake hands with the Führer (that is, if he still had a hand!) that he could hardly get the words out of his mouth.

Yours, Anne

Thursday, 25 March, 1943

Dear Kitty,

Yesterday Mummy, Daddy, Margot, and I were sitting pleasantly together when suddenly Peter came in and whispered something in Daddy's ear. I heard something about "a barrel fallen over in the warehouse" and "someone fumbling about at the door." Margot had heard it too; but when Daddy and Peter went off immediately, she tried to calm me down a bit, because I was naturally as white as a sheet and very jittery.

The three of us waited in suspense. A minute or two later Mrs. Van Daan came upstairs; she'd been listening to the wireless in the private office. She told us that Pim had asked her to turn off the wireless and go softly upstairs. But you know what that's like, if you want to be extra quiet, then each step of the old stairs creaks twice as loudly. Five minutes later Pim and Peter appeared again, white to the roots of their hair, and told us their experience.

They had hidden themselves under the stairs and waited, with no result at first. But suddenly, yes, I must tell you, they heard two loud bumps, just as if two doors were banged here in the house. Pim was upstairs in one leap. Peter warned Dussel first, who finally landed upstairs with a lot of fuss and noise. Then we all went up in stockinged feet to the Van Daans on the next floor. Mr. Van Daan had a bad cold and had already gone to bed, so we all drew up closely around his bed and whispered our suspicions to him.

Each time Mr. Van Daan coughed loudly, Mrs. Van Daan and I were so scared that we thought we were going to have a fit. That went on until one of us got the bright idea of giving him some codeine, which soothed the cough at once. Again we waited and waited, but we heard no more and finally we all came to the conclusion that the thieves had taken to their heels when they heard footsteps in the house, which was otherwise so silent.

Now it was unfortunate that the wireless downstairs was still tuned to England, and that the chairs were neatly arranged round it. If the door had been forced, and the air-raid wardens had noticed and warned the police, then the results might have been very unpleasant. So Mr. Van Daan got up and put on his coat and hat and followed Daddy cautiously downstairs, Peter took up the rear, armed with a large hammer in case of emergencies. The ladies upstairs (including Margot and me) waited in suspense, until the gentlemen reappeared five minutes later and told us that all was quiet in the house.

We arranged that we would not draw any water or pull the plug in the lavatory. But as the excitement had affected most of our tummies, you can imagine what the atmosphere was like when we had each paid a visit in succession.

When something like that happens, heaps of other things seem to come at the same time, as now. Number One was that the clock at the Westertoren, which I always find so reassuring, did not strike. Number Two was that Mr. Vossen having left earlier than usual the previous evening, we didn't know definitely whether Elli had been able to get hold of the key, and had perhaps forgotten to shut the door. It was still evening and we were still in a state of uncertainty, although we certainly did feel a bit reassured by the fact that from about eight o'clock, when the burglar had alarmed the house, until half past ten we had not heard a sound. On further reflection it also seemed very unlikely to us that a thief would have forced open a door so early in the evening, while there were still people about in the street. Moreover, one of us got the idea that it was possible that the caretaker of the warehouse next door was still at work since, in the excitement, and with the thin walls, one can easily make a mistake, and what's more, one's imagination can play a big part at such critical moments.

So we all went to bed; but none of us could get to sleep. Daddy as well as Mummy and Mr. Dussel were awake, and without much exaggeration I can say that I hardly slept a wink. This morning the men went downstairs to see whether the outside door was still shut, and everything turned out to be quite safe. We gave everyone a detailed description of the nerve-racking event. They all made fun of it, but it is easy to laugh at such things afterwards. Elli was the only one who took us seriously.

Yours, Anne

Saturday, 27 March, 1943

Dear Kitty,

We have finished our shorthand course; now we are beginning to practice speed. Aren't we getting clever? I must tell you more about my time-killing subjects (I call them such, because we have got nothing else to do but make the days go by as quickly as possible, so that the end of our time here comes more quickly); I'm mad on Mythology and especially the Gods of Greece and Rome. They think here that it is just a passing craze, they've never heard of an adolescent kid of my age being interested in Mythology. Well, then, I shall be the first!

Mr. Van Daan has a cold, or rather he has a little tickle in his throat. He makes a tremendous fuss about it. Gargling with camomile tea, painting his throat with tincture of myrrh, rubbing eucalyptus all over his chest, nose, teeth, and tongue; and then getting into an evil mood on top of it all.

Rauter, one of the German big shots, has made a speech. "All Jews must be out of the German-occupied countries before July 1. Between April 1 and May 1 the province of Utrecht must be cleaned out [as if the Jews were cockroaches]. Between May 1 and June 1 the provinces of North and South Holland." These wretched people are sent to filthy slaughterhouses like a herd of sick, neglected cattle. But I won't talk about it, I only get nightmares from such thoughts.

One good little piece of news is that the German department of the Labor Exchange has been set on fire by saboteurs. A few days after, the Registrar's Office went the same way. Men in German police uniforms gagged the guards and managed to destroy important papers.

Yours, Anne

Thursday, 1 April, 1943

Dear Kitty,

I'm really not April-fooling (see the date), but the opposite; today I can easily quote the saying: "Misfortunes never come singly." To begin with, Mr. Koophuis, the one who always cheers us up, has had hemorrhage of the stomach and has got to stay in bed for at least three weeks. Secondly, Elli has flu. Thirdly, Mr. Vossen is going to the hospital next week. He has probably got an abdominal ulcer. And fourthly, some important business conferences, the main points of which Daddy had discussed in detail with Mr. Koophuis, were due to be held, but now there isn't time to explain everything thoroughly to Mr. Kraler.

The gentlemen who had been expected duly arrived; even before they came Daddy was trembling with anxiety as to how the talks would go. "If only I could be there, if only I was downstairs" he cried. "Why don't you go and lie with one ear pressed against the floor, then you'll be able to hear everything." Daddy's face cleared, and at half past ten yesterday morning Margot and Pim (two ears are better than one!) took up their positions on the floor.

The talks were not finished in the morning, but by the afternoon Daddy was not in a fit state to continue the listening campaign. He was half paralyzed from remaining in so unusual and uncomfortable a position. I took his place at half past two, as soon as we heard voices in the passage. Margot kept me company. The talk at times was so long-winded and boring that quite suddenly I fell asleep on the cold hard linoleum floor. Margot did not dare to touch me for fear they might hear us, and talking was out of the question. I slept for a good half hour and then woke with a shock, having forgotten every word of the important discussions. Luckily Margot had paid more attention.

Yours, Anne

Friday, 2 April, 1943

Dear Kitty,

Oh dear: I've got another terrible black mark against my name. I was lying in bed yesterday evening waiting for Daddy to come and say my prayers with me, and wish me good night, when Mummy came into my room, sat on my bed, and asked very nicely, "Anne, Daddy can't come yet, shall I say your prayers with you tonight?" "No, Mummy," I answered.

Mummy got up, paused by my bed for a moment, and walked slowly towards the door. Suddenly she turned around, and with a distorted look on her face said, "I don't want to be cross, love cannot be forced." There were tears in her eyes as she left the room.

I lay still in bed, feeling at once that I had been horrible to push her away so rudely. But I knew too that I couldn't have answered differently. It simply wouldn't work. I felt sorry for Mummy; very, very sorry, because I had seen for the first time in my life that she minds my coldness. I saw the look of sorrow on her face when she spoke of love not being forced. It is hard to speak the truth, and yet it is the truth: she herself has pushed me away, her tactless remarks and her crude jokes, which I don't find at all funny, have now made me insensitive to any love from her side. Just as I shrink at her hard words, so did her heart when she realized that the love between us was gone. She cried half the night and hardly slept at all. Daddy doesn't look at me and if he does for a second, then I read in his eyes the words: "How can you be so unkind, how can you bring yourself to cause your mother such sorrow?"

They expect me to apologize; but this is something I can't apologize for because I spoke the truth and Mummy will have to know it sooner or later anyway. I seem, and indeed am, indifferent both to Mummy's tears and Daddy's looks, because for the first time they are both aware of something which I have always felt. I can only feel sorry for Mummy, who has now had to discover that I have adopted her own attitude. For myself, I remain silent and aloof; and I shall not shrink from the truth any longer, because the longer it is put off, the more difficult it will be for them when they do hear it.

Yours, Anne

Tuesday, 27 April, 1943

Dear Kitty,

Such quarrels that the whole house thunders! Mummy and I, the Van Daans and Daddy, Mummy and Mrs. Van Daan, everyone is angry with everyone else. Nice atmosphere, isn't it? Anne's usual list of failings has been brought out again and fully ventilated.

Mr. Vossen is already in the Binnengasthuis hospital. Mr. Koophuis is up again, the hemorrhage having stopped sooner than usual. He told us that the Registrar's Office received additional damage from the Fire Service who, instead of just quenching the flames, soaked the whole place with water. I'm glad!

The Carlton Hotel is smashed to bits. Two British planes loaded with incendiary bombs fell right on top of the "Offiziersheim." [1] The whole Vijzelstraat-Singel corner

---

[1] German Officers' Club.

is burned down. The air raids on German towns are growing in strength every day. We don't have a single quiet night. I've got dark rings under my eyes from lack of sleep. Our food is miserable. Dry bread and coffee substitute for breakfast. Dinner: spinach or lettuce for a fortnight on end. Potatoes twenty centimeters long and tasting sweet and rotten. Whoever wants to follow a slimming course should stay in the "Secret Annexe"! They complain bitterly upstairs, but we don't regard it as such a tragedy. All the men who fought in 1940 or were mobilized have been called up to work for "der Führer" as prisoners of war. Suppose they're doing that as a precaution against invasion.

Yours, Anne

Saturday, 1 May, 1943

Dear Kitty,

If I just think of how we live here, I usually come to the conclusion that it is a paradise compared with how other Jews who are not in hiding must be living. Even so, later on, when everything is normal again, I shall be amazed to think that we, who were so spick and span at home, should have sunk to such a low level. By this I mean that our manners have declined. For instance, ever since we have been here, we have had one oilcloth on our table which, owing to so much use, is not one of the cleanest. Admittedly I often try to clean it with a dirty dishcloth, which is more hole than cloth. The table doesn't do us much credit either, in spite of hard scrubbing. The Van Daans have been sleeping on the same flannelette sheet the whole winter; one can't wash it here because the soap powder we get on the ration isn't sufficient, and besides it's not good enough. Daddy goes about in frayed trousers and his tie is beginning to show signs of wear too. Mummy's corsets have split today and are too old to be repaired, while Margot goes about in a brassiere two sizes too small for her.

Mummy and Margot have managed the whole winter with three vests between them, and mine are so small that they don't even reach my tummy.

Certainly, these are all things which can be overcome. Still, I sometimes realize with a shock: "How are we, now going about in worn-out things, from my pants down to Daddy's shaving brush, ever going to get back to our prewar standards?"

They were banging away so much last night that four times I gathered all my belongings together. Today I have packed a suitcase with the most necessary things for an escape. But Mummy quite rightly says: "Where will you escape to?" The whole of Holland is being punished for the strikes which have been going on in many parts of the country. Therefore a state of siege has been declared and everyone gets one butter coupon less. What naughty little children!

Yours, Anne

Tuesday, 18 May, 1943

Dear Kitty,

I witnessed a terrific air battle between German and British planes. Unfortunately a couple of the Allies had to jump from burning machines. Our milkman, who lives in Halfweg, saw four Canadians sitting by the roadside, one of them spoke fluent Dutch. He asked the milkman to give him a light for his cigarette and told him that the crew had consisted of six men. The pilot was burned to death, and their fifth man had hidden himself somewhere. The German police came and fetched the four perfectly fit men. I wonder how they managed to have such clear brains after that terrifying parachute trip.

Although it is fairly warm, we have to light our fires every other day, in order to burn vegetable peelings and refuse. We can't put anything in the garbage pails, because we must always think of the warehouse boy. How easily one could be betrayed by being a little careless!

All students who wish either to get their degrees this

year, or continue their studies, are compelled to sign that they are in sympathy with the Germans and approve of the New Order. Eighty per cent have refused to go against their consciences. Naturally they had to bear the consequences. All the students who do not sign have to go to a labor camp in Germany. What will be left of the youth of the country if they have all got to do hard labor in Germany? Mummy shut the window last night because of all the banging; I was in Pim's bed. Suddenly Mrs. Van Daan jumped out of bed above us, just as if Mouschi had bitten her. A loud clap followed immediately. It sounded just as if an incendiary bomb had fallen beside my bed. I shrieked out, "Light, light!" Pim turned on the lamp. I expected nothing less than to see the room ablaze within a few minutes. Nothing happened. We all hurried upstairs to see what was going on. Mr. and Mrs. Van Daan had seen a red glow through the open window. He thought that there was a fire in the neighborhood and she thought that our house had caught fire. When the clap came Mrs. Van Daan was already on her feet with her knees knocking. But nothing more happened and we all crept back into our beds.

Before a quarter of an hour had passed the shooting started up again. Mrs. Van Daan sat bolt upright at once and then went downstairs to Mr. Dussel's room, seeking there the rest which she could not find with her spouse. Dussel received her with the words, "Come into my bed, my child!" which sent us off into uncontrollable laughter. The gunfire troubled us no longer, our fears was banished!

Yours, Anne

Sunday, 13 June, 1943

Dear Kitty,

My birthday poem from Daddy is too good to keep from you. As Pim usually writes verses in German, Margot volunteered to translate it. Judge for yourself whether Margot didn't do it brilliantly. After the usual summary of the events of the year, this is how it ran:

73

Though youngest here, you are no longer small,
But life is very hard, since one and all
Aspire to be your teacher, thus and thus:
"We have experience, take a tip from us."
"We know because we did it long ago."
"Elders are always better, you must know."
At least that's been the rule since life began!
Our personal faults are much too small to scan
This makes it easier to criticize
The faults of others, which seem double size.
Please bear with us, your parents, for we try
To judge you fairly and with sympathy.
Correction sometimes take against your will,
Though it's like swallowing a bitter pill,
Which must be done if we're to keep the peace,
While time goes by till all this suffering cease.
You read and study nearly all the day,
Who might have lived in such a different way.
You're never bored and bring us all fresh air.
Your only moan is this: "What can I wear?
I have no knickers, all my clothes are small,
My vest might be a loincloth, that is all!
To put on shoes would mean to cut off toes,
Oh dear, I'm worried by so many woes!"

There was also a bit about food that Margot could not translate into rhyme, so I shall leave it out. Don't you think my birthday poem is good? I have been thoroughly spoiled in other ways and received a lot of lovely things. Among other things a fat book on my pet subject —the mythology of Greece and Rome. I can't complain of a shortage of sweets either—everyone has broken into their last reserves. As the Benjamin of the family in hiding, I am really more honored than I deserve.

Yours, Anne

Tuesday, 15 June, 1943

Dear Kitty,

Lots of things have happened, but I often think that all my uninteresting chatter bores you very much and that you are glad not to receive too many letters. So I shall give you the news in brief.

Mr. Vossen has not been operated on for his duodenal ulcer. When he was on the operating table and they had opened him up, the doctors saw that he had cancer, which was far too advanced to operate. So they stitched him up again, kept him in bed for three weeks and gave him good food, and finally sent him home again. I do pity him terribly and think it is rotten that we can't go out, otherwise I should certainly visit him frequently to cheer him up. It is a disaster for us that good old Vossen won't be able to keep us in touch with all that goes on, and all he hears in the warehouse. He was our best helper and security adviser; we miss him very much indeed.

It will be our turn to hand in our radio next month. Koophuis has a clandestine baby set at home that he will let us have to take the place of our big Phillips. It certainly is a shame to have to hand in our lovely set, but in a house where people are hiding, one daren't, under any circumstances, take wanton risks and so draw the attention of the authorities. We shall have the little radio upstairs. On top of hidden Jews, clandestine money and clandestine buying, we can add a clandestine radio. Everyone is trying to get hold of an old set and to hand that in instead of their "source of courage." It is really true that as the news from outside gets worse, so the radio with its miraculous voice helps us to keep up our morale and to say again, "Chins up, stick it out, better times will come!"

Yours, Anne

Sunday, 11 July, 1943

Dear Kitty,

To return to the "upbringing" theme for the umpteenth time, I must tell you that I really am trying to be helpful, friendly, and good, and to do everything I can so that the rain of rebukes dies down to a light summer drizzle. It is mighty difficult to be on such model behavior with people you can't bear, especially when you don't mean a word of it. But I do really see that I get on better by shamming a bit, instead of my old habit of telling everyone exactly what I think (although no one ever asked my opinion or attached the slightest importance to it).

I often lose my cue and simply can't swallow my rage at some injustice, so that for four long weeks we hear nothing but an everlasting chatter about the cheekiest and most shameless girl on earth. Don't you think that sometimes I've cause for complaint? It's a good thing I'm not a grouser, because then I might get sour and bad-tempered.

I have decided to let my shorthand go a bit, firstly to give me more time for my other subjects and secondly because of my eyes. I'm so miserable and wretched as I've become very shortsighted and ought to have had glasses for a long time already (phew, what an owl I shall look!) but you know, of course, in hiding one cannot. Yesterday everyone talked of nothing but Anne's eyes, because Mummy had suggested sending me to the oculist with Mrs. Koophuis. I shook in my shoes somewhat at this announcement, for it is no small thing to do. Go out of doors, imagine it, in the street—doesn't bear thinking about! I was petrified at first, then glad. But it doesn't go as easily as that, because all the people who would have to approve such a step could not reach an agreement quickly. All the difficulties and risks had first to be carefully weighed, although Miep would have gone with me straight away.

In the meantime I got out my gray coat from the cupboard, but it was so small that it looked as if it belonged to my younger sister.

I am really curious to know what will come of it all, but I don't think the plan will come off because the British have landed in Sicily now and Daddy is once again hoping for a "quick finish."

Elli gives Margot and me a lot of office work; it makes us both feel quite important and is a great help to her. Anyone can file away correspondence and write in the sales book, but we take special pains.

Miep is just like a pack mule, she fetches and carries

so much. Almost every day she manages to get hold of some vegetables for us and brings everything in shopping bags on her bicycle. We always long for Saturdays when our books come. Just like little children receiving a present.

Ordinary people simply don't know what books mean to us, shut up here. Reading, learning, and the radio are our amusements.

Yours, Anne

Tuesday, 13 July, 1943

Dear Kitty,

Yesterday afternoon, with Daddy's permission, I asked Dussel whether he would please be so good (being really very polite) as to allow me to use the little table in our room twice a week in the afternoons, from four o'clock till half past five. I sit there every day from half past two till four, while Dussel sleeps, but otherwise the room plus table are out of bounds. Inside, in our common room, there is much too much going on; it is impossible to work there, and besides, Daddy likes to sit at the writing table and work too sometimes.

So it was quite a reasonable request, and the question was put very politely. Now honestly what do you think the very learned Dussel replied: "No." Just plain "No!" I was indignant and refused to be put off like that, so I asked him the reason for his "No." But I was sent away with a flea in my ear. This was the barrage which followed:

"I have to work too, and if I can't work in the afternoons, then there is no time left for me at all. I must finish my task, otherwise I've started it all for nothing. Anyway, you don't work seriously at anything. Your mythology, now just what kind of work is that; knitting and reading are not work either. I am at the table and shall stay there."

My reply was:

"Mr. Dussel, I do work seriously and there is nowhere else for me to work in the afternoons. I beg of you to kindly reconsider my request!"

With these words the offended Anne turned her back on the very learned doctor, ignoring him completely. I was seething with rage, and thought Dussel frightfully rude (which he certainly was) and myself very friendly. In the evening when I could get hold of Pim, I told him how it had gone off and discussed what I should do next, because I was not going to give in, and preferred to clear it up myself. Pim told me how I ought to tackle the problem, but warned me that it would be better to leave it till the next day, as I was so het up. I let this advice go to the winds, and waited for Dussel after the dishes were done. Pim sat in the room next to us, which had a calming influence on me. I began: "Mr. Dussel, I don't suppose you see any point in discussing the matter any more, but I must ask you to do so." Dussel then remarked with his sweetest smile: "I am always, and at all times, prepared to discuss this matter, but it has already been settled."

I went on talking, though continually interrupted by Dussel. "When you first came here we arranged that this room should be for both of us; if we were to divide it fairly, you would have the morning and I all the afternoon! But I don't even ask that much, and I think that my two afternoons are really perfectly reasonable." At this Dussel jumped up as if someone had stuck a needle into him. "You can't talk about your rights here at all. And where am I to go, then? I shall ask Mr. Van Daan whether he will build a little compartment in the attic, then I can go and sit there. I simply can't work anywhere. With you one always gets trouble. If your sister Margot, who after all has more reason to ask such a thing, would have come to me with the same questions, I should not think of refusing, but you . . ." Then followed the business about the mythology and the knitting, and Anne was insulted again. However, she did not show it and let Dussel finish speaking: "But you, one simply can't talk to you. You are so outrageously selfish, as long as you can get what you want, you don't mind pushing everyone else to one side, I've never seen such a child. But after all, I suppose I shall be obliged to give you your own way, because otherwise I shall be told later on that Anne Frank failed her exam because Mr. Dussel would not give up the table for her."

It went on and on and finally it was such a torrent I could hardly keep pace with it. At one moment I thought, "In a minute I'll give him such a smack in the face that he'll fly up to the ceiling together with his lies," but the next moment I said to myself, "Keep calm! Such a fellow isn't worth getting worked up about."

After giving final vent to his fury, Master Dussel left the room with an expression of mixed wrath and triumph, his coat stuffed with food. I dashed to Daddy and told him all that he had not already heard of the story. Pim decided to talk to Dussel the same evening, which he did. They talked for over half an hour. The theme of the conversation was something like this: first of all they talked about whether Anne should sit at the table, yes or no. Daddy said that he and Dussel had already discussed the subject once before, when he had professed to agree with Dussel, in order not to put him in the wrong in front of the young. But Daddy had not thought it fair then. Dussel thought that I should not speak as if he was an intruder who tried to monopolize everything, but Daddy stuck up for me firmly over that, because he had heard for himself that I had not breathed a word of such a thing.

To and fro it went, Daddy defending my selfishness and my "trifling" work, Dussel grumbling continually.

Finally, Dussel had to give in after all, and I had the opportunity of working undisturbed until five o'clock for two afternoons a week. Dussel looked down his nose very much, didn't speak to me for two days and still had to go and sit at the table from five till half past—frightfully childish.

A person of fifty-four who is still so pedantic and small-minded must be so by nature, and will never improve.

Yours, Anne

Friday, 16 July, 1943

Dear Kitty,

Burglars again, but real this time! This morning Peter went to the warehouse at seven o'clock as usual, and at once noticed that both the warehouse door and the door opening on to the street were ajar. He told Pim, who tuned the radio in the private office to Germany and locked the door. Then they went upstairs together.

The standing orders for such times were observed as usual: no taps to be turned on; therefore, no washing, silence, everything to be finished by eight o'clock and no lavatory. We were all very glad that we had slept so well and not heard anything. Not until half past eleven did we learn from Mr. Koophuis that the burglars had pushed in the outer door with a crowbar and had forced the warehouse door. However, they did not find much to steal, so they tried their luck upstairs. They stole two cashboxes containing forty florins, postal orders and checkbooks and then, worst of all, all the coupons for 150 kilos of sugar.

Mr. Koophuis thinks that they belonged to the same gang as the ones who tried all three doors six weeks ago. They were unsuccessful then.

It has caused rather a stir in the building, but the "Secret Annexe" can't seem to go on without sensations like this. We were very glad that the typewriters and money in our wardrobe, where they are brought upstairs every evening, were safe.

Yours, Anne

Monday, 19 July, 1943

Dear Kitty,

North Amsterdam was very heavily bombed on Sunday. The destruction seems to be terrible. Whole streets lie in ruins, and it will take a long time before all the people are dug out. Up till now there are two hundred dead and countless wounded; the hospitals are crammed. You hear of children lost in the smoldering ruins, looking for their parents. I shudder when I recall the dull droning rumble in the distance, which for us marked the approaching destruction.

Yours, Anne

Friday, 23 July, 1943

Dear Kitty,

Just for fun I'm going to tell you each person's first wish, when we are allowed to go outside again. Margot and Mr. Van Daan long more than anything for a hot bath filled to overflowing and want to stay in it for half an hour. Mrs. Van Daan wants most to go and eat cream cakes immediately. Dussel thinks of nothing but seeing Lotje, his wife; Mummy of her cup of coffee; Daddy is going to visit Mr. Vossen first; Peter the town and a cinema, while I should find it so blissful, I shouldn't know where to start! But most of all, I long for a home of our own, to be able to move freely and to have some help with my work again at last, in other words—school.

Elli has offered to get us some fruit. It costs next to nothing—grapes f.5.00 per kilo, gooseberries f.0.70 per pound, *one* peach f.0.50, one kilo melon f.1.50.[1] Then you see in the newspapers every evening in bold letters, "Play fair and keep prices down!"

Yours, Anne

Monday, 26 July, 1943

Dear Kitty,

Nothing but tumult and uproar yesterday, we are still very het up about it all. You might really ask, does a day go by without some excitement?

We had the first warning siren while we were at

[1] Equivalent prices, in order, would be approximately $1.40, twenty-one cents, fourteen cents, and forty-two cents.

breakfast, but we don't give a hoot about that, it only means that the planes are crossing the coast.

After breakfast I went and lay down for an hour as I had a bad headache, then I went downstairs. It was about two o'clock. Margot had finished her office work at half past two: she had not packed her things together when the sirens began to wail, so upstairs I went again with her. It was high time, for we had not been upstairs five minutes when they began shooting hard, so much so that we went and stood in the passage. And yes, the house rumbled and shook, and down came the bombs.

I clasped my "escape bag" close to me, more because I wanted to have something to hold than with an idea of escaping, because there's nowhere we can go. If ever we come to the extremity of fleeing from here, the street would be just as dangerous as an air raid. This one subsided after half an hour, but the activity in the house increased. Peter came down from his lookout post in the attic, Dussel was in the main office, Mrs. Van Daan felt safe in the private office, Mr. Van Daan had been watching from the loft, and we on the little landing dispersed ourselves too: I went upstairs to see rising above the harbor the columns of smoke Mr. Van Daan had told us about. Before long you could smell burning, and outside it looked as if a thick mist hung everywhere. Although such a big fire is not a pleasant sight, luckily for us it was all over, and we went about our respective tasks. That evening at dinner: another air raid alarm! It was a nice meal, but my hunger vanished, simply at the sound of the alarm. Nothing happened and three quarters of an hour later it was all clear. The dishes were stacked ready to be done: air-raid warning, ack-ack fire, an awful lot of planes. "Oh, dear me, twice in one day, that's too much," we all thought, but that didn't help at all; once again the bombs rained down, the other side this time, on Schiphol,[1] according to the British. The planes dived and climbed, we heard the hum of their engines and it was very gruesome. Each moment I thought: "One's falling now. Here it comes."

[1] Amsterdam airport.

I can assure you that when I went to bed at nine o'clock I couldn't hold my legs still. I woke up at the stroke of twelve: planes. Dussel was undressing. I didn't let that put me off, and at the first shot, I leaped out of bed, wide awake. Two hours with Daddy and still they kept coming. Then they ceased firing and I was able to go to bed. I fell asleep at half past two.

Seven o'clock. I sat up in bed with a start. Mr. Van Daan was with Daddy. Burglars was my first thought. I heard Mr. Van Daan say "everything." I thought that everything had been stolen. But no, this time it was wonderful news, such as we have not heard for months, perhaps in all the war years. "Mussolini has resigned, the King of Italy has taken over the government." We jumped for joy. After the terrible day yesterday, at last something good again and—hope. Hope for it to end, hope for peace.

Kraler called in and told us that Fokkers has been badly damaged. Meanwhile we had another air-raid alarm with planes overhead and one more warning siren. I'm just about choked with alarms, very tired and don't feel a bit like work. But now the suspense over Italy will awaken the hope that it will soon end, perhaps even this year.

Yours, Anne

Thursday, 29 July, 1943

Dear Kitty,

Mrs. Van Daan, Dussel, and I were doing the dishes and I was extraordinarily quiet, which hardly ever happens, so they would have been sure to notice.

In order to avoid questions I quickly sought a fairly neutral topic, and thought that the book *Henry from the Other Side* would meet the need. But I had made a mistake. If Mrs. Van Daan doesn't pounce on me, then Mr. Dussel does. This was what it came to: Mr. Dussel had specially recommended us this book as being excellent. Margot and I thought it was anything but excellent. The boy's character was certainly well drawn, but the rest—

I had better gloss over that. I said something to that effect while we were washing the dishes, but that brought me a packet of trouble.

"How can you understand the psychology of a man! Of a child is not so difficult (!). You are much too young for a book like that; why, even a man of twenty would not be able to grasp it." (Why did he so especially recommend this book to Margot and me?) Now Dussel and Mrs. Van Daan continued together: "You know much too much about things that are unsuitable for you, you've been brought up all wrong. Later on, when you are older, you won't enjoy anything, then you'll say: 'I read that in books twenty years ago.' You had better make haste, if you want to get a husband or fall in love—or everything is sure to be a disappointment to you. You are already proficient in the theory, it's only the practice that you still lack!"

I suppose it's their idea of a good upbringing to always try to set me against my parents, because that is what they often do. And to tell a girl of my age nothing about "grown-up" subjects is an equally fine method! I see the results of that kind of upbringing frequently and all too clearly.

I could have slapped both their faces at that moment as they stood there making a fool of me. I was beside myself with rage and I'm just counting the days until I'm rid of "those" people.

Mrs. Van Daan is a nice one! She sets a fine example ... she certainly sets one—a bad one. She is well known as being very pushing, selfish, cunning, calculating, and is never content. I can also add vanity and coquetry to the list. There is no question about it, she is an unspeakably disagreeable person. I could write whole chapters about Madame, and who knows, perhaps I will someday. Anyone can put on a fine coat of varnish outside. Mrs. Van Daan is friendly to strangers and especially men, so it is easy to make a mistake when you have only known her for a short time. Mummy thinks she is too stupid to waste words over, Margot too unimportant, Pim too ugly (literally and figuratively), and I, after long observation—

for I was never prejudiced from the start—have come to the conclusion that she is all three and a lot more! She has so many bad qualities, why should I even begin about one of them?

Yours, Anne

P.S.—Will the reader take into consideration that when this story was written the writer had not cooled down from her fury!

Tuesday, 3 August, 1943

Dear Kitty,

Political news excellent. In Italy the Fascist party has been banned. The people are fighting the Fascists in many places—even the army is actually taking part in the battle. Can a country like that wage war against England?

We've just had a third air raid; I clenched my teeth together to make myself feel courageous. Mrs. Van Daan, who has always said, "A terrible end is better than no end at all," is the greatest coward of us all now. She was shaking like a leaf this morning and even burst into tears. When her husband, with whom she has just made it up after a week's squabbling, comforted her, the expression on her face alone almost made me feel sentimental.

Mouschi has proved that keeping cats has disadvantages as well as advantages. The whole house is full of fleas, and the plague gets worse every day. Mr. Koophuis has scattered yellow powder in every nook and corner, but the fleas don't seem to mind a bit. It's making us all quite nervous; one keeps imagining an itch on one's arms, legs, and various parts of the body, which is why quite a lot of us are doing gymnastics, so as to be able to look at the back of our necks or legs while standing up. Now we're being paid back for not being more supple—we're too stiff to even turn our heads properly. We gave up real gymnastics long ago.

Yours, Anne

Dear Kitty,

Now that we have been in the "Secret Annexe" for over a year, you know something of our lives, but some of it is quite indescribable. There is so much to tell, everything is so different from ordinary times and from ordinary people's lives. But still, to give you a closer look into our lives, now and again I intend to give you a description of an ordinary day. Today I'm beginning with the evening and night.

Nine o'clock in the evening. The bustle of going to bed in the "Secret Annexe" begins and it is always really quite a business. Chairs are shoved about, beds are pulled down, blankets unfolded, nothing remains where it is during the day. I sleep on the little divan, which is not more than one and a half meters long. So chairs have to be used to lengthen it. An eiderdown, sheets, pillows, blankets, are all fetched from Dussel's bed where they remain during the day. One hears terrible creaking in the next room: Margot's concertina-bed being pulled out. Again, divan, blankets, and pillows, everything is done to make the wooden slats a bit more comfortable. It sounds like thunder above, but it is only Mrs. Van Daan's bed. This is shifted to the window, you see, in order to give Her Majesty in the pink bed jacket fresh air to tickle her dainty nostrils!

After Peter's finished, I step into the washing cubicle, where I give myself a thorough wash and general toilet; it occasionally happens (only in the hot weeks or months) that there is a tiny flea floating in the water. Then teeth cleaning, hair curling, manicure, and my cotton-wool pads with hydrogen peroxide (to bleach black mustache hairs)—all this under half an hour.

Half past nine. Quickly into dressing gown, soap in one hand, pottie, hairpins, pants, curlers, and cotton wool in the other, I hurry out of the bathroom; but usually I'm called back once for the various hairs which decorate the washbasin in graceful curves, but which are not approved of by the next person.

Ten o'clock. Put up the blackout. Good night! For at least a quarter of an hour there is creaking of beds and a sighing of broken springs, then all is quiet, at least that is if our neighbors upstairs don't quarrel in bed.

Half past eleven. The bathroom door creaks. A narrow strip of light falls into the room. A squeak of shoes, a large coat, even larger than the man inside it—Dussel returns from his night work in Kraler's office. Shuffling on the floor for ten minutes, crackle of paper (that is the food which has to be stowed away), and a bed is made. Then the form disappears again and one only hears suspicious noises from the lavatory from time to time.

Three o'clock. I have to get up for a little job in the metal pot under my bed, which is on a rubber mat for safety's sake in case of leakage. When this has to take place, I always hold my breath, as it clatters into the tin like a brook from a mountain. Then the pot is returned to its place and the figure in the white nightgown, which evokes the same cry from Margot every evening: "Oh, that indecent nightdress!" steps back into bed.

Then a certain person lies awake for about a quarter of an hour, listening to the sounds of the night. Firstly, to whether there might not be a burglar downstairs, then to the various beds, above, next door, and in my room, from which one is usually able to make out how the various members of the household are sleeping, or how they pass the night in wakefulness.

The latter is certainly not pleasant, especially when it concerns a member of the family by the name of Dussel. First, I hear a sound like a fish gasping for breath, this is repeated nine of ten times, then with much ado and interchanged with little smacking sounds, the lips are moistened, followed by a lengthy twisting and turning in bed and rearranging of pillows. Five minutes' perfect peace and then the same sequence of events unfolds itself at least three times more, after the doctor has soothed himself to sleep again for a little while. It can also happen that we get a bit of shooting in the night, varying between one o'clock and four. I never really realize it, until from habit I am already standing at my bedside. Sometimes I'm so busy dreaming that I'm thinking about French irregular verbs or a quarrel upstairs. It is some time before I begin to realize that guns are firing and that I am still in the room. But it usually happens as described above. I quickly grab a pillow and handerchief, put on my dressing gown and slippers, and scamper to Daddy, like Margot wrote in this birthday poem:

> The first shot sounds at dead of night.
> Hush, look! A door creaks open wide,
> A little girl glides into sight,
> Clasping a pillow to her side.

Once landed in the big bed, the worst is over, except if the firing gets very bad.

Quarter to seven. Trrrrr—the alarm clock that raises its voice at any hour of the day (if one asks for it and sometimes when one doesn't). Crack—ping—Mrs. Van Daan has turned it off. Creak—Mr. Van Daan gets up. Puts on water and then full speed to the bathroom.

Quarter past seven. The door creaks again. Dussel can go to the bathroom. Once alone, I take down the blackout—and a new day in the "Secret Annexe" has begun.

Yours, Anne

Thursday, 5 August, 1943

Dear Kitty,

Today I am going to take lunchtime.

It is half past twelve. The whole mixed crowd breathes again. The warehouse boys have gone home now. Above one can hear the noise of Mrs. Van Daan's vacuum cleaner on her beautiful, and only, carpet. Margot goes with a few books under her arm for her Dutch lesson "for children who make no progress," because that's Dussel's attitude. Pim goes into a corner with his inseparable Dickens to try and find peace somewhere. Mummy hurries

88

upstairs to help the industrious housewife, and I go to the bathroom to tidy it up a bit, and myself at the same time.

Quarter to one. The place is filling up. First Mr. Van Santen, then Koophuis or Kraler, Elli and sometimes Miep as well.

One o'clock. We're all sitting listening to the B.B.C., seated around the baby wireless; these are the only times when the members of the "Secret Annexe" do not interrupt each other, because now someone is speaking whom even Mr. Van Daan can't interrupt.

Quarter past one. The great share-out. Everyone from below gets a cup of soup and if there is ever a pudding, some of that as well. Mr. Van Santen is happy and goes to sit on the divan or lean against the writing table. Newspaper, cup, and usually the cat, beside him. If one of the three is missing he's sure to protest. Koophuis tells us the latest news from town, he is certainly an excellent source of information. Kraler comes helter-skelter upstairs—a short, firm knock on the door and in he comes rubbing his hands, according to his mood, in a good temper and talkative, or bad-tempered and quiet.

Quarter to two. Everyone rises from the table and goes about his own business. Margot and Mummy to the dishes. Mr. and Mrs. Van Daan to their divan. Peter up to the attic. Daddy to the divan downstairs. Dussel to his bed and Anne to her work. Then follows the most peaceful hour; everyone is asleep, no one is disturbed. Dussel dreams of lovely food—the expression on his face gives this away, but I don't look long because the time goes so fast and at four o'clock the pedantic doctor is standing, clock in hand, because I'm one minute late in clearing the table for him.

Yours, Anne

Monday, 9 August, 1943

Dear Kitty,

To continue the "Secret Annexe" daily timetable. I shall now describe the evening meal:

Mr. Van Daan begins. He is first to be served, takes a lot of everything if it is what he likes. Usually talks at the same time, always gives his opinion as the only one worth listening to, and once he has spoken it is irrevocable. Because if anyone *dares* to question it, then he flares up at once. Oh, he can spit like a cat—I'd rather not argue, I can tell you—if you've *once* tried, you don't try again. He has the best opinion, he knows the most about everything. All right then, he has got brains, but "self-satisfaction" has reached a high grade with this gentleman.

Madame. Really, I should remain silent. Some days, especially if there is a bad mood coming on, you can't look at her face. On closer examination, she is the guilty one in all the arguments. Not the subject! Oh, no, everyone prefers to remain aloof over that, but one could perhaps call her the "kindler." Stirring up trouble, that's fun. Mrs. Frank against Anne; Margot against Daddy doesn't go quite so easily.

But now at table, Mrs. Van Daan doesn't go short, although she thinks so at times. The tiniest potatoes, the sweetest mouthful, the best of everything; picking over is her system. The others will get their turn, as long as I have the best. Then talking. Whether anyone is interested, whether they are listening or not, that doesn't seem to matter. I suppose she thinks: "Everyone is interested in what Mrs. Van Daan says." Coquettish smiles, behaving as if one knew everything, giving everyone a bit of advice and encouragement, that's *sure* to make a good impression. But if you look longer, then the good soon wears off.

One, she is industrious, two, gay, three, a coquette—and, occasionally, pretty. This is Petronella Van Daan.

The third table companion. One doesn't hear much from him. Young Mr. Van Daan is very quiet and doesn't draw much attention to himself. As for appetite: a Danaïdean vessel, which is never full and after the heartiest meal declares quite calmly that he could have eaten double.

Number four—Margot. Eats like a little mouse and doesn't talk at all. The only things that go down are vegetables and fruit. "Spoiled" is the Van Daan's judgment; "not enough fresh air and games" our opinion.

Beside her—Mummy. Good appetite, very talkative. No one has the impression, as Mrs. Van Daan: this is the housewife. What is the difference? Well, Mrs. Van Daan does the cooking, and Mummy washes up and polishes.

Numbers six and seven. I won't say much about Daddy and me. The former is the most unassuming of all at table. He looks first to see if everyone else has something. He needs nothing himself, for the best things are for the children. He is the perfect example, and sitting beside him, the "Secret Annexe's" "bundle of nerves."

Dr. Dussel. Helps himself, never looks up, eats and doesn't talk. And if one must talk, then for heaven's sake let it be about food. You don't quarrel about it, you only brag. Enormous helpings go down and the word "No" is never heard, never when the food is good, and not often when it's bad. Trousers wrapping his chest, red coat, black bedroom slippers, and horn-rimmed spectacles. That is how one sees him at the little table, always working, alternated only by his afternoon nap, food, and—his favorite spot—the lavatory. Three, four, five times a day someone stands impatiently in front of the door and wriggles, hopping from one foot to the other, hardly able to contain himself. Does it disturb him? Not a bit! From quarter past seven till half past, from half past twelve till one o'clock, from two till quarter past, from four till quarter past, from six till quarter past, and from half past eleven until twelve. One can make a note of it—these are the regular "sitting times." He won't come off or pay any heed to an imploring voice at the door, giving warning of approaching disaster!

Number nine isn't a member of the "Secret Annexe" family, but rather a companion in the house and at table. Elli has a healthy appetite. Leaves nothing on her plate and is not picky-and-choosy. She is easy to please and that is just what gives us pleasure. Cheerful and good-tempered, willing and good-natured, these are her characteristics.

Yours, Anne

Tuesday, 10 August, 1943

Dear Kitty,

New idea. I talk more to myself than to the others at mealtimes, which is to be recommended for two reasons. Firstly, because everyone is happy if I don't chatter the whole time, and secondly, I needn't get annoyed about other people's opinions. I don't think my opinions are stupid and the others do; so it is better to keep them to myself. I do just the same if I have to eat something that I simply can't stand. I put my plate in front of me, pretend that it is something delicious, look at it as little as possible, and before I know where I am, it is gone. When I get up in the morning, also a very unpleasant process, I jump out of bed thinking to myself: "You'll be back in a second," go to the window, take down the blackout, sniff at the crack of the window until I feel a bit of fresh air, and I'm awake. The bed is turned down as quickly as possible and then the temptation is removed. Do you know what Mummy calls this sort of thing? "The Art of Living"—that's an odd expression. For the last week we've all been in a bit of a muddle about time, because our dear and beloved Westertoren clock bell has apparently been taken away for war purposes, so that neither by day nor night do we ever know the exact time. I still have some hope that they will think up a substitute (tin, copper or some such thing) to remind the neighborhood of the clock.

Whether I'm upstairs or down, or wherever I am, my feet are the admiration of all, glittering in a pair of (for these days) exceptionally fine shoes. Miep managed to get hold of them secondhand for 27.50 florins, wine-colored suede leather with fairly high wedge heels. I feel as if I'm on stilts and look much taller than I am.

Dussel has indirectly endangered our lives. He actually let Miep bring a forbidden book for him, one which abuses Mussolini and Hitler. On the way she happened to be run into by an S.S. car. She lost her temper, shouted, "Miserable wretches," and rode on. It is better not to think of what might have happened if she had had to go to their headquarters.

Yours, Anne

Wednesday, 18 August, 1943

Dear Kitty,

The title for this piece is: "The communal task of the day: potato peeling!"

One person fetches the newspapers, another the knives (keeping the best for himself, of course), a third potatoes, and the fourth a pan of water.

Mr. Dussel begins, does not always scrape well, but scrapes incessantly, glancing right and left. Does everyone do it the way he does? No! "Anne, look here; I take the knife in my hand like this, scrape from the top downwards! No, not like that—like this!"

"I get on better like *this*, Mr. Dussel," I remark timidly.

"But still this is the best way. But *du kannst* take *dies* from me. Naturally I don't care a bit, *aber du* must know for yourself." We scrape on. I look slyly once in my neighbor's direction. He shakes his head thoughtfully once more (over me, I suppose) but is silent.

I scrape on again. Now I look to the other side, where Daddy is sitting; for him scraping potatoes is not just a little odd job, but a piece of precision work. When he reads, he has a deep wrinkle at the back of his head, but if he helps prepare potatoes, beans, or any other vegetables, then it seems as if nothing else penetrates. Then he has on his "potato face," and he would never hand over an imperfectly scraped potato; it's out of the question when he makes that face!

I work on again and then just look up for a second; I know it already. Mrs. Van Daan is trying to attract Dussel's attention. First she looks in his direction and Dussel appears not to notice anything. Then she winks an eye; Dussel works on. Then she laughs, Dussel doesn't

look up. Then Mummy laughs too; Dussel takes no notice.
Mrs. Van Daan has not achieved anything, so she has to
think of something else. A pause and then: "Putti, do put
on an apron! Tomorrow I shall have to get all the spots
out of your suit!"

"I'm not getting myself dirty!"

Another moment's silence.

"Putti, why don't you sit down?"

"I'm comfortable standing up and prefer it!" Pause.

"Putti, look, *du spatst schon!*" ("You are making a
mess!")

"Yes, Mammy, I'm being careful."

Mrs. Van Daan searches for another subject. "I say,
Putti, why aren't there any English air raids now?"

"Because the weather is bad, Kerli."

"But it was lovely yesterday, and they didn't fly then
either."

"Let's not talk about it."

"Why, surely one can talk about it, or give one's
opinion?"

"No."

"Why ever not?"

"Do be quiet, mammi'chen."

"Mr. Frank always answers his wife, doesn't he?"

Mr. Van Daan wrestles with himself. This is his tender
spot, it's something he can't take and Mrs. Van Daan
begins again: "The invasion seems as if it will never
come!"

Mr. Van Daan goes white; when Mrs. Van Daan sees
this, she turns red, but goes on again: "The British do
nothing!" The bomb explodes!

"And now hold your tongue, *donnerwetter-noch-
einmal!*"

Mummy can hardly hold back her laughter. I look
straight in front of me.

This sort of thing happens nearly every day, unless
they have just had a very bad quarrel, because then they
both keep their mouths shut.

I have to go up to the attic to fetch some potatoes.
Peter is busy there delousing the cat. He looks up, the

cat notices—pop—he has disappeared through the open window into the gutter. Peter swears. I laugh and disappear.

Yours, Anne

Friday, 20 August, 1943

Dear Kitty,

The men in the warehouse go home sharp at half past five and then we are free.

Half past five. Elli comes to give us our evening freedom. Immediately we begin to make some headway with our work. First, I go upstairs with Elli, where she usually begins by having a bite from our second course.

Before Elli is seated, Mrs. Van Daan begins thinking of things she wants. It soon comes out: "Oh, Elli, I have only one little wish. . . ." Elli winks at me; whoever comes upstairs, Mrs. Van Daan never misses a single opportunity of letting them know what she wants. That must be one of the reasons why none of them like coming upstairs.

Quarter to six. Elli departs. I go two floors down to have a look around. First to the kitchen, then to the private office, after that the coalhole, to open the trap door for Mouschi. After a long tour of inspection I land up in Kraler's room. Van Daan is looking in all the drawers and portfolios to find the day's post. Peter is fetching the warehouse key and Boche; Pim is hauling the typewriters upstairs; Margot is looking for a quiet spot to do her office work; Mrs. Van Daan puts a kettle on the gas ring; Mummy is coming downstairs with a pan of potatoes; each one knows his own job.

Peter soon returns from the warehouse. The first question is—bread. This is always put in the kitchen cupboard by the Ladies; but it is not there. Forgotten? Peter offers to look in the main office. He crouches in front of the door to make himself as small as possible and crawls toward the steel lockers on hands and knees, so as not to be seen from outside, gets the bread, which had been put there, and disappears; at least, he wants to disappear, but before he quite realizes what has happened, Mouschi has jumped over him and gone and sat right under the writing table.

Peter looks all around—aha, he sees him there, he crawls into the office again and pulls the animal by its tail. Mouschi spits, Peter sighs. What has he achieved? Now Mouschi is sitting right up by the window cleaning himself, very pleased to have escaped Peter. Now Peter is holding a piece of bread under the cat's nose as a last decoy. Mouschi will not be tempted and the door closes. I stood and watched it all through the crack of the door. We work on. Rat, tat, tat. Three taps means a meal!

Yours, Anne

Monday, 23 August, 1943

Dear Kitty,

Continuation of the "Secret Annexe" daily timetable. As the clock strikes half past eight in the morning, Margot and Mummy are jittery: "Ssh . . . Daddy, quiet, Otto, ssh . . . Pim." "It is half past eight, come back here, you can't run any more water; walk quietly!" These are the various cries to Daddy in the bathroom. As the clock strikes half past eight, he has to be in the living room. Not a drop of water, no lavatory, no walking about, everything quiet. As long as none of the office staff are there, everything can be heard in the warehouse. The door is opened upstairs at twenty minutes past eight and shortly after there are three taps on the floor: Anne's porridge. I climb upstairs and fetch my "puppy-dog" plate. Down in my room again, everything goes at terrific speed: do my hair, put away my noisy tin pottie, bed in place. Hush, the clock strikes! Upstairs Mrs. Van Daan has changed her shoes and is shuffling about in bedroom slippers. Mr. Van Daan, too; all is quiet.

Now we have a little bit of real family life. I want to read or work, Margot as well, also Daddy and Mummy. Daddy is sitting (with Dickens and the dictionary, naturally) on the edge of the sagging, squeaky bed, where there aren't even any decent mattresses: two bolsters on top of each other will also serve the purpose, then he thinks: "Mustn't have them, then I'll manage without!"

Once he is reading he doesn't look up, or about him, laughs every now and then, takes awful trouble to get Mummy interested in a little story. Answer: "I haven't got time now." Looks disappointed for just a second, then reads on again; a little later, when he comes to something extra amusing, he tries it again. "You must read this, Mummy!" Mummy sits on the "Opklap" [1] bed, reads, sews, knits, or works, whatever she feels like. She suddenly thinks of something. Just says it quickly: "Anne, do you know . . . Margot, just jot down . . . !" After a while peace returns once more.

Margot closes her book with a clap. Daddy raises his eyebrows into a funny curve, his reading wrinkle deepens again, and he is lost in his book once more; Mummy begins to chatter with Margot, I become curious and listen too! Pim is drawn into the discussion . . . nine o'clock! Breakfast!

Yours, Anne

Friday, 10 September, 1943

Dear Kitty,

Every time I write to you something special seems to have happened, but they are more often unpleasant than pleasant things. However, now there is something wonderful going on. Last Wednesday evening, 8 September, we sat around listening to the seven o'clock news and the first thing we heard was: "Here follows the best news of the whole war. Italy has capitulated!" Italy's unconditional surrender! The Dutch program from England began at quarter past eight. "Listeners, an hour ago, I had just finished writing the chronicle of the day when the wonderful news of Italy's capitulation came in. I can tell you that I have never deposited my notes in the wastepaper basket with such joy!" "God Save the King," the American na-

[1] Dutch type of bed, which folds against the wall to look like a bookcase with curtains hanging before it.

tional anthem, and the "Internationale" were played. As always, the Dutch program was uplifting, but not too optimistic.

Still we have troubles, too; it's about Mr. Koophuis. As you know, we are all very fond of him, he is always cheerful and amazingly brave, although he is never well, has a lot of pain, and is not allowed to eat much or do much walking. "When Mr. Koophuis enters, the sun begins to shine," Mummy said just recently, and she is quite right. Now he has had to go into the hospital for a very unpleasant abdominal operation and will have to stay there for at least four weeks. You really ought to have seen how he said good-by to us just as usual—he might have simply been going out to do a bit of shopping.

Yours, Anne

Thursday, 16 September, 1943

Dear Kitty,

Relations between us here are getting worse all the time. At mealtimes, no one dares to open their mouths (except to allow a mouthful of food to slip in) because whatever is said you either annoy someone or it is misunderstood. I swallow Valerian pills every day against worry and depression, but it doesn't prevent me from being even more miserable the next day. A good hearty laugh would help more than ten Valerian pills, but we've almost forgotten how to laugh. I feel afraid sometimes that from having to be so serious I'll grow a long face and my mouth will droop at the corners. The others don't get any better either, everyone looks with fear and misgivings towards that great terror, winter. Another thing that does not cheer us up is the fact that the warehouseman, V.M., is becoming suspicious about the "Secret Annexe." We really wouldn't mind what V.M. thought of the situation if he wasn't so exceptionally inquisitive, difficult to fob off, and, moreover, not to be trusted. One day Kraler wanted to be extra careful, put on his coat at ten minutes to one, and went to the chemist round the corner. He was back in less than five minutes, and sneaked like a thief up the steep stairs that lead straight to us. At a quarter past one he wanted to go again, but Elli came to warn him that V.M. was in the office. He did a right-about turn and sat with us until half past one. Then he took off his shoes and went in stockinged feet to the front attic door, went downstairs step by step, and, after balancing there for a quarter of an hour to avoid creaking, he landed safely in the office, having entered from the outside. Elli had been freed of V.M. in the meantime, and came up to us to fetch Kraler, but he had already been gone a long time; he was still on the staircase with his shoes off. Whatever would the people in the street have thought if they had seen the Manager putting on his shoes outside? Gosh! the Manager in his socks!

Yours, Anne

Wednesday, 29 September, 1943

Dear Kitty,

It is Mrs. Van Daan's birthday. We gave her a pot of jam, as well as coupons for cheese, meat, and bread. From her husband, Dussel, and our protectors she received things to eat and flowers. Such are the times we live in!

Elli had a fit of nerves this week; she had been sent out so often; time and again she had been asked to go and fetch something quickly, which meant yet another errand or made her feel that she had done something wrong. If you just think that she still has to finish her office work downstairs, that Koophuis is ill, Miep at home with a cold, and that she herself has a sprained ankle, love worries, and a grumbling father, then it's no wonder she's at her wit's end. We comforted her and said that if she puts her foot down once or twice and says she has no time, then the shopping lists will automatically get shorter.

There is something wrong with Mr. Van Daan again, I can see it coming on already! Daddy is very angry for some reason or other. Oh, what kind of explosion is hanging over us now? If only I wasn't mixed up so much with all these rows! If I could only get away! They'll drive us crazy before long!

Yours, Anne

Sunday, 17 October, 1943

Dear Kitty,

Koophuis is back again, thank goodness! He still looks rather pale, but in spite of this sets out cheerfully to sell clothes for Van Daan. It is an unpleasant fact that the Van Daans have run right out of money. Mrs. Van Daan won't part with a thing from her pile of coats, dresses, and shoes. Mr. Van Daan's suit isn't easily disposed of, because he wants too much for it. The end of the story is not yet in sight. Mrs. Daan will certainly have to part with her fur coat. They've had a terrific row upstairs about it, and now the reconciliation period of "oh, darling Putti" and "precious Kerli" has set in.

I am dazed by all the abusive exchanges that have taken place in this virtuous house during the past month. Daddy goes about with his lips tightly pursed; when anyone speaks to him, he looks up startled, as if he is afraid he will have to patch up some tricky relationship again. Mummy has red patches on her cheeks from excitement. Margot complains of headaches. Dussel can't sleep. Mrs. Van Daan grouses the whole day and I'm going completely crazy! Quite honestly, I sometimes forget who we are quarreling with and with whom we've made it up.

The only way to take one's mind off it all is to study, and I do a lot of that.

Yours, Anne

Dear Kitty,

There have been resounding rows again between Mr. and Mrs. Van Daan. It came about like this: as I have already told you, the Van Daans are at the end of their money. One day, some time ago now, Koophuis spoke about a furrier with whom he was on good terms; this gave Van Daan the idea of selling his wife's fur coat. It's a fur coat made from rabbit skins, and she has worn it seventeen years. He got 325 florins for it—an enormous sum. However, Mrs. Van Daan wanted to keep the money to buy new clothes after the war, and it took some doing before Mr. Van Daan made it clear to her that the money was urgently needed for the household.

The yells and screams, stamping and abuse—you can't possibly imagine it! It was frightening. My family stood at the bottom of the stairs, holding their breath, ready if necessary to drag them apart! All this shouting and weeping and nervous tension are so unsettling and such a strain, that in the evening I drop into my bed crying, thanking heaven that I sometimes have half an hour to myself.

Mr. Koophuis is away again; his stomach gives him no peace. He doesn't even know whether it has stopped bleeding yet. For the first time, he was very down when he told us that he didn't feel well and was going home.

All goes well with me on the whole, except that I have no appetite. I keep being told: "You don't look at all well." I must say that they are doing their very best to keep me up to the mark. Grape sugar, cod-liver oil, yeast tablets, and calcium have all been lined up.

My nerves often get the better of me: it is especially on Sundays that I feel rotten. The atmosphere is so oppressive, and sleepy and as heavy as lead. You don't hear a single bird singing outside, and a deadly close silence hangs everywhere, catching hold of me as if it will drag me down deep into an underworld.

At such times Daddy, Mummy, and Margot leave me cold. I wander from one room to another, downstairs and up again, feeling like a songbird whose wings have been clipped and who is hurling himself in utter darkness against the bars of his cage. "Go outside, laugh, and take a breath of fresh air," a voice cries within me, but I don't even feel a response any more; I go and lie on the divan and sleep, to make the time pass more quickly, and the stillness and the terrible fear, because there is no way of killing them.

Yours, Anne

Wednesday, 3 November, 1943

Dear Kitty,

In order to give us something to do, which is also educational, Daddy applied for a prospectus from the Teachers' Institute in Leiden. Margot nosed through the thick book at least three times without finding anything to her liking or to suit her purse. Daddy was quicker, and wants a letter written to the Institute asking for a trial lesson in "Elementary Latin."

To give me something new to begin as well, Daddy asked Koophuis for a children's Bible so that I could find out something about the New Testament at last. "Do you want to give Anne a Bible for Chanuka?" asked Margot, somewhat perturbed. "Yes—er, I think St. Nicholas Day is a better occasion," answered Daddy; "Jesus just doesn't go with Chanuka." [1]

Yours, Anne

[1] See entry for 7 December, 1942.

Dear Kitty,

If you were to read my pile of letters one after another, you would certainly be struck by the many different moods in which they are written. It annoys me that I am so dependent on the atmosphere here, but I'm certainly not the only one—we all find it the same. If I read a book that impresses me, I have to take myself firmly in hand, before I mix with other people; otherwise they would think my mind rather queer. At the moment, as you've probably noticed, I'm going through a spell of being depressed. I really couldn't tell you why it is, but I believe it's just because I'm a coward, and that's what I keep bumping up against.

This evening, while Elli was still here, there was a long, loud, penetrating ring at the door. I turned white at once, got a tummy-ache and heart palpitations, all from fear. At night, when I'm in bed, I see myself alone in a dungeon, without Mummy and Daddy. Sometimes I wander by the roadside or our "Secret Annexe" is on fire, or they come and take us away at night. I see everything as if it is actually taking place, and this gives me the feeling that it may all happen to me very soon! Miep often says she envies us for possessing such tranquillity here. That may be true, but she is not thinking about all our fears. I simply can't imagine that the world will ever be normal for us again. I do talk about "after the war," but then it is only a castle in the air, something that will never really happen. If I think back to our old house, my girl friends, the fun at school, it is just as if another person lived it all, not me.

I see the eight of us with our "Secret Annexe" as if we were a little piece of blue heaven, surrounded by heavy black rain clouds. The round, clearly defined spot where we stand is still safe, but the clouds gather more closely about us and the circle which separates us from the approaching danger closes more and more tightly. Now we are so surrounded by danger and darkness that we bump against each other, as we search desperately for a means of escape. We all look down below, where people are fighting each other, we look above, where it is quiet and beautiful, and meanwhile we are cut off by the great dark mass, which will not let us go upwards, but which stands before us as an impenetrable wall; it tries to crush us, but cannot do so yet. I can only cry and implore: "Oh, if only the black circle could recede and open the way for us!"

Yours, Anne

Thursday, 11 November, 1943

Dear Kitty,
    I have a good title for this chapter:

ODE TO MY FOUNTAIN PEN
IN MEMORIAM

My fountain pen has always been one of my most priceless possessions; I value it highly, especially for its thick nib, for I can only really write neatly with a thick nib. My fountain pen has had a very long and interesting pen-life, which I will briefly tell you about.

When I was nine, my fountain pen arrived in a packet (wrapped in cotton wool) as "sample without value" all the way from Aachen, where my Grandmother, the kind donor, used to live. I was in bed with flu, while February winds howled round the house. The glorious fountain pen had a red leather case and was at once shown around to all my friends. I, Anne Frank, the proud owner of a fountain pen! When I was ten I was allowed to take the pen to school and the mistress went so far as to permit me to write with it.

When I was eleven, however, my treasure had to be put away again, because the mistress in the sixth form only allowed us to use school pens and inkpots.

When I was twelve and went to the Jewish Lyceum,[1]

---

[1] A type of secondary school specializing in the classics, common in most continental countries.

my fountain pen received a new case in honor of the great occasion; it could take a pencil as well, and as it closed with a zipper looked much more impressive.

At thirteen the fountain pen came with us to the "Secret Annexe," where it has raced through countless diaries and compositions for me.

Now I am fourteen, we have spent our last year together.

It was on a Friday afternoon after five o'clock. I had come out of my room and wanted to go and sit at the table to write, when I was roughly pushed on one side and had to make room for Margot and Daddy, who wanted to practice their "Latin." The fountain pen remained on the table unused while, with a sigh, its owner contented herself with a tiny little corner of the table, and starting rubbing beans. "Bean rubbing" is making moldy beans decent again. I swept the floor at a quarter to six and threw the dirt, together with the bad beans, into a newspaper and into the stove. A terrific flame leaped out and I thought it was grand that the fire should burn up so well when it was practically out. All was quiet again, the "Latinites" had finished, and I went and sat at the table to clear up my writing things, but look as I might, my fountain pen received a new case in honor of the great Margot looked, but there was not a trace of the thing. "Perhaps it fell into the stove together with the beans," Margot suggested. "Oh, no, of course not!" I answered. When my fountain pen didn't turn up that evening, however, we all took it that it had been burned, all the more as celluloid is terribly inflammable.

And so it was, our unhappy fears were confirmed; when Daddy did the stove the following morning the clip used for fastening was found among the ashes. Not a trace of the gold nib was found. "Must have melted and stuck to some stone or other," Daddy thought.

I have one consolation, although a slender one: my fountain pen has been cremated, just what I want later!

Yours, Anne

Dear Kitty,

Shattering things are happening. Diphtheria reigns in Elli's home, so she is not allowed to come into contact with us for six weeks. It makes it very awkward over food and shopping, not to mention missing her companionship. Koophuis is still in bed and has had nothing but porridge and milk for three weeks. Kraler is frantically busy.

The Latin lessons Margot sends in are corrected by a teacher and returned, Margot writing in Elli's name. The teacher is very nice, and witty, too. I expect he is glad to have such a clever pupil.

Dussel is very put out, none of us knows why. It began by his keeping his mouth closed upstairs; he didn't utter a word to either Mr. or Mrs. Van Daan. Everyone was struck by it, and when it lasted a couple of days, Mummy took the opportunity of warning him about Mrs. Van Daan, who, if he went on like this, could make things very disagreeable for him.

Dussel said that Mr. Van Daan started the silence, so he was not going to be the one to break it.

Now I must tell you that yesterday was the sixteenth of November, the day he had been exactly one year in the "Secret Annexe." Mummy received a plant in honor of the occasion, but Mrs. Van Daan, who for weeks beforehand had made no bones about the fact that she thought Dussel should treat us to something, received nothing. Instead of expressing, for the first time, his thanks for our unselfishness in taking him in, he didn't say a word. And when I asked him, on the morning of the sixteenth, whether I should congratulate or condole, he answered that it didn't matter to him. Mummy, who wanted to act as peacemaker, didn't get one step further, and finally the situation remained as it was.

> *Der Man hat einen grossen Geist*
> *Und ist so klein von Taten!* [1]

Yours, Anne

[1] (The spirit of the man is great,
How puny are his deeds!)

Dear Kitty,

Yesterday evening, before I fell asleep, who should suddenly appear before my eyes but Lies!

I saw her in front of me, clothed in rags, her face thin and worn. Her eyes were very big and she looked so sadly and reproachfully at me that I could read in her eyes: "Oh, Anne, why have you deserted me? Help, oh, help me, rescue me from this hell!"

And I cannot help her, I can only look on, how others suffer and die, and can only pray to God to send her back to us.

I just saw Lies, no one else, and now I understand. I misjudged her and was too young to understand her difficulties. She was attached to a new girl friend, and to her it seemed as though I wanted to take her away. What the poor girl must have felt like, I know; I know the feeling so well myself!

Sometimes, in a flash, I saw something of her life, but a moment later I was selfishly absorbed again in my own pleasures and problems. It was horrid of me to treat her as I did, and now she looked at me, oh so helplessly, with her pale face and imploring eyes. If only I could help her!

Oh, God, that I should have all I could wish for and that she should be seized by such a terrible fate. I am not more virtuous than she; she, too, wanted to do what was right, why should I be chosen to live and she probably to die? What was the difference between us? Why are we so far from each other now?

Quite honestly, I haven't thought about her for months, yes, almost a year. Not completely forgotten her, but still I had never thought about her like this, until I saw her before me in all her misery.

Oh, Lies, I hope that, if you live until the end of the war, you will come back to us and that I shall be able to take you in and do something to make up for the wrong I did you.

But when I am able to help her again, then she will not need my help so badly as now. I wonder if she ever thinks of me; if so, what would she feel?

Good Lord, defend her, so that at least she is not alone. Oh, if only You could tell her that I think lovingly of her and with sympathy, perhaps that would give her greater endurance.

I must not go on thinking about it, because I don't get any further. I only keep seeing her great big eyes, and cannot free myself from them. I wonder if Lies has real faith in herself, and not only what has been thrust upon her?

I don't even know, I never took the trouble to ask her!

Lies, Lies, if only I could take you away, if only I could let you share all the things I enjoy. It is too late now, I can't help, or repair the wrong I have done. But I shall never forget her again, and I shall always pray for her.

Yours, Anne

Monday, 6 December, 1943

Dear Kitty,

When St. Nicholas' Day approached, none of us could help thinking of the prettily decorated basket we had last year and I, especially, thought it would be very dull to do nothing at all this year. I thought a long time about it, until I invented something, something funny.

I consulted Pim, and a week ago we started composing a little poem for each person.

On Sunday evening at a quarter to eight we appeared upstairs with the large laundry basket between us, decorated with little figures, and bows of pink and blue carbon copy paper. The basket was covered with a large piece of brown paper, on which a letter was pinned. Everyone was rather astonished at the size of the surprise package.

I took the letter from the paper and read:

> *"Santa Claus has come once more,*
> *Though not quite as he came before;*
> *We can't celebrate his day*
> *In last year's fine and pleasant way.*
> *For then our hopes were high and bright,*
> *All the optimists seemed right,*
> *None supposing that this year*
> *We would welcome Santa here.*
> *Still, we'll make his spirit live,*
> *And since we've nothing left to give,*
> *We've thought of something else to do*
> *Each please look inside his shoe."*

As each owner took his shoe from the basket there was a resounding peal of laughter. A little paper package lay in each shoe with the address of the shoe's owner on it.

Yours, Anne

Wednesday, 22 December, 1943

Dear Kitty,

A bad attack of flu has prevented me from writing to you until today. It's wretched to be ill here. When I wanted to cough—one, two, three—I crawled under the blankets and tried to stifle the noise. Usually the only result was that the tickle wouldn't go away at all; and milk and honey, sugar or lozenges had to be brought into operation. It makes me dizzy to think of all the cures that were tried on me. Sweating, compresses, wet cloths on my chest, dry cloths on my chest, hot drinks, gargling, throat painting, lying still, cushion for extra warmth, hot-water bottles, lemon squashes, and, in addition, the thermometer every two hours!

Can anyone really get better like this? The worst moment of all was certainly when Mr. Dussel thought he'd play doctor, and came and lay on my naked chest with his greasy head, in order to listen to the sounds within. Not only did his hair tickle unbearably, but I was embarrassed, in spite of the fact that he once, thirty years ago, studied medicine and has the title of Doctor. Why

109

should the fellow come and lie on my heart? He's not my lover, after all. For that matter, he wouldn't hear whether it's healthy or unhealthy inside me anyway; his ears need syringing first, as he's becoming alarmingly hard of hearing.

But that is enough about illness. I'm as fit as a fiddle again, one centimeter taller, two pounds heavier, pale, and with a real appetite for learning.

There is not much news to tell you. We are all getting on well together for a change! There's no quarreling—we haven't had such peace in the home for at least half a year. Elli is still parted from us.

We received extra oil for Christmas, sweets and syrup; the "chief present" is a brooch, made out of a two-and-a-half-cent piece, and shining beautifully. Anyway, lovely, but indescribable. Mr. Dussel gave Mummy and Mrs. Van Daan a lovely cake which he had asked Miep to bake for him. With all her work, she has to do that as well! I have also something for Miep and Elli. For at least two months I have saved the sugar from my porridge, you see, and with Mr. Koophuis's help, I'll have it made into fondants.

It is drizzly weather, the stove smells, the food lies heavily on everybody's tummy, causing thunderous noises on all sides! The war at a standstill, morale rotten.

Yours, Anne

Friday, 24 December, 1943

Dear Kitty,

I have previously written about how much we are affected by atmospheres here, and I think that in my own case this trouble is getting much worse lately.

"Himmelhoch jauchzend und zum Tode betrübt" [1] certainly fits here. I am *"Himmelhoch jauchzend"* if I only think how lucky we are here compared with other Jewish children, and *"zum Tode betrübt"* comes over me when, as happened today, for example, Mrs. Koophuis comes and tells us about her daughter Corry's hockey club, canoe

[1] A famous line from Goëthe: "On top of the world, or in the depths of despair."

110

trips, theatrical performances, and friends. I don't think I'm jealous of Corry, but I couldn't help feeling a great longing to have lots of fun myself for once, and to laugh until my tummy ached. Especially at this time of the year with all the holidays for Christmas and the New Year, and we are stuck here like outcasts. Still, I really ought not to write this, because it seems ungrateful and I've certainly been exaggerating. But still, whatever you think of me, I can't keep everything to myself, so I'll remind you of my opening words—"Paper is patient."

When someone comes in from outside, with the wind in their clothes and the cold on their faces, then I could bury my head in the blankets to stop myself thinking: "When will we be granted the privilege of smelling fresh air?" And because I must not bury my head in the blankets, but the reverse—I must keep my head high and be brave, the thoughts will come, not once, but oh, countless times. Believe me, if you have been shut up for a year and a half, it can get too much for you some days. In spite of all justice and thankfulness, you can't crush your feelings. Cycling, dancing, whistling, looking out into the world, feeling young, to know that I'm free— that's what I long for; still, I mustn't show it, because I sometimes think if all eight of us began to pity ourselves, or went about with discontented faces, where would it lead us? I sometimes ask myself, "Would anyone, either Jew or non-Jew, understand this about me, that I am simply a young girl badly in need of some rollicking fun?" I don't know, and I couldn't talk about it to anyone, because then I know I should cry. Crying can bring such relief.

In spite of all my theories, and however much trouble I take, each day I miss having a real mother who understands me. That is why with everything I do and write I think of the "Mumsie" that I want to be for my children later on. The "Mumsie" who doesn't take everything that is said in general conversation so seriously, but who does take what *I* say seriously. I have noticed, though I can't explain how, that the word "Mumsie" tells you everything.

Do you know what I've found? To give me the feeling of calling Mummy something which sounds like "Mumsie" I often call her "Mum"; then from that comes "Mums"; the incomplete "Mumsie," as it were, whom I would so love to honor with the extra "ie" and yet who does not realize it. It's a good thing, because it would only make her unhappy.

That's enough about that, writing has made my *"zum Tode betrübt"* go off a bit.

Yours, Anne

Saturday, 25 December, 1943

Dear Kitty,

During these days, now that Christmas is here, I find myself thinking all the time about Pim, and what he told me about the love of his youth. Last year I didn't understand the meaning of his words as well as I do now. If he'd only talk about it again, perhaps I would be able to show him that I understand.

I believe that Pim talked about it because he who "knows the secrets of so many other hearts" had to express his own feelings for once; because otherwise Pim never says a word about himself, and I don't think Margot has any idea of all Pim has had to go through. Poor Pim, he can't make *me* think that he has forgotten everything. He will never forget this. He has become very tolerant. I hope that I shall grow a bit like him, without having to go through all that.

Yours, Anne

Monday, 27 December, 1943

Dear Kitty,

On Friday evening for the first time in my life I received something for Christmas. Koophuis, Kraler and the girls had prepared a lovely surprise again. Miep has made a lovely Christmas cake, on which was written "Peace 1944."

Elli had provided a pound of sweet biscuits of prewar quality. For Peter, Margot, and me a bottle of yoghourt, and a bottle of beer for each of the grownups. Everything was so nicely done up, and there were pictures stuck on the different packages. Otherwise Christmas passed by quickly for us.

Yours, Anne

Wednesday, 29 December, 1943

Dear Kitty,

I was very unhappy again last evening. Granny and Lies came into my mind. Granny, oh, darling Granny, how little we understood of what she suffered, or how sweet she was. And besides all this, she knew a terrible secret which she carefully kept to herself the whole time.[1] How faithful and good Granny always was; she would never have let one of us down. Whatever it was, however naughty I had been, Granny always stuck up for me.

Granny, did you love me or didn't you understand me either? I don't know. No one ever talked about themselves to Granny. How lonely Granny must have been, how lonely in spite of us! A person can be lonely even if he is loved by many people, because he is still not the "One and Only" to anyone.

And Lies, is she still alive? What is she doing? Oh, God, protect her and bring her back to us. Lies, I see in you all the time what my lot might have been, I keep seeing myself in your place. Why then should I often be unhappy over what happens here? Shouldn't I always be glad, contented, and happy, except when I think about her and her companions in distress? I am selfish and cowardly. Why do I always dream and think of the most terrible things—my fear makes me want to scream out loud sometimes. Because still, in spite of everything, I have not enough faith in God. He has given me so much—which I certainly do not deserve—and I still do so much

[1] A severe internal disease.

that is wrong every day. If you think of your fellow creatures, then you only want to cry, you could really cry the whole day long. The only thing to do is to pray that God will perform a miracle and save some of them. And I hope that I am doing that enough.

Yours, Anne

Sunday, 2 January, 1944

Dear Kitty,

This morning when I had nothing to do I turned over some of the pages of my diary and several times I came across letters dealing with the subject "Mummy" in such a hotheaded way that I was quite shocked, and asked myself: "Anne, is it really you who mentioned hate? Oh, Anne, how could you!" I remained sitting with the open page in my hand, and thought about it and how it came about that I should have been so brimful of rage and really so filled with such a thing as hate that I had to confide it all in you. I have been trying to understand the Anne of a year ago and to excuse her, because my conscience isn't clear as long as I leave you with these accusations, without being able to explain, on looking back, how it happened.

I suffer now—and suffered then—from moods which kept my head under water (so to speak) and only allowed me to see the things subjectively without enabling me to consider quietly the words of the other side, and to answer them as the words of one whom I, with my hotheaded temperament, had offended or made unhappy.

I hid myself within myself, I only considered myself and quietly wrote down all my joys, sorrows, and contempt in my diary. This diary is of great value to me, because it has become a book of memoirs in many places, but on a good many pages I could certainly put "past and done with."

I used to be furious with Mummy, and still am sometimes. It's true that she doesn't understand me, but I don't understand her either. She did love me very much and she was tender, but as she landed in so many unpleasant situations through me, and was nervous and irritable because of other worries and difficulties, it is certainly understandable that she snapped at me.

I took it much too seriously, was offended, and was rude and aggravating to Mummy, which, in turn, made her unhappy. So it was really a matter of unpleasantness and misery rebounding all the time. It wasn't nice for either of us, but it is passing.

I just didn't want to see all this, and pitied myself very much; but that, too, is understandable. Those violent outbursts on paper were only giving vent to anger which in a normal life could have been worked off by stamping my feet a couple of times in a locked room, or calling Mummy names behind her back.

The period when I caused Mummy to shed tears is over. I have grown wiser and Mummy's nerves are not so much on edge. I usually keep my mouth shut if I get annoyed, and so does she, so we appear to get on much better together. I can't really love Mummy in a dependent childlike way—I just don't have that feeling.

I soothe my conscience now with the thought that it is better for hard words to be on paper than that Mummy should carry them in her heart.

Yours, Anne

Wednesday, 5 January, 1944

Dear Kitty,

I have two things to confess to you today, which will take a long time. But I must tell someone and you are the best one to tell, as I know that, come what may, you always keep a secret.

The first is about Mummy. You know that I've grumbled a lot about Mummy, yet still tried to be nice to her again. Now it is suddenly clear to me what she lacks. Mummy herself has told us that she looked upon us more as her friends than her daughters. Now that is all very fine, but still, a friend can't take a mother's place. I need my mother as an example which I can follow, I want to be able to respect her. I have the feeling that Margot thinks differently about these things and would never be able to understand what I've just told you. And Daddy avoids all arguments about Mummy.

I imagine a mother as a woman who, in the first place, shows great tact, especially towards her children when they reach our age, and who does not laugh at me if I cry about something—not pain, but other things—like "Mums" does.

One thing, which perhaps may seem rather fatuous, I have never forgiven her. It was on a day that I had to go to the dentist. Mummy and Margot were going to come with me, and agreed that I should take my bicycle. When we had finished at the dentist, and were outside again, Margot and Mummy told me that they were going into the town to look at something or buy something—I don't remember exactly what. I wanted to go, too, but was not allowed to, as I had my bicycle with me. Tears of rage sprang into my eyes, and Mummy and Margot began laughing at me. Then I became so furious that I stuck my tongue out at them in the street just as an old woman happened to pass by, who looked very shocked! I rode home on my bicycle, and I know I cried for a long time.

It is queer that the wound that Mummy made then still burns, when I think of how angry I was that afternoon.

The second is something that is very difficult to tell you, because it is about myself.

Yesterday I read an article about blushing by Sis Heyster. This article might have been addressed to me personally. Although I don't blush very easily, the other things in it certainly all fit me. She writes roughly something like this—that a girl in the years of puberty becomes quiet within and begins to think about the wonders that are happening to her body.

I experience that, too, and that is why I get the feeling lately of being embarrassed about Margot, Mummy, and

116

Daddy. Funnily enough, Margot, who is much more shy than I am, isn't at all embarrassed.

I think what is happening to me is so wonderful, and not only what can be seen on my body, but all that is taking place inside. I never discuss myself or any of these things with anybody; that is why I have to talk to myself about them.

Each time I have a period—and that has only been three times—I have the feeling that in spite of all the pain, unpleasantness, and nastiness, I have a sweet secret, and that is why, although it is nothing but a nuisance to me in a way, I always long for the time that I shall feel that secret within me again.

Sis Heyster also writes that girls of this age don't feel quite certain of themselves, and discover that they themselves are individuals with ideas, thoughts, and habits. After I came here, when I was just fourteen, I began to think about myself sooner than most girls, and to know that I am a "person." Sometimes, when I lie in bed at night, I have a terrible desire to feel my breasts and to listen to the quiet rhythmic beat of my heart.

I already had these kinds of feelings subconsciously before I came here, because I remember that once when I slept with a girl friend I had a strong desire to kiss her, and that I did do so. I could not help being terribly inquisitive over her body, for she had always kept it hidden from me. I asked her whether, as proof of our friendship, we should feel one another's breasts, but she refused. I go into ecstasies every time I see the naked figure of a woman, such as Venus, for example. It strikes me as so wonderful and exquisite that I have difficulty in stopping the tears rolling down my cheeks.

If only I had a girl friend!

Yours, Anne

Dear Kitty,

My longing to talk to someone became so intense that somehow or other I took it into my head to choose Peter.

Sometimes if I've been upstairs into Peter's room during the day, it always struck me as very snug, but because Peter is so retiring and would never turn anyone out who became a nuisance, I never dared stay long, because I was afraid he might think me a bore. I tried to think of an excuse to stay in his room and get him talking, without it being too noticeable, and my chance came yesterday. Peter has a mania for crossword puzzles at the moment and hardly does anything else. I helped him with them and we soon sat opposite each other at his little table, he on the chair and me on the divan.

It gave me a queer feeling each time I looked into his deep blue eyes, and he sat there with that mysterious laugh playing round his lips. I was able to read his inward thoughts. I could see on his face that look of helplessness and uncertainty as to how to behave, and, at the same time, a trace of his sense of manhood. I noticed his shy manner and it made me feel very gentle; I couldn't refrain from meeting those dark eyes again and again, and with my whole heart I almost beseeched him: oh, tell me, what is going on inside you, oh, can't you look beyond this ridiculous chatter?

But the evening passed and nothing happened, except that I told him about blushing—naturally not what I have written, but just so that he would become more sure of himself as he grew older.

When I lay in bed and thought over the whole situation, I found it far from encouraging, and the idea that I should beg for Peter's patronage was simply repellent. One can do a lot to satisfy one's longings, which certainly sticks out in my case, for I have made up my mind to go and sit with Peter more often and to get him talking somehow or other.

Whatever you do, don't think I'm in love with Peter— not a bit of it! If the Van Daans had had a daughter instead of a son, I should have tried to make friends with her too.

I woke at about five to seven this morning and knew at once, quite positively, what I had dreamed. I sat on a chair and opposite me sat Peter . . . Wessel. We were looking together at a book of drawings by Mary Bos. The dream was so vivid that I can still partly remember the drawings. But that was not all—the dream went on. Suddenly Peter's eyes met mine and I looked into those fine, velvet brown eyes for a long time. Then Peter said very softly, "If I had only known, I would have come to you long before!" I turned around brusquely because the emotion was too much for me. And after that I felt a soft, and oh, such a cool kind cheek against mine and it felt so good, so good. . . .

I awoke at this point, while I could still feel his cheek against mine and felt his brown eyes looking deep into my heart, so deep, that there he read how much I had loved him and how much I still love him. Tears sprang into my eyes once more, and I was very sad that I had lost him again, but at the same time glad because it made me feel quite certain that Peter was still the chosen one.

It is strange that I should often see such vivid images in my dreams here. First I saw Grandma[1] so clearly one night that I could even distinguish her thick, soft, wrinkled velvety skin. Then Granny appeared as a guardian angel; then followed Lies, who seems to be a symbol to me of the sufferings of all my girl friends and all Jews. When I pray for her, I pray for all Jews and all those in need. And now Peter, my darling Peter—never before have I had such a clear picture of him in my mind. I don't need a photo of him, I can see him before my eyes, and oh, so well!

Yours, Anne

[1] Grandma is grandmother on Father's side, Granny on Mother's side.

Dear Kitty,

What a silly ass I am! I am quite forgetting that I have never told you the history of myself and all my boy friends.

When I was quite small—I was even still at a kinder-garten—I became attached to Karel Samson. He had lost his father, and he and his mother lived with an aunt. One of Karel's cousins, Robby, was a slender, good-looking dark boy, who aroused more admiration than the litttle, humorous fellow, Karel. But looks did not count with me and I was very fond of Karel for years.

We used to be together a lot for quite a long time, but for the rest, my love was unreturned.

Then Peter crossed my path, and in my childish way I really fell in love. He liked me very much, too, and we were inseparable for one whole summer. I can still remember us walking hand in hand through the streets together, he in a white cotton suit and me in a short summer dress. At the end of the summer holidays he went into the first form of the high school and I into the sixth form of the lower school. He used to meet me from school and, vice versa, I would meet him. Peter was a very good-looking boy, tall, handsome, and slim, with an earnest, calm, intelligent face. He had dark hair, and wonderful brown eyes, ruddy cheeks, and a pointed nose. I was mad about his laugh, above all, when he looked so mischievous and naughty!

I went to the country for the holidays; when I returned, Peter had in the meantime moved, and a much older boy lived in the same house. He apparently drew Peter's attention to the fact that I was a childish little imp, and Peter gave me up. I adored him so that I didn't want to face the truth. I tried to hold on to him until it dawned on me that if I went on running after him I should soon get the name of being boy-mad. The years passed. Peter went around with girls of his own age and didn't even think of saying "Hello" to me any more; but I —couldn't forget him.

I went to the Jewish Secondary School. Lots of boys in our class were keen on me—I thought it was fun, felt honored, but was otherwise quite untouched. Then later on, Harry was mad about me, but, as I've already told you, I never fell in love again.

There is a saying "Time heals all wounds," and so it was with me. I imagined that I had forgotten Peter and that I didn't like him a bit any more. The memory of him, however, lived so strongly in my subconscious mind that I admitted to myself sometimes I was jealous of the other girls, and that was why I didn't like him any more. This morning I knew that nothing has changed; on the contrary, as I grew older and more mature my love grew with me. I can quite understand now that Peter thought me childish, and yet it still hurt that he had so completely forgotten me. His face was shown so clearly to me, and now I know that no one else could remain with me like he does.

I am completely upset by the dream. When Daddy kissed me this morning, I could have cried out: "Oh, if only you were Peter!" I think of him all the time and I keep repeating to myself the whole day, "Oh, Petel, darling, darling Petel . . . !"

Who can help me now? I must live on and pray to God that He will let Peter cross my path when I come out of here, and that when he reads the love in my eyes he will say, "Oh, Anne, if I had only known, I would have come to you long before!"

I saw my face in the mirror and it looks quite different. My eyes look so clear and deep, my cheeks are pink—which they haven't been for weeks—my mouth is much softer; I look as if I am happy, and yet there is something so sad in my expression and my smile slips away from my lips as soon as it has come. I'm not happy, because I might know that Peter's thoughts are not with me, and

121

yet I still feel his wonderful eyes upon me and his cool soft cheek against mine.

Oh, Petel, Petel, how will I ever free myself of your image? Wouldn't any other in your place be a miserable substitute? I love you, and with such a great love that it can't grow in my heart any more but has to leap out into the open and suddenly manifest itself in such a devastating way!

A week ago, even yesterday, if anyone had asked me, "Which of your friends do you consider would be the most suitable to marry?" I would have answered, "I don't know"; but now I would cry, "Petel, because I love him with all my heart and soul. I give myself completely!" But one thing, he may touch my face, but no more.

Once, when we spoke about sex, Daddy told me that I couldn't possibly understand the longing yet; I always knew that I did understand it and now I understand it fully. Nothing is so beloved to me now as he, my Petel.

Yours, Anne

Wednesday, 12 January, 1944

Dear Kitty,

Elli has been back a fortnight. Miep and Henk were away from their work for two days—they both had tummy upsets.

I have a craze for dancing and ballet at the moment, and practice dance steps every evening diligently: I have made a supermodern dance frock from a light blue petticoat edged with lace belonging to Mansa. A ribbon is threaded through round the top and ties in a bow in the center, and a pink corded ribbon completes the creation. I tried in vain to convert my gym shoes into real ballet shoes. My stiff limbs are well on the way to becoming supple again like they used to be. One terrific exercise is to sit on the floor, hold a heel in each hand, and then lift both legs up in the air. I have to have a cushion under me, otherwise my poor little behind has a rough time.

Everyone here is reading the book *Cloudless Morn*. Mummy thought it exceptionally good; there are a lot of youth problems in it. I thought to myself rather ironically: "Take a bit more trouble with your own young people first!"

I believe Mummy thinks there could be no better relationship between parents and their children, and that no one could take a greater interest in their children's lives than she. But quite definitely she only looks at Margot, who I don't think ever had such problems and thoughts as I do. Still, I wouldn't dream of pointing out to Mummy that, in the case of her daughters, it isn't at all as she imagines, because she would be utterly amazed and wouldn't know how to change anyway; I want to save her the unhappiness it would cause her, especially as I know that for me everything would remain the same anyway.

Mummy certainly feels that Margot loves her much more than I do, but she thinks that this just goes in phases! Margot has grown so sweet; she seems quite different from what she used to be, isn't nearly so catty these days and is becoming a real friend. Nor does she any longer regard me as a little kid who counts for nothing.

I have an odd way of sometimes, as it were, being able to see myself through someone else's eyes. Then I view the affairs of a certain "Anne" at my ease, and browse through the pages of her life as if she were a stranger. Before we came here, when I didn't think about things as much as I do now, I used at times to have the feeling that I didn't belong to Mansa, Pim, and Margot, and that I would always be a bit of an outsider. Sometimes I used to pretend I was an orphan, until I reproached and punished myself, telling myself it was all my own fault that I played this self-pitying role, when I was really so fortunate. Then came the time that I used to force myself to be friendly. Every morning, as soon as someone came downstairs I hoped that it would be Mummy who would say good morning to me; I greeted her warmly, because I really longed for her to look lovingly at me. Then she made some remark or other that seemed unfriendly, and I would go off to school again feeling thoroughly disheartened. On the way home I would make excuses for her because she had so many worries, arrive home very cheerful, chatter nineteen to the dozen, until I began repeating myself, and left the room wearing a pensive expression, my satchel under my arm. Sometimes I decided to remain cross, but when I came home from school I always had so much news that my resolutions were gone with the wind and Mummy, whatever she might be doing, had to lend an ear to all my adventures. Then the time came once more when I didn't listen for footsteps on the staircase any longer, and at night my pillow was wet with tears.

Everything grew much worse at that point; *enfin*, you know all about it.

Now God has sent me a helper—Peter . . . I just clasp my pendant, kiss it, and think to myself, "What do I care about the lot of them! Peter belongs to me and no one knows anything about it." This way I can get over all the snubs I receive. Who would ever think that so much can go on in the soul of a young girl?

Yours, Anne

Saturday, 15 January, 1944

Dear Kitty,

There is no point in telling you every time the exact details of our rows and arguments. Let it suffice to tell you that we have divided up a great many things, such as butter and meat, and that we fry our own potatoes. For some time now we've been eating whole-meal bread between meals as an extra, because by four o'clock in the afternoon we are longing for our supper so much that we hardly know how to control our rumbling tummies.

Mummy's birthday is rapidly approaching. She got some extra sugar from Kraler, which made the Van Daans jealous as Mrs. Van Daan had not been favored in this way for her birthday. But what's the use of annoying each other with yet more unkind words, tears, and angry outbursts. You can be sure of one thing, Kitty, that we are even more fed up with them than ever! Mummy has expressed the wish—one which cannot come true just now—not to see the Van Daan's for a fortnight.

I keep asking myself, whether one would have trouble in the long run, whoever one shared a house with. Or did we strike it extra unlucky? Are most people so selfish and stingy then? I think it's all to the good to have learned a bit about human beings, but now I think I've learned enough. The war goes on just the same, whether or not we choose to quarrel, or long for freedom and fresh air, and so we should try to make the best of our stay here. Now I'm preaching, but I also believe that if I stay here for very long I shall grow into a dried-up old beanstalk. And I did so want to grow into a real young woman!

Yours, Anne

Saturday, 22 January, 1944

Dear Kitty,

I wonder whether you can tell me why it is that people always try so hard to hide their real feelings? How is it that I always behave quite differently from what I should in other people's company?

Why do we trust one another so little? I know there must be a reason, but still I sometimes think it's horrible that you find you can never really confide in people, even in those who are nearest to you.

It seems as if I've grown up a lot since my dream the other night. I'm much more of an "independent being." You'll certainly be amazed when I tell you that even my attitude towards the Van Daans has changed. I suddenly see all the arguments and the rest of it in a different light, and am not as prejudiced as I was.

How can I have changed so much? Yes, you see it suddenly struck me that if Mummy had been different, a real Mumsie, the relationship might have been quite different. It's true that Mrs. Van Daan is by no means a nice person, but still I do think that half the quarrels could be avoided if it weren't for the fact that when the conversation gets tricky Mummy is a bit difficult too.

Mrs. Van Daan has one good side, and that is that you can talk to her. Despite all her selfishness, stinginess, and underhandedness, you can make her give in easily, as long as you don't irritate her and get on the wrong side of her. This way doesn't work every time, but if you have patience you can try again and see how far you get.

All the problems of our "upbringing," of our being spoiled, the food—it could have been quite different if we'd remain perfectly open and friendly, and not always only on the lookout for something to seize on.

I know exactly what you'll say, Kitty: "But, Anne, do these words really come from *your* lips? From you, who have had to listen to so many harsh words from the people upstairs, from you, the girl who has suffered so many injustices?" And yet they come from me.

I want to start afresh and try to get to the bottom of it all, not be like the saying "the young always follow a bad example." I want to examine the whole matter carefully myself and find out what is true and what is exaggerated. Then if I myself am disappointed in them, I can adopt the same lines as Mummy and Daddy; if not, I shall try first of all to make them alter their ideas and if I don't succeed I shall stick to my own opinions and judgment. I shall seize every opportunity to discuss openly all our points of argument with Mrs. Van Daan and not be afraid of declaring myself neutral, even at the cost of being called a "know-all." It is not that I shall be going against my own family, but from today there will be no more unkind gossip on my part.

Until now I was immovable! I always thought the Van Daans were in the wrong, but we too are partly to blame. We have certainly been right over the subject matter; but handling of others from intelligent people (which we consider ourselves to be!) one expects more insight. I hope that I have acquired a bit of insight and will use it well when the occasion arises.

Yours, Anne

Dear Kitty,

Something has happened to me; or rather, I can hardly describe it as an event, except that I think it is pretty crazy. Whenever anyone used to speak of sexual problems at home or at school, it was something either mysterious or revolting. Words which had any bearing on the subject were whispered, and often if someone didn't understand he was laughed at. It struck me as very odd and I thought, "Why are people so secretive and tiresome when they talk about these things?" But as I didn't think that I could change things, I kept my mouth shut as much as possible, or sometimes asked girl friends for information. When I had learned quite a lot and had also spoken about it with my parents, Mummy said one day, "Anne, let me give you some good advice; never speak about this subject to boys and don't reply if they begin about it." I remember exactly what my answer was: I said, "No, of course not! The very idea!" And there it remained.

When we first came here, Daddy often told me about things that I would really have preferred to hear from Mummy, and I found out the rest from books and things I picked up from conversations. Peter Van Daan was never as tiresome over this as the boys at school—once or twice at first perhaps—but he never tried to get me talking.

Mrs. Van Daan told us that she had never talked about these things to Peter, and for all she knew neither had her husband. Apparently she didn't even know how much he knew.

Yesterday, when Margot, Peter, and I were peeling potatoes, somehow the conversation turned to Boche. "We still don't know what sex Boche is, do we?" I asked.

"Yes, certainly," Peter answered. "He's a tom."

I began to laugh. "A tomcat that's expecting, that's marvelous!"

Peter and Margot laughed too over this silly mistake.

You see, two months ago, Peter had stated that Boche would soon be having a family, her tummy was growing visibly. However, the fatness appeared to come from the many stolen bones, because the children didn't seem to grow fast, let alone make their appearance!

Peter just had to defend himself. "No," he said, "you can go with me yourself to look at him. Once when I was playing around with him, I noticed quite clearly that he's a tom."

I couldn't control my curiosity, and went with him to the warehouse. Boche, however, was not receiving visitors, and was nowhere to be seen. We waited for a while, began to get cold, and went upstairs again. Later in the afternoon I heard Peter go downstairs for the second time. I mustered up all my courage to walk through the silent house alone, and reached the warehouse. Boche stood on the packing table playing with Peter, who had just put him on the scales to weigh him.

"Hello, do you want to see him?" He didn't make any lengthy preparations, but picked up the animal, turned him over on to his back, deftly held his head and paws together, and the lesson began. "Those are the male organs, these are just a few stray hairs, and that is his bottom." The cat did another half turn and was standing on his white socks once more.

If any other boy had shown me "the male organs," I would never have looked at him again. But Peter went on talking quite normally on what is otherwise such a painful subject, without meaning anything unpleasant, and finally put me sufficiently at my ease for me to be normal too. We played with Boche, amused ourselves, chattered together, and then sauntered through the large warehouse towards the door.

"Usually, when I want to know something, I find it in some book or other, don't you?" I asked.

"Why on earth? I just ask upstairs. My father knows more than me and has had more experience in such things."

We were already on the stair, so I kept my mouth shut after that.

"Things may alter," as Brer Rabbit said. Yes. Really I shouldn't have discussed these things in such a normal way with a girl. I know too definitely that Mummy didn't mean it that way when she warned me not to discuss the subject with boys. I wasn't quite my usual self for the rest of the day though, in spite of everything. When I thought over our talk, it still seemed rather odd. But at least I'm wiser about one thing, that there really are young people —and of the opposite sex too—who can discuss these things naturally without making fun of them.

I wonder if Peter really does ask his parents much. Would he honestly behave with them as he did with me yesterday? Ah, what would I know about it!

Yours, Anne

Thursday, 27 January, 1944

Dear Kitty,

Lately I have developed a great love for family trees and genealogical tables of the royal families, and have come to the conclusion that, once you begin, you want to delve still deeper into the past, and can keep on making fresh and interesting discoveries. Although I am extraordinarily industrious over my lessons, and can already follow the English Home Service quite well on the wireless, I still devote many Sundays to sorting and looking over my large collection of film stars, which is quite a respectable size by now.

I am awfully pleased whenever Mr. Kraler brings the *Cinema and Theater* with him on Mondays. Although this little gift is often called a waste of money by the less worldly members of the household, they are amazed each time at how accurately I can state who is in a certain film, even after a year. Elli, who, on her days off, often goes to the movies with her boy friend, tells me the titles of the new films each week; and in one breath I rattle off the names of the stars who appear in them, together with what the reviews say. Not so long ago, Mum said that I wouldn't need to go to a cinema later on because I knew

129

the plots, the names of the stars, and the opinions of the reviews all by heart.

If ever I come sailing in with a new hair style, they all look disapprovingly at me, and I can be quite sure that someone will ask which glamorous star I'm supposed to be imitating. They only half believe me if I reply that it's my own invention.

But to continue about the hair style—it doesn't stay put for more than half an hour; then I'm so tired of the remarks people pass that I quickly hasten to the bathroom and restore my ordinary house-garden-kitchen hair style.

Yours, Anne

Friday, 28 January, 1944

Dear Kitty,

I asked myself this morning whether you don't sometimes feel rather like a cow who has had to chew over all the old pieces of news again and again, and who finally yawns loudly and silently wishes that Anne would occasionally dig up something new.

Alas, I know it's dull for you, but try to put yourself in my place, and imagine how sick I am of the old cows who keep having to be pulled out of the ditch again. If the conversation at mealtimes isn't over politics or a delicious meal, then Mummy or Mrs. Van Daan trot out one of the old stories of their youth, which we've heard so many times before; or Dussel twaddles on about his wife's extensive wardrobe, beautiful race horses, leaking rowboats, boys who can swim at the age of four, muscular pains and nervous patients. What it all boils down to is this—that if one of the eight of us opens his mouth, the other seven can finish the story for him! We all know the point of every joke from the start, and the storyteller is alone in laughing at his witticisms. The various milkmen, grocers, and butchers of the two ex-housewives have already grown beards in our minds, so often have they been praised to the skies or pulled to pieces; it is impossible for anything in the conversation here to be fresh or new.

Still, all this would be bearable if the grownups didn't have their little way of telling the stories, with which Koophuis, Henk, or Miep oblige the company, ten times over and adding their own little frills and furbelows, so that I often have to pinch my arm under the table to prevent myself from putting them right. Little children such as Anne must never, under any circumstances, know better than the grownups, however many blunders they make, and to whatever extent they allow their imaginations to run away with them.

One favorite subject of Koophuis's and Henk's is that of people in hiding and in the underground movement. They know very well that anything to do with other people in hiding interests us tremendously, and how deeply we can sympathize with the sufferings of people who get taken away, and rejoice with the liberated prisoner.

We are quite as used to the idea of going into hiding, or "underground," as in bygone days one was used to Daddy's bedroom slippers warming in front of the fire.

There are a great number of organizations, such as "The Free Netherlands," which forge identity cards, supply money to people "underground," find hiding places for people, and work for young men in hiding, and it is amazing how much noble, unselfish work these people are doing, risking their own lives to help and save others. Our helpers are a very good example. They have pulled us through up till now and we hope they will bring us safely to dry land. Otherwise, they will have to share the same fate as the many others who are being searched for. Never have we heard *one* word of the burden which we certainly must be to them, never has one of them complained of all the trouble we give.

They all come upstairs every day, talk to the men about business and politics, to the women about food and wartime difficulties, and about newspapers and books with the children. They put on the brightest possible faces, bring flowers and presents for birthdays and bank holi-

days, are always ready to help and do all they can. That is
something we must never forget; although others may
show heroism in the war or against the Germans, our
helpers display heroism in their cheerfulness and affection.

The wildest tales are going around, but still they are
usually founded on fact. For instance, Koophuis told us
this week that in Gelderland two football elevens met,
and one side consisted solely of members of the "underground" and the other was made up of members of the
police. New ration books are being handed out in
Hilversum. In order that the many people in hiding may
also draw rations, the officials have given instructions to
those of them in the district to come at a certain time, so
that they can collect their documents from a separate
little table. Still, they'll have to be careful that such
impudent tricks do not reach the ears of the Germans.

Yours, Anne

Thursday, 3 February, 1944

Dear Kitty,

Invasion fever in the country is mounting daily. If you
were here, on the one hand, you would probably feel the
effect of all these preparations just as I do and, on the
other, you would laugh at us for making such a fuss—who
knows—perhaps for nothing.

All the newspapers are full of the invasion and are
driving people mad by saying that "In the event of the
English landing in Holland, the Germans will do all they
can to defend the country; if necessary they will resort to
flooding." With this, maps have been published, on which
the parts of Holland that will be under water are marked.
As this applies to large parts of Amsterdam, the first
question was, what shall we do if the water in the streets
rises to one meter? The answers given by different people
vary considerably.

"As walking or cycling is out of the question, we shall
have to wade through the stagnant water."

"Of course not, one will have to try and swim. We shall

all put on our bathing suits and caps and swim under water as much as possible, then no one will see that we are Jews."

"Oh, what nonsense! I'd like to see the ladies swimming, if the rats started biting their legs!" (That was naturally a man: just see who screams the loudest!)

"We shan't be able to get out of the house anyway; the warehouse will definitely collapse if there is a flood, it is so wobbly already."

"Listen, folks, all joking apart, we shall try and get a boat."

"Why bother? I know something much better. We each get hold of a wooden packing case from the attic and row with a soup ladle!"

"I shall walk on stilts: I used to be an expert at it in my youth."

"Henk Van Santen won't need to, he's sure to take his wife on his back, then she'll be on stilts."

This gives you a rough idea, doesn't it, Kit?

This chatter is all very amusing, but the truth may be otherwise. A second question about the invasion was bound to arise: what do we do if the Germans evacuate Amsterdam?

"Leave the city too, and disguise ourselves as best we can."

"Don't go, whatever happens, stay put! The only thing to do is to remain here! The Germans are quite capable of driving the whole population right into Germany, where they will all die."

"Yes, naturally, we shall stay here, since this is the safest place. We'll try and fetch Koophuis and his family over here to come and live with us. We'll try and get hold of a sack of wood wool, then we can sleep on the floor. Let's ask Miep and Koophuis to start bringing blankets here."

"We'll order some extra corn in addition to our sixty pounds. Let's get Henk to try and obtain more peas and beans; we have about sixty pounds of beans and ten pounds of peas in the house at present. Don't forget that we've got fifty tins of vegetables."

"Mummy, just count up how much we've got of other food, will you?"

"Ten tins of fish, forty tins of milk, ten kilos of milk powder, three bottles of salad oil, four preserving jars of butter, four ditto of meat, two wicker-covered bottles of strawberries, two bottles of raspberries, twenty bottles of tomatoes, ten pounds of rolled oats, eight pounds of rice; and that's all.

"Our stock's not too bad, but if you think that we may be having visitors as well and drawing from reserves each week, then it seems more than it actually is. We have sufficient coal and firewood in the house, also candles. Let's all make little moneybags, which could easily be hidden in our clothing, in case we want to take money with us.

"We'll make lists of the most important things to take, should we have to run for it, and pack rucksacks now in readiness. If it gets that far, we'll put two people on watch, one in the front and one in the back loft. I say, what's the use of collecting such stocks of food, if we haven't any water, gas, or electricity?"

"Then we must cook on the stove. Filter and boil our water. We'll clean out some large wicker bottles and store water in them."

I hear nothing but this sort of talk the whole day long, invasion and nothing but invasion, arguments about suffering from hunger, dying, bombs, fire extinguishers, sleeping bags, Jewish vouchers, poisonous gases, etc., etc. None of it is exactly cheering. The gentlemen in the "Secret Annexe" give pretty straightforward warnings; an example is the following conversation with Henk:

"Secret Annexe": "We are afraid that if the Germans withdraw, they will take the whole population with them."

Henk: "That is impossible, they haven't the trains at their disposal."

"S.A.": "Trains? Do you really think they'd put civilians in carriages? Out of the question. They could use 'shank's mare.'" (*Per pedes apostolorum,* Dussel always says.)

H.: "I don't believe a word of it, you look on the black

134

side of everything. What would be their object in driving all the civilians along with them?"

"S.A.": "Didn't you know that Goebbels said, 'If we have to withdraw, we shall slam the doors of all the occupied countries behind us'?"

H.: "They have said so much already."

"S.A.": "Do you think the Germans are above doing such a thing or too humane? What they think is this: 'If we have got to go down, then everybody in our clutches will go down with us.'"

H.: "Tell that to the Marines; I just don't believe it!"

"S.A.": "It's always the same song; no one will see danger approaching until it is actually on top of him."

H.: "But you know nothing definite; you just simply suppose."

"S.A.": "We have all been through it ourselves, first in Germany, and then here. And what is going on in Russia?"

H.: "You mustn't include the Jews. I don't think anyone knows what is going on in Russia. The English and the Russians are sure to exaggerate things for propaganda purposes, just like the Germans."

"S.A.": "Out of the question, the English have always told the truth over the wireless. And suppose they do exaggerate the news, the facts are bad enough anyway, because you can't deny that many millions of peace-loving people were just simply murdered or gassed in Poland and Russia."

I will spare you further examples of these conversations; I myself keep very quiet and don't take any notice of all the fuss and excitement. I have now reached the stage that I don't care much whether I live or die. The world will still keep on turning without me; what is going to happen, will happen, and anyway it's no good to resist.

I trust to luck and do nothing but work, hoping that all will end well.

Yours, Anne

Dear Kitty,

The sun is shining, the sky is a deep blue, there is a lovely breeze and I'm longing—so longing—for everything. To talk, for freedom, for friends, to be alone. And I do so long . . . to cry! I feel as if I'm going to burst, and I know that it would get better with crying; but I can't, I'm restless, I go from one room to the other, breathe through the crack of a closed window, feel my heart beating, as if it is saying, "Can't you satisfy my longings at last?"

I believe that it's spring within me, I feel that spring is awakening, I feel it in my whole body and soul. It is an effort to behave normally, I feel utterly confused, don't know what to read, what to write, what to do, I only know that I am longing . . . !

Yours, Anne

Dear Kitty,

Since Saturday a lot has changed for me. It came about like this. I longed—and am still longing—but . . . now something has happened, which has made it a little, just a little, less.

To my great joy—I will be quite honest about it— already this morning I noticed that Peter kept looking at me all the time. Not in the ordinary way, I don't know how, I just can't explain.

I used to think that Peter was in love with Margot, but yesterday I suddenly had the feeling that it is not so. I made a special effort not to look at him too much, because whenever I did, he kept on looking too and then—yes, then—it gave me a lovely feeling inside, but which I mustn't feel too often.

I desperately want to be alone. Daddy has noticed that

I'm not quite my usual self, but I really can't tell him everything. "Leave me in peace, leave me alone," that's what I'd like to keep crying out all the time. Who knows, the day may come when I'm left alone more than I would wish!

Yours, Anne

Monday, 14 February, 1944

Dear Kitty,

On Sunday evening everyone except Pim and me was sitting beside the wireless in order to listen to the "Immortal Music of the German Masters." Dussel fiddled with the knobs continually. This annoyed Peter, and the others too. After restraining himself for half an hour, Peter asked somewhat irritably if the twisting and turning might stop. Dussel answered in his most hoity-toity manner, "I'm getting it all right." Peter became angry, was rude, Mr. Van Daan took his side, and Dussel had to give in. That was all.

The reason in itself was very unimportant, but Peter seems to have taken it very much to heart. In any case, when I was rummaging about in the bookcase in the attic, he came up to me and began telling me the whole story. I didn't know anything about it, but Peter soon saw that he had found an attentive ear and got fairly into his stride.

"Yes, and you see," he said, "I don't easily say anything, because I know beforehand that I'll only become tongue-tied. I begin to stutter, blush, and twist around what I want to say, until I have to break off because I simply can't find the words. That's what happened yesterday, I wanted to say something quite different, but once I had started, I got in a hopeless muddle and that's frightful. I used to have a bad habit; I wish I still had it now. If I was angry with anyone, rather than argue it out I would get to work on him with my fists. I quite realize that this method doesn't get me anywhere; and that is why I admire you. You are never at a loss for a word, you say

137

exactly what you want to say to people and are never the least bit shy."

"I can tell you, you're making a big mistake," I answered. "I usually say things quite differently from the way I meant to say them, and then I talk too much and far too long, and that's just as bad."

I couldn't help laughing to myself over this last sentence. However, I wanted to let him go on talking about himself, so I kept my amusement to myself, went and sat on a cushion on the floor, put my arms around my bent knees, and looked at him attentively.

I am very glad that there is someone else in the house who can get into the same fits of rage as I get into. I could see it did Peter good to pull Dussel to pieces to his heart's content, without fear of my telling tales. And as for me, I was very pleased, because I sensed a real feeling of fellowship, such as I can only remember having had with my girl friends.

Yours, Anne

Wednesday, 16 February, 1944

Dear Kitty,

It's Margot's birthday. Peter came at half past twelve to look at the presents and stayed talking much longer than was strictly necessary—a thing he'd have never done otherwise. In the afternoon I went to get some coffee and, after that, potatoes, because I wanted to spoil Margot for just that one day in the year. I went through Peter's room; he took all his papers off the stairs at once and I asked whether I should close the trap door to the attic. "Yes," he replied, "knock when you come back, then I'll open it for you."

I thanked him, went upstairs, and searched at least ten minutes in the large barrel for the smallest potatoes. Then my back began to ache and I got cold. Naturally I didn't knock, but opened the trap door myself, but still he came to meet me most obligingly, and took the pan from me.

"I've looked for a long time, these are the smallest I could find," I said.

"Did you look in the big barrel?"

"Yes, I've been over them all."

By this time I was standing at the bottom of the stairs and he looked searchingly in the pan which he was still holding. "Oh, but these are first-rate," he said, and added when I took the pan from him, "I congratulate you!" At the same time he gave me such a gentle warm look which made a tender glow within me. I could really see that he wanted to please me, and because he couldn't make a long complimentary speech he spoke with his eyes. I understood him, oh, so well, and was very grateful. It gives me pleasure even now when I recall those words and that look he gave me.

When I went downstairs, Mummy said that I must get some more potatoes, this time for supper. I willingly offered to go upstairs again.

When I came into Peter's room, I apologized at having to disturb him again. When I was already on the stairs he got up, and went and stood between the door and the wall, firmly took hold of my arm, and wanted to hold me back by force.

"I'll go," he said. I replied that it really wasn't necessary and that I didn't have to get particularly small ones this time. Then he was convinced and let my arm go. On the way down, he came and opened the trap door and took the pan again. When I reached the door, I asked, "What are you doing?" "French," he replied. I asked if I might glance through the exercises, washed my hands, and went and sat on the divan opposite him.

We soon began talking, after I'd explained some of the French to him. He told me that he wanted to go to the Dutch East Indies and live on a plantation later on. He talked about his home life, about the black market, and then he said that he felt so useless. I told him that he certainly had a very strong inferiority complex. He talked about the Jews. He would have found it much easier if he'd been a Christian and if he could be one after the war. I asked if he wanted to be baptized, but that wasn't

139

the case either. Who was to know whether he was a Jew when the war was over? he said.

This gave me rather a pang; it seems such a pity that there's always just a tinge of dishonesty about him. For the rest we chatted very pleasantly about Daddy, and about judging people's characters and all kinds of things, I can't remember exactly what now.

It was half past four by the time I left.

In the evening he said something else that I thought was nice. We were talking about a picture of a film star that I'd given him once, which has now been hanging in his room for at least a year and a half. He liked it very much and I offered to give him a few more sometime. "No," he replied, "I'd rather leave it like this. I look at these every day and they have grown to be my friends."

Now I understand more why he always hugs Mouschi. He needs some affection, too, of course.

I'd forgotten something else that he talked about. He said, "I don't know what fear is, except when I think of my own shortcomings. But I'm getting over that too."

Peter has a terrible inferiority complex. For instance, he always thinks that he is so stupid, and we are so clever. If I help him with his French, he thanks me a thousand times. One day I shall turn around and say: "Oh, shut up, you're much better at English and geography!"

Yours, Anne

Friday, 18 February, 1944

Dear Kitty,

Whenever I go upstairs now I keep on hoping that I shall see "him." Because my life now has an object, and I have something to look forward to, everything has become more pleasant.

At least the object of my feelings is always there, and I needn't be afraid of rivals, except Margot. Don't think I'm in love, because I'm not, but I do have the feeling all the time that something fine can grow up between us, something that gives confidence and friendship. If I get half a chance, I go up to him now. It's not like it used to be when he didn't know how to begin. It's just the opposite— he's still talking when I'm half out of the room.

Mummy doesn't like it much, and always says I'll be a nuisance and that I must leave him in peace. Honestly, doesn't she realize that I've got some intuition? She looks at me so queerly every time I go into Peter's little room. If I come downstairs from there, she asks me where I've been. I simply can't bear it, and think it's horrible.

Yours, Anne

Saturday, 19 February, 1944

Dear Kitty,

It is Saturday again and that really speaks for itself.

The morning was quiet. I helped a bit upstairs, but I didn't have more than a few fleeting words with "him." At half past two, when everyone had gone to their own rooms, either to sleep or to read, I went to the private office, with my blanket and everything, to sit at the desk and read or write. It was not long before it all became too much for me, my head drooped on to my arm, and I sobbed my heart out. The tears streamed down my cheeks and I felt desperately unhappy. Oh, if only "he" had come to comfort me. It was four o'clock by the time I went upstairs again. I went for some potatoes, with fresh hope in my heart of a meeting, but while I was still smartening up my hair in the bathroom he went down to see Boche in the warehouse.

Suddenly I felt the tears coming back and I hurried to the lavatory, quickly grabbing a pocket mirror as I passed. There I sat then, fully dressed, while the tears made dark spots on the red of my apron, and I felt very wretched.

This is what was going through my mind. Oh, I'll never reach Peter like this. Who knows, perhaps he doesn't like me at all and doesn't need anyone to confide in. Perhaps he only thinks about me in a casual sort of way. I shall

141

have to go on alone once more, without friendship and without Peter. Perhaps soon I'll be without hope, without comfort, or anything to look forward to again. Oh, if I could nestle my head against his shoulder and not feel so hopelessly alone and deserted! Who knows, perhaps he doesn't care about me at all and looks at the others in just the same way. Perhaps I only imagined that it was especially for me? Oh, Peter, if only you could see or hear me. If the truth were to prove as bad as that, it would be more than I could bear.

However, a little later fresh hope and anticipation seemed to return, even though the tears were still streaming down my cheeks.

— Yours, Anne

Wednesday, 23 February, 1944

Dear Kitty,

It's lovely weather outside and I've quite perked up since yesterday. Nearly every morning I go to the attic where Peter works to blow the stuffy air out of my lungs. From my favorite spot on the floor I look up at the blue sky and the bare chestnut tree, on whose branches little raindrops shine, appearing like silver, and at the seagulls and the other birds as they glide on the wind.

He stood with his head against a thick beam, and I sat down. We breathed the fresh air, looked outside, and both felt that the spell should not be broken by words. We remained like this for a long time, and when he had to go up to the loft to chop wood, I knew that he was a nice fellow. He climbed the ladder, and I followed, then he chopped wood for about a quarter of an hour, during which time we still remained silent. I watched him from where I stood, he was obviously doing his best to show off his strength. But I looked out of the open window too, over a large area of Amsterdam, over all the roofs and on to the horizon, which was such a pale blue that it was hard to see the dividing line. "As long as this exists," I thought, "and I may live to see it, this sunshine, the cloudless skies, while this lasts, I cannot be unhappy."

The best remedy for those who are afraid, lonely, or unhappy is to go outside, somewhere where they can be quite alone with the heavens, nature, and God. Because only then does one feel that all is as it should be and that God wishes to see people happy, amidst the simple beauty of nature. As long as this exists, and it certainly always will, I know that then there will always be comfort for every sorrow, whatever the circumstances may be. And I firmly believe that nature brings solace in all troubles.

Oh, who knows, perhaps it won't be long before I can share this overwhelming feeling of bliss with someone who feels the way I do about it.

Yours, Anne

A thought:

We miss so much here, so very much and for so long now: I miss it too, just as you do. I'm not talking of outward things, for we are looked after in that way; no, I mean the inward things. Like you, I long for freedom and fresh air, but I believe now that we have ample compensation for our privations. I realized this quite suddenly when I sat in front of the window this morning. I mean inward compensation.

When I looked outside right into the depth of Nature and God, then I was happy, really happy. And Peter, so long as I have that happiness here, the joy in nature, health and a lot more besides, all the while one has that, one can always recapture happiness.

Riches can all be lost, but that happiness in your own heart can only be veiled, and it will still bring you happiness again, as long as you live. As long as you can look fearlessly up into the heavens, as long as you know that you are pure within and that you will still find happiness.

Dearest Kitty,

From early in the morning till late at night, I really do hardly anything else but think of Peter. I sleep with his image before my eyes, dream about him and he is still looking at me when I awake.

I have a strong feeling that Peter and I are really not so different as we would appear to be, and I will tell you why. We both lack a mother. His is too superficial, loves flirting and doesn't trouble much about what he thinks. Mine does bother about me, but lacks sensitiveness, real motherliness.

Peter and I both wrestle with our inner feelings, we are still uncertain and are really too sensitive to be roughly treated. If we are, then my reaction is to "get away from it all." But as that is impossible, I hide my feelings, throw my weight about the place, am noisy and boisterous, so that everyone wishes that I was out of the way.

He, on the contrary, shuts himself up, hardly talks at all, is quiet, day-dreams and in his way carefully conceals his true self.

But how and when will we finally reach each other? I don't know quite how long my common sense will keep this longing under control.

Yours, Anne

Dearest Kitty,

It is becoming a bad dream—in daytime as well as at night. I see him nearly all the time and can't get at him, I mustn't show anything, must remain gay while I'm really in despair.

Peter Wessel and Peter Van Daan have grown into one

144

Peter, who is beloved and good, and for whom I long desperately.

Mummy is tiresome, Daddy sweet and therefore all the more tiresome, Margot the most tiresome because she expects me to wear a pleasant expression; and all I want is to be left in peace.

Peter didn't come to me in the attic. He went up to the loft instead and did some carpentry. At every creak and every knock some of my courage seemed to seep away and I grew more unhappy. In the distance a bell was playing "Pure in body, pure in soul." [1] I'm sentimental—I know. I'm desperate and silly—I know that too. Oh, help me!

Yours, Anne

Wednesday, 1 March, 1944

Dear Kitty,

My own affairs have been pushed into the background by—a burglary. I'm becoming boring with all my burglars, but what can I do, they seem to take such a delight in honoring Kolen & Co. with their visits. This burglary is much more complicated than the one in July 1943.

When Mr. Van Daan went to Kraler's office at half past seven, as usual, he saw that the communicating glass doors and the office door were open. Surprised at this, he walked through and was even more amazed to see that the doors of the little dark room were open too, and that there was a terrible mess in the main office. "There has been a burglar," he thought to himself at once, and to satisfy himself he went straight downstairs to look at the front door, felt the Yale lock, and found everything closed. "Oh, then both Peter and Elli must have been very slack this evening," he decided. He remained in Kraler's room for a while, then switched off the lamp, and went upstairs, without worrying much about either the open doors or the untidy office.

[1] The bells in old clock towers play tunes.

This morning Peter knocked at our door early and came with the not so pleasant news that the front door was wide open. He also told us that the projector and Kraler's new portfolio had both disappeared from the cupboard. Peter was told to close the door. Van Daan told us of his discoveries the previous evening and we were all awfully worried.

What must have happened is that the thief had a skeleton key, because the lock was quite undamaged. He must have crept into the house quite early and closed the door behind him, hidden himself when disturbed by Mr. Van Daan, and when he departed fled with his spoils, leaving the door open in his haste. Who can have our key? Why didn't the thief go to the warehouse? Might it be one of our own warehousemen, and would he perhaps betray us, since he certainly heard Van Daan and perhaps even saw him?

It is all very creepy, because we don't know whether this same burglar may not take it into his head to visit us again. Or perhaps it gave him a shock to find that there was someone walking about in the house?

Yours, Anne

Thursday, 2 March, 1944

Dear Kitty,

Margot and I were both up in the attic today; although we were not able to enjoy it together as I had imagined, still I do know that she shares my feelings over most things.

During dish washing Elli began telling Mummy and Mrs. Van Daan that she felt very discouraged at times. And what help do you think they gave her? Do you know what Mummy's advice was? She should try to think of all the other people who are in trouble! What is the good of thinking of misery when one is already miserable oneself? I said this too and was told, "You keep out of this sort of conversation."

Aren't the grownups idiotic and stupid? Just as if Peter,

146

Margot, Elli, and I don't all feel the same about things, and only a mother's love or that of a very, very good friend can help us. These mothers here just don't understand us at all. Perhaps Mrs. Van Daan does a little more than Mummy. Oh, I would have so liked to say something to poor Elli, something that I know from experience would have helped her. But Daddy came between us and pushed me aside.

Aren't they all stupid! We aren't allowed to have any opinions. People can tell you to keep your mouth shut, but it doesn't stop you having your own opinion. Even if people are still very young, they shouldn't be prevented from saying what they think.

Only great love and devotion can help Elli, Margot, Peter, and me, and none of us gets it. And no one, especially the stupid "know-alls" here, can understand us, because we are much more sensitive and much more advanced in our thoughts than anyone here would ever imagine in their wildest dreams.

Mummy is grumbling again at the moment—she is obviously jealous because I talk more to Mrs. Van Daan than to her nowadays.

I managed to get hold of Peter this afternoon and we talked for at least three quarters of an hour. Peter had the greatest difficulty in saying anything about himself; it took a long time to draw him out. He told me how often his parents quarrel over politics, cigarettes, and all kinds of things. He was very shy.

Then I talked to him about my parents. He defended Daddy: he thought him a "first-rate chap." Then we talked about "upstairs" and "downstairs" again; he was really rather amazed that we don't always like his parents. "Peter," I said, "you know I'm always honest, so why shouldn't I tell you that we can see their faults too." And among other things I also said, "I would so like to help you, Peter; can't I? You are in such an awkward position and, although you don't say anything, it doesn't mean that you don't care."

"Oh, I would always welcome your help."

"Perhaps you would do better to go to Daddy, he

wouldn't let anything go any further, take it from me; you can easily tell him!"

"Yes, he is a real pal."

"You're very fond of him, aren't you?" Peter nodded and I went on: "And he is of you too!"

He looked up quickly and blushed, it was really moving to see how these few words pleased him.

"Do you think so?" he asked.

"Yes," I said, "you can easily tell by little things that slip out now and then!"

Peter is a first-rate chap, too, just like Daddy!

Yours, Anne

Friday, 3 March, 1944

Dear Kitty,

When I looked into the candle this evening[1] I felt calm and happy. Oma seems to be in the candle and it is Oma too who shelters and protects me and who always makes me feel happy again.

But . . . there is someone else who governs all my moods and that is . . . Peter. When I went up to get potatoes today and was still standing on the stepladder with the pan, he at once asked, "What have you been doing since lunch?" I went and sat on the steps and we started talking. At a quarter past five (an hour later) the potatoes, which had been sitting on the floor in the meantime, finally reached their destinations.

Peter didn't say another word about his parents; we just talked about books and about the past. The boy has such warmth in his eyes; I believe I'm pretty near to being in love with him. He talked about that this evening. I went into his room, after peeling the potatoes, and said that I felt hot.

"You can tell what the temperature is by Margot and me; if it's cold we are white, and if it is hot we are red in the face," I said.

"In love?" he asked.

[1] In Jewish homes candles are lit on the Sabbath eve.

148

"Why should I be in love?" My answer was rather silly.

"Why not?" he said, and then we had to go for supper.

Would he have meant anything by that question? I finally managed to ask him today whether he didn't find my chatter a nuisance; he only said: "It's okay, I like it!"

To what extent this answer was just shyness, I am not able to judge.

Kitty, I'm just like someone in love, who can only talk about her darling. And Peter really is a darling. When shall I be able to tell him so? Naturally, only if he thinks I'm a darling too. But I'm quite capable of looking after myself, and he knows that very well. And he likes his tranquillity, so I have no idea how much he likes me. In any case, we are getting to know each other a bit. I wish we dared to tell each other much more already. Who knows, the time may come sooner than I think! I get an understanding look from him about twice a day, I wink back, and we both feel happy.

I certainly seem quite mad to be talking about him being happy, and yet I feel pretty sure that he thinks just the same as I do.

Yours, Anne

Saturday, 4 March, 1944

Dear Kitty,

This is the first Saturday for months and months that hasn't been boring, dreary, and dull. And Peter is the cause.

This morning I went to the attic to hang up my apron, when Daddy asked whether I'd like to stay and talk some French. I agreed. First we talked French, and I explained something to Peter; then we did some English. Daddy read out loud to us from Dickens and I was in the seventh heaven, because I sat on Daddy's chair very close to Peter.

I went downstairs at eleven o'clock. When I came upstairs again at half past eleven, he was already waiting for me on the stairs. We talked until a quarter to one.

If, as I leave the room, he gets a chance after a meal, for instance, and if no one can hear, he says: "Good-by, Anne, see you soon."

Oh, I am so pleased! I wonder if he is going to fall in love with me after all? Anyway, he is a very nice fellow and no one knows what lovely talks I have with him!

Mrs. Van Daan quite approves when I go and talk to him, but she asked today teasingly, "Can I really trust you two up there together?"

"Of course," I protested, "really you quite insult me!" From morn till night I look forward to seeing Peter.

Yours, Anne

Monday, 6 March, 1944

Dear Kitty,

I can tell by Peter's face that he thinks just as much as I do, and when Mrs. Van Daan yesterday evening said scoffingly: "The thinker!" I was irritated. Peter flushed and looked very embarrassed, and I was about to explode.

Why can't these people keep their mouths shut?

You can't imagine how horrible it is to stand by and see how lonely he is and yet not be able to do anything. I can so well imagine, just as if I were in his place, how desperate he must feel sometimes in quarrels and in love. Poor Peter, he needs love very much!

When he said he didn't need any friends how harsh the words sounded to my ears. Oh, how mistaken he is! I don't believe he meant it a bit.

He clings to his solitude, to his affected indifference and his grown-up ways, but it's just an act, so as never, never to show his real feelings. Poor Peter, how long will he be able to go on playing this role? Surely a terrible outburst must follow as the result of this superhuman effort?

Oh, Peter, if only I could help you, if only you would let me! Together we could drive away your loneliness and mine!

I think a lot, but I don't say much. I am happy if I

see him and if the sun shines when I'm with him. I was very excited yesterday; while I was washing my hair, I knew that he was sitting in the room next to ours. I couldn't do anything about; the more quiet and serious I feel inside, the more noisy I become outwardly.

Who will be the first to discover and break through this armor? I'm glad after all that the Van Daans have a son and not a daughter, my conquest could never have been so difficult, so beautiful, so good, if I had not happened to hit on someone of the opposite sex.

Yours, Anne

P.S. You know that I'm always honest with you, so I must tell you that I actually live from one meeting to the next. I keep hoping to discover that he too is waiting for me all the time and I'm thrilled if I notice a small shy advance from his side. I believe he'd like to say a lot just like I would; little does he know that it's just his clumsiness that attracts me.

Yours, Anne

Tuesday, 7 March, 1944

Dear Kitty,

If I think now of my life in 1942, it all seems so unreal. It was quite a different Anne who enjoyed that heavenly existence from the Anne who has grown wise within these walls. Yes, it was a heavenly life. Boy friends at every turn, about twenty friends and acquaintances of my own age, the darling of nearly all the teachers, spoiled from top to toe by Mummy and Daddy, lots of sweets, enough pocket money, what more could one want?

You will certainly wonder by what means I got around all these people. Peter's word "attractiveness" is not altogether true. All the teachers were entertained by my cute answers, my amusing remarks, my smiling face, and my questioning looks. That is all I was—a terrible flirt, coquettish and amusing. I had one or two advantages, which kept me rather in favor. I was industrious, honest, and frank. I would never have dreamed of cribbing from anyone else. I shared my sweets generously, and I wasn't conceited.

Wouldn't I have become rather forward with so much admiration? It was a good thing that in the midst of it, at the height of all this gaiety, I suddenly had to face reality, and it took me at least a year to get used to the fact that there was no more admiration forthcoming.

How did I appear at school? The one who thought of new jokes and pranks, always "king of the castle," never in a bad mood, never a crybaby. No wonder everyone liked to cycle with me, and I got other attentions.

Now I look back at that Anne as an amusing, but very superficial girl, who has nothing to do with the Anne of today. Peter said quite rightly about me: "If ever I saw you, you were always surrounded by two or more boys and a whole troupe of girls. You were always laughing and always the center of everything!"

What is left of this girl? Oh, don't worry, I haven't forgotten how to laugh or to answer back readily. I'm just as good, if not better, at criticizing people, and I can still flirt if . . . I wish. That's not it though, I'd like that sort of life again for an evening, a few days, or even a week: the life which seems so carefree and gay. But at the end of that week, I should be dead beat and would be only too thankful to listen to anyone who began to talk about something sensible. I don't want followers, but friends, admirers who fall not for a flattering smile but for what one does and for one's character.

I know quite well that the circle around me would be much smaller. But what does that matter, as long as one still keeps a few sincere friends?

Yet I wasn't entirely happy in 1942 in spite of everything; I often felt deserted, but because I was on the go the whole day long, I didn't think about it and enjoyed myself as much as I could. Consciously and unconsciously, I tried to drive away the emptiness I felt with jokes and pranks. Now I think seriously about life and what I have to do. One period of my life is over forever. The carefree schooldays are gone, never to return.

I don't even long for them any more; I have outgrown them, I can't just only enjoy myself as my serious side is always there.

I look upon my life up till the New Year, as it were, through a powerful magnifying glass. The sunny life at home, then coming here in 1942, the sudden change, the quarrels, the bickerings. I couldn't understand it, I was taken by surprise, and the only way I could keep up some bearing was by being impertinent.

The first half of 1943: my fits of crying, the loneliness, how I slowly began to see all my faults and shortcomings, which are so great and which seemed much greater then. During the day I deliberately talked about anything and everything that was farthest from my thoughts, tried to draw Pim to me; but couldn't. Alone I had to face the difficult task of changing myself, to stop the everlasting reproaches, which were so oppressive and which reduced me to such terrible despondency.

Things improved slightly in the second half of the year, I became a young woman and was treated more like a grownup. I started to think, and write stories, and came to the conclusion that the others no longer had the right to throw me about like an india-rubber ball. I wanted to change in accordance with my own desires. But *one* thing that struck me even more was when I realized that even Daddy would never become my confidant over everything. I didn't want to trust anyone but myself any more.

At the beginning of the New Year: the second great change, my dream. . . . And with it I discovered my longing, not for a girl friend, but for a boy friend. I also discovered my inward happiness and my defensive armor of superficiality and gaiety. In due time I quieted down and discovered my boundless desire for all that is beautiful and good.

And in the evening, when I lie in bed and end my prayers with the words, "I thank you, God, for all that is good and clear and beautiful," I am filled with joy. Then I think about "the good" of going into hiding, of my health and with my whole being of the "dearness" of Peter, of

153

that which is still embryonic and impressionable and which we neither of us dare to name or touch, of that which will come sometime; love, the future, happiness and of "the beauty" which exists in the world; the world, nature, beauty and all, all that is exquisite and fine.

I don't think then of all the misery, but of the beauty that still remains. This is one of the things that Mummy and I are so entirely different about. Her counsel when one feels melancholy is: "Think of all the misery in the world and be thankful you are not sharing in it!" My advice is: "Go outside, to the fields, enjoy nature and the sunshine, go out and try to recapture happiness in yourself and in God. Think of all the beauty that's still left in and around you and be happy!"

I don't see how Mummy's idea can be right, because then how are you supposed to behave if you go through the misery yourself? Then you are lost. On the contrary, I've found that there is always some beauty left—in nature, sunshine, freedom, in yourself; these can all help you. Look at these things, then you find yourself again, and God, and then you regain your balance.

And whoever is happy will make others happy too. He who has courage and faith will never perish in misery!

Yours, Anne

Sunday, 12 March, 1944

Dear Kitty,

I can't seem to sit still lately; I run upstairs and down and then back again. I love talking to Peter, but I'm always afraid of being a nuisance. He has told me a bit about the past, about his parents and about himself. It's not half enough though and I ask myself why it is that I always long for more. He used to think I was unbearable; and I returned the compliment; now I have changed my opinion, has he changed his too?

I think so; still it doesn't necessarily mean that we shall become great friends, although as far as I am concerned it would make the time here much more bearable. But

154

still, I won't get myself upset about it—I see quite a lot of him and there's no need to make you unhappy about it too, Kitty, just because I feel so miserable.

On Saturday afternoon I felt in such a whirl, after hearing a whole lot of sad news, that I went and lay on my divan for a sleep. I only wanted to sleep to stop myself thinking. I slept till four o'clock, then I had to go into the living room. I found it difficult to answer all Mummy's questions and think of some little excuse to tell Daddy, as an explanation for my long sleep. I resorted to a "headache," which wasn't a lie, as I had one . . . but inside!

Ordinary people, ordinary girls, teen-agers like myself, will think I'm a bit cracked with all my self-pity. Yes, that's what it is, but I pour out my heart to you, then for the rest of the day I'm as impudent, gay, and self-confident as I can be, in order to avoid questions and getting on my own nerves.

Margot is very sweet and would like me to trust her, but still, I can't tell her everything. She's darling, she's good and pretty, but she lacks the nonchalance for conducting deep discussion; she takes me so seriously, much too seriously, and then thinks about her queer little sister for a long time afterwards, looks searchingly at me, at every word I say, and keeps on thinking: "Is this just a joke or does she really mean it?" I think that's because we are together the whole day long, and that if I trusted someone completely, then I shouldn't want them hanging around me all the time.

When shall I finally untangle my thoughts, when shall I find peace and rest within myself again?

Yours, Anne

Tuesday, 14 March, 1944

Dear Kitty,

Perhaps it would be entertaining for you—though not in the least for me—to hear what we are going to eat today. As the charwoman is at work downstairs, I'm sitting on the Van Daans' table at the moment. I have a handkerchief soaked in some good scent (bought before we came here) over my mouth and held against my nose. You won't gather much from this, so let's "begin at the beginning."

The people from whom we obtained food coupons have been caught, so we just have our five ration cards and no extra coupons, and no fats. As both Miep and Koophuis are ill, Elli hasn't time to do any shopping, so the atmosphere is dreary and dejected, and so is the food. From tomorrow we shall not have a scrap of fat, butter, or margarine left. We can't have fried potatoes (to save bread) for breakfast any longer, so we have porridge instead, and as Mrs. Van Daan thinks we're starving, we have bought some full cream milk "under the counter." Our supper today consists of a hash made from kale which has been preserved in a barrel. Hence the precautionary measure with the handkerchief! It's incredible how kale can stink when it's a year old! The smell in the room is a mixture of bad plums, strong preservatives, and rotten eggs. Ugh! the mere thought of eating that muck makes me feel sick.

Added to this, our potatoes are suffering from such peculiar diseases that out of two buckets of *pommes de terre,* one whole one ends up on the stove. We amuse ourselves by searching for all the different kinds of diseases, and have come to the conclusion that they range from cancer and smallpox to measles! Oh, no, it's no joke to be in hiding during the fourth year of the war. If only the whole rotten business was over!

Quite honestly, I wouldn't care so much about the food, if only it were more pleasant here in other ways. There's the rub: this tedious existence is beginning to make us all touchy.

The following are the views of the five grownups on the present situation:

Mrs. Van Daan: "The job as queen of the kitchen lost its attraction a long time ago. It's dull to sit and do nothing, so I go back to my cooking again. Still, I have to complain that it's impossible to cook without any fats, and all these nasty smells make me feel sick. Nothing but ingratitude and rude remarks do I get in return for my services. I am always the black sheep, always the guilty one. Moreover, according to me, very little progress is being made in the war; in the end the Germans will still win. I'm afraid we're going to starve, and if I'm in a bad mood I scold everyone."

Mr. Van Daan: "I must smoke and smoke and smoke, and then the food, the political situation, and Keril's moods don't seem so bad. Keril is a darling wife."

But if he hasn't anything to smoke, then nothing is right, and this is what one hears: "I'm getting ill, we don't live well enough, I must have meat. Frightfully stupid person, my Keril!" After this a terrific quarrel is sure to follow.

Mrs. Frank: "Food is not very important, but I would love a slice of rye bread now, I feel so terribly hungry. If I were Mrs. Van Daan I would have put a stop to Mr. Van Daan's everlasting smoking a long time ago. But now I must definitely have a cigarette, because my nerves are getting the better of me. The English make a lot of mistakes, but still the war is progressing. I must have a chat and be thankful I'm not in Poland."

Mr. Frank: "Everything's all right. I don't require anything. Take it easy, we've ample time. Give me my potatoes and then I will keep my mouth shut. Put some of my rations on one side for Elli. The political situation is very promising, I'm extremely optimistic!"

Mr. Dussel: "I must get my task for today, everything must be finished on time. Political situation 'outschtänding' and it is 'eempossible' that we'll be caught. "I, I, I . . . !"

Yours, Anne

Wednesday, 15 March, 1944

Dear Kitty,

Phew! Oh dear, oh dear—released from the somber scenes for a moment! Today I hear nothing but "if this or that should happen, then we are going to be in difficulties . . . if he or she should become ill, then we'll be completely isolated, and then if . . ." *Enfin,* I expect you know the rest, at least I presume you know the "Secret Annexers" well enough by this time to be able to guess the trend of their conversations.

The reason for all this "if, if" is that Mr. Kraler has been called up to go digging. Elli has a streaming cold and will probably have to stay at home tomorrow. Miep hasn't fully recovered from her flu yet, and Koophuis has had such bad hemorrhage of the stomach that he lost consciousness. What a tale of woe!

The warehouse people are getting a free day tomorrow; Elli can stay at home, then the door will remain locked and we shall have to be as quiet as mice, so that the neighbors don't hear us. Henk is coming to visit the deserted ones at one o'clock—playing the role of zoo-keeper, as it were. For the first time in ages he told us something about the great wide world this afternoon. You should have seen the eight of us sitting around him; it looked exactly like a picture of grandmother telling a story. He talked nineteen to the dozen to his grateful audience about food, of course, and then Miep's doctor, and everything that we asked about. "Doctor," he said, "don't talk to me about the doctor! I rang him up this morning, had his assistant on the phone and asked for a prescription for flu. The reply was that I could come and get the prescription any time between eight and nine in the morning. If you have a very bad attack of flu, the doctor comes to the telephone himself and says 'Put out your tongue, say Aah, I can hear all right that your throat is inflamed. I'll write out a prescription for you to order from the chemist. Good-by.' And that's that." A fine practice that, run by telephone only.

But I don't want to criticize the doctors; after all, a person has but two hands, and in these days there's an abundance of patients and very few doctors to cope with them. Still, we couldn't help laughing when Henk repeated the telephone conversation to us.

I can just imagine what a doctor's waiting room must look like nowadays. One doesn't look down on panel patients any more, but on the people with minor ailments and thinks: "Hi, you, what are you doing here, end of the line, please; urgent cases have priority!"

Yours, Anne

Thursday, 16 March, 1944

Dear Kitty,

The weather is lovely, superb, I can't describe it; I'm going up to the attic in a minute.

Now I know why I'm so much more restless than Peter. He has his own room where he can work, dream, think, and sleep. I am shoved about from one corner to another. I hardly spend any time in my "double" room and yet it's something I long for so much. That is the reason too why I so frequently escape to the attic. There, and with you, I can be myself for a while just a little while. Still, I don't want to moan about myself, on the contrary, I want to be brave. Thank goodness the others can't tell what my inward feelings are, except that I'm growing cooler towards Mummy daily, I'm not so affectionate to Daddy and don't tell Margot a single thing. I'm completely closed up. Above all, I must maintain my outward reserve, no one must know that war still reigns incessantly within. War between desire and common sense. The latter has won up till now; yet will the former prove to be the stronger of the two? Sometimes I fear that it will and sometimes I long for it to be!

Oh, it is so terribly difficult never to say anything to Peter, but I know that the first to begin must be he; there's so much I want to say and do, I've lived it all in my dreams, it is so hard to find that yet another day has gone by, and none of it comes true! Yes, Kitty, Anne is a crazy child, but I do live in crazy times and under still crazier circumstances.

But, still, the brightest spot of all is that at least I can write down my thoughts and feelings, otherwise I would be absolutely stifled! I wonder what Peter thinks about all these things? I keep hoping that I can talk about it to him one day. There must be something he has guessed about me, because he certainly can't love the outer Anne, which is the one he knows so far.

How can he, who loves peace and quiet, have any liking for all my bustle and din? Can he possibly be the first and only one to have looked through my concrete armor? And will it take him long to get there? Isn't there an old saying that love often springs from pity, or that the two go hand in hand? Is that the case with me too? Because I'm often just as sorry for him as I am for myself.

I really don't honestly know how to begin and however would he be able to, when he finds talking so much more difficult than I do? If only I could write to him, then at least I would know that he would grasp what I want to say, because it's so terribly difficult to put it into words!

Yours, Anne

Friday, 17 March, 1944

Dear Kitty,

A sigh of relief has gone through the "Secret Annexe." Kraler has been exempted from digging by the Court. Elli has given her nose a talking to and strictly forbidden it to be a nuisance to her today. So everything is all right again, except that Margot and I are getting a bit tired of our parents. Don't misunderstand me, I can't get on well with Mummy at the moment, as you know. I still love Daddy just as much, and Margot loves Daddy and Mummy, but when you are as old as we are, you do want to decide just a few things for yourself, you want to be independent sometimes.

If I go upstairs, then I'm asked what I'm going to do, I'm not allowed salt with my food, every evening regularly at a quarter past eight Mummy asks whether I ought not to start undressing, every book I read must be inspected. I must admit that they are not at all strict, and I'm allowed to read nearly everything, and yet we are both sick of all the remarks plus all the questioning that go on the whole day long.

Something else, especially about me, that doesn't please them: I don't feel like giving lots of kisses any more and I think fancy nicknames are terribly affected. In short, I'd really like to be rid of them for a while. Margot said last evening, "I think it's awfully annoying, the way they ask if you've got a headache, or whether you don't feel well, if you happen to give a sigh and put your hand to your head!"

It is a great blow to us both, suddenly to realize how little remains of the confidence and harmony that we used to have at home. And it's largely due to the fact that we're all "skew-wiff" here. By this I mean that we are treated as children over outward things, and we are much older than most girls of our age inwardly.

Although I'm only fourteen, I know quite well what I want, I know who is right and who is wrong, I have my opinions, my own ideas and principles, and although it may sound pretty mad from an adolescent, I feel more of a person than a child, I feel quite independent of anyone.

I know that I can discuss things and argue better than Mummy, I know I'm not so prejudiced, I don't exaggerate so much, I am more precise and adroit and because of this—you may laugh—I feel superior to her over a great many things. If I love anyone, above all I must have admiration for them, admiration and respect. Everything would be all right if only I had Peter, for I do admire him in many ways. He is such a nice, good-looking boy!

Yours, Anne

Sunday, 19 March, 1944

Dear Kitty,

Yesterday was a great day for me. I had decided to talk things out with Peter. Just as we were going to sit down to supper I whispered to him, "Are you going to do shorthand this evening, Peter?" "No," was his reply. "Then I'd just like to talk to you later!" He agreed. After the dishes were done, I stood by the window in his parents' room awhile for the look of things, but it wasn't

161

long before I went to Peter. He was standing on the left side of the open window, I went and stood on the right side, and we talked. It was much easier to talk beside the open window in the semidarkness than in bright light, and I believe Peter felt the same.

We told each other so much, so very very much, that I can't repeat it all, but it was lovely; the most wonderful evening I have ever had in the "Secret Annexe." I will just tell you briefly the various things we talked about. First we talked about the quarrels and how I regard them quite differently now, and then about the estrangement between us and our parents.

I told Peter about Mummy and Daddy, and Margot, and about myself.

At one moment he asked, "I suppose you always give each other a good night kiss, don't you?"

"*One*, dozens, why, don't you?"

"No, I have hardly ever kissed anyone."

"Not even on your birthday?"

"Yes, I have then."

We talked about how we neither of us confide in our parents, and how his parents would have loved to have his confidence, but that he didn't wish it. How I cry my heart out in bed, and he goes up into the loft and swears. How Margot and I really only know each other well for a little while, but that, even so, we don't tell each other everything, because we are always together. Over every imaginable thing—oh, he was just as I thought!

Then we talked about 1942, how different we were then. We just don't recognize ourselves as the same people any more. How we simply couldn't bear each other in the beginning. He thought I was much too talkative and unruly, and I soon came to the conclusion that I'd no time for him. I couldn't understand why he didn't flirt with me, but now I'm glad. He also mentioned how much he isolated himself from us all. I said that there was not much difference between my noise and his silence. That I love peace and quiet too, and have nothing for myself alone, except my diary. How glad he is that my parents have children here, and that I'm glad he is here. That I

162

understand his reserve now and his relationship with his parents, and how I would love to be able to help him. "You always do help me," he said. "How?" I asked, very surprised. "By your cheerfulness." That was certainly the loveliest thing he said. It was wonderful, he must have grown to love me as a friend, and that is enough for the time being. I am so grateful and happy, I just can't find the words. I must apologize, Kitty, that my style is not up to standard today.

I have just written down what came into my head. I have the feeling now that Peter and I share a secret. If he looks at me with those eyes that laugh and wink, then it's just as if a little light goes on inside me. I hope it will remain like this and that we may have many, many more glorious times together!

Your grateful, happy Anne

Monday, 20 March, 1944

Dear Kitty,

This morning Peter asked me if I would come again one evening, and said that I really didn't disturb him, and if there's room for one there's room for two. I said that I couldn't come every evening, because they wouldn't like it downstairs, but he thought that I needn't let that bother me. Then I said that I would love to come one Saturday evening and especially asked him to warn me when there was a moon. "Then we'll go downstairs," he answered, "and look at the moon from there."

In the meantime a little shadow had fallen on my happiness. I've thought for a long time that Margot liked Peter quite a lot too. How much she loves him I don't know, but I think it's wretched. I must cause her terrible pain each time I'm with Peter, and the funny part of it is that she hardly shows it.

I know quite well that I'd be desperately jealous, but Margot only says that I needn't pity her.

"I think it's so rotten that you should be the odd one

163

out," I added. "I'm so used to that," she answered, somewhat bitterly.

I don't dare tell Peter this yet, perhaps later on, but we've got to talk about so many other things first.

I had a little ticking off yesterday evening from Mummy, which I certainly deserved. I mustn't overdo my indifference towards her. So in spite of everything, I must try once again to be friendly and keep my observations to myself.

Even Pim is different lately. He is trying not to treat me as such a child, and it makes him much too cool. See what comes of it!

Enough for now, I'm full to the brim with Peter and can do nothing but look at him!

Evidence of Margot's goodness: I received this today,

March 20th, 1944

Anne, when I said yesterday that I was not jealous of you I was only fifty per cent honest. It is like this; I'm jealous of neither you nor Peter. I only feel a bit sorry that I haven't found anyone yet, and am not likely to for the time being, with whom I can discuss my thoughts and feelings. But I should not grudge it to you for that reason. One misses enough here anyway, things that other people just take for granted.

On the other hand, I know for certain that I would never have got so far with Peter, anyway, because I have the feeling that if I wished to discuss a lot with anyone, I should want to be on rather intimate terms with him. I would want to have the feeling that he understood me through and through without my having to say much. But for that reason it would have to be someone whom I felt was my superior intellectually, and that is not the case with Peter. But I can imagine it being so with you and Peter.

You are not doing me out of anything which is my due; do not reproach yourself in the least on my account. You and Peter can only gain by the friendship.

My reply:

Dear Margot,
I thought your letter was exceptionally sweet, but I still don't feel quite happy about it and nor do I think that I shall.

At present there is no question of such confidence as you have in mind between Peter and myself, but in the twilight beside an open window you can say more to each other than in brilliant sunshine. Also it's easier to whisper your feelings than to trumpet them forth out loud. I believe that you are beginning to feel a kind of sisterly affection for Peter, and that you would love to help him, just as much as I. Perhaps you will still be able to do that sometime, although that is not the kind of confidence we have in mind. I think it must come from both sides, and I believe that's the reason why Daddy and I have never got so far.

Let's not talk about it any more; but if you still want anything please write to me about it, because I can say what I mean much better on paper.

You don't know how much I admire you, and I only hope that I may yet acquire some of the goodness that you and Daddy have, because now I don't see much difference between you and Daddy in that sense.

Yours, Anne

Wednesday, 22 March, 1944

Dear Kitty,
I received this from Margot last evening:

Dear Anne,
After your letter yesterday I have the unpleasant feeling that you will have prickings of conscience when you visit Peter; but really there is no reason for this. In my heart of hearts I feel that I have the right to share mutual confidence with someone, but I could not bear Peter in that role yet.

However, I do feel just as you say, that Peter is a bit like a brother, but—a younger brother; we have put out feelers towards each other, the affection of a brother and sister might grow if they touched, perhaps they will later—perhaps never; however, it has certainly not reached that stage yet.

Therefore you really needn't pity me. Now that you've found companionship, enjoy it as much as you can.

In the meantime it is getting more and more wonderful here. I believe, Kitty, that we may have a real great love in the "Secret Annexe." Don't worry, I'm not thinking of marrying him. I don't know what he will be like when he grows up, nor do I know whether we should ever love each other enough to marry. I know now that Peter loves me, but just how I myself don't know yet.

Whether he only wants a great friend, or whether I attract him as a girl or as a sister, I can't yet discover.

When he said that I always helped him over his parents' quarrels, I was awfully glad; it was one step towards making me believe in his friendship. I asked him yesterday what he would do if there were a dozen Annes here who always kept coming to him. His reply was, "If they were all like you, it certainly wouldn't be too bad!" He's tremendously hospitable towards me and I really believe he likes to see me. Meanwhile he is working diligently at his French, even when he's in bed, going on until a quarter past ten. Oh, when I think about Saturday evening and recall it all, word for word, then for the first time I don't feel discontented about myself; I mean that I would still say exactly the same and wouldn't wish to change anything, as is usually the case.

He is so handsome, both when he laughs and when he looks quietly in front of him; he is such a darling and so good. I believe what surprised him most about me was when he discovered that I'm not a bit the superficial worldly Anne that I appear, but just as dreamy a specimen, with just as many difficulties as he himself.

Yours, Anne

Reply:

Dear Margot,

I think the best thing we can do is simply to wait and see what happens. It can't be very long before Peter and I come to a definite decision, either to go on as before or be different. Just which way it will go I don't know myself, and I don't bother to look beyond my own nose. But I shall certainly do one thing, if Peter and I decide to be friends, I shall tell him that you are very fond of him too and would always be prepared to help him should the need arise. The latter may not be what you wish, but I don't care now; I don't know what Peter thinks about you, but I shall ask him then.

I'm sure it's not bad—the opposite! You are always welcome to join us in the attic, or wherever we are; you honestly won't disturb us because I feel we have a silent agreement to talk only in the evenings when it's dark.

Keep your courage up! Like I do. Although it's not always easy; your time may come sooner than you think.

Yours, Anne

Thursday, 23 March, 1944

Dear Kitty,

Things are running more or less normally again now. Our coupon men are out of prison again, thank goodness!

Miep returned yesterday, Elli is better, although she still has a cough; Koophuis will have to stay at home for a long time still.

A plane crashed near here yesterday; the occupants were able to jump out in time by parachute. The machine crashed onto a school, but there were no children there at the time. The result was a small fire and two people killed. The Germans shot at the airmen terribly as they were coming down. The Amsterdammers who saw it nearly exploded with rage and indignation at the cowardliness of such a deed. We—I'm speaking of the ladies— nearly jumped out of our skins, I loathe the blasted shooting.

I often go upstairs after supper nowadays and take a breath of fresh evening air. I like it up there, sitting on a chair beside him and looking outside.

Van Daan and Dussel make very feeble remarks when I disappear into his room; "Anne's second home," they call it, or "Is it suitable for young gentlemen to receive young girls in semidarkness?" Peter shows amazing wit in his replies to these so-called humorous sallies. For that matter, Mummy too is somewhat curious and would love to ask what we talk about, if she wasn't secretly afraid of being snubbed. Peter says it's nothing but envy on the part of the grownups, because we are young and we don't

167

pay much attention to their spitefulness. Sometimes he comes and gets me from downstairs, but he turns simply scarlet in spite of all precautions, and can hardly get the words out of his mouth. How thankful I am that I don't blush, it must be a highly unpleasant sensation. Daddy always says I'm prudish and vain but that's not true, I'm just simply vain! I have not often had anyone tell me I was pretty. Except a boy at school, who said I looked so attractive when I laughed. Yesterday I received a genuine compliment from Peter, and just for fun I will tell you roughly how the conversation went:

Peter so often used to say, "Do laugh, Anne!" This struck me as odd, and I asked, "Why must I always laugh?"

"Because I like it; you get such dimples in your cheeks when you laugh; how do they come, actually?"

"I was born with them. I've got one in my chin too. That's my only beauty!"

"Of course not, that's not true."

"Yes, it is, I know quite well that I'm not a beauty; I never have been and never shall be."

"I don't agree at all, I think you're pretty."

"That's not true."

"If I say so, then you can take it from me it is!"

Then I naturally said the same of him.

I hear a lot from all sides about the sudden friendship. We don't take much notice of all this parental chatter, their remarks are so feeble. Have the two sets of parents forgotten their own youth? It seems like it, at least they seem to take us seriously, if we make a joke, and laugh at us when we are serious.

Yours, Anne

Monday, 27 March, 1944

Dear Kitty,

One very big chapter of our history in hiding should really be about politics, but as this subject doesn't interest me personally very much, I've rather let it go. So for once I will devote my whole letter to politics today.

It goes without saying that there are very many different opinions on this topic, and it's even more logical that it should be a favorite subject for discussion in such critical times, but—it's just simply stupid that there should be so many quarrels over it.

They may speculate, laugh, abuse, and grumble, let them do what they will, as long as they stew in their own juice and don't quarrel, because the consequences are usually unpleasant.

The people from outside bring with them a lot of news that is not true; however, up till now our radio set hasn't lied to us. Henk, Miep, Koophuis, Elli, and Kraler all show ups and downs in their political moods, Henk least of all.

Political feeling here in the "Secret Annexe" is always about the same. During the countless arguments over invasion, air raids, speeches, etc., etc., one also always hears the countless cries of "impossible," or *"Um Gottes Willen,* if they are going to start now however long is it going to last?" "It's going splendidly, first class, good!" Optimists and pessimists, and, above all, don't let's forget the realists who give their opinions with untiring energy and, just as with everything else, each one thinking he is right. It annoys a certain lady that her spouse has such unparalleled faith in the British, and a certain gentleman attacks his lady because of her teasing and disparaging remarks about his beloved nation.

They never seem to tire of it. I have discovered something—the effects are stupendous, just like pricking someone with a pin and waiting to see how they jump. This is what I do: begin on politics. One question, one word, one sentence, and at once they're off!

Just as if the German Wehrmacht news bulletins and the English B.B.C. were not enough, they have now introduced "Special Air-Raid Announcements." In one word, magnificent; but on the other hand often disappointing too. The British are making a non-stop business of their air attacks, with the same zest as the Germans make a business of lying. The radio therefore goes on early in the morning and is listened to at all hours of the day, until nine, ten, and often eleven o'clock in the evening.

This is certainly a sign that the grownups have infinite patience, but it also means the power of absorption of their brains is pretty limited, with exceptions, of course— I don't want to hurt anyone's feelings. One or two news bulletins would be ample per day! But the old geese, well —I've said my piece!

Arbeiter-Programm, Radio "Oranje," Frank Phillips or Her Majesty Queen Wilhelmina, they each get their turn, and an ever attentive ear. And if they are not eating or sleeping, then they're sitting around the radio and discussing food, sleep, and politics.

Ugh! It gets so boring, and it's quite a job not to become a dull old stick oneself. Politics can't do much more harm to the parents!

I must mention one shining exception—a speech by our beloved Winston Churchill is quite perfect.

Nine o'clock on Sunday evening. The teapot stands, with the cozy over it, on the table, and the guests come in. Dussel next to the radio on the left, Mr. Van Daan in front of it, with Peter beside him. Mummy next to Mr. Van Daan and Mrs. Van Daan behind him, and Pim at the table, Margot and I beside. I see I haven't described very clearly how we sit. The gentlemen puff away at their pipes, Peter's eyes are popping out of his head with the strain of listening, Mummy wearing a long dark negligée, and Mrs. Van Daan trembling because of the planes, which take no notice of the speech but fly blithely on towards Essen, Daddy sipping tea, Margot and I united in a sisterly fashion by the sleeping Mouschi, who is monopolizing both our knees. Margot's hair is in curlers, I am wearing a nightdress, which is much too small, too narrow, and too short.

It all looks so intimate, snug, peaceful, and this time it is too; yet I await the consequences with horror. They can hardly wait till the end of the speech, stamping their feet, so impatient are they to get down to discussing it.

Brr, brr, brr—they egg each other on until the arguments lead to discord and quarrels.

Yours, Anne

Tuesday, 28 March, 1944

Dearest Kitty,

I could write a lot more about politics, but I have heaps of other things to tell you today. First, Mummy has more or less forbidden me to go upstairs so often, because, according to her, Mrs. Van Daan is jealous. Secondly, Peter has invited Margot to join us upstairs; I don't know whether it's just out of politeness or whether he really means it. Thirdly, I went and asked Daddy if he thought I need pay any regard to Mrs. Van Daan's jealousy, and he didn't think so. What next? Mummy is cross, perhaps jealous too. Daddy doesn't grudge us these times together, and thinks it's nice that we get on so well. Margot is fond of Peter too, but feels that two's company and three's a crowd.

Mummy thinks that Peter is in love with me; quite frankly, I only wish he were, then we'd be quits and really be able to get to know each other. She also says that he keeps on looking at me. Now, I suppose that's true, but still I can't help it if he looks at my dimples and we wink at each other occasionally, can I?

I'm in a very difficult position. Mummy is against me and I'm against her, Daddy closes his eyes and tries not to see the silent battle between us. Mummy is sad, because she does really love me, while I'm not in the least bit sad, because I don't think she understands. And Peter—I don't want to give Peter up, he's such a darling. I admire him so; it can grow into something beautiful between us; why do the "old 'uns" have to poke their noses in all the time? Luckily I'm quite used to hiding my feelings and I manage extremely well not to let them see how mad I am about him. Will he ever say anything? Will I ever feel his cheek against mine, like I felt Petel's cheek in my dream? Oh, Peter and Petel, you are one and the same!

They don't understand us; won't they ever grasp that we are happy, just sitting together and not saying a word. They don't understand what has driven us together like this. Oh, when will all these difficulties be overcome? And yet it is good to overcome them, because then the end will be all the more wonderful. When he lies with his head on his arm with his eyes closed, then he is still a child; when he plays with Boche, he is loving; when he carries potatoes or anything heavy, then he is strong; when he goes and watches the shooting, or looks for burglars in the darkness, then he is brave; and when he is so awkward and clumsy, then he is just a pet.

I like it much better if he explains something to me than when I have to teach him; I would really adore him to be my superior in almost everything.

What do we care about the two mothers? Oh, but if only he would speak!

Yours, Anne

Wednesday, 29 March, 1944

Dear Kitty,

Bolkestein, an M.P., was speaking on the Dutch News from London, and he said that they ought to make a collection of diaries and letters after the war. Of course, they all made a rush at my diary immediately. Just imagine how interesting it would be if I were to publish a romance of the "Secret Annexe." The title [1] alone would be enough to make people think it was a detective story.

But, seriously, it would seem quite funny ten years after the war if we Jews were to tell how we lived and what we ate and talked about here. Although I tell you a lot, still, even so, you only know very little of our lives.

How scared the ladies are during the air raids. For instance, on Sunday, when 350 British planes dropped half a million kilos of bombs on Ijmuiden, how the houses trembled like a wisp of grass in the wind, and who

[1] The original title of this diary was *Het Achterhuis*. There is no exact translation into English, the nearest being *The Secret Annexe*.

knows how many epidemics now rage. You don't know anything about all these things, and I would need to keep on writing the whole day if I were to tell you everything in detail. People have to line up for vegetables and all kinds of other things; doctors are unable to visit the sick, because if they turn their backs on their cars for a moment, they are stolen; burglaries and thefts abound, so much so that you wonder what has taken hold of the Dutch for them suddenly to have become such thieves. Little children of eight and eleven years break the windows of people's homes and steal whatever they can lay their hands on. No one dares to leave his house unoccupied for five minutes, because if you go, your things go too. Every day there are announcements in the newspapers offering rewards for the return of lost property, typewriters, Persian rugs, electric clocks, cloth, etc., etc. Electric clocks in the streets are dismantled, public telephones are pulled to pieces—down to the last thread. Morale among the population can't be good, the weekly rations are not enough to last for two days except the coffee substitute. The invasion is a long time coming, and the men have to go to Germany. The children are ill or undernourished, everyone is wearing old clothes and old shoes. A new sole costs 7.50 florins in the black market; moreover, hardly any of the shoemakers will accept shoe repairs or, if they do, you have to wait months, during which time the shoes often disappear.

There's one good thing in the midst of it all, which is that as the food gets worse and the measures against the people more severe, so sabotage against the authorities steadily increases. The people in the food offices, the police, officials, they all either work with their fellow citizens and help them or they tell tales on them and have them sent to prison. Fortunately, only a small percentage of Dutch people are on the wrong side.

Yours, Anne

Dear Kitty,

Think of it, it's still pretty cold, but most people have been without coal for about a month—pleasant, eh! In general public feeling over the Russian front is optimistic again, because that is terrific! You know I don't write much about politics, but I must just tell you where they are now; they are right by the Polish border and have reached the Pruth near Rumania. They are close to Odessa. Every evening here they expect an extra communiqué from Stalin.

They fire off so many salvos in Moscow to celebrate their victories that the city must rumble and shake just about every day—whether they think it's fun to pretend that the war is close at hand again or that they know of no other way of expressing their joy, I don't know!

Hungary is occupied by German troops. There are still a million Jews there, so they too will have had it now.

The chatter about Peter and me has calmed down a bit now. We are very good friends, are together a lot and discuss every imaginable subject. It is awfully nice never to have to keep a check on myself as I would have to with other boys, whenever we get on to precarious ground. We were talking, for instance, about blood and via that subject we began talking about menstruation. He thinks we women are pretty tough. Why on earth? My life has improved, greatly improved. God has not left me alone and will not leave me alone.

Yours, Anne

Dear Kitty,

And yet everything is still so difficult; I expect you can guess what I mean, can't you? I am so longing for a kiss,

174

the kiss that is so long in coming. I wonder if all the time he still regards me as a friend? Am I nothing more?

You know and I know that I am strong, that I can carry most of my burdens alone. I have never been used to sharing my troubles with anyone, I have never clung to my mother, but now I would so love to lay my head on "his" shoulder just once and remain still.

I can't, I simply can't ever forget that dream of Peter's cheek, when it was all, all so good! Wouldn't he long for it too? Is it that he is just too shy to acknowledge his love? Why does he want me with him so often? Oh, why doesn't he speak?

I'd better stop, I must be quiet, I shall remain strong and with a bit of patience the other will come too, but—and that is the worst of it—it looks just as if I'm running after him; *I* am always the one who goes upstairs, *he* doesn't come to me.

But that is just because of the rooms, and he is sure to understand the difficulty.

Oh, yes, and there's more he'll understand.

Yours, Anne

Monday, 3 April, 1944

Dear Kitty,

Contrary to my usual custom, I will for once write more fully about food because it has become a very difficult and important matter, not only here in the "Secret Annexe" but in the whole of Holland, all Europe, and even beyond.

In the twenty-one months that we've spent here we have been through a good many "food cycles"—you'll understand what that means in a minute. When I talk of "food cycles" I mean periods in which one has nothing else to eat but one particular dish or kind of vegetable. We had nothing but endive for a long time, day in, day out, endive with sand, endive without sand, stew with endive, boiled or *en casserole;* then it was spinach, and after that followed kohlrabi, salsify, cucumbers, tomatoes, sauerkraut, etc., etc.

For instance, it's really disagreeable to eat a lot of sauerkraut for lunch and supper every day, but you do it if you're hungry. However, we have the most delightful period of all now, because we don't get any fresh vegetables at all. Our weekly menu for supper consists of kidney beans, pea soup, potatoes with dumplings, potato-chalet and, by the grace of God, occasionally turnip tops or rotten carrots, and then the kidney beans once again. We eat potatoes at every meal, beginning with breakfast, because of the bread shortage. We make our soup from kidney or haricot beans, potatoes, Julienne soup in packets. French beans in packets, kidney beans in packets. Everything contains beans, not to mention the bread!

In the evening we always have potatoes with gravy substitute and—thank goodness we've still got it—beetroot salad. I must still tell you about the dumplings, which we make out of government flour, water, and yeast. They are so sticky and tough, they lie like stones in one's stomach—ah, well!

The great attraction each week is a slice of liver sausage, and jam on dry bread. But we're still alive, and quite often we even enjoy our poor meals.

Yours, Anne

Tuesday, 4 April, 1944

Dear Kitty,

For a long time I haven't had any idea of what I was working for any more; the end of the war is so terribly far away, so unreal, like a fairy tale. If the war isn't over by September I shan't go to school any more, because I don't want to be two years behind. Peter filled my days—nothing but Peter, dreams and thoughts until Saturday, when I felt so utterly miserable; oh, it was terrible. I was holding back my tears all the while I was with Peter, then laughed with Van Daan over lemon punch, was cheerful and excited, but the moment I was alone I knew that I would have to cry my heart out. So, clad in my nightdress, I let myself go and slipped down onto the floor. First I said my long prayer very earnestly, then I cried with my head on my arms, my knees bent up, on the bare floor, completely folded up. One large sob brought me back to earth again, and I quelled my tears because I didn't want them to hear anything in the next room. Then I began trying to talk some courage into myself. I could only say: "I must, I must, I must . . ." Completely stiff from the unnatural position, I fell against the side of the bed and fought on, until I climbed into bed again just before half past ten. It was over!

And now it's all over. I must work, so as not to be a fool, to get on, to become a journalist, because that's what I want! I know that I can write, a couple of my stories are good, my descriptions of the "Secret Annexe" are humorous, there's a lot in my diary that speaks, but—whether I have real talent remains to be seen.

"Eva's Dream" is my best fairy tale, and the queer thing about it is that I don't know where it comes from. Quite a lot of "Cady's Life" is good too, but, on the whole, it's nothing.

I am the best and sharpest critic of my own work. I know myself what is and what is not well written. Anyone who doesn't write doesn't know how wonderful it is; I used to bemoan the fact that I couldn't draw at all, but now I am more than happy that I can at least write. And if I haven't any talent for writing books or newspaper articles, well, then I can always write for myself.

I want to get on; I can't imagine that I would have to lead the same sort of life as Mummy and Mrs. Van Daan and all the women who do their work and are then forgotten. I must have something besides a husband and children, something that I can devote myself to!

I want to go on living even after my death! And therefore I am grateful to God for giving me this gift, this possibility of developing myself and of writing, of expressing all that is in me.

I can shake off everything if I write; my sorrows disappear, my courage is reborn. But, and that is the great question, will I ever be able to write anything great, will I ever become a journalist or a writer? I hope so, oh, I hope so very much, for I can recapture everything when I write, my thoughts, my ideals and my fantasies.

I haven't done anything more to "Cady's Life" for ages; in my mind I know exactly how to go on, but somehow it doesn't flow from my pen. Perhaps I never shall finish it, it may land up in the wastepaper basket, or the fire . . . that's a horrible idea, but then I think to myself, "At the age of fourteen and with so little experience, how can you write about philosophy?"

So I go on again with fresh courage; I think I shall succeed, because I want to write!

Yours, Anne

Thursday, 6 April, 1944

Dear Kitty,

You asked me what my hobbies and interests were, so I want to reply. I warn you, however, that there are heaps of them, so don't get a shock!

First of all: writing, but that hardly counts as a hobby.

Number two: family trees. I've been searching for family trees of the French, German, Spanish, English, Austrian, Russian, Norwegian, and Dutch royal families in all the newspapers, books, and pamphlets I can find. I've made great progress with a lot of them, as, for a long time already, I've been taking down notes from all the biographies and history books that I read; I even copy out many passages of history.

My third hobby then is history, on which Daddy has already bought me a lot of books. I can hardly wait for the day that I shall be able to comb through the books in a public library.

Number four is Greek and Roman mythology. I have various books about this too.

Other hobbies are film stars and family photos. Mad on books and reading. Have a great liking for history of art, poets and painters. I may go in for music later on. I have a great loathing for algebra, geometry, and figures.

I enjoy all the other school subjects, but history above all!

Yours, Anne

Tuesday, 11 April, 1944

Dear Kitty,

My head throbs, I honestly don't know where to begin. On Friday (Good Friday) we played Monopoly, Saturday afternoon too. These days passed quickly and uneventfully. On Sunday afternoon, on my invitation, Peter came to my room at half past four; at a quarter past five we went to the front attic, where we remained until six o'clock. There was a beautiful Mozart concert on the radio from six o'clock until a quarter past seven. I enjoyed it all very much, but especially the "Kleine Nachtmusik." I can hardly listen in the room because I'm always so inwardly stirred when I hear lovely music.

On Sunday evening Peter and I went to the front attic together and, in order to sit comfortably, we took with us a few divan cushions that we were able to lay our hands on. We seated ourselves on one packing case. Both the case and the cushions were very narrow, so we sat absolutely squashed together, leaning against other cases. Mouschi kept us company too, so we weren't unchaperoned.

Suddenly, at a quarter to nine, Mr. Van Daan whistled and asked if we had one of Dussel's cushions. We both jumped up and went downstairs with cushion, cat, and Van Daan.

A lot of trouble arose out of this cushion, because Dussel was annoyed that we had one of his cushions, one that he used as a pillow. He was afraid that there might be fleas in it and made a great commotion about his beloved cushion! Peter and I put two hard brushes in his bed as a revenge. We had a good laugh over this little interlude!

Our fun didn't last long. At half past nine Peter knocked softly on the door and asked Daddy if he would just help him upstairs over a difficult English sentence.

"That's a blind," I said to Margot, "anyone could see through that one!" I was right. They were in the act of breaking into the warehouse. Daddy, Van Daan, Dussel, and Peter were downstairs in a flash. Margot, Mummy, Mrs. Van Daan, and I stayed upstairs and waited.

Four frightened women just have to talk, so talk we did, until we heard a bang downstairs. After that all was quiet, the clock struck a quarter to ten. The color had vanished from our faces, we were still quiet, although we were afraid. Where could the men be? What was that bang? Would they be fighting the burglars? Ten o'clock, footsteps on the stairs: Daddy, white and nervous, entered, followed by Mr. Van Daan. "Lights out, creep upstairs, we expect the police in the house!"

There was no time to be frightened: the lights went out, I quickly grabbed a jacket, and we were upstairs. "What has happened? Tell us quickly!" There was no one to tell us, the men having disappeared downstairs again. Only at ten past ten did they reappear; two kept watch at Peter's open window, the door to the landing was closed, the swinging cupboard shut. We hung a jersey round the night light, and after that they told us:

Peter heard two loud bangs on the landing, ran downstairs, and saw there was a large plank out of the left half of the door. He dashed upstairs, warned the "Home Guard" of the family, and the four of them proceeded downstairs. When they entered the warehouse, the burglars were in the act of enlarging the hole. Without further thought Van Daan shouted: "Police!"

A few hurried steps outside, and the burglars had fled. In order to avoid the hole being noticed by the police, a plank was put against it, but a good hard kick from outside sent it flying to the ground. The men were perplexed at such impudence, and both Van Daan and Peter felt murder welling up within them; Van Daan beat on the ground with a chopper, and all was quiet again. Once more they wanted to put the plank in front of the hole. Disturbance! A married couple outside shone a torch through the opening, lighting up the whole warehouse. "Hell!" muttered one of the men, and now they switched over from their role of police to that of burglars. The four of them sneaked upstairs, Peter quickly opened the doors and windows of the kitchen and private office, flung the telephone onto the floor, and finally the four of them landed behind the swinging cupboard.

END OF PART ONE

The married couple with the torch would probably have warned the police: it was Sunday evening, Easter Sunday, no one at the office on Easter Monday, so none of us could budge until Tuesday morning. Think of it, waiting in such fear for two nights and a day! No one had anything to suggest, so we simply sat there in pitch-darkness, because Mrs. Van Daan in her fright had unintentionally turned the lamp right out; talked in whispers, and at every creak one heard "Sh! sh!"

It turned half past ten, eleven, but not a sound; Daddy and Van Daan joined us in turns. Then a quarter past eleven, a bustle and noise downstairs. Everyone's breath was audible, otherwise no one moved. Footsteps in the house, in the private office, kitchen, then . . . on our staircase. No one breathed audibly now, footsteps on our staircase, then a rattling of the swinging cupboard. This moment is indescribable. "Now we are lost!" I said, and could see us all being taken away by the Gestapo that very night. Twice they rattled at the cupboard, then there was nothing, the footsteps withdrew, we were saved so far. A shiver seemed to pass from one to another, I heard someone's teeth chattering, no one said a word.

There was not another sound in the house, but a light was burning on our landing, right in front of the cupboard. Could that be because it was a secret cupboard? Perhaps the police had forgotten the light? Would someone come back to put it out? Tongues loosened, there was no one in the house any longer, perhaps there was someone on guard outside.

Next we did three things: we went over again what we supposed had happened, we trembled with fear, and we

181

had to go to the lavatory. The buckets were in the attic, so all we had was Peter's tin wastepaper basket. Van Daan went first, then Daddy, but Mummy was too shy to face it. Daddy brought the wastepaper basket into the room, where Margot, Mrs. Van Daan, and I gladly made use of it. Finally Mummy decided to do so too. People kept on asking for paper—fortunately I had some in my pocket!

The tin smelled ghastly, everything went on in a whisper, we were tired, it was twelve o'clock. "Lie down on the floor then and sleep." Margot and I were each given a pillow and one blanket; Margot lying just near the store cupboard and I between the table legs. The smell wasn't quite so bad when one was on the floor, but still Mrs. Van Daan quietly brought some chlorine, a tea towel over the pot serving as a second expedient.

Talk, whispers, fear, stink, flatulation, and always someone on the pot; then try to go to sleep! However, by half past two I was so tired that I knew no more until half past three. I awoke when Mrs. Van Daan laid her head on my foot.

"For heaven's sake, give me something to put on!" I asked. I was given something, but don't ask what—a pair of woolen knickers over my pajamas, a red jumper, and a black skirt, white oversocks and a pair of sports stockings full of holes. Then Mrs. Van Daan sat in the chair and her husband came and lay on my feet. I lay thinking till half past three, shivering the whole time, which prevented Van Daan from sleeping. I prepared myself for the return of the police, then we'd have to say that we were in hiding; they would either be good Dutch people, then we'd be saved, or N.S.B.-ers,[1] then we'd have to bribe them!

"In that case, destroy the radio," sighed Mrs. Van Daan. "Yes, in the stove!" replied her husband. "If they find us, then let them find the radio as well!"

"Then they will find Anne's diary," added Daddy. "Burn it then," suggested the most terrified member of the

---

[1] The Dutch National Socialist Movement.

party. This, and when the police rattled the cupboard door, were my worst moments. "Not my diary; if my diary goes, I go with it!" But luckily Daddy didn't answer.

There is no object in recounting all the conversations that I can still remember; so much was said. I comforted Mrs. Van Daan, who was very scared. We talked about escaping and being questioned by the Gestapo, about ringing up, and being brave.

"We must behave like soldiers, Mrs. Van Daan. If all is up now, then let's go for Queen and Country, for freedom, truth, and the right, as they always say on the Dutch News from England. The only thing that is really rotten is that we get a lot of other people into trouble too."

Mr. Van Daan changed places with his wife after an hour, and Daddy came and sat beside me. The men smoked non-stop, now and then there was a deep sigh, then someone went on the pot and everything began all over again.

Four o'clock, five o'clock, half past five. Then I went and sat with Peter by his window and listened, so close together that we could feel each other's bodies quivering; we spoke a word or two now and then, and listened attentively. In the room next door they took down the blackout. They wanted to call up Koophuis at seven o'clock and get him to send someone around. Then they wrote down everything they wanted to tell Koophuis over the phone. The risk that the police on guard at the door, or in the warehouse, might hear the telephone was very great, but the danger of the police returning was even greater.

The points were these:

Burglars broken in: police have been in the house, as far as the swinging cupboard, but no further.

Burglars apparently disturbed, forced open the door in the warehouse and escaped through the garden.

Main entrance bolted, Kraler must have used the second door when he left. The typewriters and adding machine are safe in the black case in the private office.

Try to warn Henk and fetch the key from Elli, then go

and look around the office—on the pretext of feeding the cat.

Everything went according to plan. Koophuis was phoned, the typewriters which we had upstairs were put in the case. Then we sat around the table again and waited for Henk or the police.

Peter had fallen asleep and Van Daan and I were lying on the floor, when we heard loud footsteps downstairs. I got up quietly: "That's Henk."

"No, no, it's the police," some of the others said.

Someone knocked at the door, Miep whistled. This was too much for Mrs. Van Daan, she turned as white as a sheet and sank limply into a chair; had the tension lasted one minute longer she would have fainted.

Our room was a perfect picture when Miep and Henk entered, the table alone would have been worth photographing! A copy of *Cinema and Theater,* covered with jam and a remedy for diarrhea, opened at a page of dancing girls, two jam pots, two started loaves of bread, a mirror, comb, matches, ash, cigarettes, tobacco, ash tray, books, a pair of pants, a torch, toilet paper, etc., etc., lay jumbled together in variegated splendor.

Of course Henk and Miep were greeted with shouts and tears. Henk mended the hole in the door with some planks, and soon went off again to inform the police of the burglary. Miep had also found a letter under the warehouse door from the night watchman Slagter, who had noticed the hole and warned the police, whom he would also visit.

So we had half an hour to tidy ourselves. I've never seen such a change take place in half an hour. Margot and I took the bedclothes downstairs, went to the W.C., washed, and did our teeth and hair. After that I tidied the room a bit and went upstairs again. The table there was already cleared, so we ran off some water and made coffee and tea, boiled the milk, and laid the table for lunch. Daddy and Peter emptied the potties and cleaned them with warm water and chlorine.

At eleven o'clock we sat round the table with Henk,

who was back by that time, and slowly things began to be more normal and cozy again. Henk's story was as follows:

Mr. Slagter was asleep, but his wife told Henk that her husband had found the hole in our door when he was doing his tour round the canals, and that he had called a policeman, who had gone through the building with him. He would be coming to see Kraler on Tuesday and would tell him more then. At the police station they knew nothing of the burglary yet, but the policeman had made a note of it at once and would come and look round on Tuesday. On the way back Henk happened to meet our greengrocer at the corner, and told him that the house had been broken into. "I know that," he said quite coolly. "I was passing last evening with my wife and saw the hole in the door. My wife wanted to walk on, but I just had a look in with my torch; then the thieves cleared at once. To be on the safe side, I didn't ring up the police, as with you I didn't think it was the thing to do. I don't know anything, but I guess a lot."

Henk thanked him and went on. The man obviously guesses that we're here, because he always brings the potatoes during the lunch hour. Such a nice man!

It was one by the time Henk had gone and we'd finished doing the dishes. We all went for a sleep. I awoke at a quarter to three and saw that Mr. Dussel had already disappeared. Quite by chance, and with my sleepy eyes, I ran into Peter in the bathroom; he had just come down. We arranged to meet downstairs.

I tidied myself and went down. "Do you still dare to go to the front attic?" he asked. I nodded, fetched my pillow, and we went up to the attic. It was glorious weather, and soon the sirens were wailing; we stayed where we were. Peter put his arm around my shoulder, and I put mine around his and so we remained, our arms around each other, quietly waiting until Margot came to fetch us for coffee at four o'clock.

We finished our bread, drank lemonade and joked (we were able to again), otherwise everything went normally. In the evening I thanked Peter because he was the bravest of us all.

None of us has ever been in such danger as that night. God truly protected us; just think of it—the police at our secret cupboard, the light on right in front of it, and still we remained undiscovered.

If the invasion comes, and bombs with it, then it is each man for himself, but in this case the fear was also for our good, innocent protectors. "We are saved, go on saving us!" That is all we can say.

This affair has brought quite a number of changes with it. Mr. Dussel no longer sits downstairs in Kraler's office in the evenings, but in the bathroom instead. Peter goes round the house for a checkup at half past eight and half past nine. Peter isn't allowed to have his window open at nights any more. No one is allowed to pull the plug after half past nine. This evening there's a carpenter coming to make the warehouse doors even stronger.

Now there are debates going on all the time in the "Secret Annexe." Kraler reproached us for our carelessness. Henk, too, said that in a case like that we must never go downstairs. We have been pointedly reminded that we are in hiding, that we are Jews in chains, chained to one spot, without any rights, but with a thousand duties. We Jews mustn't show our feelings, must be brave and strong, must accept all inconveniences and not grumble, must do what is within our power and trust in God. Sometime this terrible war will be over. Surely the time will come when we are people again, and not just Jews.

Who has inflicted this upon us? Who has made us Jews different from all other people? Who has allowed us to suffer so terribly up till now? It is God that has made us as we are, but it will be God, too, who will raise us up again. If we bear all this suffering and if there are still Jews left, when it is over, then Jews, instead of being doomed, will be held up as an example. Who knows, it might even be our religion from which the world and all peoples learn good, and for that reason and that reason only do we have to suffer now. We can never become just Netherlanders, or just English, or representatives of any country for that matter, we will always remain Jews, but we want to, too.

Be brave! Let us remain aware of our task and not grumble, a solution will come, God has never deserted our people. Right through the ages there have been Jews, through all the ages they have had to suffer, but it has made them strong too; the weak fall, but the strong will remain and never go under!

During that night I really felt that I had to die, I waited for the police, I was prepared, as the soldier is on the battlefield. I was eager to lay down my life for the country, but now, now I've been saved again, now my first wish after the war is that I may become Dutch! I love the Dutch, I love this country, I love the language and want to work here. And even if I have to write to the Queen myself, I will not give up until I have reached my goal.

I am becoming still more independent of my parents, young as I am, I face life with more courage than Mummy; my feeling for justice is immovable, and truer than hers. I know what I want, I have a goal, an opinion, I have a religion and love. Let me be myself and then I am satisfied. I know that I'm a woman, a woman with inward strength and plenty of courage.

If God lets me live, I shall attain more than Mummy ever has done, I shall not remain insignificant, I shall work in the world and for mankind!

And now I know that first and foremost I shall require courage and cheerfulness!

Yours, Anne

Friday, 14 April, 1944

Dear Kitty,

The atmosphere here is still extremely strained. Pim has just about reached boiling point. Mrs. Van Daan is in bed with a cold and trumpeting away. Mr. Van Daan grows pale without his fags, Dussel, who is giving up a lot of his comfort, is full of observations, etc., etc.

There is no doubt that our luck's not in at the moment. The lavatory leaks and the washer of the tap has gone, but, thanks to our many connections, we shall soon be able to get these things put right.

I am sentimental sometimes, I know that, but there is occasion to be sentimental here at times, when Peter and I are sitting somewhere together on a hard, wooden crate in the midst of masses of rubbish and dust, our arms around each other's shoulders, and very close, he with one of my curls in his hand; when the birds sing outside and you see the trees changing to green, the sun invites one to be out in the open air, when the sky is so blue, then—oh, then, I wish for so much!

One sees nothing but dissatisfied, grumpy faces here, nothing but sighs and suppressed complaints; it really would seem as if suddenly we were very badly off here. If the truth is told, things are just as bad as you yourself care to make them. There's no one here that sets a good example; everyone should see that he gets the better of his own moods. Every day you hear, "If only it was all over."

My work, my hope, my love, my courage, all these things keep my head above water and keep me from complaining.

I really believe, Kits, that I'm slightly bats today, and yet I don't know why. Everything here is so mixed up, nothing's connected any more, and sometimes I very much doubt whether in the future anyone will be interested in all my tosh.

"The unbosomings of an ugly duckling" will be the title of all this nonsense. My diary really won't be much use to Messrs. Bolkestein or Gerbrandy.[1]

Yours, Anne

---

[1] Two members of the wartime Dutch Cabinet-in-Exile in London.

Dear Kitty,

"Shock upon shock. Will there ever be an end?" We honestly can ask ourselves that question now. Guess what's the latest. Peter forgot to unbolt the front door (which is bolted on the inside at night) and the lock of the other door doesn't work. The result was that Kraler and the men could not get into the house, so he went to the neighbors, forced open the kitchen window, and entered the building from the back. He is livid at us for being so stupid.

I can tell you, it's upset Peter frightfully. At one meal, when Mummy said she felt more sorry for Peter than anyone else, he almost started to cry. We're all just as much to blame as he is, because nearly every day the men ask whether the door's been unbolted and, just today, no one did.

Perhaps I shall be able to console him a bit later on; I would so love to help him.

Yours, Anne

Sunday morning, just before eleven o'clock,
16 April, 1944

Darlingest Kitty,

Remember yesterday's date, for it is a very important day in my life. Surely it is a great day for every girl when she receives her first kiss? Well, then, it is just as important for me too! Bram's kiss on my right cheek doesn't count any more, likewise the one from Mr. Walker on my right hand.

How did I suddenly come by this kiss? Well, I will tell you.

Yesterday evening at eight o'clock I was sitting with Peter on his divan, it wasn't long before his arm went

189

round me. "Let's move up a bit," I said, "then I don't bump my head against the cupboard." He moved up, almost into the corner, I laid my arm under his and across his back, and he just about buried me, because his arm was hanging on my shoulder.

Now we've sat like this on other occasions, but never so close together as yesterday. He held me firmly against him, my left shoulder against his chest; already my heart began to beat faster, but we had not finished yet. He didn't rest until my head was on his shoulder and his against it. When I sat upright again after about five minutes, he soon took my head in his hands and laid it against him once more. Oh, it was so lovely, I couldn't talk much, the joy was too great. He stroked my cheek and arm a bit awkwardly, played with my curls and our heads lay touching most of the time. I can't tell you, Kitty, the feeling that ran through me all the while. I was too happy for words, and I believe he was as well.

We got up at half past eight. Peter put on his gym shoes, so that when he toured the house he wouldn't make a noise, and I stood beside him. How it came about so suddenly, I don't know, but before we went downstairs he kissed me, through my hair, half on my left cheek, half on my ear; I tore downstairs without looking round, and am simply longing for today!

Yours, Anne

Monday, 17 April, 1944

Dear Kitty,

Do you think that Daddy and Mummy would approve of my sitting and kissing a boy on a divan—a boy of seventeen and a half and a girl of just under fifteen? I don't really think they would, but I must rely on myself over this. It is so quiet and peaceful to lie in his arms and to dream, it is so thrilling to feel his cheek against mine, it is so lovely to know that there is someone waiting for me. But there is indeed a big "but," because will Peter be content to leave it at this? I haven't forgotten his promise already, but . . . he *is* a boy!

I know myself that I'm starting very soon, not even fifteen, and so independent already! It's certainly hard for other people to understand, I know almost for certain that Margot would never kiss a boy unless there had been some talk of an engagement or marriage, but neither Peter nor I have anything like that in mind. I'm sure too that Mummy never touched a man before Daddy. What would my girl friends say about it if they knew that I lay in Peter's arms, my heart against his chest, my head on his shoulder and with his head against mine!

Oh, Anne, how scandalous! But honestly, I don't think it is; we are shut up here, shut away from the world, in fear and anxiety, especially just lately. Why, then, should we who love each other remain apart? Why should we wait until we've reached a suitable age? Why should we bother?

I have taken it upon myself to look after myself; he would never want to cause me sorrow or pain. Why shouldn't I follow the way my heart leads me, if it makes us both happy? All the same, Kitty, I believe you can sense that I'm in doubt, I think it must be my honesty which rebels against doing anything on the sly! Do you think it's my duty to tell Daddy what I'm doing? Do you think we should share our secret with a third person? A lot of the beauty would be lost, but would my conscience feel happier? I will discuss it with "him."

Oh, yes, there's still so much I want to talk to him about, for I don't see the use of only just cuddling each other. To exchange our thoughts, that shows confidence and faith in each other, we would both be sure to profit by it!

Yours, Anne

Tuesday, 18 April, 1944

Dear Kitty,

Everything goes well here. Daddy's just said that he definitely expects large-scale operations to take place before the twentieth of May, both in Russia and Italy, and also in the West; I find it more and more difficult to imagine our liberation from here.

Yesterday Peter and I finally got down to our talk, which had already been put off for at least ten days. I explained everything about girls to him and didn't hesitate to discuss the most intimate things. The evening ended by each giving the other a kiss, just about beside my mouth, it's really a lovely feeling.

Perhaps I'll take my diary up there sometime, to go more deeply into things for once. I don't get any satisfaction out of lying in each other's arms day in, day out, and would so like to feel that he's the same.

We are having a superb spring after our long, lingering winter; April is really glorious, not too hot and not too cold, with little showers now and then. Our chestnut tree is already quite greenish and you can even see little blooms here and there.

Elli gave us a treat on Saturday, by bringing four bunches of flowers, three bunches of narcissus and one of grape hyacinths, the latter being for me.

I must do some algebra, Kitty—good-by.

Yours, Anne

Wednesday, 19 April, 1944

My darling,

Is there anything more beautiful in the world than to sit before an open window and enjoy nature, to listen to the birds singing, feel the sun on your cheeks and have a darling boy in your arms? It is so soothing and peaceful to feel his arms around me, to know that he is close by and yet to remain silent, it can't be bad, for this tranquillity is good. Oh, never to be disturbed again, not even by Mouschi.

Yours, Anne

Friday, 21 April, 1944

Dear Kitty,

Yesterday afternoon I was lying in bed with a sore throat, but since I was already bored on the first day and did not have a temperature, I got up again today. It's the eighteenth birthday of Her Royal Highness Princess Elizabeth of York. The B.B.C. has said that she will not be declared of age yet, though it's usually the case with royal children. We have been asking ourselves what prince this beauty is going to marry, but cannot think of anyone suitable. Perhaps her sister, Princess Margaret Rose, can have Prince Baudouin of Belgium one day.

Here we are having one misfortune after another, Scarcely had the outside doors been strengthened than the warehouse man appeared again. In all probability it was he who stole the potato meal and wants to put the blame on to Elli's shoulders. The whole "Secret Annexe" is understandably het up again. Elli is beside herself with anger.

I want to send in to some paper or other to see if they will take one of my stories, under a pseudonym, of course.

Till next time, darling!

Yours, Anne

Tuesday, 25 April, 1944

Dear Kitty,

Dussel has not been on speaking terms with Van Daan for ten days and just because, ever since the burglary, a whole lot of fresh security measures have been made that don't suit him. He maintains that Van Daan has been shouting at him.

"Everything here happens upside down," he told me. "I am going to speak to your father about it." He is not supposed to sit in the office downstairs on Saturday afternoons and Sundays any more, but he goes on doing it just the same. Van Daan was furious and Father went downstairs to talk to him. Naturally, he kept on inventing excuses, but this time he could not get around even Father. Father now talks to him as little as possible, as Dussel has insulted him. None of us know in what way, but it must have been very bad.

I have written a lovely story called "Blurr, the Explorer," which pleased the three to whom I read it very much.

Yours, Anne

Thursday, 27 April, 1944

Dear Kitty,

Mrs. Van Daan was in such a bad mood this morning, nothing but complaints! First, there's her cold, and she can't get any lozenges, and so much nose-blowing is unendurable. Next, it's that the sun's not shining, that the invasion doesn't come, that we can't look out of the windows, etc., etc. We all had to laugh at her; and she was sporting enough to join in. At the moment I'm reading *The Emperor Charles V*, written by a professor at Göttingen University; he worked at the book for forty years. I read fifty pages in five days; it's impossible to do more. The book has 598 pages, so now you can work out how long it will take me—and there is a second volume to follow. But very interesting.

What doesn't a schoolgirl get to know in a single day! Take me, for example. First, I translated a piece from Dutch into English, about Nelson's last battle. After that, I went through some more of Peter the Great's war against Norway (1700-1721), Charles XII, Augustus the Strong,

194

Stanislavs Leczinsky, Mazeppa, Von Görz, Brandenburg, Pomerania and Denmark, plus the usual dates.

After that I landed up in Brazil, read about Bahia tobacco, the abundance of coffee and the one and a half million inhabitants of Rio de Janeiro, of Pernambuco and Sao Paulo, not forgetting the river Amazon; about Negroes, Mulattos, Mestizos, Whites, more than fifty per cent of the population being illiterate, and the malaria. As there was still some time left, I quickly ran through a family tree. Jan the Elder, Willem Lodewijk, Ernst Casimir I, Hendrik Casimir I, right up to the little Margriet Franciska (born in 1943 in Ottawa).

Twelve o'clock: In the attic, I continued my program with the history of the Church—Phew! Till one o'clock.

Just after two, the poor child sat working ('hm, 'hm!) again, this time studying narrow- and broad-nosed monkeys. Kitty, tell me quickly how many toes a hippopotamus has! Then followed the Bible, Noah and the Ark, Shem, Ham, and Japheth. After that Charles V. Then with Peter: *The Colonel*, in English by Thackeray. Heard my French verbs and then compared the Mississippi with the Missouri.

I've still got a cold and have given it to Margot as well as to Mummy and Daddy. As long as Peter doesn't get it! He called me his "Eldorado" and wanted a kiss. Of course, I couldn't! Funny boy! But still, he's a darling.

Enough for today, good-by!

Yours, Anne

Friday, 28 April, 1944

Dear Kitty,

I have never forgotten my dream about Peter Wessel (see beginning of January). If I think of it, I can still feel his cheek against mine now, and recall that lovely feeling that made everything good.

Sometimes I have had the same feeling here with Peter, but never to such an extent, until yesterday, when we were, as usual, sitting on the divan, our arms around each other's waists. Then suddenly the ordinary Anne slipped away and a second Anne took her place, a second Anne who is not reckless and jocular, but one who just wants to love and be gentle.

I sat pressed closely against him and felt a wave of emotion come over me, tears sprang into my eyes, the left one trickled onto his dungarees, the right one ran down my nose and also fell onto his dungarees. Did he notice? He made no move or sign to show that he did. I wonder if he feels the same as I do? He hardly said a word. Does he know that he has two Annes before him? These questions must remain unanswered.

At half past eight I stood up and went to the window, where we always say good-by. I was still trembling, I was still Anne number two. He came towards me, I flung my arms around his neck and gave him a kiss on his left cheek, and was about to kiss the other cheek, when my lips met his and we pressed them together. In a whirl we were clasped in each other's arms, again and again, never to leave off. Oh, Peter does so need tenderness. For the first time in his life he has discovered a girl, has seen for the first time that even the most irritating girls have another side to them, that they have hearts and can be different when you are alone with them. For the first time in his life he has given of himself and, having never had a boy or girl friend in his life before, shown his real self. Now we have found each other. For that matter, I didn't know him either, like him having never had a trusted friend, and this is what it has come to. . . .

Once more there is a question which gives me no peace: "Is it right? Is it right that I should have yielded so soon, that I am so ardent, just as ardent and eager as Peter himself? May I, a girl, let myself go to this extent?" There is but *one* answer: "I have longed so much and for so long —I am so lonely—and now I have found consolation."

In the mornings we just behave in an ordinary way, in the afternoons more or less so (except just occasionally); but in the evenings the suppressed longings of the whole day, the happiness and the blissful memories of all the previous occasions come to the surface and we only think of each other. Every evening, after the last kiss, I would like to dash away, not to look into his eyes any more—away, away, alone in the darkness.

And what do I have to face, when I reach the bottom of the staircase? Bright lights, questions, and laughter; I have to swallow it all and not show a thing. My heart still feels too much; I can't get over a shock such as I received yesterday all at once. The Anne who is gentle shows herself too little anyway, and, therefore, will not allow herself to be suddenly driven into the background. Peter has touched my emotions more deeply than anyone has ever done before—except in my dreams. Peter has taken possession of me and turned me inside out; surely it goes without saying that anyone would require a rest and a little while to recover from such an upheaval?

Oh Peter, what have you done to me? What do you want of me? Where will this lead us? Oh, now I understand Elli; now, now that I am going through this myself, now I understand her doubt; if I were older and he should ask me to marry him, what should I answer? Anne, be honest! You would not be able to marry him, but yet, it would be hard to let him go. Peter hasn't enough character yet, not enough will power, too little courage and strength. He is still a child in his heart of hearts, he is no older than I am; he is only searching for tranquillity and happiness.

Am I only fourteen? Am I really still a silly little school-girl? Am I really so inexperienced about everything? I have more experience than most; I have been through things that hardly anyone of my age has undergone. I am afraid of myself, I am afraid that in my longing I am giving myself too quickly. How, later on, can it ever go right with other boys? Oh, it is so difficult, always battling with one's heart and reason; in its own time, each will speak, but do I know for certain that I have chosen the right time?

Yours, Anne

Dear Kitty,

On Saturday evening I asked Peter whether he thought that I ought to tell Daddy a bit about us; when we'd discussed it a little, he came to the conclusion that I should. I was glad, for it shows that he's an honest boy. As soon as I got downstairs I went off with Daddy to get some water; and while we were on the stairs I said, "Daddy, I expect you've gathered that when we're together Peter and I don't sit miles apart. Do you think it's wrong?" Daddy didn't reply immediately, then said, "No, I don't think it's wrong, but you must be careful, Anne, you're in such a confined space here." When we went upstairs, he said something else on the same lines. On Sunday morning he called me to him and said, "Anne, I have thought more about what you said." I felt scared already. "It's not really very right—here in this house; I thought that you were just pals. Is Peter in love?"

"Oh, of course not," I replied.

"You know that I understand both of you, but you must be the one to hold back. Don't go upstairs so often, don't encourage him more than you can help. It is the man who is always the active one in these things; the woman can hold him back. It is quite different under normal circumstances, when you are free, you see other boys and girls, you can get away sometimes, play games and do all kinds of other things; but here, if you're together a lot, and you want to get away, you can't; you see each other every hour of the day—in fact, all the time. Be careful, Anne, and don't take it too seriously!"

"I don't, Daddy, but Peter is a decent boy, really a nice boy!"

"Yes, but he is not a strong character; he can be easily influenced, for good, but also for bad; I hope for his sake that his good side will remain uppermost, because, by nature, that is how he is."

We talked on for a bit and agreed that Daddy should talk to him too.

On Sunday morning in the attic he asked, "And have you talked to your father, Anne?"

"Yes," I replied, "I'll tell you about it. Daddy doesn't think it's bad, but he says that here, where we're so close together all the time, clashes may easily arise."

"But we agreed, didn't we, never to quarrel; and I'm determined to stick to it!"

"So will I, Peter, but Daddy didn't think that it was like this, he just thought we were pals; do you think that we still can be?"

"I can—what about you?"

"Me too, I told Daddy that I trusted you. I do trust you, Peter, just as much as I trust Daddy, and I believe you to be worthy of it. You are, aren't you, Peter?"

"I hope so." (He was very shy and rather red in the face.)

"I believe in you, Peter," I went on, "I believe that you have good qualities, and that you'll get on in the world."

After that, we talked about other things. Later I said, "If we come out of here, I know quite well that you won't bother about me any more!"

He flared right up. "That's not true, Anne, oh no, I won't let you think that of me!"

Then I was called away.

Daddy has talked to him; he told me about it today. "Your father thought that the friendship might develop into love sooner or later," he said. But I replied that we would keep a check on ourselves.

Daddy doesn't want me to go upstairs so much in the evenings now, but I don't want that. Not only because I like being with Peter; I have told him that I trust him. I do trust him and I want to show him that I do, which can't happen if I stay downstairs through lack of trust.

No, I'm going!

In the meantime the Dussel drama has righted itself again. At supper on Saturday evening he apologized in beautiful Dutch. Van Daan was nice about it straight away; it must have taken Dussel a whole day to learn that little lesson off by heart.

Sunday, his birthday, passed peacefully. We gave him a bottle of good 1919 wine, from the Van Daans (who could give their presents now after all), a bottle of piccalilli and a packet of razor blades, a jar of lemon jam from Kraler, a book, *Little Martin*, from Miep, and a plant from Elli. He treated each one of us to an egg.

Yours, Anne

Wednesday, 3 May, 1944

Dear Kitty,

First, just the news of the week. We're having a holiday from politics; there is nothing, absolutely nothing to announce. I too am gradually beginning to believe that the invasion will come. After all, they can't let the Russians clear up everything; for that matter, they're not doing anything either at the moment.

Mr. Koophuis comes to the office every morning again now. He's got a new spring for Peter's divan, so Peter will have to do some upholstering, about which, quite understandably, he doesn't feel a bit happy.

Have I told you that Boche has disappeared? Simply vanished—we haven't seen a sign of her since Thursday of last week. I expect she's already in the cats' heaven, while some animal lover is enjoying a succulent meal from her. Perhaps some little girl will be given a fur cap out of her skin. Peter is very sad about it.

Since Saturday we've changed over, and have lunch at half past eleven in the morning, so we have to last out with one cupful of porridge; this saves us a meal. Vegetables are still very difficult to obtain: we had rotten boiled lettuce this afternoon. Ordinary lettuce, spinach, and boiled lettuce, there's nothing else. With these we eat rotten potatoes, so it's a delicious combination!

As you can easily imagine we often ask ourselves here

despairingly: "What, oh, what is the use of the war? Why can't people live peacefully together? Why all this destruction?"

The question is very understandable, but no one has found a satisfactory answer to it so far. Yes, why do they make still more gigantic planes, still heavier bombs and, at the same time, prefabricated houses for reconstruction? Why should millions be spent daily on the war and yet there's not a penny available for medical services, artists, or for poor people?

Why do some people have to starve, while there are surpluses rotting in other parts of the world? Oh, why are people so crazy?

I don't believe that the big men, the politicians and the capitalists alone, are guilty of the war. Oh no, the little man is just as guilty, otherwise the peoples of the world would have risen in revolt long ago! There's in people simply an urge to destroy, an urge to kill, to murder and rage, and until all mankind, without exception, undergoes a great change, wars will be waged, everything that has been built up, cultivated, and grown will be destroyed and disfigured, after which mankind will have to begin all over again.

I have often been downcast, but never in despair; I regard our hiding as a dangerous adventure, romantic and interesting at the same time. In my diary I treat all the privations as amusing. I have made up my mind now to lead a different life from other girls and, later on, different from ordinary housewives. My start has been so very full of interest, and that is the sole reason why I have to laugh at the humorous side of the most dangerous moments.

I am young and I possess many buried qualities; I am young and strong and am living a great adventure; I am still in the midst of it and can't grumble the whole day long. I have been given a lot, a happy nature, a great deal of cheerfulness and strength. Every day I feel that I am developing inwardly, that the liberation is drawing nearer and how beautiful nature is, how good the people are about me, how interesting this adventure is! Why, then, should I be in despair?

Yours, Anne

Friday, 5 May, 1944

Dear Kitty,

Daddy is not pleased with me; he thought that after our talk on Sunday I automatically wouldn't go upstairs every evening. He doesn't want any "necking," a word I can't bear. It was bad enough talking about it, why must he make it so unpleasant now? I shall talk to him today. Margot has given me some good advice, so listen; this is roughly what I want to say:

"I believe, Daddy, that you expect a declaration from me, so I will give it you. You are disappointed in me, as you had expected more reserve from me, and I suppose you want me to be just as a fourteen-year-old should be. But that's where you're mistaken!

"Since we've been here, from July 1942 until a few weeks ago, I can assure you that I haven't had an easy time. If you only knew how I cried in the evening, how unhappy I was, how lonely I felt, then you would understand that I want to go upstairs!

"I have now reached the stage that I can live entirely on my own, without Mummy's support or anyone else's for that matter. But it hasn't just happened in a night; it's been a bitter, hard struggle and I've shed many a tear, before I became as independent as I am now. You can laugh at me and not believe me, but that can't harm me. I know that I'm a separate individual and I don't feel in the least bit responsible to any of you. I am only telling you this because I thought that otherwise you might think that I was underhand, but I don't have to give an account of my deeds to anyone but myself.

"When I was in difficulties you all closed your eyes and stopped up your ears and didn't help me; on the contrary, I received nothing but warnings not to be so boisterous. I was only boisterous so as not to be miserable all the time.

202

I was reckless so as not to hear that persistent voice within me continually. I played a comedy for a year and a half, day in, day out, I never grumbled, never lost my cue, nothing like that—and now, now the battle is over. I have won! I am independent both in mind and body. I don't need a mother any more, for all this conflict has made me strong.

"And now, now that I'm on top of it, now that I know that I've fought the battle, now I want to be able to go on in my own way too, the way that I think is right. You can't and mustn't regard me as fourteen, for all these troubles have made me older; I shall not be sorry for what I have done, but shall act as I think I can. You can't coax me into not going upstairs; *either* you forbid it, *or* you trust me through thick and thin, but then leave me in peace as well!"

Yours, Anne

Saturday, 6 May, 1944

Dear Kitty,

I put a letter, in which I wrote what I explained to you yesterday, in Daddy's pocket before supper yesterday. After reading it, he was, according to Margot, very upset for the rest of the evening. (I was upstairs doing the dishes.) Poor Pim, I might have known what the effect of such an epistle would be. He is so sensitive! I immediately told Peter not to ask or say anything more. Pim hasn't said any more about it to me. Is that yet in store, I wonder?

Here everything is going on more or less normally again. What they tell us about the prices and the people outside is almost unbelievable, half a pound of tea costs 350 florins,[1] a pound of coffee 80 florins, butter 35 florins per pound, an egg 1.45 florin. People pay 14 florins for an ounce of Bulgarian tobacco! Everyone deals in the black market, every errand boy has something to offer. Our baker's boy got hold of some sewing silk, 0.9 florin for a

[1] A florin is equal to approximately twenty-eight cents.

thin little skein, the milkman manages to get clandestine ration cards, the undertaker delivers the cheese. Burglaries, murders, and theft go on daily. The police and night watchmen join in just as strenuously as the professionals, everyone wants something in their empty stomachs and because wage increases are forbidden the people simply have to swindle. The police are continually on the go, tracing girls of fifteen, sixteen, seventeen and older, who are reported missing every day.

Yours, Anne

Sunday morning, 7 May, 1944

Dear Kitty,

Daddy and I had a long talk yesterday afternoon, I cried terribly and he joined in. Do you know what he said to me, Kitty? "I have received many letters in my life, but this is certainly the most unpleasant! You, Anne, who have received such love from your parents, you, who have parents who are always ready to help you, who have always defended you whatever it might be, can you talk of feeling no responsibility towards us? You feel wronged and deserted; no, Anne, you have done us a great injustice!

"Perhaps you didn't mean it like that, but it is what you wrote; no, Anne, we haven't deserved such a reproach as this!"

Oh, I have failed miserably; this is certainly the worst thing I've ever done in my life. I was only trying to show off with my crying and my tears, just trying to appear big, so that he would respect me. Certainly, I have had a lot of unhappiness, but to accuse the good Pim, who has done and still does do everything for me—no, that was too low for words.

It's right that for once I've been taken down from my inaccessible pedestal, that my pride has been shaken a bit, for I was becoming much too taken up with myself again. What Miss Anne does is by no means always right! Anyone who can cause such unhappiness to someone else, someone he professes to love, and on purpose, too, is low, very low!

And the way Daddy has forgiven me makes me feel more than ever ashamed of myself, he is going to throw the letter in the fire and is so sweet to me now, just as if he had done something wrong. No, Anne, you still have a tremendous lot to learn, begin by doing that first, instead of looking down on others and accusing them!

I have had a lot of sorrow, but who hasn't at my age? I have played the clown a lot too, but I was hardly conscious of it; I felt lonely, but hardly ever in despair! I ought to be deeply ashamed of myself, and indeed I am.

What is done cannot be undone, but one can prevent it happening again. I want to start from the beginning again and it can't be difficult, now that I have Peter. With him to support me, I can and will!

I'm not alone any more; he loves me. I love him, I have my books, my storybook and my diary, I'm not so frightfully ugly, not utterly stupid, have a cheerful temperament and want to have a good character!

Yes, Anne, you've felt deeply that your letter was too hard and that it was untrue. To think that you were even proud of it! I will take Daddy as my example, and I *will* improve.

Yours, Anne

Monday, 8 May, 1944

Dear Kitty,

Have I ever really told you anything about our family?

I don't think I have, so I will begin now. My father's parents were very rich. His father had worked himself right up and his mother came from a prominent family, who were also rich. So in his youth Daddy had a real little rich boy's upbringing, parties every week, balls, festivities, beautiful girls, dinners, a large home, etc., etc.

After Grandpa's death all the money was lost during the World War and the inflation that followed. Daddy was therefore extremely well brought up and he laughed very much yesterday when, for the first time in his fifty-five years, he scraped out the frying pan at table.

Mummy's parents were rich too and we often listen openmouthed to stories of engagement parties of two hundred and fifty people, private balls and dinners. One certainly could not call us rich now, but all my hopes are pinned on after the war.

I can assure you I'm not at all keen on a narrow, cramped existence like Mummy and Margot. I'd adore to go to Paris for a year and London for a year to learn the languages and study the history of art. Compare that with Margot, who wants to be a midwife in Palestine! I always long to see beautiful dresses and interesting people.

I want to see something of the world and do all kinds of exciting things. I've already told you this before. And a little money as well won't do any harm.

Miep told us this morning about a party she went to, to celebrate an engagement. Both the future bride and bridegroom came from rich families and everything was very grand. Miep made our mouths water telling us about the food they had: vegetable soup with minced meat balls in it, cheese, rolls, hors d'oeuvre with eggs and roast beef, fancy cakes, wine and cigarettes, as much as you wanted of everything (black market). Miep had ten drinks—can that be the woman who calls herself a teetotaler? If Miep had all those, I wonder however many her spouse managed to knock back? Naturally, everyone at the party was a bit tipsy. There were two policemen from the fighting squad, who took photos of the engaged couple. It seems as if we are never far from Miep's thoughts, because she took down the addresses of these men at once, in case anything should happen at some time or other, and good Dutchmen might come in useful.

She made our mouths water. We, who get nothing but two spoonfuls of porridge for our breakfast and whose tummies were so empty that they were positively rattling, we, who get nothing but half-cooked spinach (to preserve the vitamins) and rotten potatoes day after day, we, who get nothing but lettuce, cooked or raw, spinach and yet again spinach in our hollow stomachs. Perhaps we may yet grow to be as strong as Popeye, although I don't see much sign of it at present!

If Miep had taken us to the party we shouldn't have left any rolls for the other guests. I can tell you, we positively drew the words from Miep's lips, we gathered round her, as if we'd never heard about delicious food or smart people in our lives before!

And these are the granddaughters of a millionaire. The world is a queer place!

Yours, Anne

Tuesday, 9 May, 1944

Dear Kitty,

I've finished my story of Ellen the fairy. I have copied it once on nice note paper. It certainly looks very attractive, but is it really enough for Daddy's birthday? I don't know. Margot and Mummy have both written poems for him.

Mr. Kraler came upstairs this afternoon with the news that Mrs. B., who used to act as demonstrator for the business, wants to eat her box lunch in the office here at two o'clock every afternoon. Think of it! No one can come upstairs any more, the potatoes cannot be delivered, Elli can't have any lunch, we can't go to the W.C., we mustn't move, etc., etc. We thought up the wildest and most varied suggestions to wheedle her away. Van Daan thought that a good laxative in her coffee would be sufficient. "No," replied Koophuis, "I beg of you not, then we'd never get her off the box!" Resounding laughter. "Off the box," asked Mrs. Van Daan, "what does that mean?" An explanation followed. "Can I always use it?" she then asked stupidly. "Imagine it," Elli giggled, "if one asked for the box in Bijenkorf's[1] they wouldn't even understand what you mean!"

Oh, Kit, it's such wonderful weather, if only I could go outdoors!

Yours, Anne

[1] "Bijenkorf" is a large store in Amsterdam.

Dear Kitty,

We were sitting in the attic doing some French yesterday afternoon when I suddenly heard water pattering down behind me. I asked Peter what it could be, but he didn't even reply, simply tore up to the loft, where the source of the disaster was, and pushed Mouschi, who, because of the wet earth box, had sat down beside it, harshly back to the right place. A great din and disturbance followed, and Mouschi, who had finished by that time, dashed downstairs.

Mouschi, seeking the convenience of something similar to his box, had chosen some wood shavings. The pool had trickled down from the loft into the attic immediately and, unfortunately, landed just beside and in the barrel of potatoes. The ceiling was dripping, and as the attic floor is not free from holes either, several yellow drips came through the ceiling into the dining room between a pile of stockings and some books, which were lying on the table. I was doubled up with laughter; it really was a scream. There was Mouschi crouching under a chair, Peter with water, bleaching powder, and floor cloth, and Van Daan trying to soothe everyone. The calamity was soon over, but it's a well-known fact that cats' puddles positively stink. The potatoes proved this only too clearly and also the wood shavings that Daddy collected in a bucket to be burned. Poor Mouschi! How were you to know that peat is unobtainable?

Yours, Anne

P.S. Our beloved Queen spoke to us yesterday and this evening. She is taking a holiday in order to be strong for her return to Holland. She used words like "soon, when I am back, speedy liberation, heroism, and heavy burdens."

A speech by Gerbrandy followed. A clergyman concluded with a prayer to God to take care of the Jews, the people in concentration camps, in prisons, and in Germany.

Yours, Anne

Thursday, 11 May, 1944

Dear Kitty,

I'm frightfully busy at the moment, and although it sounds mad, I haven't time to get through my pile of work. Shall I tell you briefly what I have got to do? Well, then, by tomorrow I must finish reading the first part of *Galileo Galilei*, as it has to be returned to the library. I only started it yesterday, but I shall manage it.

Next week I have got to read *Palestine at the Crossroads* and the second part of *Galilei*. Next I finished reading the first part of the biography of *The Emperor Charles V* yesterday, and it's essential that I work out all the diagrams and family trees that I have collected from it. After that I have three pages of foreign words gathered from various books, which have all got to be recited, written down, and learned. Number four is that my film stars are all mixed up together and are simply gasping to be tidied up; however, as such a clearance would take several days, and since Professor Anne, as she's already said, is choked with work, the chaos will have to remain a chaos.

Next Theseus, Oedipus, Peleus, Orpheus, Jason, and Hercules are all awaiting their turn to be arranged, as their different deeds lie crisscross in my mind like fancy threads in a dress; it's also high time Myron and Phidias had some treatment, if they wish to remain at all coherent. Likewise it's the same with the seven and nine years' war; I'm mixing everything up together at this rate. Yes, but what can one do with such a memory! Think how forgetful I shall be when I'm eighty!

Oh, something else, the Bible, how long is it still going to take before I meet the bathing Suzanna? And what do they mean by the guilt of Sodom and Gomorrah? Oh, there is still such a terrible lot to find out and to learn. And in the meantime I've left Lisolette of the Pfalz completely in the lurch.

Kitty, can you see that I'm just about bursting?

Now, about something else: you've known for a long time that my greatest wish is to become a journalist some-day and later on a famous writer. Whether these leanings towards greatness (or insanity?) will ever materialize remains to be seen, but I certainly have the subjects in my mind. In any case, I want to publish a book entitled *Het Achterhuis* after the war. Whether I shall succeed or not, I cannot say, but my diary will be a great help. I have other ideas as well, besides *Het Achterhuis*. But I will write more fully about them some other time, when they have taken a clearer form in my mind.

Yours, Anne

Saturday, 13 May, 1944

Dearest Kitty,

It was Daddy's birthday yesterday. Mummy and Daddy have been married nineteen years. The charwoman wasn't below and the sun shone as it has never shone before in 1944. Our horse chestnut is in full bloom, thickly covered with leaves and much more beautiful than last year.

Daddy received a biography of the life of Linnaeus from Koophuis, a book on nature from Kraler, *Amsterdam by the Water* from Dussel, a gigantic box from Van Daan, beautifully done up and almost professionally decorated, containing three eggs, a bottle of beer, a bottle of yoghourt, and a green tie. It made our pot of syrup seem rather small. My roses smelled lovely compared with Miep's and Elli's carnations, which had no smell, but were very pretty too. He was certainly spoiled. Fifty fancy pastries have arrived, heavenly! Daddy himself treated us to spiced gingerbread, beer for the gentlemen, and yoghourt for the ladies. Enjoyment all around!

Yours, Anne

Tuesday, 16 May, 1944

Dearest Kitty,

Just for a change, as we haven't talked about them for so long, I want to tell you a little discussion that went on between Mr. and Mrs. Van Daan yesterday.

Mrs. Van Daan: "The Germans are sure to have made the Atlantic Wall very strong indeed, they will certainly do all in their power to hold back the English. It's amazing how strong the Germans are!"

Mr. Van Daan: "Oh, yes, incredibly."

Mrs. Van Daan: "Ye-es."

Mr. Van Daan: "The Germans are so strong they're sure to win the war in the end, in spite of everything!"

Mrs. Van Daan: "It's quite possible, I'm not convinced of the opposite yet."

Mr. Van Daan: "I won't bother to reply any more."

Mrs. Van Daan: "Still you always do answer me, you can't resist capping me every time."

Mr. Van Daan: "Of course not, but my replies are the bare minimum."

Mrs. Van Daan: "But still you do reply, and you always have to be in the right! Your prophecies don't always come true by a long shot."

Mr. Van Daan: "They have up till now."

Mrs. Van Daan: "That's not true. The invasion was to have come last year, and the Finns were to have been out of the war by now. Italy was finished in the winter, but the Russians would already have Lemberg; oh, no, I don't think much of your prophecies."

Mr. Van Daan (standing up): "It's about time you shut your mouth. One day I'll show you that I'm right; sooner or later you'll get enough of it. I can't bear any more of your grousing. You're so infuriating but you'll stew in your own juice one day."

End of Part I.

I really couldn't help laughing. Mummy too, while Peter sat biting his lip. Oh, those stupid grownups, they'd do better to start learning themselves, before they have so much to say to the younger generation!

Yours, Anne

Friday, 19 May, 1944

Dear Kitty,

I felt rotten yesterday, really out of sorts (unusual for Anne!), with tummy-ache and every other imaginable misery. I'm much better today, feel very hungry, but I'd better not touch the kidney beans we're having today.

All goes well with Peter and me. The poor boy seems to need a little love even more than I do. He blushes every evening when he gets his good-night kiss and simply begs for another. I wonder if I'm a good substitute for Boche? I don't mind, he is so happy now that he knows that someone loves him.

After my laborious conquest I've got the situation a bit more in hand now, but I don't think my love has cooled off. He's a darling, but I soon closed up my inner self from him. If he wants to force the lock again he'll have to work a good deal harder than before!

Yours, Anne

Saturday, 20 May, 1944

Dear Kitty,

Last evening I came downstairs from the attic and as I entered the room saw at once the lovely case of carnations lying on the floor, Mummy down on hands and knees mopping up and Margot fishing up some papers from the floor.

"What's happened here?" I asked, full of misgivings and, not even waiting for their answer, tried to sum up the damage from a distance. My whole portfolio of family trees, writing books, textbooks, everything was soaked. I nearly wept and was so worked up that I can hardly remember what I said, but Margot said that I let fly something about "incalculable loss, frightful, terrible, can never be repaired," and still more. Daddy burst out laughing, Mummy and Margot joined in, but I could have cried over all the toil that was wasted, and the diagrams I'd so carefully worked out.

On closer inspection the "incalculable loss" didn't turn out to be as bad as I'd thought. I carefully sorted out all the papers that were stuck together and separated them in the attic. After that I hung them all up on the clothes lines to dry. It was a funny sight and I couldn't help laughing myself. Maria de Medici beside Charles V, William of Orange and Marie Antoinette; it's a "racial outrage," was Mr. Van Daan's joke on the subject. After I'd entrusted my papers into Peter's care I went downstairs again.

"Which books are spoiled?" I asked Margot, who was checking up on them. "Algebra," she said. I hurried to her side, but unfortunately not even the algebra book was spoiled. I wish it had fallen right in the vase; I've never loathed *any* other book so much as that one. There are the names of at least twenty girls in the front, all previous owners; it is old, yellow, full of scribbles and improvements. If I'm ever in a really very wicked mood, I'll tear the blasted thing to pieces!

Yours, Anne

Monday, 22 May, 1944

Dear Kitty,

On May 20th Daddy lost five bottles of yoghourt on a bet with Mrs. Van Daan. The invasion still hasn't come yet; it's no exaggeration to say that all Amsterdam, all Holland, yes, the whole west coast of Europe, right down to Spain, talks about the invasion day and night, debates about it, and makes bets on it and . . . hopes.

The suspense is rising to a climax. By no means everyone we had regarded as "good" Dutch have stuck to their faith in the English; by no means everyone thinks the English bluff a masterly piece of strategy, oh no, the people want to see deeds at last, great, heroic deeds. Nobody sees beyond his own nose, no one thinks that the English are fighting for their own land and their own people, everyone thinks that it's their duty to save Holland, as quickly and as well as they can.

What obligations have the English towards us? How have the Dutch earned the generous help that they seem so explicitly to expect? Oh no, the Dutch will have made a big mistake, the English, in spite of all their bluff, are certainly no more to blame than all the other countries, great and small, which are not under occupation. The English really won't offer us their apologies, for even if we do reproach them for being asleep during the years when Germany was rearming, we cannot deny that all the other countries, especially those bordering Germany, also slept. We shan't get anywhere by following an ostrich policy. England and the whole world have seen that only too well now, and that is why, one by one, England, no less than the rest, will have to make heavy sacrifices.

No country is going to sacrifice its men for nothing and certainly not in the interests of another. England is not going to do that either. The invasion, with liberation and freedom, will come sometime, but England and America will appoint the day, not all the occupied countries put together.

To our great horror and regret we hear that the attitude of a great many people towards us Jews has changed. We hear that there is anti-Semitism now in circles that never thought of it before. This news has affected us all very, very deeply. The cause of this hatred of the Jews is understandable, even human sometimes, but not good. The Christians blame the Jews for giving secrets away to the Germans, for betraying their helpers and for the fact that, through the Jews a great many Christians have gone the way of so many others before them, and suffered terrible punishments and a dreadful fate.

214

This is all true, but one must always look at these things from both sides. Would Christians behave differently in our place? The Germans have a means of making people talk. Can a person, entirely at their mercy, whether Jew or Christian, always remain silent? Everyone knows that is practically impossible. Why, then, should people demand the impossible of the Jews?

It's being murmured in underground circles that the German Jews who emigrated to Holland and who are now in Poland may not be allowed to return here; they once had the right of asylum in Holland, but when Hitler has gone they will have to go back to Germany again.

When one hears this one naturally wonders why we are carrying on with this long and difficult war. We always hear that we're all fighting together for freedom, truth, and right! Is discord going to show itself while we are still fighting, is the Jew once again worth less than another? Oh, it is sad, very sad, that once more, for the umpteenth time, the old truth is confirmed: "What *one* Christian does is his own responsibility, what *one* Jew does is thrown back at all Jews."

Quite honestly, I can't understand that the Dutch, who are such a good, honest, upright people, should judge us like this, we, the most oppressed, the unhappiest, perhaps the most pitiful of all peoples of the whole world.

I hope *one* thing only, and that is that this hatred of the Jews will be a passing thing, that the Dutch will show what they are after all, and that they will never totter and lose their sense of right. For anti-Semitism is unjust!

And if this terrible threat should actually come true, then the pitiful little collection of Jews that remain will have to leave Holland. We, too, shall have to move on again with our little bundles, and leave this beautiful country, which offered us such a warm welcome and which now turns it back on us.

I love Holland. I who, having no native country, had hoped that it might become my fatherland, and I still hope it will!

Yours, Anne

215

Dear Kitty,

There's something fresh every day. This morning our vegetable man was picked up for having two Jews in his house. It's a great blow to us, not only that those poor Jews are balancing on the edge of an abyss, but it's terrible for the man himself.

The world has turned topsy-turvy, respectable people are being sent off to concentration camps, prisons, and lonely cells, and the dregs that remain govern young and old, rich and poor. One person walks into the trap through the black market, a second through helping the Jews or other people who've had to go "underground"; anyone who isn't a member of the N.S.B. doesn't know what may happen to him from one day to another.

This man is a great loss to us too. The girls can't and aren't allowed to haul along our share of potatoes, so the only thing to do is to eat less. I will tell you how we shall do that; it's certainly not going to make things any pleasanter. Mummy says we shall cut out breakfast altogether, have porridge and bread for lunch, and for supper fried potatoes and possibly once or twice per week vegetables or lettuce, nothing more. We're going to be hungry, but anything is better than being discovered.

Yours, Anne

Dear Kitty,

At last, at last I can sit quietly at my table in front of a crack of window and write you everything.

I feel so miserable, I haven't felt like this for months; even after the burglary I didn't feel so utterly broken. On the one hand, the vegetable man, the Jewish question, which is being discussed minutely over the whole house, the invasion delay, the bad food, the strain, the miserable atmosphere, my disappointment in Peter; and on the other hand, Elli's engagement, Whitsun reception, flowers, Kraler's birthday, fancy cakes, and stories about cabarets, films, and concerts. That difference, that huge difference, it's always there; one day we laugh and see the funny side of the situation, but the next we are afraid, fear, suspense, and despair staring from our faces. Miep and Kraler carry the heaviest burden of the eight in hiding, Miep in all she does, and Kraler through the enormous responsibility, which is sometimes so much for him that he can hardly talk from pent-up nerves and strain. Koophuis and Elli look after us well too, but they can forget us at times, even if it's only for a few hours, or a day, or even two days. They have their own worries, Koophuis over his health, Elli over her engagement, which is not altogether rosy, but they also have their little outings, visits to friends, and the whole life of ordinary people. For them the suspense is sometimes lifted, even if it is only for a short time, but for us it never lifts for a moment. We've been here for two years now; how long have we still to put up with this almost unbearable, ever increasing pressure?

The sewer is blocked, so we mustn't run water, or rather only a trickle; when we go to the W.C. we have to take a lavatory brush with us, and we keep dirty water in a large Cologne pot. We can manage for today, but what do we do if the plumber can't do the job alone? The municipal scavenging service doesn't come until Tuesday.

Miep sent us a currant cake, made up in the shape of a doll, with the words "Happy Whitsun" on the note attached to it. It's almost as if she's ridiculing us; our present frame of mind and our uneasiness could hardly be called "happy." The affair of the vegetable man has made us more nervous, you hear "shh, shh" from all sides again, and we're being quieter over everything. The police forced the door there, so they could do it to us too! If one day we too should . . . no, I mustn't write it, but I can't put the question out of my mind today. On the contrary, all the fear I've already been through seems to face me again in all its frightfulness.

This evening at eight o'clock I had to go to the downstairs lavatory all alone; there was no one down there, as everyone was listening to the radio; I wanted to be brave, but it was difficult. I always feel much safer here upstairs than alone downstairs in that large, silent house; alone with the mysterious muffled noises from upstairs and the tooting of motor horns in the street. I have to hurry for I start to quiver if I begin thinking about the situation.

Again and again I ask myself, would it not have been better for us all if we had not gone into hiding, and if we were dead now and not going through all this misery, especially as we shouldn't be running our protectors into danger any more. But we all recoil from these thoughts too, for we still love life; we haven't yet forgotten the voice of nature, we still hope, hope about everything. I hope something will happen soon now, shooting if need be—nothing can crush us *more* than this restlessness. Let the end come, even if it is hard; then at least we shall know whether we are finally going to win through or go under.

Yours, Anne

Wednesday, 31 May, 1944

Dear Kitty,

It was so frightfully hot on Saturday, Sunday, Monday, and Tuesday that I simply couldn't hold a fountain pen in my hand. That's why it was impossible to write to you. The drains went shut again on Friday, were mended again on Saturday; Mr. Koophuis came to see us in the afternoon and told us masses about Corry and her being in the same hockey club as Jopie.

On Sunday Elli came to make sure no one had broken in and stayed for breakfast, on Whit Monday Mr. Van Santen acted as the hide-out watchman, and, finally, on Tuesday the windows could be opened again at last.

There's seldom been such a beautiful, warm, one can even say hot, Whitsun. The heat here in the "Secret Annexe" is terrible; I will briefly describe these warm days by giving you a sample of the sort of complaints that arise:

Saturday: "Lovely, what perfect weather," we all said in the morning. "If only it wasn't quite so warm," in the afternoon when the windows had to be closed.

Sunday: "It's positively unbearable, this heat. The butter's melting, there's not a cool spot anywhere in the house, the bread's getting so dry, the milk's going sour, windows can't be opened, and we, wretched outcasts, sit here suffocating while other people enjoy their Whitsun holiday."

Monday: "My feet hurt me, I haven't got any thin clothes. I can't wash the dishes in this heat," all this from Mrs. Van Daan. It was extremely unpleasant.

I still can't put up with heat and am glad that there's a stiff breeze today, and yet the sun still shines.

Yours, Anne

Monday, 5 June, 1944

Dear Kitty,

Fresh "Secret Annexe" troubles, a quarrel between Dussel and the Franks over something very trivial: the sharing out of the butter. Dussel's capitulation. Mrs. Van Daan and the latter very thick, flirtations, kisses and friendly little laughs. Dussel is beginning to get longings for women. The Fifth Army has taken Rome. The city has been spared devastation by both armies and air forces, and is undamaged. Very few vegetables and potatoes. Bad weather. Heavy bombardments against the French coast and Pas de Calais continue.

Yours, Anne

Tuesday, 6 June, 1944

Dear Kitty,

"This is D-day," came the announcement over the English news and quite rightly, "this is *the* day." [1] The invasion has begun!

[1] Original English.

The English gave the news at eight o'clock this morning: Calais, Boulogne, Le Havre, and Cherbourg, also the Pas de Calais (as usual), were heavily bombarded. Moreover, as a safety measure for all occupied territories, all people who live within a radius of thirty-five kilometers from the coast are warned to be prepared for bombardments. If possible, the English will drop pamphlets one hour beforehand.

According to German news, English parachute troops have landed on the French coast, English landing craft are in battle with the German Navy, says the B.B.C.

We discussed it over the "Annexe" breakfast at nine o'clock: Is this just a trial landing like Dieppe two years ago?

English broadcast in German, Dutch, French, and other languages at ten o'clock: "The invasion has begun!" that means the "real" invasion. English broadcast in German at eleven o'clock, speech by the Supreme Commander, General Dwight Eisenhower.

The English news at twelve o'clock in English: "This is D-day." General Eisenhower said to the French people: "Stiff fighting will come now, but after this the victory. The year 1944 is the year of complete victory; good luck." [1]

English news in English at one o'clock (translated): 11,000 planes stand ready, and are flying to and fro nonstop, landing troops and attacking behind the lines; 4000 landing boats, plus small craft, are landing troops and matériel between Cherbourg and Le Havre incessantly. English and American troops are already engaged in hard fighting. Speeches by Gerbrandy, by the Prime Minister of Belgium, King Haakon of Norway, De Gaulle of France, the King of England, and last, but not least, Churchill.

Great commotion in the "Secret Annexe"! Would the long-awaited liberation that has been talked of so much, but which still seems *too* wonderful, *too* much like a fairy tale, ever come true? Could we be granted victory this year, 1944? We don't know yet, but hope is revived within us; it gives us fresh courage, and makes us strong

[1] Original English.

220

again. Since we must put up bravely with all the fears, privations, and sufferings, the great thing now is to remain calm and steadfast. Now more than ever we must clench our teeth and not cry out. France, Russia, Italy, and Germany, too, can all cry out and give vent to their misery, but we haven't the right to do that yet!

Oh, Kitty, the best part of the invasion is that I have the feeling that friends are approaching. We have been oppressed by those terrible Germans for so long, they have had their knives so at our throats, that the thoughts of friends and delivery fills us with confidence!

Now it doesn't concern the Jews any more; it concerns Holland and all occupied Europe. Perhaps, Margot says, I may yet be able to go back to school in September or October.

Yours, Anne

P.S. I'll keep you up to date with all the latest news!

Friday, 9 June, 1944

Dear Kitty,

Super news of the invasion. The Allies have taken Bayeux, a small village on the French coast, and are now fighting for Caen. It's obvious that they intend to cut off the peninsula where Cherbourg lies. Every evening war correspondents give news from the battle front, telling us of the difficulties, courage, and enthusiasm of the army; they manage to get hold of the most incredible stories. Also some of the wounded who are already back in England again came to the microphone. The air force is up all the time in spite of the miserable weather. We heard over the B.B.C. that Churchill wanted to land with the troops on D-Day, however, Eisenhower and the other generals managed to get him out of the idea. Just think of it, what pluck he has for such an old man—he must be seventy at least.

The excitement here has worn off a bit; still, we're hoping that the war will be over at the end of this year.

It'll be about time too! Mrs. Van Daan's grizzling is absolutely unbearable; now she can't any longer drive us crazy over the invasion, she nags us the whole day long about the bad weather. It really would be nice to dump her in a bucket of cold water and put her up in the loft.

The whole of the "Secret Annexe" except Van Daan and Peter have read the trilogy *Hungarian Rhapsody*. This book deals with the life history of the composer, virtuoso, and child prodigy, Franz Liszt. It is a very interesting book, but in my opinion there is a bit too much about women in it. In his time Liszt was not only the greatest and most famous pianist, but also the greatest ladies' man —right up to the age of seventy. He lived with the Duchess Marie d'Agould, Princess Caroline Sayn-Wittgenstein, the dancer Lola Montez, the pianist Agnes Kingworth, the pianist Sophie Menter, Princess Olga Janina, Baroness Olga Meyendorff, the actress Lilla what's-her-name, etc., etc.; it is just endless. The parts of the book that deal with music and art are much more interesting. Among those mentioned are Schumann, Clara Wieck, Hector Berlioz, Johannes Brahms, Beethoven, Joachim, Richard Wagner, Hans von Bülow, Anton Rubinstein, Frédéric Chopin, Victor Hugo, Honoré de Balzac, Hiller, Hummel, Czerny, Rossini, Cherubini, Paganini, Mendelssohn, etc., etc.

Liszt was personally a fine man, very generous, and modest about himself though exceptionally vain. He helped everyone, his art was everything to him, he was mad about cognac and about women, could not bear to see tears, was a gentleman, would never refuse to do anyone a favor, didn't care about money, loved religious liberty and world freedom.

Yours, Anne

Tuesday, 13 June, 1944

Dear Kitty,
Another birthday has gone by, so now I'm fifteen. I received quite a lot of presents.

All five parts of Sprenger's *History of Art,* a set of underwear, a handkerchief, two bottles of yoghourt, a pot of jam, a spiced gingerbread cake, and a book on botany from Mummy and Daddy, a double bracelet from Margot, a book from the Van Daans, sweet peas from Dussel, sweets and exercise books from Miep and Elli and, the high spot of all, the book *Maria Theresa* and three slices of full-cream cheese from Kraler. A lovely bunch of peonies from Peter; the poor boy took a lot of trouble to try and find something, but didn't have any luck.

There's still excellent news of the invasion, in spite of the wretched weather, countless gales, heavy rains, and high seas.

Yesterday Churchill, Smuts, Eisenhower, and Arnold visited French villages which have been conquered and liberated. The torpedo boat that Churchill was in shelled the coast. He appears, like so many men, not to know what fear is—makes me envious!

It's difficult for us to judge from our secret redoubt how people outside have reacted to the news. Undoubtedly people are pleased that the idle (?) English have rolled up their sleeves and are doing something at last. Any Dutch people who still look down on the English, scoff at England and her government of old gentlemen, call the English cowards, and yet hate the Germans deserve a good shaking. Perhaps it would put some sense into their woolly brains.

I hadn't had a period for over two months, but it finally started again on Saturday. Still, in spite of all the unpleasantness and bother, I'm glad it hasn't failed me any longer.

Yours, Anne

Wednesday, 14 June, 1944

Dear Kitty,

My head is haunted by so many wishes and thoughts, accusations and reproaches. I'm really not as conceited as so many people seem to think, I know my own faults and shortcomings better than anyone, but the difference is that I also know that I want to improve, shall improve, and have already improved a great deal.

Why is it then, I so often ask myself, that everyone still thinks I'm so terribly knowing and forward? Am I so knowing? Is it that I really am, or that maybe the others aren't? That sounds queer, I realize now, but I shan't cross out the last sentence, because it really isn't so crazy. Everyone knows that Mrs. Van Daan, one of my chief accusers, is unintelligent. I might as well put it plainly and say "stupid." Stupid people usually can't take it if others do better than they do.

Mrs. Van Daan thinks I'm stupid because I'm not quite so lacking in intelligence as she is; she thinks I'm forward because she's even more so; she thinks my dresses are too short, because hers are even shorter. And that's also the reason that she thinks I'm knowing, because she's twice as bad about joining in over subjects she knows absolutely nothing about. But one of my favorite sayings is "There's no smoke without fire," and I readily admit that I'm knowing.

Now the trying part about me is that I criticize and scold myself far more than anyone else does. Then if Mummy adds her bit of advice the pile of sermons becomes so insurmountable that in my despair I become rude and start contradicting and then, of course, the old well-known Anne watchword comes back: "No one understands me!" This phrase sticks in my mind; I know it sounds silly, yet there is some truth in it. I often accuse myself to such an extent that I simply long for a word of comfort, for someone who could give me sound advice and also draw out some of my real self; but, alas, I keep on looking, but I haven't found anyone yet.

I know that you'll immediately think of Peter, won't you, Kit? It's like this: Peter loves me not as a lover but as a friend and grows more affectionate every day. But what is the mysterious something that holds us both back? I don't understand it myself. Sometimes I think that my terrible longing for him was exaggerated, yet that's really not it, because if I don't go up to see him for two days, then I long for him more desperately than ever before. Peter is good and he's a darling, but still there's no denying that there's a lot about him that disappoints me. Especially his dislike of religion and all his talk about food and various other things don't appeal to me. Yet I feel quite convinced that we shall never quarrel now that we've made that straightforward agreement together. Pete is a peace-loving person; he's tolerant and gives in very easily. He lets me say a lot of things to him that he would never accept from his mother, he tries most persistently to keep his things in order. And yet why should he keep his innermost self to himself and why am I never allowed there? By nature he is more closed-up than I am, I agree, but I know—and from my own experience—that at some time or other even the most uncommunicative people long just as much, if not more, to find someone in whom they can confide.

Both Peter and I have spent our most meditative years in the "Secret Annexe." We often discuss the future, the past, and the present, but, as I've already said, I still seem to miss the real thing and yet I know that it's there.

Yours, Anne

Thursday, 15 June, 1944

Dear Kitty,

I wonder if it's because I haven't been able to poke my nose outdoors for so long that I've grown so crazy about everything to do with nature? I can perfectly well remember that there was a time when a deep blue sky, the song of the birds, moonlight and flowers could never have kept me spellbound. That's changed since I've been here.

At Whitsun, for instance, when it was so warm, I stayed awake on purpose until half past eleven one evening in order to have a good look at the moon for once by myself. Alas, the sacrifice was all in vain, as the moon gave far too much light and I didn't dare risk opening a window. Another time, some months ago now, I happened to be upstairs one evening when the window was open. I didn't go downstairs until the window had to be shut. The dark, rainy evening, the gale, the scudding clouds held me entirely in their power; it was the first time in a year and a half that I'd seen the night face to face. After that evening my longing to see it again was greater than my fear of burglars, rats, and raids on the house. I went downstairs all by myself and looked outside through the windows in the kitchen and the private office. A lot of people are fond of nature, many sleep outdoors occasionally, and people in prisons and hospitals long for the day when they will be free to enjoy the beauties of nature, but few are so shut away and isolated from that which can be shared alike by rich and poor. It's not imagination on my part when I say that to look up at the sky, the clouds, the moon, and the stars makes me calm and patient. It's a better medicine than either Valerian or bromine; Mother Nature makes me humble and prepared to face every blow courageously.

Alas, it has had to be that I am only able—except on a few rare occasions—to look at nature through dirty net curtains hanging before very dusty windows. And it's no pleasure looking through these any longer, because nature is just the one thing that really must be unadulterated.

Yours, Anne

Friday, 16 June, 1944

Dear Kitty,

New problems: Mrs. Van Daan is desperate, talks about a bullet through her head, prison, hanging, and suicide. She's jealous that Peter confides in me and not her. She's offended that Dussel doesn't enter into her flirtations with him, as she'd hoped, afraid that her husband is smoking all the fur-coat money away, she quarrels, uses abusive language, cries, pities herself, laughs, and then starts a fresh quarrel again. What on earth can one do with such a foolish, blubbering specimen? No one takes her seriously, she hasn't any character, and she grumbles to everyone. The worst of it is that it makes Peter rude, Mr. Van Daan irritable, and Mummy cynical. Yes, it's a frightful situation! There's *one* golden rule to keep before you: laugh about everything and don't bother yourself about the others! It sounds selfish, but it's honestly the only cure for anyone who has to seek consolation in himself.

Kraler has received another call-up to go digging for four weeks. He's trying to get out of it with a doctor's certificate and a letter from the business. Koophuis wants to have an operation on his stomach. All private telephones were cut off at eleven o'clock yesterday.

Yours, Anne

Friday, 23 June, 1944

Dear Kitty,

Nothing special going on here. The English have begun their big attack on Cherbourg; according to Pim and Van Daan, we're sure to be free by October 10. The Russians are taking part in the campaign, and yesterday began their offensive near Vitebsk; it's exactly three years to a day since the Germans attacked. We've hardly got any potatoes; from now on we're going to count them out for each person, then everyone knows what he's getting.

Yours, Anne

Tuesday, 27 June, 1944

Dearest Kitty,

The mood has changed, everything's going wonderfully. Cherbourg, Vitebsk, and Sloben fell today. Lots of prisoners and booty. Now the English can land what they want now they've got a harbor, the whole Cotentin Peninsula three weeks after the English invasion! A tremendous achievement! In the three weeks since D-day not a day has gone by without rain and gales, both here and in France, but a bit of bad luck didn't prevent the English and Americans from showing their enormous strength, and how! Certainly the "wonder weapon" is in full swing, but of what consequence are a few squibs apart from a bit of damage in England and pages full of it in the Boche newspapers! For that matter, when they really realize in "Bocheland" that the Bolshevists really are on the way, they'll get even more jittery.

All German women not in military service are being evacuated to Groningen, Friesland, and Gelderland with their children. Mussert [1] has announced that if they get as far as here with the invasion he'll put on a uniform. Does the old fatty want to do some fighting? He could have done so in Russia before now. Some time ago Finland turned down a peace offer, now the negotiations have just been broken off again, they'll be sorry for it later, the silly fools!

How far do you think we'll be on July 27?

Yours, Anne

Friday, 30 June, 1944

Dear Kitty,

Bad weather, or *bad weather at a stretch to the thirtieth of June*.[2] Isn't that well said! Oh yes, I have a smattering of English already; just to show that I can, I'm reading *An Ideal Husband* with the aid of a dictionary. War going wonderfully! Bobroisk, Mogilef, and Orsa have fallen, lots of prisoners.

Everything's all right here and tempers are improving. The superoptimists are triumphing. Elli has changed her hair style, Miep has the week off. That's the latest news.

Yours, Anne

---

[1] Mussert was the Dutch National Socialist leader.
[2] In English in the original.

Dear Kitty,

It strikes fear to my heart when Peter talks of later being a criminal, or of gambling; although it's meant as a joke, of course, it gives me the feeling that he's afraid of his own weakness. Again and again I hear from both Margot and Peter: "Yes, if I was as strong and plucky as you are, if I always stuck to what I wanted, if I had such persistent energy, yes then . . . !"

I wonder if it's really a good quality not to let myself be influenced. Is it really good to follow almost entirely my own conscience?

Quite honestly, I can't imagine how anyone can say: "I'm weak," and then remain so. After all, if you know it, why not fight against it, why not try to train your character? The answer was: "Because it's so much easier not to!" This reply rather discouraged me. Easy? Does that mean that a lazy, deceitful life is an easy life? Oh, no, that can't be true, it mustn't be true, people can so easily be tempted by slackness . . . and by money.

I thought for a long time about the best answer to give Peter, how to get him to believe in himself and, above all to try and improve himself; I don't know whether my line of thought is right though, or not.

I've so often thought how lovely it would be to have someone's complete confidence, but now, now that I'm that far, I realize how difficult it is to think what the other person is thinking and then to find the *right* answer. More especially because the very ideas of "easy" and "money" are something entirely foreign and new to me. Peter's beginning to lean on me a bit and that mustn't happen under any circumstances. A type like Peter finds it difficult to stand on his own feet, but it's even harder to stand on your own feet as a conscious, living being. Because if you do, then it's twice as difficult to steer a right path through the sea of problems and still remain constant through it all. I'm just drifting around, have been searching for days, searching for a good argument against that terrible word "easy," something to settle it once and for all.

How can I make it clear to him that what appears easy and attractive will drag him down into the depths, depths where there is no comfort to be found, no friends and no beauty, depths from which it is almost impossible to raise oneself?

We all live, but we don't know the why or the wherefore. We all live with the object of being happy; our lives are all different and yet the same. We three have been brought up in good circles, we have the chance to learn, the possibility of attaining something, we have all reason to hope for much happiness, but . . . we must earn it for ourselves. And that is never easy. You must work and do good, not be lazy and gamble, if you wish to earn happiness. Laziness may *appear* attractive, but work *gives* satisfaction.

I can't understand people who don't like work, yet that isn't the case with Peter; he just hasn't got a fixed goal to aim at, and he thinks he's too stupid and too inferior to achieve anything. Poor boy, he's never known what it feels like to make other people happy, and I can't teach him that either. He has no religion, scoffs at Jesus Christ, and swears, using the name of God; although I'm not orthodox either, it hurts me every time I see how deserted, how scornful, and how poor he really is.

People who have a religion should be glad, for not everyone has the gift of believing in heavenly things. You don't necessarily even have to be afraid of punishment after death; purgatory, hell, and heaven are things that a lot of people can't accept, but still a religion, it doesn't matter which, keeps a person on the right path. It isn't the fear of God but the upholding of one's honor and conscience. How noble and good everyone could be if, every evening before falling asleep, they were to recall to their minds the events of the whole day and consider exactly what has been good and bad. Then, without realizing it, you try to improve yourself at the start of each new day; of course, you achieve quite a lot in the course of time. Anyone can do this, it costs nothing and is certainly very helpful. Whoever doesn't know it must learn and find by experience that: "A quiet conscience makes one strong!"

Yours, Anne

Saturday, 8 July, 1944

Dear Kitty,

The chief representative of the business, Mr. B., has been in Beverwijk and managed, just like that, to get strawberries at the auction sale.[1] They arrived here dusty, covered with sand, but in large quantities. No less then twenty-four trays for the office people and us. That very same evening we bottled six jars and made eight pots of jam. The next morning Miep wanted to make jam for the office people.

At half past twelve, no strangers in the house, front door bolted, trays fetched, Peter, Daddy, Van Daan clattering on the stairs: Anne, get hot water; Margot, bring a bucket; all hands on deck! I went into the kitchen, which was chock-full, with a queer feeling in my tummy, Miep, Elli, Koophuis, Henk, Daddy, Peter: the families in hiding and their supply column, all mingling together, and in the middle of the day too!

People can't see in from outside because of the net curtains, but, even so, the loud voices and banging doors positively gave me the jitters. Are we really supposed to be in hiding? That's what flashed through my mind, and it gives me a very queer feeling to be able to appear in the world again. The pan was full, and I dashed upstairs again. The rest of the family was seated round our table in the kitchen busy stalk-picking—at least that's what they were supposed to be doing; more went into mouths than into buckets. Another bucket would soon be required. Peter went to the downstairs kitchen again—the

[1] It is compulsory in Holland for all growers to sell their produce at public auction.

bell rang twice; the bucket stayed where it was, Peter tore upstairs, locked the cupboard door. We were kicking our heels impatiently, couldn't turn on a tap, even though the strawberries were only half washed; the rule: "If anyone in the house, use no water, because of the noise," was strictly maintained.

At one o'clock Henk came and told us that it was the postman. Peter hurried downstairs again. Ting-a-ling . . . the bell, right about turn. I go and listen to see if I can hear anyone coming, first at our cupboard door and then creep to the top of the stairs. Finally Peter and I both lean over the banisters like a couple of thieves, listening to the din downstairs. No strange voices, Peter sneaks down, stops halfway, and calls out: "Elli!" No answer, one more: "Elli!" Peter's voice is drowned by the din in the kitchen. He goes right down and into the kitchen. I stand looking down tensely. "Get upstairs at once, Peter, the accountant is here, clear out!" It was Koophuis speaking. Peter comes upstairs sighing, the cupboard door closes. Finally Kraler arrives at half past one. "Oh, dearie me, I see nothing but strawberries, strawberries at breakfast, strawberries stewed by Miep, I smell strawberries, must have a rest from them and go upstairs—what is being washed up here . . . strawberries."

The remainder are being bottled. In the evening: two jars unsealed. Daddy quickly makes them into jam. The next morning: two more unsealed and four in the afternoon. Van Daan hadn't brought them to the right temperature for sterilizing. Now Daddy makes jam every evening.

We eat strawberries with our porridge, skimmed milk with strawberries, bread and butter with strawberries, strawberries for dessert, strawberries with sugar, strawberries with sand. For two whole days strawberries and nothing but strawberries, then the supply was finished or in bottles and under lock and key.

"I say, Anne," Margot calls out, "the greengrocer on the corner has let us have some green peas, nineteen pounds." "That's nice of him," I replied. And it certainly is, but oh, the work . . . ugh!

"You've all got to help shelling peas on Saturday morning," Mummy announced when we were at table. And, sure enough, the big enamel pan duly appeared this morning, filled to the brim. Shelling peas is a boring job, but you ought to try "skinning" the pods. I don't think many people realize how soft and tasty the pod is when the skin on the inside has been removed. However, an even greater advantage is that the quantity which can be eaten is about triple the amount of when one only eats the peas. It's an exceptionally precise, finicky job, pulling out this skin; perhaps it's all right for pedantic dentists or precise office workers, but for an impatient teen-ager like me, it's frightful. We began at half past nine, I got up at half past ten, at half past eleven I sat down again. This refrain hummed in my ears: bend the top, pull the skin, remove the string, throw out the pod, etc., etc., they dance before my eyes, green, green, green maggots, strings, rotten pods, green, green, green. Just for the sake of doing something, I chatter the whole morning, any nonsense that comes into my head, make everyone laugh, and bore them stiff. But every string that I pull makes me feel more certain that I never, never want to be just a housewife only!

We finally have breakfast at twelve o'clock, but from half past twelve until quarter past one we've got to go skinning pods again. I'm just about seasick when I stop, the others a bit too. I go and sleep till four o'clock, but I'm still upset by those wretched peas.

Yours, Anne

Saturday, 15 July, 1944

Dear Kitty,

We have had a book from the library with the challenging title of: *What Do You Think of the Modern Young Girl?* I want to talk about this subject today.

The author of this book criticizes "the youth of today" from top to toe, without, however, condemning the whole of the young brigade as "incapable of anything good." On the contrary, she is rather of the opinion that if young people wished, they have it in their hands to make a bigger, more beautiful and better world, but that they occupy themselves with superficial things, without giving a thought to real beauty.

In some passages, the writer gave me very much the feeling she was directing her criticism at me, and that's why I want to lay myself completely bare to you for once and defend myself against this attack.

I have one outstanding trait in my character, which must strike anyone who knows me for any length of time, and that is my knowledge of myself. I can watch myself and my actions, just like an outsider. The Anne of every day I can face entirely without prejudice, without making excuses for her and watch what's good and what's bad about her. This "self-consciousness" haunts me, and every time I open my mouth I know as soon as I've spoken whether "that ought to have been different" or "that was right as it was." There are so many things about myself that I condemn; I couldn't begin to name them all. I understand more and more how true Daddy's words were when he said: "All children must look after their own upbringing." Parents can only give good advice or put them on the right paths, but the final forming of a person's character lies in their own hands.

In addition to this, I have lots of courage, I always feel so strong and as if I can bear a great deal, I feel so free and so young! I was glad when I first realized it, because I don't think I shall easily bow down before the blows that inevitably come to everyone.

But I've talked about these things so often before. Now I want to come to the chapter of "Daddy and Mummy don't understand me." Daddy and Mummy have always thoroughly spoiled me, were sweet to me, defended me, and have done all that parents could do. And yet I've felt so terribly lonely for a long time, so left out, neglected, and misunderstood. Daddy tried all he could to check my rebellious spirit, but it was no use, I have cured myself, by seeing for myself what was wrong in my behavior and keeping it before my eyes.

How is it that Daddy was never any support to me in

my struggle, why did he completely miss the mark when he wanted to offer me a helping hand? Daddy tried the wrong methods, he always talked to me as a child who was going through difficult phases. It sounds crazy, because Daddy's the only one who has always taken me into his confidence, and no one but Daddy has given me the feeling that I'm sensible. But there's one thing he's omitted: you see, he hasn't realized that for me the fight to get on top was more important than all else. I didn't want to hear about "symptoms of your age," or "other girls," or "it wears off by itself"; I didn't want to be treated as a girl-like-all-others, but as Anne-on-her-own-merits. Pim didn't understand that. For that matter, I can't confide in anyone, unless they tell me a lot about themselves, and as I know very little about Pim, I don't feel that I can tread upon more intimate ground with him. Pim always takes up the older, fatherly attitude, tells me that he too has had similar passing tendencies. But still he's not able to feel with me like a friend, however hard he tries. These things have made me never mention my views on life nor my well-considered theories to anyone but my diary and, occasionally, to Margot. I concealed from Daddy everything that perturbed me; I never shared my ideals with him. I was aware of the fact that I was pushing him away from me.

I couldn't do anything else. I have acted entirely according to my feelings, but I have acted in the way that was best for my peace of mind. Because I should completely lose my repose and self-confidence, which I have built up so shakily, if, at this stage, I were to accept criticisms of my half-completed task. And I can't do that even from Pim, although it sounds very hard, for not only have I not shared my secret thoughts with Pim but I have often pushed him even further from me, by my irritability.

This is a point that I think a lot about: why is it that Pim annoys me? So much so that I can hardly bear him teaching me, that his affectionate ways strike me as being put on, that I want to be left in peace and would really prefer it if he dropped me a bit, until I felt more certain in my attitude towards him. Because I still have a gnawing feeling of guilt over that horrible letter that I dared to write him when I was so wound up. Oh, how hard it is to be really strong and brave in every way!

Yet this was not my greatest disappointment; no, I ponder far more over Peter than Daddy. I know very well that I conquered him instead of he conquering me. I created an image of him in my mind, pictured him as a quiet, sensitive, lovable boy, who needed affection and friendship. I needed a living person to whom I could pour out my heart; I wanted a friend who'd help to put me on the right road. I achieved what I wanted, and slowly but surely, I drew him towards me. Finally, when I had made him feel friendly, it automatically developed into an intimacy which, on second thought, I don't think I ought to have allowed.

We talked about the most private things, and yet up till now we have never touched on those things that filled, and still fill, my heart and soul. I still don't know quite what to make of Peter, is he superficial, or does he still feel shy, even of me? But dropping that, I committed one error in my desire to make a real friendship: I switched over and tried to get at him by developing it into a more intimate relation, whereas I should have explored all other possibilities. He longs to be loved and I can see that he's beginning to be more and more in love with me. He gets satisfaction out of our meetings, whereas they just have the effect of making me want to try it out with him again. And yet I don't seem able to touch on the subjects that I'm so longing to bring out into the daylight. I drew Peter towards me, far more than he realizes. Now he clings to me, and for the time being, I don't see any way of shaking him off and putting him on his own feet. When I realized that he could not be a friend for my understanding, I thought I would at least try to lift him up out of his narrow-mindedness and make him do something with his youth.

"For in its innermost depths youth is lonelier than old age." I read this saying in some book and I've always remembered it, and found it to be true. Is it true then that grownups have a more difficult time here than we do? No. I know it isn't. Older people have formed their opinions about everything, and don't waver before they act. It's twice as hard for us young ones to hold our ground, and maintain our opinions, in a time when all ideals are being shattered and destroyed, when people are showing their worst side, and do not know whether to believe in truth and right and God.

Anyone who claims that the older ones have a more difficult time here certainly doesn't realize to what extent our problems weigh down on us, problems for which we are probably much too young, but which thrust themselves upon us continually, until, after a long time, we think we've found a solution, but the solution doesn't seem able to resist the facts which reduce it to nothing again. That's the difficulty in these times: ideals, dreams, and cherished hopes rise within us, only to meet the horrible truth and be shattered.

It's really a wonder that I haven't dropped all my ideals, because they seem so absurd and impossible to carry out. Yet I keep them, because in spite of everything I still believe that people are really good at heart. I simply can't build up my hopes on a foundation consisting of confusion, misery, and death. I see the world gradually being turned into a wilderness, I hear the ever approaching thunder, which will destroy us too, I can feel the sufferings of millions and yet, if I look up into the heavens, I think that it will all come right, that this cruelty too will end, and that peace and tranquillity will return again.

In the meantime, I must uphold my ideals, for perhaps the time will come when I shall be able to carry them out.

Yours, Anne

Dear Kitty,

Now I am getting really hopeful, now things are going well at last. Yes, really, they're going well! Super news! An attempt has been made on Hitler's life and not even by Jewish communists or English capitalists this time, but by a proud German general, and what's more, he's a count, and still quite young. The Führer's life was saved by Divine Providence and, unfortunately, he managed to get off with just a few scratches and burns. A few officers and generals who were with him have been killed and wounded. The chief culprit was shot.

Anyway, it certainly shows that there are lots of officers and generals who are sick of the war and would like to see Hitler descend into a bottomless pit. When they've disposed of Hitler, their aim is to establish a military dictator, who will make peace with the Allies, then they intend to rearm and start another war in about twenty years' time. Perhaps the Divine Power tarried on purpose in getting him out of the way, because it would be much easier and more advantageous to the Allies if the impeccable Germans kill each other off; it'll make less work for the Russians and the English and they'll be able to begin rebuilding their own towns all the sooner.

But still, we're not that far yet, and I don't want to anticipate the glorious events too soon. Still, you must have noticed, this is all sober reality and that I'm in quite a matter-of-fact mood today; for once, I'm not jabbering about high ideals. And what's more, Hitler has even been so kind as to announce to his faithful, devoted people that from now on everyone in the armed forces must obey the Gestapo, and that any soldier who knows that one of his superiors was involved in this low, cowardly attempt upon his life may shoot the same on the spot, without court-martial.

What a perfect shambles it's going to be. Little Johnnie's

feet begin hurting him during a long march, he's snapped at by his boss, the officer, Johnnie grabs his rifle and cries out: "You wanted to murder the Führer, so there's your reward." One bang and the proud chief who dared to tick off little Johnnie has passed into eternal life (or is it eternal death?). In the end, whenever an officer finds himself up against a soldier, or having to take the lead, he'll be wetting his pants from anxiety, because the soldiers will dare to say more than they do. Do you gather a bit what I mean, or have I been skipping too much from one subject to another? I can't help it; the prospect that I may be sitting on school benches next October makes me feel far too cheerful to be logical! Oh, dearie me, hadn't I just told you that I didn't want to be too hopeful? Forgive me, they haven't given me the name "little bundle of contradictions" all for nothing!

Yours, Anne

Tuesday, 1 August, 1944

Dear Kitty,

"Little bundle of contradictions." That's how I ended my last letter and that's how I'm going to begin this one. "A little bundle of contradictions," can you tell me exactly what it is? What does contradiction mean? Like so many words, it can mean two things, contradiction from without and contradiction from within.

The first is the ordinary "not giving in easily, always knowing best, getting in the last word," *enfin*, all the unpleasant qualities for which I'm renowned. The second nobody knows about, that's my own secret.

I've already told you before that I have, as it were, a dual personality. One half embodies my exuberant cheerfulness, making fun of everything, my high-spiritedness, and above all, the way I take everything lightly. This includes not taking offense at a flirtation, a kiss, an embrace, a dirty joke. This side is usually lying in wait and pushes away the other which is much better, deeper and purer.

You must realize that no one knows Anne's better side and that's why most people find me so insufferable.

Certainly I'm a giddy clown for one afternoon, but then everyone's had enough of me for another month. Really, it's just the same as a love film is for deep-thinking people, simply a diversion, amusing just for once, something which is soon forgotten, not bad, but certainly not good. I loathe having to tell you this, but why shouldn't I, if I know it's true anyway? My lighter superficial side will always be too quick for the deeper side of me and that's why it will always win. You can't imagine how often I've already tried to push this Anne away, to cripple her, to hide her, because after all, she's only half of what's called Anne: but it doesn't work and I know, too, why it doesn't work.

I'm awfully scared that everyone who knows me as I always am will discover that I have another side, a finer and better side. I'm afraid they'll laugh at me, think I'm ridiculous and sentimental, not take me seriously. I'm used to not being taken seriously but it's only the "light-hearted" Anne that's used to it and can bear it; the "deeper" Anne is too frail for it. Sometimes, if I really compel the good Anne to take the stage for a quarter of an hour, she simply shrivels up as soon as she has to speak, and lets Anne number one take over, and before I realize it, she has disappeared.

Therefore, the nice Anne is never present in company, has not appeared one single time so far, but almost always predominates when we're alone. I know exactly how I'd like to be, how I am too . . . inside. But, alas, I'm only like that for myself. And perhaps that's why, no, I'm sure it's the reason why I say I've got a happy nature within and why other people think I've got a happy nature without. I am guided by the pure Anne within, but outside I'm nothing but a frolicsome little goat who's broken loose.

As I've already said, I never utter my real feelings about anything and that's how I've acquired the name of chaser-after-boys, flirt, know-all, reader of love stories. The cheerful Anne laughs about it, gives cheeky answers, shrugs her shoulders indifferently, behaves as if she doesn't care, but, oh dearie me, the quiet Anne's reactions are just the opposite. If I'm to be quite honest, then I must admit that it does hurt me, that I try terribly hard to change myself, but that I'm always fighting against a more powerful enemy.

A voice sobs within me: "There you are, that's what's become of you: you're uncharitable, you look supercilious and peevish, people dislike you and all because you won't listen to the advice given you by your own better half." Oh, I would like to listen, but it doesn't work; if I'm quiet and serious, everyone thinks it's a new comedy and then I have to get out of it by turning it into a joke, not to mention my own family, who are sure to think I'm ill, make me swallow pills for headaches and nerves, feel my neck and my head to see whether I'm running a temperature, ask if I'm constipated and criticize me for being in a bad mood. I can't keep that up: if I'm watched to that extent, I start by getting snappy, then unhappy, and finally I twist my heart round again, so that the bad is on the outside and the good is on the inside and keep on trying to find a way of becoming what I would so like to be, and what I could be, if . . . there weren't any other people living in the world.

Yours, Anne

EPILOGUE

Anne's diary ends here. On August 4, 1944, the Grüne Polizei made a raid on the "Secret Annexe." All the occupants, together with Kraler and Koophuis, were arrested and sent to German and Dutch concentration camps.

The "Secret Annexe" was plundered by the Gestapo. Among a pile of old books, magazines, and newspapers which were left lying on the floor, Miep and Elli found Anne's diary. Apart from a very few passages, which are of little interest to the reader, the original text has been printed.

Of all the occupants of the "Secret Annexe," Anne's father alone returned. Kraler and Koophuis, who withstood the hardships of the Dutch camp, were able to go home to their families.

In March 1945, two months before the liberation of Holland, Anne died in the concentration camp at Bergen-Belsen.

AFTERWORD

Anne Frank's diary is a work utterly complete in itself, and its eloquence requires no further comment. But the experiences Anne described become perhaps even more meaningful when seen in their immediate historical context. It is the purpose of this brief afterword to provide at least the outlines of that context and to bring Anne's own story to its conclusion.

I

The German Empire, which since the beginning of the twentieth century had been the strongest power in Europe, collapsed in 1918 as a result of its defeat in World War I. The Emperor, or Kaiser, fled to Holland and a group of democratic politicians in Berlin proclaimed the establishment of a German republic.

The leaders of the new republic sued for peace, and in April, 1919, sent a delegation to the Versailles Peace Conference. Contrary to their expectations, the German representatives were not permitted to help frame the Treaty of Versailles, by which peace was restored to Europe. Instead, the victorious Allies—among them Great Britain, France, Italy, and the United States—submitted the finished treaty to the German delegates who were told that if they did not sign, Germany would be invaded. The treaty placed upon Germany sole responsibility for the war. It stripped Germany of its overseas colonies and of valuable territories in Europe. It virtually disarmed the once great military power, and it demanded that Germany pay the cost of all civilian damage caused by the war. The leaders of the German republic had no choice but to accept these terms.

Within Germany, the Treaty of Versailles was the subject of widespread indignation. Many Germans thought that their nation was no more responsible for causing the war than any other and that Germany had been unfairly singled out for blame. Nationalists spread the false belief that republican politicians had administered a "stab in the back" to the undefeated German army in November, 1918, and branded these politicians the "November criminals." To many Germans this theory proved a comforting rationalization for their country's defeat.

The new German government, which became known as the Weimar republic because its constitution was drawn up at Weimar, faced a number of serious problems. One of these problems was its identification with the unpopular Treaty of Versailles. Another was the fact that no political party was able to achieve a majority in the Reichstag, or parliament, so that the government was always a combination of several parties.

Opposition to the republic came from many quarters. Middle class Germans who had lost everything in the inflation of the early 1920's blamed the republican government for their distress. Unemployed workers, impatient with the conservative republic, looked for solutions to their problems in radical movements of both the left and right. Industrialists, landowners, and army officers longed to replace the republic with a regime more in keeping with the autocratic and militaristic traditions of the old empire.

Although there were also many in Germany who hoped that the experiment in democratic government would succeed, the years immediately following the war saw the establishment of a number of political parties dedicated to the destruction of the republic and the reversal of the Treaty of Versailles. One of these was the National Socialist German Workers—or Nazi—Party. Like other extremist groups, the Nazis appealed to all sorts of discontented people—to demobilized soldiers and youthful idealists, to unemployed workingmen hostile to "the interests", and to businessmen and property owners fearful of a Communist revolution, to cranks and criminals and outcasts of every kind. The Nazi program combined the strong appeals of nationalism and socialism. It promised to restore Germany's power through the establishment of a totalitarian state; it also promised to redistribute the national wealth and to provide jobs for everyone.

The man who became leader, or Führer, of the Nazi party in 1921 was an Austrian-born former house painter named Adolf Hitler. Shrewd, fanatical, never hesitating to use lies or brute force to achieve his ends, Hitler had the ability to rouse an audience to hysterical enthusiasm. Hitler and the Nazis blamed the decline in Germany's power on Jews and radicals and preached the supremacy of the so-called German or Aryan race. The Germans, Hitler declared, were the "master race," creators of all civilization, and fitted by nature to rule the world. To provide ample living space for this race, Hitler planned to expand Germany's frontiers in the east, carving out a great empire in Poland and Russia at the expense of the Slavic inhabitants of those lands. The Slavs, he said, were a subhuman people fit only to be slaves. In Hitler's New Order, they would either serve the "master race" or be exterminated.

During the 1920s the Nazis were prominent only in the southern German state of Bavaria. In the increasingly prosperous years between 1924 and 1929 most Germans regarded them as ruffians and clowns of no great importance. But with the onset of the world-wide depression in 1929, ever greater numbers of Germans began to listen to Hitler. His simplifications of complex issues satisfied them. His promise of a glorious national future appealed to their pride. His willingness to assume total responsibility if given total power relieved them of the unaccustomed burdens of citizenship in a democracy. In the elections of 1930 and 1932, the Nazis became the largest party in the Reichstag.

Hitler's most violent racial attacks were directed against the Jews. Despite the many distinguished contributions Jews had made to German life over the centuries, Hitler's propaganda described them as an alien, inferior race. Not only were they non-Aryan, he said, but they were the originators of all those doctrines hostile to Nazi aims— Communism, pacifism, internationalism, Christianity. In

Hitler's view, as long as Jews remained in Germany, they were a constant source of ideological infection and a threat to German racial purity.

The racial theories Hitler adopted, like his nationalism, had deep roots in the German past and appealed strongly to many Germans. After 1930, the thousand-year-old Jewish community in Germany, numbering half a million people, watched the rapid rise of the Nazis with mixed disbelief and foreboding.

On January 30, 1933, the aged president of the republic, Field Marshal Paul von Hindenburg, appointed Hitler Chancellor of Germany. Hitler proceeded to bring the republic to an end and to establish in Germany a totalitarian regime. Shortly after becoming Chancellor, Hitler demanded that the Reichstag grant him emergency powers for four years. On March 23 the Reichstag gave in to his demands, and then dissolved itself. Thereafter Hitler ruled by decree. All political parties but the Nazis were outlawed. Churches, labor unions, youth organizations became organs of the state. Every medium of communication—radio, newspapers, motion pictures, books—was used to manipulate public opinion. The majority of Germans supported Hitler or acquiesced in his government, though many were disturbed by his methods. Those who did not support him were suppressed by Storm Troopers or by the dreaded secret police, the Gestapo. Midnight arrests, beatings and torture at the hands of the Gestapo, imprisonment without trial in concentration camps soon silenced most of Hitler's opponents, or drove them underground.

Hitler did not long delay putting into effect his anti-Jewish program. Jews were promptly dismissed from public office and the civil service. They were not allowed to teach in schools or universities or to work in journalism, radio, the movies, or the theater. Later they were barred from practicing law or medicine or engaging in business. Even private employment was increasingly denied them, so that many lost all means of livelihood. Both by law and by unofficial police terror, Jews were segregated from their Aryan neighbors. Jewish children could not attend school with Aryans. Jews were forbidden to marry or employ Aryans. Many stores and shops refused to serve Jews or hotels to accommodate them. Emigration, which had been relatively easy for Jews at first, was made increasingly difficult. Many of those who managed to escape from Germany in later years were compelled to leave all their possessions behind.

In September, 1939, Hitler launched in the east the war for which he had been preparing since soon after becoming Chancellor. Convinced at last that appeasement of the German dictator would lead only to further aggression, England and France declared war and prepared for the inevitable attack in the west. In eighteen days the German army, spearheaded by tanks and dive bombers, conquered Poland. In April, 1940, the Germans seized Denmark and invaded Norway. On May 10 Hitler struck in the west. Within a few days his armies had crushed neutral Holland and Belgium and were pouring into France. Unable to withstand the highly mobilized German assault, France surrendered on June 22. The British miraculously rescued their badly mauled expeditionary force from the beaches at Dunkirk and made preparations for the expected German invasion of England. Hitler was now master of most of Europe, and in June, 1941, after unsuccessfully attempting to bomb Britain into submission, Germany attacked the Soviet Union despite the non-aggression pact that Hitler had signed with Stalin in 1939.

Nazi-dominated Europe was a virtual slave empire. On farms and in factories, hungry populations toiled for their Nazi overlords. Thousands of men and women were taken to Germany as slave laborers. The Germans dealt ruthlessly with resistance. The shooting of a German soldier or policeman was avenged by the slaughter of hostages. Captured partisans were tortured and killed in Gestapo prisons. Listening to British broadcasts or possession of anti-German literature were made crimes punishable by imprisonment and death.

Everywhere in conquered Europe the German occupation forces vigorously implemented Hitler's racial policies.

For the "Jewish question", as he called it, Hitler adopted the "final solution"—extermination. Special SS (Elite Guard) units following in the wake of the German army in Russia killed hundreds of thousands of Jews. To deal with the Jews of occupied Europe, the Germans created an efficient apparatus that rounded up Jews and transported them to special extermination camps, many of them in Poland. There the prisoners were worked to exhaustion before being shot or gassed. To Treblinka, Belsec, Sibibor, Chelmo, but especially to Auschwitz, the long, slow trains began to move in 1941, carrying their wretched human freight to destruction. Before the Nazi nightmare had passed, an estimated six million Jews—men, women, and children—had been systematically murdered. Millions of non-Jews in Poland, Czechoslovakia, Russia, and elsewhere, most of them Slavs, were also victims of the Nazis.

II

Anne Frank was born on June 12, 1929 in the historic German city of Frankfurt. Frankfurt owed much of its commercial and cultural preeminence to its Jewish community, of which the Franks were members; the founders of the great Jewish banking family, the Rothschilds, had been natives of Frankfurt. Anne's father, Otto Frank, a respected businessman, could trace his family in the city's archives back to the seventeenth century. For Anne and her older sister Margot, the world of early childhood was a secure place inhabited by loving parents, relatives, and nurses.

Beyond the nursery, beyond the comfortable five-room flat on Ganghoferstrasse, the world was not so pleasant. Otto Frank did not wait for the full force of Nazi persecution to make itself felt. In the summer of 1933 the Franks left Frankfurt. Mrs. Frank with the two girls joined her mother in Aachen, near the Belgian border. Otto Frank went directly to Holland, where he established himself in a food products business. For centuries Holland had provided a refuge for the persecuted. In the 1930s it received many German Jews as it had welcomed French Huguenots in the sixteenth century and English Puritans in the seventeenth. By the spring of 1934, the Franks were reunited and settled in Amsterdam.

During the next few years, while crisis followed crisis and the threat of a second world war increased, Anne Frank lived happily in Amsterdam like any Dutch girl. She attended the Montessori School, had a host of friends, and discovered with delight that boys liked her.

But all of this began to change once the Germans invaded Holland in 1940. Shortly after the invasion Queen Wilhelmina and her cabinet escaped to England, where they formed a government in exile to cooperate with the Allies. Occupied Holland was ruled by a German high commissioner, Arthur Seyss-Inquart, who would one day be hanged as a major war criminal. The Germans terrorized and exploited Holland as they did other conquered countries. They banned listening to Allied broadcasts, muzzled the press, and suppressed political parties and trade unions. They closed the universities and imprisoned the country's political, military, and intellectual leaders. Thousands of persons were sent to Germany as slave laborers. As the resistance movement grew stronger, the Germans exacted savage reprisals. In Holland as elsewhere, they imposed harsh anti-Jewish measures. Despite strikes and protests by the brave Dutch, the roundup and deportation of Jews to extermination camps began.

For Anne Frank, life under the German occupation was at first not greatly different from what it had been before. She was compelled to leave the Montessori School and to attend the Jewish Lyceum. But she still had her family and friends, and she was absorbed in the experiences of everyday life. The growing number of anti-Jewish decrees did not weigh heavily upon her.

Her father, however, perceived the direction of events clearly enough. In February, 1941, the Nazis launched their first roundup of Jews in Amsterdam. Those arrested were taken to reception camps at Westerbork and Vught and from there shipped eastward into Germany. As the roundups continued, Otto Frank made plans for his family's safety. He had been forced by a German decree to leave his business, but his Dutch associates and employees remained loyal friends. Secretly, a group of rooms at the top and back of a building on the Prinsengracht Canal, that served as a warehouse and office for the business, was prepared as a hiding place. On July 5, 1942, the Germans summoned 16-year-old Margot to report for deportation. The following morning the Franks slipped away from their home and went into hiding in the "secret annexe." They were soon joined there by a business associate of Otto Frank, Mr. Van Daan, and by the latter's wife and 15-year-old son Peter. Later, they invited an elderly dentist, Albert Dussel, to share their refuge.

The eight Jews in the "secret annexe" remained quiet during the day while business was conducted as usual in the lower part of the building. They stirred only at night when the building was deserted. Their friends in the office below—Mr. Koophuis and Mr. Kraler, Miep van Santen and Elli Vossen—kept their secret, brought food and even gifts, provided what news they could of events in the city. That news, in the fall of 1942, was terrifying. The roundup and deportation of Jews from Holland was proceeding according to plan.

When the Franks went into hiding, Germany was at the height of its conquests. Hitler's empire extended from the English Channel deep into Russia, from the Arctic Circle to North Africa. Gradually, the tide began to turn. In the fall of 1942, the German advance into Russia was checked at Stalingrad. At the same time, in North Africa, the British drove the Germans back from Egypt and, with their French and American allies—the United States having entered the war in December, 1941—landed in Morocco and Algeria behind the German forces. While the Russians counterattacked along the eastern front in 1943, the western Allies cleared Africa of Hitler's *Afrika Korps*, conquered Sicily, and invaded Italy, toppling Hitler's Fascist partner, Benito Mussolini. Daily, Allied air raids over Europe grew in intensity. In June, 1944, came the long awaited Allied invasion of France. For two long years the little group in the "secret annexe" followed these events over their illegal radio. Joyfully, they looked forward to the day when the Germans would be driven from Holland and they could emerge from hiding.

But on August 4, 1944, following information provided by a Dutch informer, the Gestapo penetrated into the Franks' hiding place. The eight Jews, together with Mr. Koophuis and Mr. Kraler, were taken to Gestapo headquarters in Amsterdam. After a few weeks' imprisonment, Mr. Koophuis was released for medical care. Mr. Kraler spent eight months in a forced labor camp. The Franks, the Van Daans, and Mr. Dussel were sent to Westerbork.

On September 3, the day the Allies captured Brussels, these eight were among the last shipment of a thousand Jews to leave Holland. The prisoners were herded aboard a freight train, seventy-five people to a car. The cars, each with only a small, barred window high on one side, were sealed. For three days and nights the train wandered eastward across Germany, often stopping, backing, detouring. On the third night it reached Auschwitz in Poland. In the glare of searchlights, watched by black-uniformed SS men tightly reining their police dogs, the Jews left the train. On the platform men and women were separated. It was the last Otto Frank saw of his family.

At Auschwitz the healthier prisoners, their heads shaved, worked twelve hours a day digging sod, driven relentlessly by the sadistic *Kapos*, criminals who served the SS as labor overseers. At night they were locked into crowded barracks. Outside the windows they could see the sky glow red above the crematories.

Through the research of Ernst Schnabel, a German writer whose book *Anne Frank, A Portrait in Courage*, was published in 1958, some of the events of the last few months of Anne's life have been reconstructed. Auschwitz, a former inmate told Mr. Schnabel, was "fantastically well-organized, spick-and-span hell. The food was bad, but it was distributed regularly. We kept our barracks so clean that you could have eaten off the floor. Anyone who died in the barracks was taken away first thing in the morning. Anyone who fell ill disappeared also. Those who were gassed did not scream. They just were no longer there. The crematories smoked, but we received our rations and had roll calls. The SS harassed us at roll call and kept guard with machine guns from the watchtowers, and the camp fences were charged with high-tension electricity, but we could wash every day and sometimes even take showers. If you could forget the gas chambers, you could manage to live.'"

The prisoners moved like sleep walkers, half dead, protected somehow from seeing anything, from feeling anything. "'But Anne had no such protection,'" another survivor recalled. "'I can still see her standing at the door and looking down the camp street as a herd of naked gypsy girls was driven by to the crematory, and Anne watched them go and cried. And she cried also when we marched past the Hungarian children who had already been waiting half a day in the rain in front of the gas chambers because it was not yet their turn. And Anne nudged me and said: "Look, look. Their eyes. . . ." '"

In October, 1944, Anne, Margot, and Mrs. Van Daan were among a group of the youngest and strongest women selected to be moved to Belsen in Germany. Left alone, refusing to eat, her mind wandering, Mrs. Frank died in the infirmary barracks at Auschwitz on January 6, 1945. Otto Frank, in the men's camp, saw Mr. Van Daan taken off to be gassed. Mr. Dussel was sent back to Germany and died in the Neuengamme camp. When the SS abandoned Auschwitz in February, 1945, to escape the advancing Russians, they took Peter Van Daan with them on the winter march to the west; he was never heard from again. Otto Frank survived to be liberated by the Russians.

Belsen, Anne discovered, was different from Auschwitz. There was no organization, no roll call, no food or water, only the barren, frozen heath and the starving people looking like ghosts. By January, 1945, the Allies had reached the Rhine, but at Belsen typhus raged and hope was dead.

At Belsen, Anne found her school friend, Lies Goosens. "'I waited shivering in the darkness,'" Lies related of the night when Anne was brought to her. " 'It took a long time. But suddenly I heard a voice: "Lies, Lies? Where are you?"

" 'It was Anne, and I ran in the direction of the voice, and then I saw her beyond the barbed wire. She was in rags. I saw her emaciated, sunken face in the darkness. Her eyes were very large. We cried and cried, for now there was only the barbed wire between us, nothing more. And no longer any difference in our fates.

" 'I told Anne that my mother had died and my father was dying, and Anne told me that she knew nothing about her father, but that her mother had stayed behind in Auschwitz. Only Margot was still with her, but she was already very sick. They had seen Mrs. Van Daan again only after their arrival here in Belsen.' "

Mrs. Van Daan died at Belsen, but no witness marked the date. Margot died at the end of February or beginning of March, 1945. " 'Anne, who was already sick at the time,' " recalled a survivor, " 'was not informed of her sister's death; but after a few days she sensed it, and soon afterwards she died, peacefully, feeling that nothing bad was happening to her.' " She was not yet 16.

III

In May, 1945, the war ended. Months later, Otto Frank returned to Amsterdam by way of Odessa and Marseilles. Miep and Elli gave him the notebooks and papers in Anne's handwriting that they had found strewn over the floor of the "secret annexe" after the Gestapo had gone. These were Anne's diary, stories, and sketches. They were all that remained.

At first Otto Frank had copies of the diary privately circulated as a memorial to his family. It was a Dutch university professor who urged formal publication of the book, and with only slight excisions by Mr. Frank *Het Achterhuis (The Secret Annexe)* was published in Amsterdam by Contact Publishers in June, 1947. The book soon went through several editions. In 1950 it was published in

Germany by the Heidelberg firm of Lambert Schneider. The first printing was only 4500 copies, and many booksellers were actually afraid to show it in their windows; but the book caught on rapidly, and sales of the pocket edition, published by S. Fischer Verlag, totaled 900,000. In 1950 the diary was published in France; in 1952, in England and the United States under the title *Anne Frank: The Diary of a Young Girl.* Now, twenty years after its original publication, the book has been translated into thirty-one languages, including Bengali, Slovene, and Esperanto. It has been published in thirty countries, and has sold more than one million copies in hard-cover alone. In the United States the diary and *The Works of Anne Frank,* both published by Doubleday & Company, have sold well over 150,000 copies and the Pocket Book edition of the diary has sold almost four million copies. The diary was also distributed by the Teen Age Book Club and the Book Find Club and was reprinted in the Modern Library. It was serialized by an American newspaper syndicate with an estimated audience of ten million readers, and millions more read it when it was condensed in *Omnibook* and *Compact* magazines. A German translation of the book has been used in the United States as a school reader, and a large-type edition has been published by Franklin Watts, Inc.

In 1955 a play by Frances Goodrich and Albert Hackett based on the diary and called simply *The Diary of Anne Frank* opened at the Cort Theatre in New York. A great success, it received the Pulitzer Prize, the Critics Circle Prize, and the Antoinette Perry Award for 1956. On October 1, 1956, *The Diary of Anne Frank* opened simultaneously in seven German cities. Audiences there greeted it in stunned silence. The play released a wave of emotion that finally broke through the silence with which Germans had treated the Nazi period. For the first time there were widespread expressions of guilt and shame for what Germans had done to the Jews only a few years before.

In Amsterdam, Queen Juliana attended the play's opening on November 27. This was the city where the events of the play had actually occurred, and many Netherlanders who had lost families and friends in the extermination of the Dutch Jews were in the audience. "There were audible sobs," *The New York Times* correspondent reported, "and one strangled cry as the drama struck its climax and conclusion—the sound of the Germans hammering at the door of the hideout. The audience sat in silence for several minutes after the curtain went down and then rose as the royal party left. There was no applause."

In the United States, *The Diary of Anne Frank* was made into a motion picture in 1959 and adapted for television in 1967.

But still the story was not finished. With the passing of the years, more and more details of Anne Frank's life became known. In 1958 Ernst Schnabel published his moving book, for which he interviewed forty-two people who had known Anne or whose lives had touched hers. In 1963 a Viennese police inspector, Karl Silberbauer, was identified as the Gestapo sergeant who had arrested the Franks in 1944. Silberbauer protested that he had merely followed orders. He was suspended from his post but was later acquitted of the charge of having concealed his past. In January, 1966, the Nazi police chief in the Netherlands during World War II, former SS lieutenant general Wilhelm Harster, together with two former aides, was arrested in Munich. The three were charged with having directed the deportation of nearly 100,000 Dutch Jews to Auschwitz. One of their victims had been Anne Frank. At their trial a year later, a former SS major, Wilhelm Zopf, testified that the Franks' betrayer—probably an employee in the warehouse—had received the usual reward of five gulden (about $1.40) for each of the persons taken from the "secret annexe." The German court sentenced Harster to fifteen years in prison, his accomplices to nine years and five years.

Anne Frank's wish—"I want to go on living even after my death"—has come true. Today the Anne Frank Foundation maintains the building on the Prinsengracht Canal where the Franks hid for twenty-five months as a memorial to Anne Frank. Each year the house is visited by thousands of people from all over the world. The Foundation is also working toward the future by helping to promote better understanding among young people from every part of the world. To this end it has established the International Youth Center, which serves as a meeting place for young people and which holds lectures, discussions, and conferences covering a wide range of international problems.

The Montessori School in Amsterdam is now the Anne Frank school. There are other memorials to her in Germany, Israel, and elsewhere to atone for the unmarked grave at Belsen. But above all, the diary remains. "Her voice was preserved," Ernst Schnabel wrote, "out of the millions that were silenced, this voice no louder than a child's whisper. . . . It has outlasted the shouts of the murderers and has soared above the voices of time."